Dragon Thunder

DRAGON THUNDER

My Life with Chögyam Trungpa

Diana J. Mukpo

with Carolyn Rose Gimian

Shambhala
Boston & London
2006

SHAMBHALA PUBLICATIONS, INC.
Horticultural Hall
300 Massachusetts Avenue
Boston, Massachusetts 02115
www.shambhala.com

9 8 7 6 5 4 3 2

Printed in the United States of America

♾ This edition is printed on acid-free paper that meets
the American National Standards Institute z39.48 Standard.
Distributed in the United States by Random House, Inc.,
and in Canada by Random House of Canada Ltd

Designed by Jeff Baker

Library of Congress Cataloging-in-Publication Data
Mukpo, Diana J.
Dragon thunder: my life with Chögyam Trungpa/Diana J. Mukpo; with
Carolyn Rose Gimian.—1st ed.
p. cm.
ISBN: 978-1-59030-256-9 (alk. paper)
1. Trungpa, Chögyam, 1939–1987. 2. Lamas—Biography. 3. Mukpo, Diana J.
I. Gimian, Carolyn Rose. II. Title.
BQ990.R867M86 2006
294.3'923092—dc22
[B]
2006013421

To my family

Bringing together sun and moon,
Dragon thunder proclaims
Let us rejoice in the name of the Great Eastern Sun.

—CHÖGYAM TRUNGPA, FROM THE UNPUBLISHED MANUSCRIPT
    "THE MEMOIRS OF SIR NYIMA SANGPO, W.O.D.S."

CONTENTS

Dragon Thunder

ONE

This is the story of my life, and it is also an intimate portrait of my husband, Chögyam Trungpa Rinpoche. The two things are quite intertwined for me. My husband was a Tibetan Buddhist lama, the eleventh incarnation in the Trungpa lineage and the abbot of Surmang, a major group of monasteries in Eastern Tibet. *Rinpoche* (pronounced RIM-poach-eh), the name by which I usually called him, is a title for great lamas and incarnate teachers, which means "precious one." Rinpoche left Tibet in 1959 because of the communist Chinese invasion of his country, and after spending a few years in India, he came to England. I met him there when he was twenty-eight and I was fifteen. We were married when I was sixteen, which was quite shocking to both my family and to Rinpoche's Tibetan colleagues. We loved each other deeply, and we had a very special connection. However, our marriage was highly unconventional by most standards, and it was not without heartbreak or difficulty. In the end I have no regrets.

Rinpoche was one of the first Tibetan Buddhist teachers in the West and one of the very first to teach Westerners in the English language. The time that he spent in the West—between 1963, when he arrived in England, and 1987, when he died in North America—was an important period for the transplantation of Buddhism to the West, and I hope that my viewpoint as his wife may offer a unique perspective on that period. A lot of what my life was about during those years was about him and what happened to him. So a main objective for telling my story is so that the memory of him and of all those things that happened can be preserved.

I also want to talk about our life together and our relationship because it was so human and so intimate. Ultimately I think that this is the essence of the Buddhist teachings: they are about how to live our lives as human beings, intimately, moment by moment. So I will try to share with you what it was really like to love such a person. It was quite extraordinary.

The first time I saw Rinpoche was in December of 1968, during my Christmas break from Benenden School, an elite English boarding school for girls. I was fifteen at the time, and I was spending the holidays at home with my mother and my sister in London. The previous summer, my sister Tessa and I had traveled with Mother to Malta. At that point in my life, I couldn't communicate at all with my mother, and I felt claustrophobic around her. While we were in Malta, I withdrew more and more into myself, and I read many books about Theravada, Zen, and Tibetan Buddhism. When we got back to London, I started to go to lectures and other events at the Buddhist Society in Eccleston Square. Buddhism was not particularly popular at that time, and none of my friends were interested in it. However, my father had had an interest in Buddhism and after his death, when I was thirteen, I began to question and explore my own spirituality, first reading about comparative religion and then focusing on Buddhist writings. In the autumn of 1968, I read *Born in Tibet,* Rinpoche's book about his upbringing in Tibet and his escape from the Chinese. I thought it was an exciting and somewhat exotic story. However, the book was nowhere near as thrilling as meeting the author proved to be!

Over the Christmas holidays, I went to St. George's Hall to attend a rally for the liberation of Tibet, sponsored by the Buddhist Society. The program went on for several hours, with one speaker after another. I found it quite boring. One of the last speakers on the schedule was the author of *Born in Tibet,* Chögyam Trungpa Rinpoche, who appeared onstage in the maroon and saffron robes of a Tibetan monk. I looked up at him from the audience, and much to my amazement, I felt an immediate and intense connection. Before he could say anything, however, he collapsed and was carried offstage. We were told that Rinpoche had taken ill, but I imagine that alcohol may have been involved.

Although he was only onstage for a few minutes, I knew that I had a very deep and old connection with him, and it stirred up a great deal of emotion for me. The only way I can describe this experience is that it was like coming home. Nothing in my life had hit me in such a powerful way. I said to myself, "This is what I've been missing all my life. Here he is again." This wasn't just some exciting, powerful experience. I *knew* him, and as soon as I saw him, I realized how much I'd been missing him. From that moment on, I wanted desperately to meet him.

Since the age of thirteen, shortly after my father's death, I had had several very vivid dreams about previous lives in Tibet. I didn't tell anyone about them because I didn't know what to say about them, and I thought that people might misunderstand. I didn't really understand these dreams myself, although somehow I knew that the location was Tibet and these were about previous lives. When I saw Rinpoche, I knew that he was connected to the world that I had encountered in my dreams.

In one of the most vivid dreams, I lived in a nunnery on a large white lake in Tibet. At first I lived in a dormitory with other nuns, but then I was given my own living quarters in a large room dominated by a huge white statue of a Buddha. I stayed in the nunnery for several years, practicing meditation and studying. Then, I left to go on retreat in a cave in the mountains.

In retreat I wore a heavy woolen nun's robe, which is called a *chuba,* and it was lined with fur. The furnishings in the cave were spartan, with a small bed in one corner, an area for cooking, and a simple shrine in front of which I practiced, seated cross-legged on a small raised platform. At one time, I could remember the deity that I visualized in retreat, although that memory has faded now. Later, when I described this to my husband, he knew exactly what practice I was doing.

I was terrified of wild animals in the vicinity. I started building a fire near the front of the cave every night to keep the animals away. Eventually, people from a nearby village raised the money to build a white facade to the cave, and then I felt safe staying there alone.

Once, I saw some Westerners passing through the area. I was amazed and fascinated by them. They had boots that were like nothing I had ever seen before, hiking boots, I suppose. When I recall them, the memories are as clear as any part of the past.

To get water, I had to walk down the valley to a little stream. It was peaceful there, and I enjoyed these outings. One day, I was sitting by the water holding a pomegranate. I have no idea where I got it. Pomegranates grow in Northern India, and perhaps they grew in this part of Tibet as well. It's quite tropical in some of the valleys. I distinctly remember the feel of the fruit in my hand. Then, suddenly, I died—just like that. I think I must have had a heart attack. Then I saw my body from a long way away. I felt as if I were in a vacuum hose, being vacuumed up and out of this world through a tunnel. That is the last thing that I can remember.

When I described all of this to my husband, he said that with a little more discussion he could tell me exactly who I had been but that it wouldn't be a good thing for me to know that. He thought it might become an obstacle. He told me that probably I was given my own room in the nunnery because I was the relative of an important person, possibly a high lama. He thought I might have been related to his own predecessor, the Tenth Trungpa. He never said anything further about it.

I only told Rinpoche about this dream after we were married, but he said that he'd known about my past life in Tibet from the first time we met. I have told very few people about all of this, but it seems that it might be helpful now to understanding our connection.

After seeing Rinpoche in London, I continued to read anything about Tibet or Tibetan Buddhism that I could get my hands on. Not long after the rally, I was able to attend a program that he was teaching at the Buddhist Society, which is one of the oldest Buddhist organizations in England. It was founded by Christmas Humphries, a very colorful and well-known judge. When Rinpoche first arrived in England, the Buddhist Society often invited him to teach there, and they published some of his early lectures in their journal, *The Middle Way*. However, at some point, the Buddhist Society and Rinpoche had a falling-out. I heard that, after they discovered he was drinking alcohol during a program, they never invited him back.

The particular program that I attended was a series of lectures on Padmasambhava, or Guru Rinpoche, the Indian teacher who was instrumental in bringing Buddhism to Tibet in the eighth century. Rinpoche told us stories of Padmasambhava's life and the lessons that one could take from it. Frankly, I don't remember the talks that well; I mainly remember staring at the teacher. I thought that he looked beautiful in his monks' robes, and although he had rather thick reading glasses, I found him quite good-looking.

The participants were told that we could have a private interview with the teacher if we requested one. Although I felt a bit shy and intimidated, of course I asked to see him. The lectures were conducted in a large room upstairs in the Buddhist Society, across from which was a small interview room. During the interview, Rinpoche was incredibly sweet. He gave me instruction in meditation, which I don't remember very well. I was just so hungry for *him*. To me, he seemed to be a very special being: so kind, so pure, so sharp. During the interview, I had the sense that he was touching my mind with his. There was absolutely no barrier in our communication. He seemed to fall in love with the mind of whomever he worked with. I felt that he had no personal agenda except to be kind and helpful.

In the interview room, Rinpoche sat on a cushion on the floor, and I sat across from him. There was a bowl of grapes in front of him, and at a certain point, he offered me some. Even though we had just met, I think there was already some sexual feeling between us, but I didn't really pick up on it. I was only fifteen and quite naive at that point. After the interview, I felt enchanted by the experience and by how close I felt to him. I resolved to spend more time with him.

In 1967 Rinpoche had cofounded a rural meditation center in Scotland, named Samye Ling. He spent most of his time there, and one could go to the center to practice meditation and hear lectures on Buddhism. Early in 1969, I heard about a program at Samye Ling that I wanted to attend during a long weekend that I had off from school. Being only fifteen, I had to have my mother's permission. When I asked her, she told me that the only way she would allow me to go was if she came too. The prospect of her accompanying me was unpleasant. Our relationship was not good, to say the least, and my mother also was extremely prejudiced against anybody who wasn't white and a member of the English upper class. She would have had a problem with Rinpoche if he were Italian, let alone an Asian who was an adherent of some strange religion—as far as she was concerned. However, I felt that I had no choice, so I told her that it would be fine if she came along. I think she was mildly intrigued by something as exotic as a Tibetan lama.

Mother, Tessa, and I took the long drive up from London to Scotland. Although I wasn't looking forward to spending the weekend with my mother, I was excited to be going to Samye Ling, especially with Tessa, with whom I was quite close. The drive took us more than six hours. Most of the roads weren't good, which made it slow going. We crossed the border from England into Dumfriesshire, in the southwest of Scotland. From the city of Dumfries, we turned northeast onto a two-lane highway, which we followed for about twenty miles until we came into Lockerbie, a town of a few thousand residents. We passed through an area forested with short pine trees and then came into a part of the Scottish lowlands with almost no trees at all. We headed north on a small country road. The countryside there feels quite empty, but also quite romantic in a desolate way.

We continued north to Eskdalemuir, a tiny village composed of a few houses here and there. A few miles further north, we found ourselves at Samye Ling. The main building was a large white stone house, several hundred years old, set starkly in the middle of its lawn. There were several small buildings spread around the property, for people doing retreats. The well-tended grounds were surrounded by barren terrain, windswept hills with a mixture of green and brown long grass now flattened by the wind. Little clouds in the sky seemed to mirror the scattered sheep on the hillsides.

When we entered the house, we were directed down the main corridor. On our left was a room with large windows that looked out into the garden. Sherab Palden Beru used this room as his painting studio. He was one of the Tibetan monks in residence there and was a talented painter of traditional Tibetan religious paintings, which are called *thangkas*. The room was filled with his drawings and paintings in various stages of completion. They depicted Tibetan mandalas and deities, some of them quite fierce. I was somewhat familiar with these images, but it must have been quite strange to my mother's eyes.

Farther down the hall on the left was the main shrine room, a large room set aside for meditation and the conduct of various Tibetan practices and ceremonies. It was painted in deep reds, yellows, oranges, and gold, and a number of shrines were set up around the room. In addition to the more elaborate central shrine, there were smaller shrines in various parts of the room. There were butter lamps burning, and we noticed a number of bronze and gold statues. *Thangka* paintings hung on the backdrops to the shrines and on the walls of the room, and there was a heavy smell of Tibetan incense. There were low benches and cushions for people to sit on as well as a sort of throne covered in brocade. We were told that this was where Rinpoche sat, as the presiding lama. Early morning services, or *pujas,* were held every day in the shrine room. Rinpoche used to come down to morning *puja.* There were stories about him falling asleep on the throne, and people used to drive around the driveway honking the horn to wake him up.

On the right was a room with nothing in it but a rug, a small table, and a few cushions on the floor. This was where Rinpoche conducted personal interviews. I can't imagine what my mother thought, as the whole place had the feeling of a Tibetan monastery.

We were given a room on the second floor with windows overlooking the grounds. Soon after we arrived, Rinpoche invited Mother to come for an interview. Most of the people who came to Samye Ling were not from my mother's social class and were much younger than she was, so I'm sure that Rinpoche was intrigued to meet her. My sister and I snuck down while she was talking with him and stood outside the room wondering what was going on in there. We had a good laugh, because my mother's high-heeled snakeskin shoes were neatly placed beside the closed door. We thought it was a hilarious image: my mother taking off her shoes and going barefoot to meet with somebody. We found it amusing and incongruous to see these two worlds coming together in that way.

When my mother came out of her meeting, she said, "He asked me to stay." She was absolutely enamored of Rinpoche. This was surprising, to say the least, but it was fantastic news for my sister and me. We all settled into the routine at Samye Ling. We took our meals at one of the long wooden tables in the dining room set aside for Western students. The food was quite simple; I remember we had soup and bread for supper. There were a number of other Westerners there for the weekend, as well as a number of resident students. There were several practice sessions every day. We got up around 6:30 and practice started at 7:00. My sister and I were asked to help with simple chores, such as doing dishes.

I also had an interview with Rinpoche while we were there. I remember telling him about my anxieties and my problems with my mother. He seemed very understanding. I asked him questions about his new book, *Meditation in Action,* which had just been published in England by Stuart and Watkins. However, the main thing for me was just being in his presence. I was pretty blissed out.

Most of the Western students at Samye Ling were English or Scottish. I don't remember meeting any Americans at that time. In addition to Rinpoche and the painter Sherab Palden Beru, we were introduced to another Tibetan: Akong Rinpoche, Trungpa Rinpoche's longtime companion and the cofounder of the center. Akong had escaped from Tibet with Trungpa Rinpoche and had lived with him at Oxford University, where Rinpoche had studied for several years after he arrived in England. Akong at this time was not teaching very much, although Akong was a *rinpoche* as well. He was in charge of the administration of Samye Ling, while Rinpoche was the spiritual head of the center. Apparently, they had known each other for several lifetimes (the Trungpa *tulkus,* or incarnations, and the Akong *tulkus* had been very close in previous lives), and the two had been very close in this lifetime as well, like brothers. However, by the time I visited Samye Ling, they were having major disagreements, though I didn't know this at the time. During our stay there was no evidence of discord. As far as I could see, it was a peaceful scene.

I was also interested to meet an English Buddhist nun, Josie Wechsler, who was a student of Rinpoche's and very fond of him. There was an area of the house upstairs where the Tibetans lived, which was generally off-limits to Westerners. Josie, however, was allowed to stay in that part of the house when she was not in retreat.

Both the morning and the evening services were chanted in Tibetan. The main emphasis at that time was on a traditional Tibetan approach to meditation practice, quite different from what Rinpoche eventually developed. Things were already in transition, however. Rinpoche had introduced a new liturgy that was practiced in English almost every day, and the atmosphere was changing rapidly.

In the summer of 1968, Rinpoche had gone to India for a visit. It was the first time he had returned to Asia since coming to the West five years earlier. While he was there, he went to Bhutan at the invitation of the queen, who was a devout Buddhist practitioner. She and Rinpoche were both students of the revered teacher Dilgo Khyentse Rinpoche. She was very friendly and extended her courtesy to Rinpoche when she heard he was coming to India. While at Oxford, he had been a tutor to Jigme Singye Wangchuck, her eldest son and the future (now current) king of Bhutan. In addition to an invitation to visit the royal family in Bhutan, Rinpoche was permitted to do a meditation retreat at Taktsang, a famous cave where Padmasambhava meditated before entering Tibet.

While Rinpoche was in retreat there, he uncovered a liturgy entitled the *Sadhana of Mahamudra*. I say that he uncovered it because, according to traditional Tibetan belief, he didn't write it himself. Instead, Rinpoche discovered this text—a text that Padmasambhava was believed to have composed hundreds of years ago—hidden in the recesses of his own mind. Meditating in the cave where Padmasambhava had practiced centuries ago unlocked this precious text, which is about the spiritual degeneration and materialism of the current age and how this darkness can be overcome by an ecumenical approach to presenting genuine spirituality. My husband was considered to be a *tertön,* a Tibetan title that means "treasure finder" or "treasure revealer." A *tertön* is a little bit like a prophet, in the Western biblical sense. Many of Tibet's greatest teachers have been *tertöns.* This title is given to those who discover teachings— and sometimes actual texts and ritual objects—that Padmasambhava is said to have hidden in various places to help people in future generations. I think of such teachings as time bombs, in the sense that they often reveal a new understanding, or wisdom, at the appropriate time. The *Tibetan Book of the Dead* is a famous example of one of these hidden teachings. Some of these texts are discovered hidden in a rock in a cave or are found in a container left at the bottom of a river, or in other unusual places. Some of them are said to be hidden in the mind, and they arise or are discovered there, in the mind of a *tertön.* Rinpoche was considered to be the kind of *tertön* who was able to find such mind *terma* or mind "treasures" as well as physically concealed *terma.* He had already discovered a number of *terma* as a young lama in Tibet, but the *Sadhana of Mahamudra,* I believe, was the first *terma* he found after leaving his country.

When we were at Samye Ling, Rinpoche had only recently returned from his trip to Bhutan, bringing this text with him, newly translated into English. Now, in addition to chanting in Tibetan, students at Samye Ling practiced the *Sadhana of Mahamudra* in English. I remember that the text was crudely mimeographed on colored sheets of paper.

One afternoon, after we'd been there for several days, I walked into the bedroom to find Mother sitting on the bed, absolutely frozen. She seemed to be in shock. She didn't move or say anything for several minutes. Then she said, "My God, I've been hypnotized. I've been hypnotized by this Asian. Pack your bags immediately. It's black magic. We have to get out of here."

Looking back, I realize that it was amazing that she stayed at Samye Ling as long as she did. In a way, it *was* magic. She had completely set aside her normal concepts of propriety during this period of time. I don't actually understand why this was possible. Whatever the spell was, it was now broken.

At the time, I didn't appreciate how remarkable her behavior had been. Rather, I was focused on wanting to stay longer and distraught that she insisted we leave. Both my sister and I tried to convince her that everything was all right, that it wasn't black magic, and that we could stay. I pleaded with her, but she said that we had to go *immediately*. I went to say good-bye to Rinpoche, whom I felt I'd barely seen while we were there. I told him that, because of my mother freaking out, we had to leave. He reassured me and told me not to worry, that it would be all right, and that we could get together in the future.

My sister had friends nearby in Scotland, and since she was older, Mother allowed her to stay with them for the rest of the weekend. I had to drive home alone with Mother. I loaded our cases into the car, a Jaguar sedan, and the two of us drove back to London. I didn't speak; I didn't open my mouth on the whole trip, except to give monosyllabic replies to direct questions. Several hours into the journey, Mother stopped and bought me an ice cream cone, thinking it might change my mood. I waited until we were on the road again; then I opened the window and threw the cone out. I remember her pleading with me, "We'll move to South Africa. You'll like it there. I'll buy you a horse farm. You can have as many horses as you want. Just please, please forget your interest in Buddhism and this strange man." Of course, I did nothing of the kind.

Soon after this, I went back to school at Benenden. It was the spring of 1969, and I didn't see Rinpoche again for almost six months. During the spring term, I was shocked to hear that he had had a terrible car accident and was paralyzed on his left side. Shortly after that, I heard that he was slowly recuperating and was planning to marry a young Englishwoman by the name of Maggie Russell. That was another shock. Then, a little bit after that, I heard that Maggie had decided not to marry him. Strangely enough, that was the most disturbing news. I couldn't believe it. I remember thinking, "How could somebody say no to him? How could he want to marry somebody and they would turn him down like that? She has to be out of her mind." I thought to myself that if I ever had the opportunity to marry him, I wouldn't hesitate. I would have no second thoughts.

When Rinpoche later wrote about his car accident, he talked about overcoming hesitation, doubt, and self-deception. In the epilogue to *Born in Tibet*, "Planting the Dharma in the West," he wrote about the message that came through to him from this accident:

When plunging completely and genuinely into the teachings, one is not allowed to bring along one's deceptions. I realized that I could no longer attempt to preserve any privacy for myself, any special identity or legitimacy. I should not hide behind the robes of a monk, creating an impression of inscrutability which, for me, turned out to be only an obstacle. With a sense of further involving myself with the sangha, I determined to give up my monastic vows. More than ever, I felt myself given over to serving the cause of Buddhism.[1]

At the time, I knew nothing about the implications of the accident. For my part, I simply thought about Rinpoche constantly and couldn't wait to see him again. A young girl of fifteen, I was infatuated with him and caught up in my own life, my own dramas. I didn't stop to think about the deeper meaning of what he was going through.

During this period, my schoolwork started to slip. I had never been that comfortable at Benenden, and now having met Rinpoche, my view of life was changing drastically, and I seemed to be increasingly out of place and out of step. Benenden was where the British upper class, the children of foreign diplomats, and royalty from around the world sent their daughters. It offered the best education in the style of British public schools—which is what the most exclusive private schools in England are called. Frankly, I never felt that I fit that well into English society, from early childhood, so at its best, Benenden was not an easy place for me to be. At this point, I couldn't relate to the situation at school at all, and I became more and more disconnected from life there. I was becoming quite a problem child by that point. I remember feeling that I just wanted to get away. Especially after the falling-out with my mother at Samye Ling, I felt desperate and somewhat depressed.

During this time, a friend, who was in school near Cambridge, started to send me drugs in the mail. Periodically, she would send marijuana, which I enjoyed smoking—anything to take the edge off of my life. Then, she sent me some opium in the mail. I had never tried that. I thought I would save it for a special occasion. A few weeks later, we were told that Queen Elizabeth was coming to Benenden to visit Princess Anne, who was one of the girls in my house at school. I thought this was the perfect opportunity, and I ate the opium before the queen arrived. I remember having a really good time, feeling very relaxed and enjoying myself immensely during her visit. At a certain point, I was standing in formation to say good-bye to the queen in the parking lot, and I felt as though I were floating.

The next thing I remember is that I was lying down in a corridor in the school because my legs were suddenly so heavy. My housemistress was standing over me, saying, "Diana Pybus, get up immediately. Stand up. Why are you lying there?" I looked up at her and said, "What's the problem, man? I'm just stoned." Of course, that got a reaction out of her. She reported me immediately to the headmistress and then put me to bed, because I was quite incoherent at that point. The next morning I was sent to explain myself to the headmistress. I told her that, no, of course it wasn't drugs. I said that I had drunk my first glass of wine ever, feeling despondent about my father's death and how much I missed him. I didn't receive a very serious punishment. Either they believed my explanation or they felt sorry for me. Actually, I had lain in bed the entire night having hallucinations and enjoying it.

At one point during the term, I asked to see the headmistress and told her that I was becoming a vegetarian because I was now a Buddhist. She told me that she wasn't about to enter into a philosophical discussion with me but that I simply must eat meat. I also told her that I didn't want to go to church anymore. We were required at Benenden to attend services twice on Sundays. Being a Buddhist was not considered an acceptable excuse. I was told that I absolutely must attend.

I stopped going anyway, and eventually I got caught. As a punishment, I was told to walk about two miles to the church in the village, where I was to sit quietly by myself, memorize a psalm, and then walk back to school where I was to recite the psalm to our housemistress and all the monitors in my house at school. My friend Veronica Bruce Jones decided to come with me. When we got to the church, there was no one around. It wasn't the regular hour for services, so the church was empty. We were, however, able to get into the main sanctuary, and behind the altar I found the vicar's robes. Veronica and I also found a bottle of sacramental wine, which we drank. Then I put on the robes and stood in the pulpit, where I delivered a sermon to the empty pews on the meaning of impermanence and the Buddha's teaching of the Four Noble Truths. At the end, I remember standing there and saying, "Well, I'm a Buddhist, and Buddhism is better than this!" After that, we walked back to school, rather sloshed.

Somehow I finished out the year at school, but I knew that I didn't want to go back to Benenden in the fall. I asked my mother if I could transfer to Kirby Lodge, where my sister had spent her last two years of school. Although I longed to go to Samye Ling in the summer of 1969, I was away all summer with Mother and Tessa on a trip to Mijas, Spain, where my mother rented a villa for our vacation. I investigated where to buy local drugs cheaply and also enjoyed shoplifting in the marketplace. I stole a number of caftans, colorful long dresses worn by women in some countries of the Near East. I took to wearing these as the perfect sort of hippie clothes. While we were in Spain, I had a pet goat that I named Pan. I used to walk him around the village on a leash.

In the fall of 1969, I started school at Kirby Lodge, a small school for sixteen- to eighteen-year-old girls located in a village outside of Cambridge. At Benenden I had done best in sciences, but at Kirby Lodge I decided to do my A-levels (advanced coursework and examinations) in languages: Sanskrit, Spanish, and English. I wanted to study Sanskrit because of my interest in Eastern religion. There were no courses in Sanskrit offered at the school, but they arranged for me to have a tutorial with one of the professors at Cambridge. I used to take the bus into

Cambridge once a week to have my Sanskrit lesson. However, I didn't do the assigned work, so eventually the professor refused to teach me any longer. Altogether, I'm afraid that I didn't do very well at Kirby Lodge. I had changed schools, but that didn't solve anything because that wasn't the real source of my problems.

There was one bright light in my studies during this period. I had also wanted to learn Tibetan, of course, and I heard about a Tibetan lama, Ato Rinpoche, living in Cambridge. I approached him, and he agreed to give me Tibetan lessons. His wife, Alithea, was the English daughter of an Anglican bishop, and I believe she has remained a Christian. He was absolutely devoted to her and she to him, calling him Rinpoche-la. At that time, although he occasionally lectured on Buddhism, Ato Rinpoche made his living as a nurse in a psychiatric hospital. I went to his house in Cambridge once a week for my Tibetan lesson. He was very patient, and both of them were very sweet to me. He knew Trungpa Rinpoche and respected him very much, so I loved going to visit him.

On the home front, I was still having terrible problems with my mother, and our communication—or lack of it—did not improve. The custom at Kirby Lodge was that on your birthday your parents would bring up a cake and other food. I had my sixteenth birthday coming up on the eighth of October. At the last minute, my mother decided not to come for it at all. Sixteen is an important milestone in a young girl's life, so it was particularly devastating that she wasn't going to be there. I had already invited people to a party when I found out that Mother wasn't planning to come up. Mother told me to go out and buy things for the party myself.

Throughout this dismal autumn term at Kirby Lodge, I thought about going up to Samye Ling to see Rinpoche again. It was out of the question to discuss this with Mother, so I decided to find my own way there, the first chance I got. At the end of October I decided to leave school for the weekend without permission. I asked my friends at school to cover for me, and I hitchhiked up to Scotland. Before I left, I went to a nearby greengrocer and bought Rinpoche a pomegranate as a gift. I didn't consciously know why I chose that, but it seemed appropriate, and I put it in my bag.

When I arrived at Samye Ling, I discovered that Rinpoche wasn't staying there. He was living about a mile down the road to recuperate from his accident, at a residence called Garwald House, an old Scottish home owned by Christopher and Pamela Woodman, two students who were quite devoted to him. .

Rinpoche also left Samye Ling because he and Akong had had a major falling-out. After his trip to Bhutan, but even more so after his accident, Rinpoche started to reach out to his Western students. He really wanted to explore the world beyond monastic constraints, and he didn't want to be typecast as a Tibetan monk. He wanted to go beyond all of the cultural boundaries. Akong became frightened of what Rinpoche was doing, and as Rinpoche told me later, Akong's fear became controlling. There was a huge discrepancy in the way that they wanted to treat Westerners and to be treated by them as well. Akong didn't mind Rinpoche's behavior—which included some sexual activity and the consumption of alcohol—as long as it was kept very private. But after the accident, Rinpoche was no longer willing to hide behind the pretense of religiosity. The only way that Akong seemed able to deal with Rinpoche's behavior was to say that Trungpa Rinpoche had gone crazy. Akong often would not allow Rinpoche to teach at Samye Ling, and it became a very limited existence for him there.

But at this time, I knew nothing about all this. Rinpoche's students who lived in and around Samye Ling may have known what was going on, but publicly everyone, except Rinpoche, was trying to keep things very hush-hush.

The first evening I was at Samye Ling, Rinpoche came by to have dinner with the Tibetans. After dinner, as he was getting ready to return to Garwald House, I saw him outside by the car. He was no longer wearing monks' robes. Instead he had on a layman's *chuba,* or robe, and he was walking slowly in a labored way with the aid of a walker. He was quite crippled from the accident. I managed to get close to him, and as he walked past me, he stopped to greet me. I had the pomegranate with me to present to him as a gift. I pulled it out of my bag and extended it to him. He took it graciously and thanked me for it, commenting that it was a very significant gesture. At that point, I hadn't told him about my dreams of life as a nun in Tibet.

Although I only saw Rinpoche that evening for a few minutes, in that short period of time I realized that he was a completely different person than he had been before his accident. Of course, he looked quite different physically because he was paralyzed on one side and had obviously been through a lot. However, it wasn't just his physical being that had changed. He manifested differently now, which I found fascinating. Before the accident, he had been so youthful, pure, and light. Now he was much more heavy and solid, and there was a well-processed feeling about him. He seemed much older, and he had an unfathomable quality that I hadn't experienced before. He was transformed.

His earlier manifestation had been one that Westerners, especially the proper English Buddhists, were more comfortable with. He was obviously powerful and accomplished, but not in a way that was threatening. He radiated loving kindness. Now, although his kindness was still apparent, there was a wrathful quality. It was a little bit scary to approach him, and when he looked at you, it was penetrating and disconcerting. But for me, he was magnetic.

I desperately wanted to have an audience with him, but the people I spoke to at Samye Ling told me it would be impossible. Nevertheless, the next day I decided to visit him at Garwald House. I walked a little over a mile to the turnoff to the house, and then began to walk down the long driveway that wound through the Woodmans' property. I was wearing a red caftan, part of the collection I had shoplifted the previous summer.

Near Garwald House, I met one of Rinpoche's American students who was helping to care for him after the accident. When she asked me what I was doing there, I told her I had come to see Rinpoche. She said that he simply wasn't having any visitors. She was adamant, but so was I. I told her that if he didn't want to see me, I wanted to hear that from him directly.

I walked on down the driveway, and when I got to the house, someone went upstairs to tell Rinpoche that he had an unexpected visitor. A few minutes later, she came down and said that I would be allowed to go up to his bedroom for a few minutes. I was told to keep it short. I was led up the main stairs to a large room, whose only furnishings were a double bed and a small nightstand. When I entered the room, Rinpoche was in bed, and he was wearing maroon cotton pajamas. He spent a great deal of time in bed during this period, as he was still recovering from the accident itself and from the pneumonia and pleurisy that he had developed as side effects of the original trauma. However, as I soon found out, his injury didn't stop him from being sexually active.

I sat down on the side of the bed and we started to chat. I was so happy to see him. I couldn't believe that I'd finally found my way to him. He was very friendly, and I felt closer to him than I had ever felt before. Somewhat unexpectedly, but also much to our mutual delight, one thing led to the next between us. I reached out my hand to him, and he took it and we kissed each other. He sat up in bed, put his arm around me, and invited me to get into bed with him. I accepted with no hesitation. It was in fact exactly the invitation I was hoping for at that moment.

I had barely turned sixteen, and I knew very little about sex or about men, having grown up in a sheltered environment, having my father pass away when I was just thirteen, and having attended boarding schools from the age of nine, where there were no boys. I had a boyfriend in Cambridge, but we hadn't done anything much more than kiss. As I was climbing into bed, Rinpoche started to take off his pajamas. I remember saying to him, "Where are your knickers?" And he replied, "Well, men don't wear knickers." I also was shocked to discover that men had pubic hair.

Once I entered his bedroom, his manner was so intimate that it seemed natural for us to take the relationship to this new level. I had never been with a man before, but I didn't have any qualms about making love with him. When I visited him again a few weeks later, I asked him a number of questions about a religious teacher having sexual relationships and why he had given up his robes. But we didn't talk about any of that the first time we were together. I was so happy being there with him that I didn't question anything. Later on, I realized that it was rather outrageous for us to be sleeping together, but I also thought it was terrific.

After we made love, we stayed in bed and talked. In fact, we spent the entire weekend in bed together. Being with him made complete sense to me, in a way that nothing in my life had before. I had never connected with English culture, and I had always felt like an outsider. Basically, I thought the whole English thing was crackers, from day one. I had felt emotionally repressed my entire life. Suddenly here was this person who I could connect with, who could go anywhere with you in your mind. I felt that I had been rescued—and liberated, because it wasn't just that I could go anywhere with him; he would go anywhere with me, too. During that weekend with Rinpoche, I discovered this tremendously vast playground. There was so much space, and I felt the freedom to be myself. That was one of the things that I always most appreciated about him: that fathomless quality.

I remember that at some point he turned to me and said, "Maybe one day, someday, we could get married." I pretty much melted at that point, and I said, "Yes, yes, I'd love to marry you." While we were together, he wrote me a beautiful poem. It began, "This marriage is the marriage of sun and moon."

People have many naive ideas about tantric sex and what it must be like to sleep with the guru. It was certainly amazing to be with him, but not because of exotic sexual positions or super orgasms. What was extraordinary about it wasn't the physicality at all. Rather, it was the atmosphere of pervasive gentleness and compassion. There was, I would almost say, a sense of being zapped by the huge space of his mind. I can only describe the experience as a combination of profundity and sweetness.

By the end of the weekend, I was in a fog, but it was a soft, velvet fog unlike the cold spaces I usually inhabited. It was difficult to leave, but I pulled myself away and caught a ride south with someone leaving Samye Ling. I managed to slip back into school undetected. I think they never knew that I'd been gone.

This Marriage

This marriage is the marriage of sun and moon.
It is the marriage of ocean and sky.
What can I say if the universal force demonstrates it?

Today there is a big storm;
The autumn leaves are swept by the force of wind.
That is the meeting of wind and tree.

Emotion, what is that?
Longing for you is something deeper than my impression of you
And the memory could be carved on rock, something substantial.

Your letter is beautiful because it is written by you.
I hear Krishna playing his flute
In the long distance.

There needs to be courage from both you and me.
The words that I said will not fade
Because they are carved on this gigantic rock.
Your presence in my chamber
Still remains
As the presence of my Guru
In my mind.

Let's dance together
In the nondualistic air.
Let's sing together
In the silent clarity.

Still there is sorrow
As oneness crowned with thorns and crucified.
But it's not the fault of Pontius Pilate;
It's beyond his stature and his power.

There have been many discoveries
Like a child collecting pebbles.
I'm so pleased that you are the source of happiness.
You radiate light.

This is the gateway for you:
As you enter this gate
You will find openness without effort.

Faith is most important.
Nothing else matters.
It is the channel for everything.

Come my darling,
Be open.
There is tremendous discovery.
It is not you alone
If we both make the effort.[2]

NOVEMBER 2, 1969

Two

A few weeks later, I decided to go up to see Rinpoche again. Unless your parents made special arrangements, on weekends you were expected to stay at school. My mother, of course, had no idea what I was up to and hadn't given her permission for me to go anywhere, but I decided to leave school for the weekend anyway. This time, I didn't cover my tracks so well. I just split.

My mother wouldn't give me any spending money because she thought that I would use it to buy drugs. So there I was in the south of England, and I had to find a way to get up to Scotland without any cash. I called Rinpoche, and he said that if I could get to the Carlisle train station, which was the station nearest to Samye Ling, he would pay for my taxi the rest of the way.

I hitchhiked part of the way up to Scotland. A truck driver picked me up and drove me all the way up to Yorkshire. There I boarded the train to Carlisle. In England in those days, you had to give your ticket to the conductor at your destination. Since I had no ticket, I waited until the train slowed down coming into Carlisle Station, and I opened the door and jumped off the train. I remember hitting the ground with a big *thonk* and rolling down an embankment. Then I had to climb over several fences, which led me into a chicken farm. There were hundreds of chickens running around in the yard. When I got out of the farm, I walked around to the front of the train station, relatively unscathed, and took the hour-long taxi drive up to Garwald House. Rinpoche, as he'd promised, paid for the taxi.

We had a fabulous weekend together. It only deepened my connection with him, and we were able to talk about a lot of things. I had some questions about our relationship and whether it was appropriate for a Tibetan lama to be sexually active. When Rinpoche and I were in bed together that second weekend, I said to him, "You know, I thought sex was bad, especially for people like you." I told him that I'd heard that the Dalai Lama had spoken about the value of sexual abstinence. Rinpoche told me that was true for some people, but that it wasn't true for everyone. He pointed out to me that he was no longer a monk.

In Tibetan Buddhism there is quite an old established tradition of married lamas, who can be revered spiritual teachers. Khyentse Rinpoche, one of my husband's main mentors, was one of these married teachers. It is often the case, for some reason, that *tertöns* marry. When Rinpoche began finding hidden treasures, *terma,* in Tibet, some of the older monks at his monastery speculated that he might take a consort in the future.

Speaking more broadly, I believe that sexuality is viewed differently in Buddhism than it is within the Judeo-Christian tradition. I think that many Oriental teachers who've come to the West have hidden their views on sex from their Western disciples because they've realized that these attitudes, which are cultural as well as religious, would be misconstrued. Some Western adherents of Buddhism advocate a very conservative, almost moralistic, approach, but that doesn't come from the Buddhist tradition itself. There is, of course, an emphasis on not causing harm to others, which applies to one's sexual behavior as well as to other areas of conduct. But that doesn't mean that one must have a prudish approach toward sex.

In any case, Rinpoche and I spent the entire weekend in bed together, just as we had the first time we were together. I can remember lying awake one of the nights that I was there feeling how special it was to be with him. I was very much in love. The time went by quickly, and I was sad to have to leave. When I had to go, Rinpoche found someone to drive me partway, and then I hitchhiked the rest of the way back to school. This time, when I got back, the school officials as well as the police were waiting for me, and they demanded to know where I'd been. I refused to tell them. There were two or three policemen trying to intimidate me. I dug in my heels and didn't say anything. I knew that if I told them where I'd been or that I had been with Rinpoche or anything like that, it would destroy my chances of ever seeing him again. Finally, they told me, "All right, but if you ever leave school again without permission, you'll be expelled and put into juvenile detention."

At school they were now aware that I was in real trouble. I had reached a point where I was not functioning, not doing anything. The housemistress was very sweet and not judgmental at all. She tried to be helpful. She knew that I was in a difficult family situation, my father having died and my mother being so unstable at this point.

During this time, I went home for a few days. I had an appointment with our family physician, and I told him that I was sexually active. He immediately wanted to give me contraception. He told me that my mother was having a nervous crisis and that if I became pregnant, it would finish her off. My mother had many psychological problems even before my father died. The biggest problem for me was that she wanted me to be a particular way, and what I did was never good enough for her. During this period, she ignored the fact that I was in psychological distress myself and just kept saying, "Oh why can't you be like so and so?" She wanted me to be, not even who *she* was, but who she had always *wanted* to be.

She was trying to advance me socially, to have me marry the right man and do the right things and have the right sort of feminine attitude and all of that. She didn't seem to appreciate how unhappy and miserable and confused I was. All I wanted to do was to be with Rinpoche and I couldn't relate to anything else.

My mother did send me to a psychiatrist in London during this period. He opened our session by saying, "Your mother tells me that you want to be a dropout from society." I replied eagerly, "Yes, I do!" So he said, "Oh, do tell me about it." He was so enthusiastic that I felt that he was about ready to drop out himself. We talked about Buddhism and other things, and finally he said to me, "You know something, I have to confide in you. Your mother is a very troubled person. She has alienated a lot of people around her, including you. I actually think you're doing quite fine." For a short time, this made me feel a bit better about myself.

Throughout the term at Kirby Lodge, I continued to be out of touch with the academic situation. I maintained a vegetarian diet at school, eating the rather disgusting English boarding school food, but not meat or eggs. I became somewhat disconnected from the world around me. The more I thought about it, the more I felt that I couldn't continue to live with my mother. My sister had already moved out, and the spectacle of being alone in London with Mother over the upcoming Christmas holiday was unbearable. I talked to my housemistress about this, and she seemed very understanding. We talked about alternatives, and we came up with the idea that I could stay with my aunt and uncle in Northumberland. I asked to be put in their custody. I thought that was a good option. They seemed to be fairly stable people, and I felt that I'd be in a more neutral situation with them.

Shortly thereafter I got a telephone call from my mother. The housemistress had obviously phoned her. Mother was furious and told me, "I can't believe you've done this. I'm expecting you home for the Christmas holidays, and I've already bought flowers for the house. I can't believe you're thinking of not coming back." That was the depth of our communication at that point. I felt that I had no choice but to give in to her, so I ended up going home for Christmas. I had a shrine in my bedroom there, with a picture of Rinpoche, a statue of the Buddha, and some butter lamps on it. My sister had painted my room in bright Tibetan colors: orange and maroon and deep blue, which I loved. While I was away at school, my mother had my bedroom redecorated. She repainted, did away with my shrine, and put up curtains with a Chinese design on them. She said to me, "Well, you should like this. It has an Asian theme." It was just Mother and me for Christmas. Did we celebrate? I don't even remember.

Right after Christmas, Rinpoche called me in London, pleading with me to come up to Scotland for the New Year. I didn't know how to persuade my mother to let me go, but then I hatched a plan. I called some friends who were also students of Rinpoche's, Stash and Amalie, who lived near Eskdalemuir, and told them that I needed a cover so that I could see Rinpoche. Stash knew how to do the English upper-crust thing really well, so he called my mother and said that he and his wife were having a lovely New Year's Eve party at their home in Scotland. He told my mother, "I'd really like Diana to come for it. But please be very careful about train tickets, because of all the drunken people on the train this time of year. I think you'll have to spend the money on a first-class ticket, and we'll pick her up at the station in Carlisle." My mother was quite charmed, so this time I ended up having my way paid first class to Carlisle.

I had an instinct that I would never be coming back. When I was packing, my mother walked into the bedroom and said, "You're taking so many things. You're packing as if you're leaving home." I laughed and said, "Oh well, I just don't know what I'm going to need to wear."

When I got off the train, I got a taxi directly to Garwald House and met Rinpoche there. I never even saw Stash and Amalie that night. I arrived on December 30. The next night, New Year's Eve, was wild. Rinpoche and I drove around with some friends to visit various people. The first place we stopped, the people had put hashish in their Christmas cake. After they'd eaten it, they'd had a terrible fight and had broken every piece of china in the house. We went on from there to visit Stash and Amalie, who lived in a cottage in a remote area. We continued making the rounds at Eskdalemuir, stopping at a number of friends' houses.

Halfway through the evening, we joined up with the Woodmans, who owned the house where Rinpoche was living. After that, I remember encountering a lot of negativity toward Rinpoche, and some that was directed at the two of us. I don't know exactly what had happened, whether Rinpoche had gone one step too far for them at that point, or if there was jealousy because of me, or what. However, the situation felt hostile and rather weird.

For Rinpoche at that time, there was so much personal crisis and personal growth taking place simultaneously. He was quite young, if you think about it, just twenty-eight, and he was dealing with incredible forces of change in his life. He'd lost his own culture in a horribly brutal way and had been exiled to a strange land. Then he'd had the big message of his car accident and the subsequent paralysis, which was a major turning point for him spiritually. He used to say to me that there was a point in your spiritual development where you could either go crazy or become enlightened. He was right there, on that point.

I think that he felt abandoned to a large extent, misunderstood both by the Tibetans and by his students. Most of the English students, even those who had been quite close to him, couldn't go along with him at this point. He just didn't fit the mold of a spiritual teacher that the English people wanted. They found him brilliant, but they were also intimidated by him. They could venerate an Asian guru if he remained a holy little man, but a powerful figure like Rinpoche was threatening.

So when I came into his life, there weren't very many people there for him. At the same time, although this era was terribly bleak, he was giving birth to something much more powerful than what had happened in the past. It was a very pregnant time. In October of 1969, Rinpoche had sent a letter to the lawyer for Samye Ling, who was also one of his students, in which he talked frankly about the whole situation. Early in the letter he talks about his decision to disrobe:

> I have decided to give up the robe, which I feel stood as a subtle obstacle to the formulation of my teaching in the West. The monk's robe confused many here as a glorious image of spirituality. However, my teaching concerns actual experience. I don't feel that I need to hide behind something, though some people are critical of me for coming out and showing myself as a human being.[1]

He continues,

> To be quite frank with you, I feel that I must make it quite clear that the disapproval which has been directed toward me from some so-called Buddhists, including some of my compatriots, has been a fear of plunging in in this way. My very existence becomes an enormous threat to them because I am utterly without fear in this world of violent change.[2]

That New Year's Eve, after we went round and visited Rinpoche's students in Eskdalemuir, we went back to Garwald House. Rinpoche got on the phone, and at first I thought he was calling people to wish them a happy New Year. I finally realized that he was calling his old girlfriends and inviting them up to the house. Four or five young women arrived within the hour, and they were each put up in a different bedroom for the night, while I slept with Rinpoche in his room. When I asked him what on earth he was doing, he said, "I'm trying to decide which of you I'm going to marry." Somehow I knew that it would be me, so I didn't feel threatened, as strange as that might sound. But what a bizarre spectacle!

In the morning when I woke up, I wanted to go down to the kitchen to get something to eat, but I couldn't find my nightgown or a robe to put on, so I grabbed Rinpoche's Tibetan robe, his *chuba,* wrapped it around myself, and went downstairs. Pamela Woodman was there, and when she saw me, she started screaming at me, "Who do you think you are? Who do you think you are that you can wear his *chuba?*" There was tremendous black negativity in the air.

Later that day, after saying goodbye to all the assembled ladies, Rinpoche and I decided to escape the whole scene at Garwald House and go to Edinburgh. I thought that we might be getting married there. Rinpoche just said, "Let's get out of here," and I agreed. I phoned my sister, and she and her boyfriend Roderick arrived at Garwald House to drive us. We packed a few things, got in their car, and headed north. We stopped in Glasgow for the night. We didn't have much money, so we stayed in a tiny, disgusting little place where every hour or two the heater would go off and you had to spend a half-crown to get it to come back on. Rinpoche and I would fall asleep, only to be woken up when it was freezing in the room. Then we'd have to find another half-crown and put it in the heater. We spent the whole night like that. The next night we moved into a nicer hotel in Edinburgh.

The period from Rinpoche's accident until we married and left for America a year later was one of the darkest times in his life. Rinpoche was often in the depths of depression. He was sick with pleurisy and pneumonia, he was crippled, his Tibetan compatriots were trying to control him, and many of his students had left him. He felt that his only reason for existence was to present the Buddhist teachings. Akong refused to support him in teaching the way that he wanted to, and he had very few students in England who could hear what he had to say. For Rinpoche, if he had no opportunity to present the buddhadharma, the Buddhist teachings, life was not worth living. He told me at several points that if he couldn't teach, he had no reason to go on.

That night in the hotel, Rinpoche had a big jar of Seconals, which are sleeping pills. I don't know where he had obtained them. At one point that night, he turned to me and said, "Let's take all these pills. Let's just do it." I grabbed the bottle out of his hand and threw the pills out of the hotel window, saying, "We're not going to do that. There's a future for us." Then we went to bed.

I'm not sure if Rinpoche really meant it, if he actually would have taken an overdose. One might think he was testing me somehow, but I'm not so sure. If I had said, "Okay, yes, let's kill ourselves," I think he might have gone ahead. He loved those Japanese movies where the star-crossed lovers commit double suicide, a bit like *Romeo and Juliet*.

I'm sure it's difficult to understand how a spiritual teacher could even contemplate taking his own life. But Rinpoche was just so real. He wasn't like anybody's concept of a spiritual teacher. Of course, I found the suggestion that we take all those pills quite shocking, although I felt tremendous sympathy for what Rinpoche was going through. In a way, it seemed like a very human response to his situation. Thank heavens I kept my faith in our ability to transcend this awful situation. I don't mean to suggest that I saved his life, exactly. It was more that I was part of the circumstances or the atmosphere that gave him a future. I don't know if you can understand this, but there were many times in my husband's life when circumstances intervened and helped him. I felt as though I were part of that support system—which almost felt like a cosmic coincidence of some kind.

Later, I heard about another great Tibetan teacher who was driven to the brink of self-destruction. In the eleventh century in Tibet, there was a famous meditator named Milarepa, who is probably the greatest saint in the Tibetan Buddhist tradition. He spent years trying to receive the highest teachings from his guru. Because of Milarepa's particularly stubborn and difficult nature and because of his many misdeeds in the past, his teacher made him undergo many tests and trials. Nothing seemed to please his guru. Finally, Milarepa became so discouraged and convinced that he would never receive the final spiritual empowerment that he decided he would take his own life. His teacher appeared just as he was about to hurl himself over a cliff. At that point, feeling that Milarepa had finally surrendered completely, his guru gave him the ultimate transmission. My husband always said that he admired Milarepa because everything he did was undertaken with an attitude of complete warriorship.

My husband lived his life in the same way. He was an extreme human being, and he lived his life with extreme and immaculate concern for others. When he became depressed and suicidal, it was not out of self-pity.

The next morning, January 3, 1970, we decided that we were going to get married. What an outrageous time to make this decision! Most people, looking back on their courtship and marriage, would see a happy picture, I think. Our bond, obviously, was not forged out of any such cheerful circumstances. What we had, however, was a true connection, and I never doubted my love for Rinpoche or his genuine love for me.

On January 1, a law had gone into effect in Scotland that made it legal to get married at sixteen years of age without your parents' consent. The morning of the third, Rinpoche called Akong and Sherab Palden at Samye Ling and told them that we were getting married. They came up to Edinburgh right away, but it was like they'd come for a funeral. That's the only way I can describe it. Our marriage was a huge mistake as far as Rinpoche's Tibetan colleagues were concerned, further proof that he was not going to remain securely within the fold. Akong was sullen and wouldn't look me in the eye. I think the icing on the cake for him, so to speak, was that Rinpoche was going to marry a white girl. At that point, Akong might have given in and softened to the situation, but instead he seemed to become more rigid. In doing so, he sealed shut a door of intimacy that had been open between Rinpoche and him, not just in this life, but for many lifetimes. In the letter I quoted from earlier, Rinpoche also addressed his relationship with Akong:

> There is much that I think you ought to know about the situation at Samye Ling. . . . Most of the difficulty boils down to a basic disagreement between Akong and myself. I have not acted more forcefully as of yet because I feel that he is involved in a deep personal crisis through which I want him to discover his own way himself. At heart the problem is that same lack of courage and lack of faith which I have tried to impress on you as the ultimate danger. . . .
>
> The point is that Akong wishes to control me and use me in a very limited way. He feels that my "becoming Western" is a

"disgrace to Tibet"—(pride lies very near the surface here). But my role is a far deeper one than a mere cultural mission, a representative of the East in the West. I am not Tibetan but *Human* and my mission is to teach others as effectively as I can in the world in which I find myself. Therefore, I refuse to be bound by any "national" considerations whatsoever. And if Akong wishes to work effectively now, he too must have the courage to break through his Tibetanness, to stop hiding behind our national background. . . .[3]

I think that Akong was hoping that at the last minute Trungpa Rinpoche would change his mind about marrying me, but that didn't happen. Akong and Sherab went with Rinpoche and me to a very formal old Scottish building to apply for our marriage licenses. Rinpoche and I must have been quite a sight as we approached the registrar: a rather short, crippled Tibetan man, age twenty-nine, wearing a special caliper on his leg and a cumbersome walker to support him, and a tall, sixteen-year-old English girl with long blonde hair. The registrar had a Bible, and he said to Rinpoche, "Put your hand on this Bible and swear before God." And Rinpoche said, "I'm sorry, I can't do that. I'm a Buddhist." That was all right for him, but then the registrar gave me the same instruction, and I said, "I'm also sorry I can't do this. I'm a Buddhist." This absolutely appalled him. Here I was, a young English girl who had obviously run away from home and a good family, and on top of that I had renounced Christianity. I thought for a moment that he might not give us the marriage licenses, but he did.

After we got the license, we had to go to the justice of the peace to perform the actual wedding. Before the ceremony, Akong and Sherab bowed out and went back to Samye Ling. Rinpoche had taken me shopping earlier in the day and had bought me a beige camel-hair suit, so at least I didn't get married in one of my hippie caftans. I think he was trying to clean up my act a little. He wore a dark gray flannel suit and tie. Before we got married, we got our picture taken in one of those booths where you put in a coin and take four pictures really quickly.

My sister, her boyfriend, and a couple of other friends went with us to a little hall where we were married by a justice of the peace. We took our vows sitting on folding chairs. We said all the traditional things: we promised to honor, obey, and love one another. I got two gifts: a muslin shirt and a bunch of daffodils. Later, Rinpoche said that we should get married again and have a proper wedding, but we never did.

When we came out of the hall after the ceremony, there was a scene with the press. Because of the new law, a number of reporters were hanging around to see who was getting married, and as we left the hall, they took photographs and tried to interview us. After we escaped the reporters, we went out to eat with our friends and then went back to the hotel and got in bed.

Shortly thereafter, our hotel room door burst open and more reporters came into the bedroom. They said to me, "We want to get some information. You've married your *gobo*. We need information. Tell us all about it." They didn't know what a guru was, so they kept calling Rinpoche my "gobo," a meaningless word. We were both horrified. That was one of the few times in those early days that I saw Rinpoche become really angry. He yelled at them, "Get out of here before I smash your cameras." And they left.

There were other dramas that evening. The press went to my mother's house in London and said that they wanted to ask her some questions about the daughter who'd just married a Tibetan guru—or *gobo*. My mother went into shock and said, "Oh my God, oh my God, Tessa got married. I can't believe it." Then they told her, "No, no, it's not Tessa, it's Diana." My mother fainted.

Rinpoche and I received a telephone call later that night from a friend of my mother's, saying that my mother was having the marriage annulled because I was underage. Rinpoche kept telling me not to worry, that it was okay, and that she wouldn't be able to do that because the marriage was legal and we had the marriage license to prove it. But it was still frightening.

The next morning we got the newspapers and discovered that our marriage had made the front page of the *People* and the *Express,* as well as the back page of the *Sunday Mirror,* none of which are among the better English papers. The *Sunday Mirror* featured a picture of Rinpoche and me, with the caption "Diana, 16, Runs Away to Marry a Monk." Seeing our picture in the tabloids must have been terribly humiliating for my mother.

However, for me, the most outrageous event occurred after all the reporters had gone away and the phone calls had ended. Late that morning, while we were lying in bed, Rinpoche decided he would call some friends to announce our marriage. His first call was to a friend in Wales, and I remember him saying, "Mary, a very exciting thing has happened to me. I'm married." And then he said, "Yes, yes, she's sixteen years old." Then I could hear her talking on the other end of the line, but I couldn't hear what she was saying. Rinpoche looked slightly quizzical, there was a pause, and then he said, "Hold on a minute." He put his hand over the mouthpiece of the telephone, and he turned to me and said, "Excuse me, Sweetheart, but what's your name?"

He had actually forgotten my name! Rinpoche lived his life without the conventional reference points that most of us cling to as the anchors of our sanity. I don't know if you can possibly imagine what I felt at this moment. It wasn't that I felt he didn't care about me or that fundamentally he didn't know who I was. In fact, he knew me better than anyone else did. But on the morning after our wedding, he couldn't remember my name. Not at all. Not Diana, not Pybus, not any of it. So I told him my name, and he happily went back to his phone conversation as though nothing had happened.

I, meanwhile, was freaking out. There was no regret on my part, but I realized that I had gotten myself into the wildest situation possible. I lay in bed thinking, "I don't know what's going to happen in my life. You know, I really at this point do not know at all what lies in my future. But I do know one thing: my life will never be boring. It definitely is going to be amazing and unusual." On the whole, I was both excited and terrified at the prospect of spending my life with such a person.

That was how our marriage began. I don't really blame my parents for the unusual path I've taken. They had something to do with it, but it is also the result of who I am. I chose this marriage and this life. As I said before, until I met Rinpoche, I never could connect with the world as a whole. I always felt different. I never felt like I was one of "them" at all. Meeting Rinpoche and being in his world were the first real things that happened for me in my life.

Once I entered his world, I didn't have any objective reference points, nothing to fall back on and say, "Well, this is normal, this is civilized. This isn't." For me, there was absolutely no other reference point. Just him. Just us. Just our marriage. I spent a lot of years married to Rinpoche operating in that space with him.

Later, when I started my intensive dressage training, I knew that I had to acknowledge the conventional world and some sort of conventional wisdom and behavior if I was going to find a place for myself in the riding world. I tried to keep those two worlds, my marriage and my career, separate so that I would be accepted in the riding world. Rinpoche's world was not a problem for me. It was just a bit of a balancing act.

THREE

To understand the cultural divide between my background and my life with Rinpoche, it might be helpful to know something about my childhood and upbringing. I was born Diana Judith Pybus at Queen Charlotte's Hospital in London, England, on October 8, 1953, at midnight on the new moon. My great-great grandfather was the first British ambassador to Ceylon and a member of the Council of Madras. When he returned to England, the king honored him by adding an elephant to the family coat of arms, which is also part of the Pybus seal on the family signet ring.

David Humphrey Pybus, my father, grew up in a large country house in the village of Hexham in Northumberland in the north of England. The house was close to Hadrian's Wall and in fact was made out of stones from the wall, so it had enormously thick walls. Denton Hall, as it was called, is one of the famous haunted houses in England. During the reign of Elizabeth I, when many Protestants were being persecuted, a young woman who lived nearby was murdered by Catholics, and she became the ghost of Denton Hall. My father's family called her "Silky," because of the silky white dress she wore as an apparition. Silky was a very active ghost, somewhat of a poltergeist. According to some stories, she was looking for a treasure that was buried somewhere in Denton Hall. Although she usually inhabited the family home, she was also seen in the coal mines in Newcastle that were owned by the Pybus family. The miners used to say that Silky appeared when there was about to be a fall in the mine.

My father had a speech impediment, which he thought was due to his terror of Silky as a young child. The youngest of three boys, he was often sent to bed before his brothers John and Michael. When he was alone in the bedroom, the curtains would begin to move, and he would hear strange moans and groans. Sometimes his dresser would move of its own accord.

Visitors to Denton Hall often reported encounters with Silky. Once when a woman and her son were staying with my father's family, the boy came down to breakfast and asked, "Oh, Mummy, who was that nice lady in the pointed hat who covered me up last night?" Most of the Pybus family saw this ghost on a fairly regular basis, so they realized that the little boy was talking about Silky, but they laughed it off, pretending that he was only dreaming. Another time, when a Catholic bishop came to stay in the house, Silky tore his covers off the bed during the night and terrified him by rattling things and moving them around in his room. Remember, she was a Protestant ghost. The bishop left the house early the next morning. Eventually, after many incidents, the family arranged for an exorcism, which was apparently successful, as Silky disappeared from Denton Hall. They say, however, that she still appears in the church in the little village of Hexham.

Following the completion of his public school education at English boarding schools, which he described as a miserable experience, my father attended Cambridge, where he took a degree in law. For generations, the Pybus men have been barristers and judges, so my father followed in the family tradition, even though his speech impediment did not make him an ideal candidate for the legal profession. After graduating, he enlisted in the British army and became the commander of a squadron that was part of the Normandy invasion in World War II. My father had terrible memories of the war. When I was a young girl, he told me how he and his squad had run over a German soldier with their tank. This memory haunted him. He would say, "I wish we hadn't done it. We could have gone around him. What happened to his family? Did he have children? This was a human being." Shortly after the invasion, he was seriously wounded by a sniper in France, the bullet passing an eighth of an inch from his optic nerve. Father was evacuated to England where he had a long convalescence.

My mother, Elizabeth Cornelia Smith, was born in 1910 in Bloemfontein, South Africa. Her mother was a baroness from Dutch nobility, while her father was an English businessman. When my grandmother decided to marry an Englishman, her family disowned her, for the Boers detested the English. My grandmother never spoke to her family again. (Estrangement seems a recurrent theme throughout our recent family history.)

My mother, Elizabeth, was the eleventh of thirteen children. Many of the older siblings had already left home before she was born. When she was five years old, her father contracted pneumonia and died, leaving a sizable estate to my grandmother. However, shortly after his death, the family discovered that he had cosigned on a large loan for a friend's business. The business went bankrupt, the friend defaulted on the loan, and the family lost everything.

My mother had a tough childhood in many ways. There was often not enough to eat; the children were lucky to have bread and milk for supper. Although my grandmother was a devout member of the Dutch Reform Church—on the Sabbath, the curtains were drawn and everyone had to spend the day sitting quietly in the living room—after she became so poor, she stopped taking the children to church because she didn't have money for shoes for all of them. My mother was also physically abused by one of her older brothers, who used to tie her to the bed and beat her. She never said this, but I always wondered if she had been sexually abused as well.

When she turned sixteen, my mother moved out of the house and became a hairdresser. She had her own salon in Johannesburg within a year. At eighteen she got involved with an older man who owned diamond mines in Rhodesia. After a brief courtship, she married him and moved to Rhodesia, but she was never happy there. Her husband had grown children and didn't want any more, whereas my mother was ready to start a family. After a short time, he took up with her seamstress. When my mother found out about the affair, she briefly contemplated poisoning her husband or killing herself, but she decided to leave him instead. She had never been off the African continent but had always dreamed of traveling to London. So she told him she wanted to travel by steamship to England, and he agreed to send her. On the boat, she met my father, who was on a holiday, and fell in love with him (my father had been in Africa). When she reached London, she wrote to her husband asking for a divorce.

My parents married a few years before World War II. My mother was eight years older than my father, and their marriage was not well accepted by my father's family. The Pybuses were not at all pleased that my father was marrying a divorcée from South Africa.

During the war, my mother was on her own in London for several years. While my father was away at war, she made attempts to educate herself. To disguise her South African accent, she took elocution lessons. She wanted to be accepted as a member of the British upper classes. She also read voraciously to make up for her lack of formal education. It wasn't so much that she wanted to know more; rather, she wanted to be able to make good conversation with my father's English friends.

While my father was away, my mother also made her professional debut as an opera singer, and she had a short but successful career during the war. A talented mezzo-soprano, she had been taking voice lessons for several years, and during wartime there was a shortage of divas in London. She was given the lead in a number of operas, including Mimi in *La Bohème* and Violeta in *La Traviata*. She sang at Covent Garden, the premier opera house in London.

When my father returned to England to convalesce from his war injury, he and my mother moved to a small cottage in the south of England, where he could recuperate. My mother wrote to the Pybus family asking them for financial support during this difficult period, but they sent no money. Instead, my grandmother sent down some old discarded linens that had been used by the servants in Denton Hall. The towels were embroidered with the word "Tweeney," which stands for "Between Maid" (between upstairs and downstairs in rank). My mother never forgot this insult.

Some time later, she persuaded my father to move to South Africa, thinking that life would be better for them there. They bought a beautiful old farm on the east coast, which they named Willowstream Park. During their years in South Africa, my mother and father started their family. They lost the first child, a little girl named Carol, who died three days after she was born from a medical condition that would have been easily remedied in England. In 1950, when my mother became pregnant for the second time, she and my father returned to England for the birth of my older sister Tessa. When I was born in 1953, my parents moved back to England for good.

When I was four months old, we moved into a Queen Anne house in the village of Cobham in the county of Surrey in the south of England. The house was called Ham Manor and was situated in a walled garden on one acre of grounds just on the outskirts of the village.

I have heard that only psychotic people remember their infancies, but I remember a great deal about mine, and from my earliest memories I remember feeling disconnected from my mother. I can remember lying in my perambulator on the lawn at Ham Manor, screaming. I had some booties on, and I didn't like their color. I wanted to take them off but I couldn't sit up, and I couldn't remove them myself. I must have been very small. I remember thinking about my mother, saying to myself, "She's in the house. She's not going to bother to come out and help me."

English babies spend a lot of time in their navy blue prams, which are made of coach metal and lacquered like an automobile. The baby's bed is large and sits quite high off the ground, with a luxuriously padded interior. There is a little seatback that you can set up in the bed, so that when the baby is awake, he or she can sit up and look around. I remember being wheeled by the nanny down to the village. I loved to daydream in my pram, and I can still remember the fantasy worlds I inhabited.

When I was about a year-and-a-half old, I remember standing in my bedroom, looking up at my dresses hanging in the wardrobe. They seemed tiny to me, and I thought, "Look at that. How ridiculously small they are! I don't know how I got myself into this situation. What on earth happened?" I thought it was quite amusing to be so small. My husband used to say that children before the age of five often have memories from past lives. When I look back on this incident, it seems that I was looking at my wardrobe through grown-up eyes from a previous life.

There was an apple orchard at Ham Manor, and in the middle of the orchard the children had a playhouse, which we called the Wendy House. There were terraced lawns in front of the house, and I was very good at riding my bicycle down the lawn and into the one and only tree on the front lawn, a large spreading oak.

As you entered Ham Manor, there was a large drawing room on the left and a library on the right. My parents were avid antique collectors, so the house was furnished with a lot of dark wood and Chippendale antiques. If you continued past the front hallway, you entered the formal dining room, behind which were the kitchen, pantries, and the laundry rooms. There was nothing remarkable about the second floor, where my parents had their bedrooms. But on the top floor there was a central room completely encased in glass. It had been built as a wig room. When you powdered your wig, the powder would adhere to the glass. The children had their nursery on the top floor, and my father's study was there. The nanny's quarters were also on the top floor, next to the nursery.

In our family the nanny was the chief caregiver. She took care of my sister and me twenty-four hours a day, and that was her only responsibility. The nanny always wore a uniform, a pale blue or green dress that buttoned down the front and looked like a nurse's uniform. Over the dress she wore an apron and a starched white collar.

When I was three years old, we had a rather elderly woman as our nanny for a brief period of time. She was stocky and wore black stockings. I can remember riding my tricycle in the lane behind the house while she watched me. At some point, I escaped and took off down the lane. She came running after me, yelling at me to stop. I got as far as a new housing development in the village, where there was a circular traffic island. I rode around and around the island, while she chased me in her uniform and black stockings.

Our next nanny stayed with the family, on and off, for a number of years. Frieda Kopfli, a young Swiss woman, was very kind to us, and my sister and I loved her, although she was a bit eccentric. She used to play the violin for us while we were going to the bathroom. It was an unusual toilet training technique. Once, she came into the nursery and started pulling all the jigsaw puzzles off the shelves, throwing the pieces in the air, dancing and singing and mixing all the puzzle pieces up. Finally, my father came in and stopped her. She was sent back to Switzerland for six months to recover from her nervous breakdown, after which she returned to us.

Frieda left the family when my sister was eight and I was five. My mother felt that we no longer needed a nanny when I was sent to a nearby private day school to attend kindergarten. After Frieda's departure, the live-in housekeeper looked after us when Mother was busy. Mrs. Wills, the housekeeper, was also the cook. Although she was quite a good cook, she herself seemed to survive on large tins of English biscuits, and she drank voluminous quantities of very sweet tea. She must have weighed close to three hundred pounds. Once or twice a year there would be a big drama when Mrs. Wills fell down in the lane behind the house. She was unable to get up by herself, so the men would have to be summoned from the garden to help Mrs. Wills up. She would then retire to bed for several days to nurse her bruises.

Mrs. Wills was a temperamental cook. If she was in a good mood, she would allow us to come into the kitchen and even help her with the baking, but at other times, she would scream at us, "You get out of my kitchen!" We ate breakfast every morning in the dining room, and we always knew what to expect for breakfast because Mrs. Wills had a weekly menu that never varied. Mondays would be tomatoes on toast, Tuesdays would be egg and bacon, Thursdays we had kidneys on toast, and Fridays we had cereal. I loved her puddings and the mince pies that she made at Christmas.

Once when Mother was giving a dinner party, she and Mrs. Wills prepared a special apple meringue pudding, which was put into the oven to bake just as the guests were arriving. While everyone was sitting at the table having their main course, my mother heard a crash coming from the kitchen. Excusing herself, she disappeared into the kitchen, closing the door behind her, only to find that Mrs. Wills had dropped the pudding on the floor as it came out of the oven. They conferred and my mother returned to the table. A little while later, apple meringue was brought to the table in dessert glasses. When one of the guests complimented my mother on the dessert and asked her how it was made, she replied, "You take an apple meringue, you bake it in the oven, you drop it on the floor, and finally you put it in glasses." Everyone found this amusing, not suspecting that she was telling the truth.

When we moved down to London when I was seven, Mrs. Wills came along and stayed with the family until shortly after my father's death when I was thirteen. When my mother discovered that Mrs. Wills had a heart condition, she let her go, telling us that it would be really unfortunate if Mrs. Wills were to have a heart attack during a dinner party. Mrs. Wills retired to a trailer park in the south of England. I felt terrible that this was how her loyalty to the family was rewarded.

Since my mother had been an opera singer, she had great hopes that her children would be musical. I was completely tone deaf and hated my piano lessons, which were forced on me at the age of four. However, when I was four, I was also allowed to start riding lessons, which I adored. My mother dropped me off at my first lesson at a stable near Ham Manor. She couldn't believe how excited I was. I can remember her saying, "Diana, I don't understand why you want to ride. You'll be out in the weather all the time and it will ruin your complexion."

At my first lesson, I was given a little white pony to ride. When it was over, I hung around the stall where my pony was stabled while I waited for Mother to pick me up. I was wearing a brand new outfit that Mother had bought me for my riding lessons. I took off my new velvet hard hat and filled it with water from a nearby trough. Then I invited the pony to drink out of my hat. After he finished his drink, he nibbled some of the buttons off my new blue sweater and chewed on the sweater as well. By the time my mother arrived, my clothes were pretty well ruined. When we got home, I was sent to my bedroom for the rest of the day as punishment. However, this didn't faze me at all. Horses were to become a lifelong passion.

My father had been working as a barrister, and he had prosecuted some rather important murder trials. But because he had such a terrible stutter, he became embarrassed about having to present arguments in court. When I was four, he went to work for a pharmaceutical company in London, about an hour from our home. By the time I was seven, my mother was bored with country life and wanted to move into the city. My father was glad to move into London; he was overtired from the commute and his long hours of work. I, on the other hand, had never known any other home, and I was sad to leave Ham Manor.

I had chronic bronchitis during my childhood, so when my parents made the decision to move into the city, it was decided that while they were getting the household set up in London, I would go for several months to South Africa to stay with my aunt Carol. My parents thought that the sunshine would do me good. I was sent by myself on the plane, and it was a really long trip. We stopped in Rome and in Nairobi on the way down.

Aunt Carol had a little bungalow outside of Johannesburg. There was a peach orchard in the back of her house, and she had several little dogs, with which I played during the day. I have fond memories of those months. Later, when I was thirteen, I returned to South Africa and at that time realized the extent of the racial prejudice. As a young child, however, I didn't take notice of it. My aunt was nurturing and caring in a way that I wish my mother had been. Tessa came down for the last month that I was there, and at the end of the summer we flew back to London together. I never saw Aunt Carol again. When I was nine, she developed lung cancer. My mother went back to South Africa and cared for her for six months until she died.

When Tessa and I returned to London, my parents had moved us into a large flat in the city. I found London claustrophobic. To my mind, it couldn't match life in the country. Our flat was located in Thorney Court, a Victorian block of apartments overlooking Kensington Gardens. The rooms were quite large, with high ceilings and tall windows, many of them facing the gardens, including those in my bedroom. The central hallway in the apartment was large enough to hold a grand piano and several wingback chairs.

My relationship with Mother deteriorated significantly at Thorney Court. I didn't feel that I could share anything with her because I found her so critical. She was never what I would call understanding or accepting of any pain or discomfort that I experienced, so I kept those things to myself. Occasionally, I would talk about my feelings with my father, with whom I shared more closeness and warmth. But he wasn't around much, so most of what I felt had to be buried.

After we had moved up to London, my parents purchased a small sixteenth-century thatched cottage in Cambridgeshire. We used the cottage during the school holidays, especially the summers. It was near Newmarket in the small village of Snailwell. It was quite primitive, with no electricity or central heating. It was set in the middle of a field. We would park in the field, where there often would be Jersey cows grazing, and walk from there through a gate that led into a small garden in front of the cottage. I loved being there in the countryside. I was able to go riding, as there was a stable nearby. My sister and I had a tree house at the cottage, and we had a fort in a hollow tree.

I have wonderful childhood memories of times spent at the cottage. My sister and I had more freedom when we were there. We used to ride our bicycles down to a nearby stream to go fishing. Once some gypsies came in a horse-drawn, brightly painted caravan and camped there, and I remember spying on them. Because we were children of the British upper class, in London we were not allowed to play with what my parents called "common" children. However, when we were at the cottage, the parents relaxed this rule. I used to go up to the nearby farm to see the Jersey calves and to play with several children who lived there.

One summer, my sister and I started the Red Riders Club. We invited our local friends to join, and we held our meetings in an empty house in the neighborhood. We broke into a house that was for sale, and we met in the attic. Initiations into the club were held there. To become a member, you had to sign your name in blood. At a certain point, one of the girls, Jenny, the farm manager's daughter, told on us. We all got into trouble for breaking into this house. I was furious at Jenny, and I decided to get back at her. There are natural deposits of chalk in that area, and I got hold of a piece. When Jenny and her family were away on holiday, I chalked a message onto the front door of their cottage. I wrote, "Jenny is a pig and we all hate her." When the family came home, they found the message, and it turned out I'd pressed so hard into the wood that I'd actually carved those words into the door. Understandably, my parents were furious.

From that time on, Tessa and I were not allowed to play with any of the children there. It seemed that my parents blamed the incident on the fact that we had been playing with the local village children, who were a bad influence, according to my parents. They were in fact quite prejudiced. As a young child, I had a music teacher who came to the house each week. Once, she brought another piano student with her, a young black boy. I liked him, and we got along very well. However, when I told my mother I wanted to invite him over to play, she told me that I wasn't allowed to see colored children. When I asked her why, she said, "If you play with colored children, you get familiar with them, and when you grow up you might end up marrying one." Intermarriage, apparently, would be a great tragedy. (In my mother's view, Rinpoche was a black man, so her fears did come to fruition.)

Just before my ninth birthday, my parents made plans to send Tessa to boarding school at Benenden School. The thought of being at home without her was frightening. My mother criticized and belittled me, and my father worked long hours and was rarely at home. I got the idea that I would like to go away to school as well. I remember the day this thought crystallized in my head. I had been out playing tennis with a friend. When I returned, my mother was in the lobby of Thorney Court, and we got in the elevator together to go up to the apartment. All of a sudden she started slapping me on one side of the head and the other. She was angry because I had a spot on my shirt. I remember thinking, "I've got to get out of here. I can't be left alone with Mother."

That night I asked my parents if I could go to boarding school too. I presented it as a positive idea, and although they were a little taken aback and worried because I was so young, they agreed. It was not that unusual for English children my age to go off to school. Before I left for school that autumn, Mrs. Wills taught me how to make a bed with perfect hospital corners, a skill that she knew I would need in the school environment.

I was too young to attend Benenden with Tessa, so I was sent to Portsdown Lodge, in Bexhill-on-Sea, in Sussex. It was an old, very long brick building that looked more like a hospital than a school. The educational system they followed there could only be described as archaic. We learned to write with quill pens, which we dipped in the inkwells on our desks. Once we mastered writing with a quill, we were allowed to use a metal nib that we also dipped into the inkwell. Finally, we were given fountain pens to write with. For our uniforms, we wore navy blue tunics with white shirts and dark ties.

The children were put to bed at six o'clock in the evening, even in the summertime. There was no talking after lights out, and if you cried in your bed at night, you were punished. You had to spend the next day in silence, no one was allowed to speak to you, and you were not allowed any dessert. That was the punishment for the first offence. I was terrified to talk, and I would lay awake in bed for hours.

After a few weeks in this repressive situation, I became spaced out and disoriented. I can remember feeling terrible about myself. The staff had my hearing tested because I was so unresponsive; they thought maybe I was partially deaf. Although life at boarding school was stark and lonely, I honestly wouldn't say that it was worse than my life at home. Leaving home and going to boarding school was perhaps exchanging one prison for the next, but I preferred being in an emotionally non-committal situation. In many respects, it was better to be free of the feeling of intimate personal attack from my mother.

At the same time, I missed my home and family terribly. One day, I saw my parents' car parked outside the school, and I was so excited, thinking that they were there for a visit. I waited expectantly, but they left without coming to see me. That was devastating. When I asked my father about it afterward, he said that they had a meeting with the headmistress, who was concerned about me because I was so remote and withdrawn. They were trying to figure out what to do. He thought it wouldn't be good for me to see them because it wasn't a visiting day.

Portsdown Lodge closed after my first term there. I think they had financial problems. I transferred to Sibton Park in the village of Lyminge, in Kent. It was also a repressive environment, but after I adjusted to it, I liked it better because of the facilities and some of the activities they provided. I was especially excited about the opportunities for riding at the school. There was a large stable, and they also had tennis courts and swimming pools.

Sibton Park was a large, sprawling Georgian building, with a beautiful facade onto the road. The students there, particularly the older girls, were especially cruel to new girls, in the best tradition of English prep schools. When I arrived at Sibton Park, one of my most precious possessions was a black doll with long hair, which I called my golliwog. At that time, golliwogs were very popular dolls in England; there were many children's stories written about them. Later, they largely disappeared because of the racist implications. For me, my golliwog was a precious possession, for which I felt great affection. Tessa had made the doll, and I always took it to bed with me. My first night at Sibton Park, the older girls ripped the golliwog out of my hands and shaved his hair off.

There were other incidents, some relatively harmless (such as tearing the covers off my bed just before our rooms were inspected), some sadistic. We bathed in cubicles lined up one next to the other. While I was in the tub, the girls would throw dead birds and insects over the top of the wall into my bathwater. During my first term, many early mornings around five A.M. a particularly nasty group of girls would gather at my bedside. One of them would grab me by the hair and yank me out of bed so that they could pour a pitcher of ice water over my head.

When I went home for the first school holidays, I tried to talk with my mother about what was happening at school. She laughed and treated it as a joke. She said to me, "Oh Darling, don't worry. If they aren't nice to you, just kill them." I took her advice quite literally. When I got back to school, I was determined not to let the girls tease me anymore. There was one especially nasty girl who abused me verbally. She was twelve, one of the oldest girls in our dorm, and she was the prefect, the girl in charge in our dormitory. She went out of her way to be mean to me, constantly teasing and making fun of me.

One night when she started in on me, I got out of bed and grabbed her hair with one hand while I punched her time after time. She started screaming, but I kept hitting her over and over again, on her body and her head. Finally, the girls ran to get the school matron, who burst into the room shouting at me to stop. I told her that I wouldn't. I said, "Oh no, I'm not stopping. My mother told me to kill her, and she's not dead yet." At that point, several of the staff pulled me off her and dragged me downstairs, where I was held until my mother came and picked me up. I was suspended for two weeks. When I went back to school, however, nobody gave me any more trouble.

The approach to many things at Sibton Park was old-fashioned. When I came down with chicken pox, I was put into isolation in a sick room and wasn't allowed to eat anything for twenty-four hours. I remember being so hungry. They felt it was bad to feed you very much if you had chicken pox. I was kept in isolation for two weeks with another girl who also had chicken pox. Her name was Sonam, and she and her sister Dechen both attended Sibton Park. She was a Bhutanese princess, the sister of Jigme Singye Wangchuck, who is now the king of Bhutan. She told me magical stories about Bhutan and its crystal mountains. She talked a lot about her brother, how tireless he was and how he could ride for days on end. I found her stories exciting. She also told me that she could do black magic, so if I didn't give her all my candy, she would do black magic on me. I believed her and gave her my whole stash of candy. I believe this was the first time I heard anything about Bhutan, a country closely connected with Tibet and Tibetan Buddhism.

At Sibton Park, the stables were across the courtyard from our class-rooms. When classes were done for the day, I would go and help in the stables, and I could ride the horses there. After I'd been at the school for a while, my parents told me that if my marks were really good, they would get me my own horse. My father, being a lawyer, drew up a de-tailed document in Latin promising me an *equus callibus unum,* which means "one horse" in Latin, if I got a certain number of high marks dur-ing the term. This was a great motivator. I decided that I was definitely going to obtain my pony, whatever it took, so I got the equivalent of all A's in school that term.

My mother took me to a dealer's yard, where there were a number of ponies of different sizes and colors all running around in a field. Not knowing anything about horses at all, my mother picked one based on its color. She picked out a Welsh bay pony, with four white stockings and a blaze. Appropriately enough, it was named Blaze. We arranged for the horse to be delivered to the school. When he arrived, it quickly became apparent that he had never been ridden and was totally untrained. After he was turned out into the field, nobody could catch him for several weeks. Eventually we did catch him, however, and he proved rather easy to train. It was the fulfillment of my dreams to have my own horse. In the spring and early summer, after school, I would ride Blaze through the woods and across the fields.

In the spring of 1966, when I was twelve, I took the common en-trance examination so that I could attend Benenden School in the fall. Benenden was—and I think still is—one of the top private schools in England. When I was there, Princess Anne, who was three years older than me, was a student there. The sister of King Hussein of Jordan and his daughter also attended Benenden, as did the Princess of Malaysia and Hailie Selassie's grandchildren, Princesses Mary and Saheen. The school was housed in an old building with beautiful grounds near the village of Benenden, in Kent. You had to perform quite well academically to be admitted, so I was very happy that I passed the entrance examination and was admitted to go there. I looked forward to joining Tessa, who was three years ahead of me.

When I came home for the summer holidays in 1966, it was appar-ent that the relationship between my mother and father had grown quite difficult. My father looked stressed, and he had aged considerably in a short period of time. Because his mother had treated Mother so badly, he was forbidden by Mother to see Grandmother or take us to see her. Secretively, my father would go with my sister and me to visit Grandmother. He told us that we absolutely mustn't tell Mother about this; she had threatened to divorce him if he defied her. Father told me that he actually wished he could divorce my mother, but that he wasn't going to do that because of how it would affect his children. There was a terrible stigma attached to divorce. It was not as it is in this day and age. He felt that if he were to divorce my mother, we would become known as the children of divorce and become less socially acceptable.

The family took a holiday that summer in Portugal. We stayed at a villa about fifty miles from Lisbon, up in the mountains above the beach. Our house was on a road opposite a convent for a silent order of nuns. One day when my sister and I were sitting in the villa garden, a man came by driving a herd of turkeys with a stick. We felt sorry for the turkeys, so we went out and bought two of them, which we kept in the garden for the rest of the summer. They made unbelievably loud screeching noises. It must have been very unpleasant for the nuns.

We were there with my mother for about two months, during which Father came out for a three-week visit. When he was there it was even more evident that my parents were having a great deal of difficulty. He cut his stay short, in fact, and went back to England to stay by himself and work.

When I think back on it, I realize that my mother had tremendous anxieties and insecurities that arose from trying to secure her position in English society. It was quite a stigma for her to have come from South Africa. In fact, she didn't tell anybody that she had grown up there. She was always struggling with her past. She really was not who she presented herself to be, because she felt that she wouldn't be accepted for who she was. As a result, she had an extremely strong desire to mold us into perfect, British upper-class children, her perfect products.

I realize now why she was incapable of having good communication with her children. Her overriding need for us to succeed where she could not prevented her from seeing who we were or what we needed. She had no ability to connect with our emotional life at all. The heavy burden from her past produced many of her emotional problems and made her dysfunctional as a parent.

I don't seem to have a single memory from childhood of feeling nurtured by my mother. In fact, it's difficult for me to think of even one time that my mother and I spoke openly and honestly to one another. I was always afraid of her, and I was afraid of exposing myself to her. If I let down my guard and allowed her to see my vulnerability, she was extremely critical and would tell me who I should be, what I should be, and why everything else was bad. I was never able to break through that. When she died, I realized, standing over her deathbed, that I had never in my entire life communicated with this woman, my mother, even once. That was both poignant and painful.

In 1966, after we came back from Portugal, I was lying in bed one morning in London when I had a very strong flash that one of my parents was going to die. Throughout my life, I've had these premonitions, usually in dreams, but this was not a dream. I lay there for a while looking at the sun coming through the curtains, thinking, "I hope it's my mother." When I caught myself having that thought, I felt tremendously guilty. Obviously, it was a very unpleasant thought. I tried to put it out of my mind.

My father was having a professional as well as a personal crisis at that time. He had started his own company a few years earlier, a company that was producing a new type of children's vitamin. He had used almost all his savings in the start-up. The product went on the market at almost exactly the same time that the problems with thalidomide came out, and this gravely affected sales because customers were afraid to try anything new and untested on the market. The company failed, and he lost everything he had invested. He was under tremendous financial strain. To keep my sister and me in private school, my father and my mother realized that they had to buy a smaller flat. While we were at school that fall, they moved into a modest flat in the Kensington area of London.

It was on that note that I started at Benenden School in September 1966. When you were accepted at Benenden, you received a long list of clothes that you had to purchase. There was a special department store in London where you went to get the things for your uniform. You had to have long-sleeved viyella shirts, and the younger children wore navy blue tunics with a tie. After the first two years, you didn't wear a tunic anymore. You had a navy blue pleated skirt. I was assigned to Guldeford

House, and Guldeford wore orange ties. There were six houses, and each house had its own color.

For outings, we had to have navy blue straw boaters, hats with brims that stood straight out. Men used to wear them in the 1930s. You had a band around your boater that was also the color of your house. Just by looking at a girl's tie or her hat, you could always tell what house she was from. The younger children wore navy blue overcoats. When you were a bit older, you wore a long woolen cloak. We also had regulation shoes. There were four or five styles that you were allowed to choose from. We wore navy blue stockings with our uniforms. In the afternoon, we could change into a velveteen dress. The dresses were exactly the same for all the girls, but you had a few colors to choose from.

When you got into the sixth form, which Tessa was in, you were finally allowed to change into your own clothes in the afternoon. I remember that Princess Anne had quite unfashionable clothes. I believe that she was only allowed to wear clothes made by the tailor for the Royal family. She wasn't allowed to wear the sort of hip clothes that other girls had.

Three houses at Benenden were located in the main building, and the other three were in freestanding buildings on the grounds. Guldeford was in the main building. Each house had its own dormitory and common rooms. You tended to identify with your house and socialize with girls from that house. I didn't have many friends in the other houses. There were about fifty children in each house, of all ages, and there was a housemistress for each house.

I did fairly well academically at Benenden, but in other respects I was a less than model student. The new girls were all expected to play lacrosse. We went to practice several afternoons each week, and in the evenings after practice, we would look at a bulletin board to see how well we'd done that day. Next to your name on the board were five empty squares. If you did very well at lacrosse practice, you would find that one square had been filled in with the color of your house. If you performed adequately, half of one square would be filled in. If you had done poorly, the square would be empty. After about two weeks, the girls who were quite good at lacrosse got five squares, and they were allowed to play in a house game. Girls who were unathletic might take three or

four weeks to fill in their squares. I managed to go three months without getting my squares filled. Finally, they gave up and allowed me into
a game. During the first game, I managed to do an over pass and hit the
teacher on the head with a lacrosse stick. My school report card at the
end of the term said, "Diana is a complete and thorough danger on the
lacrosse field." Eventually I found my way into the position of goalie. I
could wear a lot of padding and just sit in the goal and let the balls fly by.

Once again, at Benenden I found myself becoming disoriented and
unhappy. In part I think this was due to continuing problems at home,
but I can't blame it all on that. I came into this world feeling disconnected. At school, I didn't feel I was one of *them*. Fundamentally, I didn't
know why I was there; as a result, I failed to engage with my world.

My sister was also at Benenden for the first three months I was there.
She was a monitor, which is like a prefect. I had been looking forward to
being at school with Tessa, but in fact we didn't get along well at school.
I'm afraid that I was a bit of a pest and I think it embarrassed Tessa. She
decided that after the Christmas holiday, she was going to transfer to
Kirby Lodge, near Cambridge, to prepare for her A-levels.

When we came home for Christmas, there was still a lot of tension
between my parents, although they put on a good face so that we could
enjoy the holiday. On New Year's Eve, 1966, the family stayed up together to welcome in the New Year. Just past midnight, after we made
toasts to the New Year, my father took me aside and said that he wanted
to give me the family seal, the Pybus signet ring with the elephant on it.
He said, "This is always handed down in our family, and I want you to
have this." I was shocked. I said, "Why? I'm so young. Why now?" He
simply said again, "I want you to have it." I felt terrible about this because
it brought back my premonition that one of my parents was going to
die. Suddenly, I felt that he was going to die—quite soon. That night, Father slept on the couch in my bedroom. I asked him why he was sleeping in my room, and he said, "Life is precious. I don't have that many
opportunities to be with you." There seemed to be a certain unspoken
understanding between us that he was nearing the end of his life.

Two days later he left to take my sister to school. After dropping Tessa
at Kirby Lodge, he was going to spend the night at our cottage. He told
me that he wanted to get it ready to open up in the spring, so that I
could come out and go riding. Perhaps he also wanted a night or two

away from my mother. I remember hugging him good-bye. He was a heavy smoker, and I still remember the smoky smell of his cashmere overcoat as we embraced, the touch and the feel of it as we said good-bye. Later that evening, he called my mother and wanted to talk to me to wish me good night. I told Mother that I didn't want to talk to him. I couldn't bear to speak with him on the phone. Somehow I knew this would be the last time I would ever talk to him, and I just couldn't do it.

The following morning, I was in the flat with my mother, and she was having a fit because I had lost one of the rollers that she used to curl her hair. She was screaming and throwing the curlers at me one by one. The doorbell rang, and I went to answer it. It was the police, and I knew why they were there. They said to Mother and me, "You need to sit down. We have to talk to you." Immediately I said, "I know. My father's dead. How did it happen?" They told us that he had made a mistake when he turned on the gas, which we used for the stove in the house. Apparently, he had a fire going in the fireplace to heat the cottage. Gas from the tank leaked in the house and built up, and eventually the open flame in the fireplace ignited it, and the house caught on fire. My father apparently ran upstairs when the fire started to try to escape the flames, and he was overcome with smoke inhalation. By the time the fire engines got there, my father was dead. The cottage was completely destroyed.

In the days after his death, I felt a sense of unreality, as though there had been a mistake and he was going to show up again, just walk through the door at any moment. At the funeral, when I saw the coffin, I accepted that he was dead. Nobody talked to my sister or me, however, about how we felt.

After the funeral, we all stayed together in the flat for about a week, then Tessa and I were sent back to boarding school. My mother seemed overcome by her grief during this time. For my part, I was never able to express my feelings. I didn't cry much at all. There was the lingering feeling of unreality. From that time onward, the sense of being disconnected from my life became stronger.

A few months after Father's death, my mother moved into an ugly little house, which today we would say had terrible *feng shui*. It was off Exhibition Road in London, behind a block of large flats that overshadowed it. During the school holidays of 1967, the summer after my father died, my mother decided that it might do us all good to take a cruise to

South Africa. We were on the boat for about ten days, traveling on the Union Castle Line on one of the magnificent English ships of that era. I remember drawing into Cape Town and seeing Table Mountain rising behind the city as we docked. As we were preparing to disembark, I noticed that there was an area cordoned off, where we were supposed to walk. As the captain was walking down the center of this gangway, a black porter was walking in the opposite direction. Suddenly the captain grabbed this fellow, kicked him, and said, "Don't you dare get in my way. Don't you dare walk so close to me." I was shocked. Initially, I thought this man was crazy. I thought he was just some horrible, aggressive, out-of-control person, but as the visit went on, I realized that this went on all the time in this country.

When I'd been in South Africa at the age of seven, I hadn't noticed the racial climate. I was now starting to see that many things in the adult world were not as I had thought before. I think this is a fairly common part of growing up. At some point, you begin to question things that you took for granted as a child. Throughout this visit, I became acutely aware of the atrocities in the apartheid system in South Africa.

I also remember feeling psychologically dissociated from my world and depressed during our time there and thinking to myself, "Maybe I should just kill myself and get out of this misery." On the other hand, I was terrified of dying. I felt groundless.

After we toured around Cape Town, my mother wanted a few days by herself, so she sent my sister and me, along with a boy that Tessa had met, to Victoria Falls in Rhodesia—by ourselves. In retrospect, this seems like an irresponsible thing for my mother to have done. I was only thirteen, my sister was sixteen, and Tessa's boyfriend Charles was seventeen. However, we thought it was a great idea at the time.

Shortly after we arrived at the hotel in Rhodesia, we learned there was a casino near the hotel, but you had to be twenty-one to get in. So my sister went to work with all sorts of eye shadow and other makeup. We did ourselves up and managed to get into the casino, where we spent all of our money. We had money set aside for the return trip, which we also gambled with. We put the money for the tickets home on number thirteen on the roulette table, and amazingly enough, thirteen came up. We were lucky; it could have been disastrous.

We met up with my mother in Johannesburg, and she took us on a tour of the area. We visited Willowstream Park, the farm where she and my father lived with my sister when she was an infant. My mother told us stories about being there with Father when he was recuperating from his war injury. When they first moved there, he had bandages over his eyes and was very ill. My godfather, Walter Westhead, a retired naval commander, lived with them during that period. He was a bit of an alcoholic. One time when the car broke down, he was so desperate to get his gin that he drove the tractor twenty miles to town.

My mother was completely pro-apartheid, but I knew, even at the age of thirteen, that this was absolutely wrong. I began to hear terrible stories about the racial situation there. For example, when the people in the neighboring farm went to town to purchase groceries, they brought along their black servant to help them with the packages, but they didn't want him in the car, because they said he smelled. They made him ride in the trunk. We heard lots of stories like that.

When we returned to Johannesburg, we visited my mother's relatives, who were very religious. We visited her mother, who was ninety-eight at the time. She had taken to bed at the age of eighty-five, having decided that she was dying. She had spent the last thirteen years in bed. She was moved from one daughter's house to the next. When we were there, she was staying with Aunt Sarah, one of my mother's oldest sisters. Sarah would call to have her groceries delivered, but she wouldn't let the black deliveryman into the house with them. She made him put the box of groceries outside the door because no black people were allowed in her house. Altogether, I felt that South Africa, an exquisitely beautiful country, was ruined for me by the terrible prejudice that was prevalent at that time.

At the end of the summer, my sister went back to Kirby Lodge, and I returned for my second year at Benenden. This is when I began to look into approaches to religion and spirituality beyond the Christian beliefs I had grown up with. I had always had questions about the nature of existence, even as a young child. Something felt out of sync to me, right from the beginning. When, as most children do, I questioned my parents about why things are the way they are in the world, I didn't believe the religious explanations they gave me. When I was about six, I asked my mother, "Why am I me?" I had thought about this for a while. She said to me, "You're you because God made you you." Even at that age, I thought, "This doesn't work for me. I must have a little bit more responsibility in this than that!"

I could never connect with the Christianity with which I grew up. I found it impossible to believe in an unseen God. God was supposed to make all the decisions and know what people were thinking and feeling and help people through their hardships. To me it seemed like a fairy story. It never made sense to me.

We went to church, in the Church of England, every Sunday when I was growing up. A few years before my father died, he had a crisis of faith, and my parents started going to Billy Graham rallies and got rather fanatical about religion for a short time. This lasted for less than a year. In the last few years of his life, my father got interested in Eastern religion, and specifically in Tibetan Buddhism, but I only discovered that after his death.

Throughout the school year at Benenden, I read books on comparative and Eastern religion. The first Buddhist book I picked up was one by Christmas Humphries. When I read something like "The goal is to have no ego" or "You have no ego; you don't really exist"—or something along those lines—I put the book down and I thought, "I'm not going to read about Buddhism any more." I went back to reading about other religions. However, I came back to the books on Buddhism because they made the most sense to me, in spite of my fears. I connected with the emphasis on taking personal responsibility for your own state of mind. Beyond that, I was drawn to the Buddhist teachings because they talk about a path, a real means, to work with yourself and your state of mind. This felt more real and grounded than anything else I had encountered.

As I mentioned earlier, in the summer of 1968, when I was almost fifteen, we traveled to Malta. That summer I became convinced that Mother was trying to poison me. It was a ridiculous idea, but I couldn't get it out of my mind. When I did something she didn't like, she would yell, "I could kill you!" I took her at her word and I absolutely refused to eat anything she cooked. I spent my summer holiday being paranoid about Mother and reading books about Buddhism. It was just four months later that I first saw Rinpoche at the Buddhist Society. My life was about to change in ways I could never have anticipated.

Four

My husband, Chögyam Trungpa Rinpoche, was born in Tibet in 1940, the Year of the Dragon. His parents were Tibetan nomads living on the high arid plateau of eastern Tibet, and he had several siblings. When he was about eighteen months old, some monks from Surmang Dutsi Tel Monastery came to the encampment where he lived, looking for the reincarnation of their abbot, the Tenth Trungpa, who had died the year before. The Tibetan Buddhist belief is that when great, realized teachers die, they reincarnate and return, so that they can continue their work teaching and helping others. In their old age, some teachers write a letter about where they will be reborn, but in this case, no letter was found, and the monks were relying on a vision that His Holiness the Gyalwang Karmapa, the head of their lineage, had had. He told them where to look, the name of the child's father and mother, and gave them other details.

The first time they came to my husband's encampment, they interviewed people and made a list of the families with a child about a year old. However, they didn't talk to Rinpoche's parents because they were among the poorest families there, and the monks expected the next

Trungpa to come from a more well-to-do situation. When they presented the list to the Karmapa, he told them they must have overlooked someone and they should go back and try again. This time, when they got close to the village, they saw a little boy waving at them, and this was Rinpoche. They talked to his parents, and at first they were confused. The mother's name was right, but the father's name was not. Then, finally, the mother told them that her husband was not the father of this child, and she gave them the name of her first husband, which was the name they were looking for. The family also had a red dog and the door of their tent faced south, which were other details the Karmapa had seen in his vision.

The monks then tested the little boy to see if this was indeed the right child. They had a painted mandala that depicted six different realms of existence, and they asked the little boy which one he was from. He pointed to the human realm, rather than any of the others—the hell realm, the realm of hungry ghosts, the animal realm, the realm of the jealous gods, or the realm of the gods. That was the right answer, so they kept going. They took out two different bells, two ritual scepters (called *dorjes*), two walking sticks, and two *malas* (Tibetan rosaries), and they asked him which ones he would like. In each case, he chose the object that his predecessor, the Tenth Trungpa, had used.

The monks were delighted. Here was their abbot, this little nomad living in a yak-skin tent. He and his parents were invited back to Surmang. There are a number of monasteries that are all part of Surmang, spread over an area of perhaps fifty square miles in eastern Tibet. The monastery where my husband would spend most of his childhood was called Surmang Dutsi Tel. Dutsi Tel was an important monastery, but was not the largest. Surmang Namgyal Tse was the biggest monastery in the group, with close to a thousand monks living there. Rinpoche and his parents were taken to Namgyal Tse for the enthronement ceremony. His Holiness the Karmapa was visiting in that area, and thus he was able to perform the enthronement himself. More than thirteen thousand monks and nuns, plus many laypeople, attended the ceremony. It began with the refuge ceremony, which included cutting a lock of the young child's hair and giving him a Buddhist name.

Rinpoche then moved to Surmang Dutsi Tel, where he would live and study in the quarters of his predecessor. His father went back to the family encampment, but his mother stayed nearby until Rinpoche was five years old and began his formal studies. She was allowed to visit him every day, and he looked forward to these visits with great anticipation.

The Tenth Trungpa had been an austere, saintly man. His lifestyle was quite ascetic. For example, although he had received a beautiful white horse as a gift, when he went to another monastery to teach or went into the villages to see people, he refused to ride and always walked, until he was very old. His quarters at Surmang Dutsi Tel were likewise very spare. The bursar there—and bursars were very powerful people in the monastic hierarchy—wanted to redo the apartment completely in a more colorful and comfortable style now that the Eleventh Trungpa, the new abbot, had been found. Up to that point, they kept the rooms exactly the way they had been when the last incarnation had lived there. However, traditionally, when the new person is enthroned, he can make whatever changes he would like. In this case, Rinpoche was much too young to make those kinds of decisions, so his bursar had a free rein.

Rinpoche was delighted by the renovations, not so much because he wanted a fancier place to live, but because he was so interested in the work that all the craftspeople were doing. They painted the wood beams in his apartment in bright colors and designs, and Rinpoche and a little friend stole some of the paints so that they could make their own drawings. He had an interest in art that continued throughout his life.

Until he was five, Rinpoche's life at Dutsi Tel was fairly relaxed and pleasant. He was sometimes allowed to play with other young monks, and not much was required of him. He was a curious little boy, and somewhat mischievous. He got in trouble once for setting off firecrackers on the roof of the monastic kitchens. When there was fresh snow, he and the other little boys would sometimes have snowball fights in the courtyard.

At five, life changed quite a lot for him. There was a ceremony to mark the beginning of his education, and he started to learn how to read and write with a tutor, who stayed with him in his rooms at the monastery and watched his every move. Every detail of what he did was now observed and corrected: his posture, how he ate, how he sat, how he chanted, how he walked. The only time Rinpoche was alone was if his tutor took a break or when Rinpoche was in the privy. Sometimes he stayed there a long time, just to have some time to himself.

Life was both claustrophobic and lonely for him. His mother came less and less frequently to see him, and eventually she went home to their village and didn't return for months at a time. Those few times that Rinpoche was in his quarters by himself, he often would cry with loneliness.

At the same time, his tutor was a kind man, who occasionally disciplined Rinpoche but was generally very sweet and cheerful. If he needed to punish Rinpoche, he would excuse himself and go wash his hands, then he would light a stick of incense on the shrine in Rinpoche's bedroom, he would bow to Rinpoche—in fact, I think he might have done a prostration to him—and then he would proceed to spank him. As soon as his tutor lit the incense, Rinpoche knew what was going to follow.

He taught Rinpoche how to read and write by telling him stories about all the Tibetan letters, how this one looked like a man walking, and this one looked like a person sticking out his tongue, this one like a worm, things like that. Rinpoche found it easy to pick up, and everyone was impressed with how quickly he learned to read and write. His tutor also told him stories about the Buddha and about great Buddhist teachers in India and Tibet, which Rinpoche loved. In the evenings he would practice chanting. He was also allowed occasionally to draw, if the subject was a religious figure. On special afternoons, they would have a picnic or go for walks. However, he was no longer allowed to play with other children. In fact, he and his tutor moved up to a retreat center above the main monastery, so that he wouldn't have so many distractions from his studies.

Life went on like this for several years, and Rinpoche thought that things were going pretty well. He loved his tutor as though he were his father. He learned things much faster than anyone expected, and he thought he was doing a good job. But then, when he was about seven, the monastic committee in charge of his education decided that his tutor was being much too soft on him and that he needed greater discipline. So they brought in another man, who was quite harsh. He never administered corporal punishment, but his attitude was so severe that Rinpoche found him much more difficult to deal with. He too corrected Rinpoche's behavior constantly, but his approach was to belittle him with no encouragement, which made Rinpoche feel generally that he wasn't doing such a good job after all. At first, Rinpoche was quite intimidated by his new tutor, but then he decided that the way to deal with him was to be an absolutely exceptional student in every respect, so that there would be less to criticize. So he started to discipline himself and to study diligently, and within a couple of years he found that he could read better than his tutor and that he understood more than his tutor did about many of the topics they were studying. This intimidated the man, although he would pretend that he still knew more than his pupil.

Around the time that his new tutor arrived, Rinpoche began to have dreams about Western technology. He had never seen an airplane or a taxi, but he had dreams about both, and he saw lots of Western clothing, as well as boots and shoes in some of his dreams. His tutor told him that these dreams were nonsense.

Rinpoche felt that, through applying himself, he was becoming quite successful at his studies and he was doing what his elders wanted, but he didn't understand why they were making such a big deal about him. He thought that they were trying to make him into something that he wasn't and that he was supposed to pretend to be somebody. He found this strange and somewhat disheartening, but he tried to go along, to please everyone.

When he was eight years old, there was great excitement at Dutsi Tel because Jamgön Kongtrul, a very great teacher, was coming to conduct important ceremonies and give teachings at the monastery. He would become Rinpoche's root guru, his main teacher. This meant that he was going to be Rinpoche's primary spiritual mentor, who would work intensely and one-on-one with him and impart the most profound teachings to him. Rinpoche expected someone serious and stern, someone very learned and wise whom he would be expected to imitate. But when he met Jamgön Kongtrul, he found that he was not at all like that. He was completely open, kind, and warm, and not at all solemn. Nevertheless, everyone seemed to be slightly afraid of him because he also seemed to exude a lot of power. Rinpoche found that every movement that Jamgön Kongtrul made was very beautiful, not in an artistic way, but everything he did seemed to come from a deep well of genuineness.

Rinpoche thought, "Ah! This is what they want. This is what they've been trying to teach me." He saw that there was real wisdom embodied here and a genuine state of being that he could emulate, and he began to get an entirely different idea of what spirituality might be.

While Jamgön Kongtrul was visiting, Rinpoche had several private interviews with him. Jamgön Kongtrul gave him instruction in the sitting practice of meditation. It was very simple; in fact, it felt almost as though nothing happened. They simply sat in the space together. Jamgön Kongtrul seemed very pleased with their meetings, and he said that he was very happy to be able to give back to Rinpoche the wisdom that he, Jamgön Kongtrul, had received from Rinpoche's predecessor, the Tenth Trungpa—who had been his teacher. He told Rinpoche that he shouldn't discuss their meetings with anyone else. Rinpoche understood that his teacher was giving him something precious, something that couldn't be described in words. After Jamgön Kongtrul left, Rinpoche applied himself more and more to his studies, and he began to get a true sense of what the teachings were really about, which went beyond the rules and the outward discipline that he was expected to follow.

Around this time, Rinpoche spent several months studying with Rölpe Dorje, who was the regent abbot of Surmang, which meant that he was the acting abbot of the monastery until Rinpoche reached the age and had the maturity where he could assume these duties. Rölpe Dorje was quite a realized teacher in his own right. He was staying in a cave at his retreat center in the area, away from the main monastery at Dutsi Tel.

Rinpoche found his time with Rölpe Dorje very powerful. Rinpoche started what are called the preliminary practices, or the *ngöndro,* in preparation for more advanced tantric practice. The preliminaries include performing a hundred thousand full prostrations while visualizing the Buddhist lineage and taking refuge in the Buddha, the teachings, and the *sangha,* or the Buddhist community. Rinpoche also did other practices that involve purifying oneself and surrendering one's ego so that it is possible to connect with the wisdom of the Buddhist lineage. Although he found all of this very helpful, he wanted more than anything to go to Jamgön Kongtrul's monastery to study with his guru. Jamgön Kongtrul had told him that he had much more to learn and that he should come and spend time with him when he was ready, and Rinpoche felt that indeed the time was approaching for him to go to his teacher.

Rinpoche was now nine years old. It was 1949, and the influence of the communist Chinese began to be felt in this region of Tibet. Nothing had actually happened to disrupt their way of life, but the Tibetans were very distrustful of the situation. Around this time, Rinpoche's mother left her husband and was able to move to Surmang permanently. Rinpoche was very happy to have her return. She was given a position working in the dairy farm just outside the walls of the monastery. She worked with the yaks in the dairy and helped take care of the horses. Whenever he could, Rinpoche would go down and spend time with her. Once, when they were in the horse stables, he found some of the salty pickles that were given to the horses as treats. He started eating them, and he found them delicious. He was chewing on one of them, and he asked his mother what their family name was. She said, "You are Rinpoche. Your name is Rinpoche." And he said, "Yes, I know that, but what is our family name?" And she said, "Why do you want to know that?" He replied, "Well, you're my mother and I came out of your body, and I want to know who I am." He was very persistent. Finally, she said, "Well, you shouldn't think about that. But if you will stop eating those pickles, I'll tell you our name." And he stopped, so she said, "Our name is Mukpo. But forget about that. You are Rinpoche."

Rinpoche was very proud to be a Mukpo. In Tibet, Mukpo is one of the six main clans. His Holiness Karmapa was from the Mukpo clan, as was Dilgo Khyentse Rinpoche, another of my husband's teachers. Gesar of Ling, who is a famous folk hero in Tibet, was also a Mukpo. So Rinpoche took great pride in the Mukpo name. He used the name C. T. Mukpo on his British passport and passed on that family name to me and to our children.

When he was twelve, Rinpoche talked to the monastic committee about going to Sechen Monastery to study with Jamgön Kongtrul. They convinced him to first do a tour around the Surmang area, as there had been several invitations for him to visit neighboring towns and monasteries. These tours were one way that the monastery raised money for its operations, so the committee was very interested in having Rinpoche do this. The tour took about three months, and while he was traveling around, for the first time, he saw Chinese soldiers encamped around some of the monasteries to the south of Surmang. It was a troubling sign.

Finally, having completed his obligations, he left for Sechen with several attendants, including his tutor, who insisted on coming along. It took ten days to reach the monastery. He arrived on his thirteenth birthday.

Jamgön Kongtrul was delighted to see Rinpoche and immediately had him start a rigorous course of study. His main tutor at Sechen was a *khenpo,* the equivalent of a Ph.D. in the West. Khenpo Gangshar was a very learned man. Over the course of time, he became a somewhat wild and crazy yogi who would impart much more than book learning to Rinpoche.

Rinpoche was able to stay a full year at Sechen. During that time, Jamgön Kongtrul conducted an extensive transmission of important Buddhist texts, called the *Rinchen Terdzö,* which takes about six months to complete. All the students receiving these teachings had to be up and in the shrine room by five A.M. every day, when the morning session began. Several hundred monks attended this presentation of the teachings. At the end of the whole program, Rinpoche was selected from all the participants to receive a special empowerment that made him the holder of these teachings and gave him the permission to transmit them to others. He was somewhat overwhelmed by this honor, which is only extended to one person at an event like this. He was just a young monk, and there were many older, much more learned teachers attending this cycle of teachings.

When the *Rinchen Terdzö* teachings were finished, Rinpoche continued his studies under Khenpo Gangshar. He lived in the monastic college, or *shedra,* which housed about a hundred students at Sechen Monastery. He would finish his breakfast before five A.M. and then study for three hours. At eight A.M., Khenpo Gangshar would begin the day's lecture. The studies were demanding, but Rinpoche found that he enjoyed them. The material was quite advanced and presented in depth, and Rinpoche loved the challenge and the vitality with which the Khenpo taught. He also was able to continue his private instruction with Jamgön Kongtrul, which was not just about learning the doctrine but was about actualizing the teachings in one's personal experience.

One of the aspects of the training that Jamgön Kongtrul emphasized was teaching Rinpoche how to compose *dohas,* which are spontaneous songs or poems that express your experience or immediate realization of the teachings. They are quite different from traditional Tibetan poetry, which is prescribed and formal. Rinpoche also learned those strict poetic forms, but having to compose *dohas* in the presence of his teacher was both more intimidating and more profound for him. Jamgön

Kongtrul could see through him right away if he was not completely genuine and on the spot.

Just after his fourteenth birthday, Rinpoche's monastery sent word that they wanted him to return to Surmang Namgyal Tse, the large monastery where he had been enthroned, to conduct the funeral rites for an important lama who had just died. He would have preferred to stay at Sechen, but his tutor insisted that they must go. When Rinpoche went to tell Jamgön Kongtrul that they were leaving, his guru told him that he should return as soon as he possibly could. Jamgön Kongtrul had a dream in which he saw a half moon that others said was full. "This means that you are not fully ripened," his guru said.

On the way back to Surmang, Rinpoche and his party saw a Chinese airfield and soldiers riding around on newly built roads in their jeeps. After Rinpoche performed the requisite ceremonies at Namgyal Tse, he received an invitation to visit Drölma Lhakhang, a monastery about six days from Surmang. Several days after arriving there, he was requested to give the *Rinchen Terdzö* empowerment. This was a great honor, although Rinpoche felt intimidated to be asked to do this when he had so recently received it. As well, he was only fourteen years old. It was at Drölma Lhakhang that he first met Akong Rinpoche, in this lifetime at least. Akong was the young abbot there, and he and Rinpoche became close friends in a short period of time.

Rinpoche was fifteen when he finally returned to Surmang Dutsi Tel. He had been gone for more than two years. Now, there were many signs of the influence of the Chinese. They were building roads in the area, and they appeared at the monastery and sat in on many events. Clearly, they were advancing their objectives in this part of Tibet. It was in this atmosphere that Rinpoche continued his duties and his training at Surmang.

He was now old enough to begin learning the tradition of monastic dance, for which his monastery was, and still is, quite famous. It is a contemplative form of dance that incorporates the meaning of some of the highest Buddhist teachings from the *Chakrasamvara Tantra,* a very advanced Vajrayana text, in the gestures and movements that are performed by the dancers. It is extremely physically demanding. Rinpoche threw himself wholeheartedly into the training, and by the time of the Tibetan New Year's celebration at the end of that year, he was able to join in the dances, although he felt that his training was certainly not complete.

The Chinese were now visiting the surrounding monasteries to show propaganda films to the monks. Many senior teachers were becoming quite worried about what the Chinese would do next. Both His Holiness the Karmapa and His Holiness the Dalai Lama made visits to eastern Tibet around this time, ostensibly to give teachings and blessings to the people, but also to warn them of what might be to come. They were not able to speak out directly, of course, because they were being watched, and in fact they now had to travel with a Chinese escort who observed and listened to everything they said.

It was extremely moving to Rinpoche to meet His Holiness the Dalai Lama. He was able to have a brief private interview with the Dalai Lama, and Rinpoche talked at greater length with the Karmapa, who urged Rinpoche to complete his education and to build a monastic college at Surmang, which Rinpoche took to heart. There was no actual discussion about what the Chinese might be up to, but when the Dalai Lama and the Karmapa described their recent trips to Beijing, reading between the lines, it was clear that all of Tibet was in a precarious situation. Some Tibetan teachers were already making plans to escape to India, but Rinpoche hoped at this stage to remain. He still wanted to return to his teacher one more time, and thankfully, he was able to do so. He traveled back to Sechen and spent a few months with Jamgön Kongtrul, where he received the final teachings from him. Jamgön Kongtrul told him that he would now have to make decisions for himself, and that he should always be guided by the wisdom of the teachings and the lineage in whatever he did. His guru said that he had seen that Rinpoche might indeed be going to the West.

Rinpoche returned to Surmang where he began work on building a *shedra,* the college for advanced Buddhist studies that His Holiness Karmapa had recommended he create, similar to the *shedra* at Sechen that so inspired him.

Things were now in an uproar, with the Chinese beginning to take over some of the monasteries, burning books from the monastic libraries, destroying religious treasures, forcing the monks to do manual labor on the roads, and so forth. Some laypeople were organizing a Tibetan militia in eastern Tibet to fight the Chinese. There had been no problems yet at Surmang, but almost everyone felt that it was only a matter of time.

During this difficult period, Jamgön Kongtrul sent Khenpo Gangshar to Surmang to help Rinpoche with the work of establishing the college. While at Surmang, Khenpo Gangshar became convinced that it was time to take drastic measures. My husband told me many stories about the time that he spent with Khenpo Gangshar and the amazing teachings that he received from him. Rinpoche told me that while at Surmang, Khenpo Gangshar had taken ill and seemingly died. After remaining in a meditative state for several days, he got up, as though life had come back to his body. Before that, he had been a gentle, quiet man, a perfect monk and extremely learned. But from that time on he exhibited wild and wrathful energy. Rinpoche said that indeed Khenpo Gangshar was the embodiment of what is called the "crazy wisdom" lineage in Tibet. Such teachers are known for displaying their wisdom through unconventional and often unpredictable behavior, which is the expression of compassion without bounds. Crazy wisdom is not indulging in wild behavior just to have a good time or to be shocking and provocative for no reason. As Rinpoche once said, first you get the wisdom; then you get the crazy. The idea is that there is no boundary to the energy of egolessness and that whatever is called for in a situation, even if the means are extremely unconventional, will be used to help beings who are suffering in samsara, the endless cycle of confused existence. Rinpoche himself became known as one of the foremost crazy wisdom teachers in the West.

At this time at Surmang, Khenpo Gangshar insisted that it was time to break down the barriers between the monastic and the lay communities and that everyone should work together to understand the Buddha's message of compassion, so that hopefully they would be able to change the attitude and the intentions of the Chinese. He held meetings with everyone in the neighboring area, bringing people together from all of the monastic and lay communities. This was an outrageous thing to do in Tibet, where everything was so stratified and there was such a big divide between monastic and lay life. Khenpo gave teachings to everyone. He allowed women to come into the monastery for these teachings, which was unheard of. He also went and visited many monks in solitary retreat and told them that, during this time, they should come out of retreat, return to their monasteries and villages, and work with others. He told them that in their hearts they could remain in retreat but that their help was needed in the world.

In spite of the chaos of the time, construction went forward with the *shedra,* and the Khenpo worked closely with Rinpoche so that he was able to complete his studies and take the examination to become a *khenpo* himself. This was very meaningful for my husband; even though the times were so dire, he wanted to go forward with this project and with his own education.

Then, they heard that Jamgön Kongtrul had left Sechen and gone into hiding. It was becoming increasingly clear that the Chinese would not be dissuaded. There were reports of many more monasteries being invaded, sacked, or completely destroyed. Surmang was spared for some months and Rinpoche waited and waited, not wanting to disappoint anyone or leave anyone behind, but eventually it became clear that for his own safety, he too would have to go into hiding. He left Surmang, not really knowing but feeling that it was for the last time. His parting with his mother was especially poignant. He never saw her again.

He spent some time in retreat and also gave teachings at another monastery some days away from Surmang, performing the *Rinchen Ter-dzö* for the second and last time in Tibet. At the very end of the empowerment—which they shortened because of the political crisis, so that it could be completed in three months—he learned that Jamgön Kongtrul had been captured by the Chinese. Then, while in retreat, Rinpoche learned that Surmang Dutsi Tel had been sacked. The tomb of the Tenth Trungpa had been opened by the Chinese and the remains spread around the courtyard. Rinpoche's bursar, who was at Surmang at the time, gathered and cremated the remains and brought them to Rinpoche in a reliquary box. The bursar also carried the news that Surmang had largely been destroyed and that there was a price on Rinpoche's head. In the end, Rinpoche had no choice but to leave for India. Before his departure, he heard that his mother and other members of his family had gone to a small, very remote monastery, and they sent word that they were safe. His mother wrote and told him not to worry about her. He should go.

So he set off for India, a trip that would last ten months and take him over many of the highest passes in the Himalayas. When word got out that he was leaving, many joined his party. He had hoped to travel with a small group, but in the end close to two hundred Tibetans joined him. Akong was one of the party, as were several other young *rinpoches*. They walked out of Tibet, leaving in April 1959.

When the snow was very deep going over the passes, the largest, most burly monks in the party would go ahead and throw their bodies in the snow to make a pathway for the others. When one group tired, a second group of men would take over this task. At times they had to cross fast-flowing rivers on rickety hand-built bridges, one by one.

They took a circuitous route, to avoid the main roads used by the Chinese and the areas of greatest Chinese occupation. Often they traveled at night, especially if they had to cross a highway. Their journey was amazingly successful, especially considering the number in the party, and they avoided any encounters with the Chinese until the very end. Several times, they made camp for a few days of rest and meditation at Rinpoche's urging. He wanted people to keep up their strength as much as possible and not to lose contact with their meditative insight. When the path ahead was uncertain, Rinpoche would often use forms of Tibetan divination, in which he was trained, to decide which way they should go.

After many months of travel, the party, which had grown now to almost three hundred, reached the wide, swiftly running Brahmaputra River in the southern part of Tibet. There were only a few crossing points. Some of the monks fashioned boats made of yak skins to get them across, and they chose a crossing that was just outside of a small village. They hid in bushes around the village during the day, and on the night of December 15, 1959, under a full moon, they set out to cross.

Villagers, however, had alerted the Chinese that there was a group of Tibetans hiding near the town who might attempt to cross the river, and when Rinpoche and the first party had just made it across and the boatmen were about to go back for the next group, the Chinese attacked. Of the three hundred in the party, only a few dozen escaped and continued on. The remainder were captured, and many were shot. The group of those who successfully escaped traveled for another month through southern Tibet. They had almost run out of food and at the end had to boil leather to eat. They saved a small amount of barley flour for Rinpoche so that he would not have to eat these provisions. Toward the end, they passed through valleys where bananas were growing on trees along the side of the path, but not knowing what a banana was, they didn't eat them. On January 17, 1960, they crossed the border into India.

Rinpoche spent nearly four years in India, where he encountered a world vastly different from Tibet. He had grown up in an essentially medieval culture, and a very unusual one at that. It was one of the very few places on earth, at least in the twentieth century, where spirituality was uppermost in the minds and hearts of almost the entire population. Tibet was certainly not an idyllic society. Rinpoche often said that there was a great deal of corruption in Tibet, and that this was a contributing factor in its occupation by the communist Chinese. At the same time, he loved the land and the people, and he was completely immersed in a Buddhist world there.

In Tibet, he had been a very special and privileged person. In India, the Tibetans were refugees and were not generally treated very well, although kindness was extended to them by the Indian government and many individuals living in India. However, Rinpoche was no longer a person of high status, as he had been. He told me that, not long after arriving in India, he was invited to an English garden party. The hostess was passing around a tray of cucumber sandwiches, which she offered first to Rinpoche. He took the whole tray, thinking that she had made a nice lunch for him. Later, he was quite embarrassed by this.

Many of the Tibetan refugees ended up in camps. He stayed in the camps for a short time, but then he was able to relocate to Kalimpong, which was close to the seat that His Holiness the Karmapa established in Sikkim after escaping from Tibet. While he was in Kalimpong, Rinpoche studied *thangka* painting, and he produced beautiful paintings of Padmasambhava and his consort Yeshe Tsogyal, as well as other subjects. Later, he was able to bring these paintings with him to the West, and one of them hangs in my house today. He became friends with Tendzin Rongae, a wonderful *thangka* painter who had also recently arrived from Tibet and helped Rinpoche with his painting. Rinpoche became close to the entire Rongae family. While in Kalimpong, he learned that Dilgo Khyentse Rinpoche had also recently entered India and was living a few miles away, about an hour away by foot. Rinpoche used to walk over to see Khyentse Rinpoche and to receive teachings from him. Dilgo Khyentse was over six feet tall, very unusual for a Tibetan, and he had enormous warmth and presence. During this time, Rinpoche became friends with Khyentse Rinpoche's nephew Ato Rinpoche.

India is a significant place for Tibetans because it was the home of the Buddha and of many of the great teachers whose works are studied in Tibet. One could say that India is for Tibetans what the Middle East is for Jews, Muslims, and Christians. There are many Buddhist pilgrimage sites in India. Rinpoche was able to visit Bodhgaya, where the Buddha attained enlightenment, and other important sites.

In India, Rinpoche was also exposed to many non-Buddhist cultures for the first time. He came to love Indian food and to appreciate many things about the Indian culture. He encountered people from all over the world there. In particular, he met several English Buddhists who were extremely kind and helpful to him. Freda Bedi was one of these. She was an Englishwoman who had married an Indian, Baba Bedi. She worked for the Central Social Welfare Board of the Indian government helping Tibetan refugees, and she was so affected by her involvement with the Tibetans that she became a Buddhist herself. After her husband's death, she was one of the first Westerners to become a Tibetan Buddhist nun.

Rinpoche met her at the refugee camp in Bir, and she formed an immediate bond with him. From the earliest contacts he had with Westerners, he shone out like a light or a beacon to them. Lama Govinda, a Westerner and an early writer about Tibetan Buddhism, reported this quality. Lama Govinda met Rinpoche in northern India, just after Rinpoche's escape from Tibet. Many Tibetan refugees stayed at Lama Govinda's house in the Himalayas on their way south, and he said that Trungpa Rinpoche was the brightest of them all.

Freda Bedi helped Rinpoche resettle in Kalimpong, and later she asked him to help her establish a school to train young Tibetan monks, the Young Lamas Home School, in New Delhi, which moved to Dalhousie after about a year. He was delighted to do this, and with the blessings of His Holiness the Dalai Lama, Rinpoche became the spiritual advisor to the young monks at the school.

This was the first time that Rinpoche had ever lived in a secular society, and although at first he found it quite strange, he soon took to it. He went to meetings of a British women's club so that he could hear the poetry of T. S. Eliot read, and he used to go to the cinema in New Delhi. On his way out of Tibet, close to the border with India, he was exposed to alcoholic beverages for the first time. In one of the villages where they stopped, you couldn't drink the water, and everyone drank a kind of Tibetan beer. He had been hesitant to imbibe any alcohol since it was a violation of his monastic vows, but once he gave in, he enjoyed the experience, and in India he started to drink occasionally, though not openly. Tendzin Rongae and Rinpoche liked to get together and drink from time to time.

On the way out of Tibet, Rinpoche had fallen in love with a young Tibetan nun, Könchok Paldrön, who was part of the escape party. He became clandestinely involved with her while he was in India. She was living in the refugee camp in Bir. She visited him at the Young Lamas Home School, and they took a mattress up on the roof of the building, where they spent the night together. She became pregnant and gave birth to Rinpoche's eldest son, Ösel Rangdröl Mukpo, a short time before Rinpoche left for England. When she was pregnant, she made a pilgrimage to Bodhgaya, and their son was born there. She could no longer be a nun, so after Ösel was born, she worked as a road laborer to support herself for some time. Later, she married and had another child.

Around this time, Rinpoche received a Spaulding Scholarship to attend Oxford University. This had come through the intercession of Freda Bedi and John Driver, an Englishman who tutored Rinpoche in the English language in India and helped him with his studies later at Oxford. The Tibet Society in the United Kingdom had also helped him to get the scholarship. To go to England, Rinpoche needed the permission of the Dalai Lama's government. They would never have allowed him to leave if they had known about his sexual indiscretion, nor do I think it would have gone over very well with the Tibet Society or his English friends in New Delhi. He and Könchok Paldrön kept their relationship a secret, and it was a long time before anyone knew that Rinpoche was the father of her child. This caused him a great deal of pain, although I also think that he hadn't yet entirely faced up to the implications of the direction he was going in his relationships with women. At that time, in spite of the inconsistencies in his behavior, he still seemed to think that he could make life work for himself as a monk. Rinpoche continued to stay in touch with Könchok Paldrön and his son Ösel, and a few years later, he returned to see them and to make arrangements for his son to come to England.

Rinpoche sailed from Bombay for England early in 1963, on the P&O Line, accompanied by his close friend Akong, who was to be a helper and companion to him at Oxford. Rinpoche had been working very hard on his English, but when he left India, he was still struggling with the language, speaking what would be called a form of pidgin English. When Rinpoche and Akong docked in England, they were welcomed by members of the Tibet Society, and before his studies started at Oxford in the fall, Rinpoche spent time in London, where he met many of the most prominent members of the English Buddhist community. He was invited to give several talks at the Buddhist Society, and he attended a kind of summer camp they sponsored each year, where he gave a number of lectures.

While still in Tibet, Rinpoche was fascinated by any Western objects that he saw. He received a watch as a gift when he was a teenager, and he had taken it completely apart to see, literally, what made it tick. He couldn't get it to work when he put it back together. Later, when he was given a clock that chimed, he took that apart as well, to discover what mistakes he had made the first time. He was successful putting the clock—and then the watch—back together so that they both kept time. He said of his arrival in England: "Coming to the Western world, I encountered the makers of the clocks, big and small, and the makers of other machines that do wondrous things—such as airplanes and motor cars. It turned out that there was not so much wisdom in the West, but there was lots of knowledge."[1] That, I think, was one of his dominant impressions of England: the technology and the knowledge about how things work in the world were very impressive, but there was not so much interest in a deeper spiritual understanding. There was, however, quite a lot of fascination with Eastern spirituality.

In England, among some people, Rinpoche found himself the object of that fascination. It was almost as though he were an exotic species of bird. He said that he found it very strange to be looked at as though he were a biological oddity rather than a human being. I think this was his first inkling that there might have to be major changes in his life if he wanted to break through the cultural distance and the polite veneer.

There was also quite a distinction between the older generation of English Buddhists Rinpoche met, who were prim and proper and highly philosophical, and the younger generation, who were part of the broad exploration and revolution in thinking that was spreading like a virus through Western youth in the mid-1960s. The young English students were certainly less extreme in their counterculture than those in America, but young people in Great Britain were also questioning many aspects of their society. Rinpoche found this quite alluring from early on. He was brought to England by the older, somewhat stodgy generation, but they weren't going to be able to corral him for long.

When he went up to Oxford, he had quite a challenge trying to bring his English up to speed so that he could understand the lectures and the books he was given to read. Rinpoche wanted to learn as much as he could about English history, philosophy, religion, and politics, but it was pretty tough going for him at the beginning. John Driver, whom he had met in India and who had been instrumental in bringing him to England, returned to England and helped Rinpoche a great deal with his lessons, and Rinpoche never forgot this kindness. In the evenings, Rinpoche attended classes in the town of Oxford to improve his English. Years later, he still remembered how his teacher had made the class say words over and over, to improve their elocution, such as "policeman, policeman, policeman." Rinpoche proved himself a brilliant student of the English language. By the time he left England for America, his English vocabulary exceeded that of many of his students.

At Oxford Rinpoche was befriended by the Jesuits, who thought that his tremendous enthusiasm for learning about the Christian religion made him a good candidate for conversion. Of course, nothing could be further from the truth, but Rinpoche enjoyed their company and felt that here at least he had found Westerners who had some understanding of a wisdom tradition, even though it was not his own.

When he first arrived in England, he was still haunted by memories of the atrocities he had witnessed in Tibet and by the sadness of losing his country. At this point, he had no idea what had happened to many of his teachers, compatriots, and members of his family. He didn't know if he would ever find out what happened to them or be able to return to Tibet. He felt it was unlikely. A way of life, a whole culture, was gone, as far as he knew, except for the remnants that survived in India. Rinpoche wanted to make sure that the wisdom of that culture was not lost, so his commitment to the Buddhist teachings and to bringing them to the West was beyond, I think, what we can imagine.

At first, he tried to hold onto what he sometimes called "Tibetan-ness." As much as he was fascinated by Western culture, he also could see how materialistic it was and how lacking in some of the values that he held most dear. For quite a while, he tried to befriend Westerners while holding onto his cultural identity. He felt this was being loyal, true to his heritage. But then he began to realize that it was only by going much further into the ways of the West that he would be able to communicate what he knew. He became determined to let go of the trappings of the past and to embrace the Western approach to life in order to preserve the wisdom of his heritage, paradoxical as that might seem.

This transition was not entirely gloomy or forced, but for a period of time it was very painful for him because he had left so much behind in Tibet, and now he was giving up even more. At the same time, he was drawn to the West, and he remembered things that Jamgön Kongtrul had said to him the last time they were together in Tibet. His guru had told him that he thought Rinpoche would go to the West, and that he would find people there who would remind him of the sanity and soft heart embodied in his teachers. He also told him that in India, the Buddha was born a prince and became a monk, but that in the West, a monk might have to become a prince. Rinpoche took this to mean that a secular approach to Buddhism might be the best way to proceed in the West.

I think that one of the most painful things for him was that he and Akong saw this so differently. The more Rinpoche was attracted to a Western way of life, the more Akong wanted to preserve the Tibetan style and culture. More fundamentally, Rinpoche started to make deep connections with Westerners, especially some of the younger students who made their way to him. He went beyond viewing them as a foreign species or as barbarians. Many Westerners were also looking at him that way, but he found the ones that weren't. They were the ones that reminded him of his teachers. They were the ones he wanted to spend time with. Akong couldn't get past those cultural barriers, nor did he seem to want to. At least, that is how Rinpoche came to see it. Even before they came up to Samye Ling, there was a huge divide between them. Rinpoche kept a diary in Tibetan during this period, and he wrote about these things.

Rinpoche found that most of the English Buddhists kept a certain distance from him because he was a monk. This made him an even stranger being in their eyes, different from them by yet another degree. They would probably have treated a Christian monk this way as well. However, while this kind of deference was comfortable for a lot of the other Tibetans, including Akong, Rinpoche was not interested in maintaining that distance. For many, it was quite nice to be treated as a special person again, even if you were regarded as a representative of an exotic species.

Rinpoche came from a tradition where wisdom is awakened through an intimate and direct transmission between the teacher and the student. He began to see that in order to communicate the depth of the teachings, he had to build such truly intimate relationships with Western students. Otherwise, he might be able to give little blessings, perform ceremonies that Westerners would find exotic, and give teachings that they would find fascinating, but he wouldn't be able to make a real dent in their mentality or their understanding. What they would retain would be superficial, and quite possibly much of the depth of his tradition would be lost to future generations. Being treated with a diffident respect might be more comfortable and lucrative, but it wasn't worth anything to him if he couldn't transmit what he knew and if he didn't connect with students with whom he could work.

Rinpoche also saw that he wouldn't be able to work with anyone or help people in any way if he didn't understand Western culture and the Western mind from the inside out. Of course, essentially there is no difference between the mind of a Western practitioner and the mind of an Eastern practitioner. But there are a lot of cultural trappings covering over the basic mind, the basic intelligence, which one has to penetrate if one is going to truly communicate with others. Rinpoche knew that he was taking a huge risk; he didn't always know how to do it and he wasn't always skillful, but he was prepared to jump in and make the effort.

When he and Akong started Samye Ling, Rinpoche wanted to call it a meditation center, not a Tibetan Buddhist center—precisely so that people wouldn't view it as something exotic. The two of them were already on quite bad terms when the center opened, and it only got worse. One might wonder why they stayed together throughout those difficult years. I don't know exactly what the reason was for Akong. I think perhaps he hoped that Rinpoche would come to his senses. They certainly had had a deep friendship. For his part, Rinpoche always displayed an amazing ability to assimilate things and to move forward while still remaining loyal to the past. Even as a young child, he learned so quickly that it astounded people around him. That was true in his encounter with the West as well. He witnessed things, he integrated them, and he moved on to the next challenge, the next frontier. At the same time, he never gave up on anyone or anything in his life. He was grateful to Akong for having worked to support him in England and for having been his dear friend when he had had no others. They had shared things that no one else would ever understand, such as life in Tibet before the Chinese invasion and the difficulties of the escape and coming to a new world. So it was painful to grow apart.

When I met Rinpoche, even though many things in his relationships with Akong and many of his English students seemed far beyond salvaging, he was still thinking about how he could bring people along. Although there was tremendous disagreement and tension between Akong and himself, Rinpoche thought they should be able to work it out.

From his point of view, he wasn't abandoning the Tibetan culture or the Buddhist tradition of Tibet. He wanted to bring it all along. But he also wanted to reach out to find a new way to integrate the past with the present. He saw that this would create a genuine meeting point for the teachings to take root in the West.

In 1968, when he returned to India and did his retreat at Taktsang, it was everything that had come before, up to that point, that allowed him to find the *Sadhana of Mahamudra,* the *terma* teachings that would set the tone for the future. He was already well into the transformation that would make him the powerful figure he became in the transmission of Buddhism to the West. In a sense, it was the last gesture, the end of a process, when he gave up his robes, although it was also the beginning.

It was just at that point that I met him, as all of this that had been unfolding in a more internal way began to play itself out on a bigger stage. I think that no one, including Rinpoche, could have predicted what was to come.

FIVE

January 4, 1970, the day after our wedding: When my mother recovered somewhat from the shock of hearing the news of our marriage, she moved quickly. She called relatives and friends to ask them to help her get the marriage annulled. She also phoned us the next morning, in a fairly hysterical state. I wrote in my diary, "Mummy said she would turn the press against Ami (my special name for Rinpoche), and we'd be arrested in England." This did not prove to be true, but it was a worrisome threat.

My aunt and uncle also phoned that morning, and they arranged to meet us for lunch that day. My mother had asked my Aunt Veronica and Uncle Michael to drive up to Edinburgh from their home in Northumberland, which was only an hour or two away. She wanted them to find out more about what was happening and to see if they could persuade me to give up the marriage. They drove up to our hotel in their big brown Bentley, and Rinpoche and I got in the back seat. My aunt and uncle were in the front, and they proceeded to have an awful fight about how to get to the hotel where we were going to have drinks. In the middle of this, my aunt turned to me and said, "You know, marriage isn't easy under the best of circumstances. I don't know how you can expect this to work out."

My uncle ordered drinks for us at the bar. Rinpoche had whiskey, and given the circumstances, he drank a fair amount. My uncle tried to open a conversation with him, saying, "Well, now, do tell me about yourself. When did you become a priest?" Rinpoche answered, "Oh, I was a year old." Of course, this was incomprehensible to my uncle, and he began to sputter. He didn't know where to begin to get a handle on the whole situation. The conversation degenerated from there, and he and Rinpoche proceeded to get drunk. My uncle started yelling at him, calling him a cradle robber and a baby snatcher.

Then, seemingly out of the blue, my uncle looked across the street and said in his most arch English accent, "Well, there's a Chinese restaurant. That looks appropriate! Let's eat there." We all got up and walked across the street, which was not that easy for Rinpoche, who was still using a walker after his accident. My uncle seemed to have no idea that going to a Chinese restaurant would not necessarily be the most pleasant experience for a Tibetan. However, Rinpoche loved Chinese food and had no particular animosity toward the Chinese people as a whole. Nevertheless, my uncle's lack of sensitivity struck me as a reflection of his narrow-mindedness. To my uncle, one Oriental was the same as another regardless of whether they were Chinese, Japanese, Burmese, or Tibetan.

After we sat down at the restaurant, my uncle started yelling at the waiter, "Boy, boy, come over here." When the waiter came along, my uncle said, "Bring something Chinese!" The waiter said, "I'm very happy to bring you a menu, sir," to which my uncle replied, "Just bring something Chinese. Anything Chinese. It's all the same anyway." Not surprisingly, nothing was resolved at dinner. Toward the end of the meal, my uncle said to Rinpoche, "Well, you'd better go to America. You'll do well in America, because anything goes there."

After this painful evening with my aunt and uncle, Rinpoche and I felt quite alienated from my family, and we thought about driving to Samye Ling the next day. (We had already decided that we would not be going back to the ugly scene at Garwald House.) However, the next morning, Tessa and her boyfriend Roderick arrived at our hotel. They had traveled to Samye Ling the day after the wedding, where they had spent the night. They told us that people there were having a terribly difficult time accepting the marriage and that we shouldn't return right away. We decided to take a short honeymoon to Findhorn, a spiritual community in northern Scotland. We invited Roderick and my sister to drive up with us. That day we drove all the way to Inverness, which was a beautiful drive through the landscape of northern Scotland, much of which reminded Rinpoche of Tibet. I remember sitting in the car as we went through the highlands, staring at Rinpoche, thinking, "I can't believe I'm married to you. This is amazing. I can't believe this has happened." I felt like the luckiest person in the world, even though the situation definitely had taken some bizarre twists and turns.

The Findhorn community is famous for growing huge vegetables in the rocky highland soil and for talking to the fairies. It was started by Peter Caddy and his wife Eileen, who greeted us when we arrived. Rinpoche and I were given a nicely appointed trailer, and Tessa and her boyfriend also stayed on the property. It was a brief but delightful honeymoon. We took walks around the property, and Peter Caddy showed us artwork done by people there, which had something to do with extraterrestrials.

While we were there, I consulted the I Ching, and I got "The Marrying Maiden," with the first line a changing line, which mentions "the lame man who is able to tread." I found this amusing, thinking of it literally as referring to Rinpoche and his difficulties walking. The line said that undertakings would bring good fortune.

During our time at Findhorn, I was introduced to Rinpoche's custom of waking up in the middle of the night wanting something to eat. He had this habit for years, for most of his life in the West, in fact. While we were at Findhorn, I got up every night and made him a sandwich.

We also visited an ancient Benedictine monastery nearby, Pluscarden Priory. After Rinpoche mentioned that he was a Tibetan lama, the monks were very interested in him, and they gave us a complete tour of the facilities. We attended services there and had an interview with the prior. Rinpoche particularly enjoyed the Gregorian chanting used in the service, as well as the sweet-smelling incense, and he purchased some to take back to Samye Ling. He felt the monks were following a valid contemplative tradition there and that they were practicing the heart of Christianity. He was quite impressed by their contemplative lifestyle and was inspired to see people practicing an authentic Christian monastic tradition.

At the priory, Rinpoche talked to the monks about his relationship with Thomas Merton, whom he had met in India in 1968, a short time before Father Merton's sudden death. They had drinks together in a bar in Calcutta and were quite taken with one another. Merton commented in the journal he kept at the time, "Chögyam Trungpa is a completely marvelous person. Young, natural, without front or artifice, deep, awake, wise. I am sure we will be seeing a lot more of each other." Rinpoche, looking back years later on their meeting, said of it, "I had the feeling that I was meeting an old friend, a genuine friend. In fact, we planned to work on a book containing selections from the sacred writings of Christianity and Buddhism. . . . He was the first genuine person I met from the West."[1]

After our visit to Pluscarden, Rinpoche and I discussed the Christian contemplative tradition. I think it was the first time we ever talked about the relationship between Christianity and Buddhism. We joked that our children could become Christians as their rebellion against their parents. I asked Rinpoche, "What would you do if one of our sons said he wanted to become a Christian priest?" And he said, "I would encourage him to become the best Christian priest that ever existed; he would have to do it completely, fully." He certainly didn't feel that he had cornered the market on wisdom. He appreciated the wisdom and discipline in other traditions. I didn't have a very good impression of the Christian faith, based on my own repressive experiences, but he helped me to see that there was more to it than the conventional approach.

Our time at Findhorn came to an end all too quickly, and we reluctantly resolved to go to Samye Ling, not knowing what to expect. When we arrived there, we were pleasantly surprised to find that a very nice bedroom had been prepared for us. An elaborate *thangka* of the Buddha had been hung in our room, filling an entire wall. It was a gift to Rinpoche from the queen of Bhutan, Ashi Kesang, when he visited there in 1968. Having this magnificent painting in our bedroom gave me a feeling of acceptance. One of the young monks living at Samye Ling, Samten, presented us with the traditional Tibetan offering of white scarves, or *khatas,* and talked about the positive significance of our marriage. Superficially at least, there was a sense of being welcomed.

Although we tried to settle in at Samye Ling, almost immediately we began making plans for our departure. Rinpoche gave some thought to returning to live in Asia since things had become so difficult in Scotland. He had me write to a university in Hong Kong, asking if they had a teaching position for him. They wrote back and said that if he could teach Tibetan, they would like him to join the faculty. I convinced him, however, that this was not the direction we should go. He also had been talking about making a visit to America, to do a lecture tour and to receive additional medical care there. Several close students who had left Samye Ling were in the United States looking for land for a meditation center on the East Coast. I encouraged him to think about going to America as soon as possible.

We stayed at Samye Ling for about two-and-a-half months. While we were there, I took Tibetan lessons with one of the monks, Phende Rinpoche, and studied *thangka* painting with Sherab Palden Beru. He was always very warm toward me, and he adored Rinpoche. He had some initial difficulty with the idea of our marriage, but after he adjusted, he was very kind to both of us. Rinpoche spent most of his time in our room, although occasionally he would come down to the shrine room during the *pujas,* or religious services. During this period, he sometimes wore monks' robes, tied with a yellow sash to indicate that he was a married lama. I learned to help him dress. Because of the accident, he needed my help. Other times, he wore Western-style dress, men's trousers with a blue button-down shirt and a maroon cashmere sweater. In that era, even his Western clothing often had a little bit of monastic feeling. He loved to wear a turtleneck that was the color of a monk's saffron robe.

During this period, Rinpoche still had to wear a caliper, or a brace, for his left foot and lower leg, which I used to help him put on. When we were first married, he used a walker, but he soon graduated to a walking stick, and eventually he was able to walk just with the caliper. In the long run, he didn't even need that, although he always had orthopedic shoes specially made for him.

Akong would not allow Rinpoche to lecture at Samye Ling. It seemed to be a control issue. Rinpoche, however, did travel to other parts of Britain to teach. Once he was invited to speak at Bristol University. We stayed the night with an Indian family who was hosting the talk. Another time, we went down to Cambridge for Rinpoche to give a talk. We visited Ato Rinpoche and Alithea while we were there. Since meeting in India, Trungpa Rinpoche and Ato Rinpoche had remained close colleagues and friends. Perhaps because Ato Rinpoche had experienced obstacles to his marrying an Englishwoman, he and his wife were very understanding of our situation.

Since Rinpoche could not give talks or group teachings at Samye Ling, most of his personal contact with students was in the form of private interviews, which were held in our room. He often set aside several hours a day for interviews. During that time, I practiced meditation, worked on my *thangka* painting, or handled Rinpoche's correspondence for him. We were preparing for the celebration of Losar, the Tibetan New Year, which would occur that year in early February, and I helped address New Year's cards for Rinpoche. Akong even gave me a typewriter and a place to work. A postcard came from a Mr. Karl Usow in Boulder, Colorado, inviting Rinpoche to visit there and teach at the University of Colorado. We both liked the mountains shown on the front of the card, and Rinpoche said it reminded him of the mountains in Tibet. I wrote back to Karl on Rinpoche's behalf, saying that we would try to come to Colorado for a visit.

One morning at Samye Ling, Rinpoche's interviews went on much longer than expected. Finally, I returned to our room to see what was up. I walked in on him passionately embracing a young woman. I was devastated. I locked myself in our bathroom and sat on the floor crying for hours. I didn't know what to do. I wondered if I should leave Rinpoche. He kept knocking on the bathroom door, but I repeatedly told him to go away.

After several hours, I came out, and we talked. Rinpoche was very sweet. He didn't seem to be avoiding or concealing anything, neither did he seem embarrassed. In some respects, it was an absolutely intimate and direct moment. He said that our connection was very deep and important to him. He told me openly that he expected that he was going to have intimate relationships with some of his female students, but that it didn't mean there was a problem with our relationship. Rinpoche said that in fact it was only because he had such trust in our relationship that he felt it would be possible for him to have these other relationships.

This is a very personal example, from my own life, of Rinpoche's truthfulness. He never lied to me about what he was doing. He was quite willing to talk about what had happened. The communication was so direct and real that I felt I could relax, and I started to let go of my conventional reference points. Rinpoche and I were deeply in love, and I didn't feel that he was using another relationship to blackmail me emotionally in some way.

On a fundamental level, Rinpoche was the most loyal husband I can imagine. In fact, our relationship went much deeper than many conventional marriages. My heart connection with him went far beyond the issue of sexuality, and I knew this from these very early times. As time went on, I felt that many relative difficulties were not fundamental problems—if I let myself feel that deeper connection.

Although I had the formality of marriage with Rinpoche, my union with him was unique. We called it marriage, whatever it was, but Rinpoche was much too big a personality to trap into a monogamous relationship. It just couldn't be. Rinpoche was not an ordinary husband. He was not an ordinary man. I couldn't be possessive of him. I know that this may be difficult for people to accept, but it is my experience.

His life was dedicated to working with other people and their state of mind. In answering a letter from a student in 1971, he wrote: "I work with people—that seems to be my reason for existence."[2] I came to feel that if that sometimes carried over into sexual intimacy, that was okay. I never felt these relationships were an exploitation of his students. It was a way for him to create further intimacy with people. From a broad perspective, I came to realize that Rinpoche definitely was not here on this earth solely to be my sexual partner. It was not always easy or pleasant for me to accept this, but it was really okay.

In Rinpoche's monastery, the monks did a chant invoking the incarnations of the Trungpas, of which Rinpoche was the eleventh. Rinpoche's students in the West now do this chant as well. There is one stanza for each new Trungpa. In the stanza for the Eleventh Trungpa—my husband—he is compared to the Mad Yogi of Bhutan, a revered teacher who lived in the nineteenth century. He was famous both for the depth of his wisdom and for being very wild—drunken and bawdy. This was a very unusual reference because the other Trungpas were generally saintly monks, quite reserved in their behavior. This lineage supplication was written when Rinpoche was about ten years old, so it must somehow have been obvious to the revered lama who wrote this text that this Trungpa would be an unconventional person, another mad yogi.

In fact, Rinpoche's sexual experiences began before he left Tibet. A little while after we were married, I had a dream that he had a daughter in Tibet. I woke up and I said, "I had this ridiculous dream." "Oh," he said when I told him the dream, "It might be true." Then he told me about a night he spent with a Tibetan princess. He was in a procession with a beautiful princess from an outlying area, and he became infatuated with her. He managed to get close to her and suggested that she climb in through his window that night. She did, and they slept together. Before leaving Tibet, Rinpoche saw her again at some public event and she was clearly pregnant. So he might have had a daughter somewhere in Tibet.

As much as I appreciated my husband, I wasn't always accepting of his behavior. When we were first married, Rinpoche told me that it was normal for Tibetan men to beat their wives. I told him this was barbaric, but he said that it was just common practice. In the first few months of our marriage, he tried—not very convincingly—to slap me a couple of times when we were arguing. I said to him, "What do you think you're doing?" And he said to me, "This is just what Tibetans do." I felt that this was definitely not okay. I waited until he was asleep one day, and I took his walking stick and began hitting him as hard as I could. He woke up, and he was quite shocked, and he said, "What are you doing?" I said, "This is just what Western women do." He got the message, and it was never an issue again.

If you think about it, Rinpoche had no idea how to be a husband. He went to live in a monastery when he was thirteen months old, and although his mother came and stayed nearby until he was five, he had virtually no experience of family life. His role models were his gurus, and he had great examples in that area. He grew up as a monk, a student, and a Buddhist teacher, but he had to learn what it meant to be a householder, a husband, and a father.

In fact, at the time that we married, Rinpoche's seven-year-old son, Ösel Mukpo, was living at Samye Ling. When Rinpoche visited India and Bhutan in 1968, he told Könchokla, Ösel's mother, that he wanted to bring their son back to Scotland to live with him. It took a while to arrange this, but eventually he was able to come over. The first time I saw Ösel at Samye Ling, I was struck by his physical beauty and small stature, the latter probably a result of malnutrition in India. He was very shy and spoke only Tibetan at the time. I remember him going off to his first day in kindergarten in a jeep with a local Scottish fellow, Mr. McTaggert. This beautiful, small, and very shy child was sobbing as the car left.

Ösel arrived in England around the time of Rinpoche's accident. They had a very affectionate relationship, although Ösel was shy around his father, understandably so. Rinpoche had asked the monks to look after his son while he was recuperating at Garwald House, since he was in no position to personally care for his son. When we arrived at Samye Ling after the wedding, Ösel was living in the monks' quarters. In addition to attending the local school, he was being tutored in literary Tibetan by Akong and the other monks. They were apparently very rough with him. It seemed to be some sort of archaic method of Tibetan education.

Soon after I married Rinpoche, Ösel had a high fever, and the monks put him to bed with no pajama top on. I felt that this was not the proper thing to do, so I asked one of the monks to put a top on him. The monk replied, "Oh no, it's good if he's cold. He'll get rid of the fever quickly." At that point, I said, "This is enough," and I got an extra mattress and moved him into our bedroom with us. He stayed in our room with us until we left for America.

In general, Rinpoche and I were very isolated from others during this period. Few of Rinpoche's close students remained at Samye Ling. Josie Wechsler, the English nun, was devoted to Rinpoche, and a few other close students were still around. A few friends would occasionally visit or invite us over, such as Ato Rinpoche and Alithea. Stash and Amalie lived nearby, and we would get together with them sometimes. Maggie Russell, whom Rinpoche had wanted to marry, came to visit once. I thought it was great that she had her own car. We spent a great deal of time alone, however, and there was a terrible underlying atmosphere of aggression toward us at Samye Ling.

During this time, Rinpoche's relationship with Akong continued to degenerate. In addition to their disagreement over the presentation of Buddhism in the West, there were other points of contention. Rinpoche was quite disappointed with how Akong related to the mental illness of one of the young monks at Samye Ling. He had to be hospitalized because of a nervous breakdown. Rinpoche felt that, rather than working with this person, Akong's main concern seemed to be to hide the situation from everyone. Rinpoche and I went to visit this monk in the mental hospital.

Akong was terribly mean to me. He put me on the work schedule to do dinner dishes almost every night. If he didn't like the way I did the dishes, he would knock on the bedroom door and tell me to come down and do them again. It felt like a humiliation tactic. This, of course, added to the tension that was building between Rinpoche and Akong.

Akong insisted that Rinpoche should come down for meals rather than eating in our room. Rinpoche often preferred to spend time alone while he was recovering from his accident. He was going through a lot of personal trauma—much of which had to do with his relationship with Akong. It was not very pleasant for him to come downstairs, as you can imagine. He also didn't keep normal hours—which was true throughout much of his life. Often he was not awake when dinner was being served, but he would be hungry late at night. If I came to a meal, Akong would not allow me to take a plate upstairs to Rinpoche. Akong used to say, "He can't have food if he doesn't come down and get it." Rinpoche absolutely refused to give in to this kind of intimidation. Eventually, I got an electric frying pan and started to cook for Rinpoche in our bedroom. I knew almost nothing about cooking, but I learned how to cook meat for him in the frying pan. Although many Buddhists, especially in Southeast Asia, are vegetarian, Buddhists in Tibet could not have survived without meat in their diet. Rinpoche was always a meat eater, and I gave up my somewhat idealistic approach to diet when I married him.

To take care of Rinpoche's needs, I sometimes would steal food from downstairs. Akong kept the pantry locked, and he kept the keys with him. I would hide in the kitchen and wait for Akong to unlock the door to the pantry, which was a long narrow room. When Akong would walk to the back of the pantry, I would run in, grab things off the shelves, and take them upstairs to our bedroom. Sometimes Rinpoche and I would go into town to shop. If we could get a beef tongue, which he particularly enjoyed, I would boil it for him in the room.

Things between Rinpoche and Akong reached a point where they were barely speaking to one another. One day some major donors were coming to Samye Ling. Rinpoche was very turned off to the idea that Akong was putting on a fake front for these wealthy people so that they would give money. He didn't feel that genuine spirituality was being practiced at Samye Ling at that point, and he thought that under the surface the whole situation was corrupt. Just before the donors arrived, while Akong was downstairs waiting to greet them, Rinpoche went into Akong's bedroom upstairs and completely destroyed Akong's personal shrine with his walking stick. Then he went and urinated all over the top of the stairwell, after which he lay down and passed out at the top of the stairs. He had had a lot to drink that afternoon, perhaps to work himself up to doing this. The whole event was extremely shocking, to me and everyone else there. But at the same time, because we had been treated terribly by Akong, I felt okay about it. Akong's way of controlling the situation was to use passive aggression. In his mind, there was always a good reason why he did this to us or that to us. It was very hard to get through to him.

Rinpoche didn't explain his actions to me, but I personally felt that destroying Akong's shrine and then making a big stink, literally, was Rinpoche's way of sending a message to Akong that he couldn't ignore. The sacredness of the situation there was being destroyed and the atmosphere was rotten for us at that point. Looking back now, I think that Rinpoche was willing to go to extreme ends to expose the hypocrisy he saw. Based on other things he said about Akong, I feel that Rinpoche was trying to wake him up. Of course I can't speak for Rinpoche and I don't know what was going on in his mind, but that was definitely the feeling that I had about it at the time.

Rinpoche's behavior was at times outrageous. I think this was probably the first time I had seen this side of him so graphically displayed. On the one hand, he was absolutely brilliant. On the other hand, his behavior could be so unconventional that he seemed rather crazy at times. It was like two sides of a coin: brilliant, or wise, on one side; unfathomable, or crazy from a conventional viewpoint, on the other. Of course, there's crazy and then there's *crazy*. As far as I'm concerned, in my entire association with him, he never did anything to harm another human being. He used to use the term "idiot compassion" to refer to being kind to someone when something more drastic was called for. He was never guilty of that! At times, he could be black and wrathful, but it was always with the agenda of waking people up. He would push people so that they would recognize their self-deception. His mind and actions were fearless and often quite fathomless. There were certain times when it was difficult to understand the motive behind his actions. Those things usually became clarified for me, and I think often for others, with time.

The situation at Samye Ling was becoming unbearably claustrophobic for us, to say the least. One morning Rinpoche suggested that we go to Glasgow to have a holiday and escape the dark atmosphere at the center. We checked into a nice hotel there and had a lovely time. Every night we would eat in the steak house nearby, which was a real treat for us compared to scrounging food at Samye Ling. When it came time to pay the bill, we realized that we didn't have enough money with us, so we had to go to the bank. The people at the hotel were very nice about this. We took a taxi to the bank. When I checked our balance, I was shocked that there was so little money in the account. I realized that we had forgotten to deposit one of Rinpoche's royalty checks for *Born in Tibet,* so there actually wasn't enough in the account to pay our hotel bill. We decided to take a taxi all the way back to Samye Ling, which was more than an hour's drive. The plan was that I would get the check, deposit it in our bank in Lockerbie, and wire the money to the hotel. Unfortunately, we didn't phone the hotel to let them know what we were doing. It never occurred to either of us that this would be a problem. I don't know if Rinpoche fully understood how the banking system worked in England, since most of his finances had been handled by Akong. For my part, I was a naive teenager.

By the time we reached the bank in Lockerbie with the check, the bank was closed. So we went back to Samye Ling for the night. The next morning, I took a taxi with Rinpoche into town. We deposited the check, and I wired the money. Then we went to the pub for lunch. We were there eating lunch when the Glasgow police arrived and arrested us for not having paid the hotel bill. We were put in the back of a black Mariah and driven to Glasgow.

They took mug shots of us at the police station. Rinpoche refused to let me call anyone about what had happened. He knew that Akong would use this event to humiliate us and fuel his view that Rinpoche had gone off the deep end. After the police booked us, we were put in jail. We had to spend the night in separate cells, filthy cold jail cells with ratty blankets and a broken toilet seat in the corner. I begged to be with Rinpoche, but the jailer said that I couldn't be in the same cell with him. He had only recently recovered from the complications of his accident, and I feared that he would become ill again because of the cold. Finally, the jailer agreed to give him some of my blankets.

The jailer asked me about my background and where I had been to school. I told him that I had gone to Benenden, and he said, "I've heard of Benenden." Then he said, "Why have I heard of Benenden?" And I said, "Probably because Princess Anne went there." And he replied, "Yes, that's right." It was hard for him to believe that an English girl who'd been at school with Princess Anne was being held overnight for not paying her hotel bill.

It was a bleak, bleak night, an absolute low point. It seemed that no matter what we did at this time, we were going to encounter terrible difficulties. The next morning we were taken to court. After I explained to the magistrate what had happened, he released us. We went back to Samye Ling, and no one ever knew about our night in jail. It would have been just the confirmation that Akong needed to reinforce his opinion of Rinpoche and me. The next day we received a telegram saying that all charges had been dropped because the hotel had received the money. So there were no lasting repercussions.

However, at this point, we realized that we needed to get out of Britain as soon as possible. During this period, Rinpoche would sometimes wake up in the night, experiencing some sort of panic. I actually don't know if it was panic exactly. He would wake up and he couldn't breathe. Sometimes, he would seem to be in another realm, I would almost say, and I would sort of have to bring him back by talking to him and insisting that he come back and listen to me. He told me that I was able to provide ground for him, which helped him to stay on the earth, somewhat literally. I don't want to psychoanalyze Rinpoche, but I think this was a very difficult period for him, in many ways. It was a momentous decision to leave behind his Tibetan identity and to strike out in the world. I think he was absolutely fraught with loneliness and sometimes with despair. At this point he didn't know how well things would go in America. He didn't know what was going to happen. To me, Rinpoche was the ultimate warrior. He was willing to jump off the edge of the cliff, not knowing where he would land.

On the other hand, he also had tremendous dedication to his world. Even though others might abandon him, he never wanted to abandon anyone else. For quite a while, even though it had been such a bad scene in Scotland, Rinpoche continued to talk about returning to Great Britain after the lecture tour in America. He had incredible loyalty to people there, even to Akong, whom he hoped would eventually open up to Westerners and come to appreciate the way in which Rinpoche wanted to live and teach. I, however, was convinced that we should leave for good. I told him that we weren't coming back. I was quite vocal about this, saying that the scene in Scotland was not a healthy situation for us. After our night in jail, Rinpoche didn't resist at all. He consulted the I Ching, using yarrow sticks, which is the traditional method, and it indicated that "it furthers one to cross the big water." This was the turning point for us.

Years later, at a public event, he made a spontaneous toast to me, thanking me for helping us to get out of Great Britain: "You have cheered me up many times. In the past, I have gone through all kinds of depressing occasions and dungeons and an unspeakably unliberated world, pure and simple, a world that was not purified at all. We went through that together, with you leading the way ahead of me. I appreciate that very much. You are an extremely brave lady, I must say. Such an extremely kind lady and an extremely resourceful lady as well, she managed to get us to this goddamned place called America!"[3]

Unfortunately, there were still obstacles to our departure. Earlier, Rinpoche had obtained a multiple entry visa to the United States. While we were making our final plans, we went to the American consulate in Glasgow to get information. When Rinpoche presented his British passport at the desk, the person behind the counter took it and stamped a huge "cancelled" across the visa. We were shocked. We discovered that Christopher Woodman had been to the consulate and told them dreadful stories, saying that Rinpoche was unfit to go to the United States.

Ever since our marriage, Rinpoche's relationship with Christopher and his wife Pamela had degenerated. After the wedding, we never went back to Garwald House, and we had barely seen the Woodmans. It seemed that Christopher and Pamela were jealous of the intimacy between Rinpoche and me. Also, Christopher in particular seemed to have developed tremendous anger and what seemed like a complex about controlling Rinpoche or reforming him. Rinpoche said that in part it was the result of the confusion generated by his falling-out with Akong, which forced students to take sides in this dharmic controversy. However, he also referred to it as a problem that sometimes arose for students in relating to their teacher, a phenomenon that he described as "hunting the guru." He had witnessed this personally in Tibet, when some of Jamgön Kongtrul's main students decided that their guru needed to be reformed. Rinpoche wrote about this in the first epilogue to *Born in Tibet,* which he wrote soon after we left Scotland for North America. He said there:

> When a guru makes a great change in his life, it is often an open-ing for great chaos among the pupils who regard him as an object of security. Very few are able to go along with the change. . . . My marriage to my wife Diana took place in January 1970. This brought a . . . reaction among the more possessive followers who regarded their guru as "lover." They began what may be called "hunting the guru." When this occurs the person is no longer open to teaching. The ego game is so strong that everything nourishes it and the person wants only to manipulate, so that in a sense he kills the guru with his own ignorance.
>
> This situation reminded me of the time when Jamgön Kongtrul's disciples tried, with the best of intentions, to reinter-pret with their scholarly research Jamgön Kongtrul's own words in order to show him their real meaning. They attempted to help him out with tremendous violence and feelings of superiority. This ignorance of one's real purpose can be called the basic twist of ego.[4]

Christopher Woodman seemed to be "hunting" Rinpoche in this way. He convinced himself that Rinpoche should not be allowed to go to America. His stated purpose for containing him was that he seemed to think that Rinpoche was a disturbed individual who needed to re-main in England. I think, in fact, that Christopher was very frightened about losing Rinpoche. However, his attempts to hold onto Rinpoche only drove a wedge between them. Later there would be further reper-cussions. For the time being, we had to decide what to do now that Rin-poche's visa had been cancelled.

Without him having a valid visa, we weren't sure that we could get into the United States, but Rinpoche still wanted to book tickets to

New York. He thought we might be able to gain admission. So we decided to proceed with our plans to leave.

However, we needed money for the tickets. We barely had enough to cover a few nights in a hotel in Glasgow. How could we possibly come up with the money to travel to America? Having no other choice, we decided to go to Akong and ask him to please give us the money for our plane tickets. I volunteered to approach Akong on our behalf, as he and Rinpoche were barely able to be together in the same room at this time.

Although Rinpoche's activities generated most of the income at Samye Ling, Akong kept complete control of the finances, and he gave Rinpoche almost no money for his personal account. Akong refused to give us the money, but he said that he would "loan" us the funds for the tickets if Rinpoche would sign over the seals of his lineage. These were the official marks of Rinpoche's position in Tibet. There were seven seals, some of them dating back centuries. Among them were two seals that were given to one of the early Trungpas by the emperor of China. Leaving them behind was like being stripped of his authority. Certainly, this was the message that Akong seemed to be sending, although ultimately Rinpoche's authority had nothing to do with any outer trappings. Akong also demanded that Rinpoche leave behind other religious treasures that he had carried with him from his monastery in Surmang. They included a gold statue of a protector, or *mahakala,* that was very precious to him, small statues of Milarepa and Padmasambhava, and other important relics. He had been able to bring only these few small but significant objects from Tibet, and now Akong demanded that we leave many of them at Samye Ling. We convinced him to let us bring some of these along with us, but all others had to remain with him. When you consider that the vast majority of the art and religious treasures at Rinpoche's monastery had been destroyed, it was quite devastating for Rinpoche to be asked to leave behind the last few things that connected him to Surmang. Akong was not even from the Surmang monastery, so for him to take control of the Surmang seals and treasures was quite outrageous.

I was so upset that I called my uncle—the same uncle who took us out for lunch after we married—and told him this terrible thing was happening. He was completely unhelpful and unsupportive. He was a lawyer, so I'd been hoping that he might give us some assistance, but he just said, "Too bad for you." So Rinpoche left the seals from the Surmang monastery with Akong, and we used the money to get our tickets. It was not until 1975 that we were able to recover them.

Even though the situation was so negative and circumstances seemed so difficult, Rinpoche had a sense of promise about what was to come. As he wrote later, "I do not believe that there is a divine Providence as such, but the situation of karma and the wildness of Khenpo Gangshar and Jamgön Kongtrul directed me to cross the Atlantic with my wife in the spring of 1970."[5]

As we made preparations to leave, we secured a promise from Akong to take care of Rinpoche's son until we were able to send for him. Ösel did not have a British passport, and with our visa difficulties, we could not bring him with us. As well, we had no money for a third ticket. I wish that he had been able to accompany us, as there were terrible difficulties bringing him over later on.

Finally, in early March 1970, the day arrived for us to depart. We had only been at Samye Ling for a little more than two months, but it seemed an eternity. In the taxi on the way to Prestwick Airport, for some reason that I absolutely could not fathom, Rinpoche decided that he wanted to stop off at the pub in Langholm, very close to Samye Ling, for lunch. I was completely beside myself because there were only two flights a week to New York from Glasgow. He got mad at me for harassing him, so I gave in. Of course, with our luck, we got all the way to Prestwick and missed the flight. We had to go back to Samye Ling for four more days. However, we made it on the next flight. Looking back on it, I think that perhaps Rinpoche realized, more than I did, that in leaving Great Britain, he was saying his final goodbye to an important part of his life. He was saying goodbye to Akong, who had been his heart companion in the escape from Tibet. He was saying goodbye to England, where he had mastered the English language, made many discoveries about Westerners and their relationship to mind, and made his first connection with Western students. So he took his time in leaving, frustrating as that was for me.

Rinpoche left Scotland with a ritual dagger, called a *phurba,* strapped to his midsection with a long scarf. A *phurba* is supposed to cut through obstacles and assassinate ego on the spot. This was one of the treasures from his monastery in Tibet that Rinpoche refused to surrender to Akong. He left Great Britain with at least this one piece of his heritage intact. It had belonged to the founder of Buddhism in Tibet, Padmasambhava. Rinpoche often carried it on his body in those days, almost as if it gave him the strength and protection that he needed to make this change in his life. It being a very different era, it didn't set off any metal detectors or alarms at the airport.

On the plane we were both very cheerful and, as Rinpoche wrote later, "We talked of conquering the American continent, and we were filled with a kind of constant humor."[6] We flew into New York, hoping to enter the United States, but we were told that without the proper visas we wouldn't be admitted. However, since we were both British citizens, we were allowed to continue on to Canada. We took a flight to Toronto. We had finally arrived in the New World.

Looking back on the dreadful times we endured in Great Britain, part of me would like to forget about the whole thing and that part of me says, "Why tell people about these black times?" But then I remember what Rinpoche said about this. As my husband wrote, just a few months after we left:

> Upon being asked to do an epilogue for the new edition of *Born in Tibet*, I began to think about the nature of these last years. Their most outstanding quality has been the strength of the teachings, which have been a constant source of inspiration during this time in India, Britain, and America.
>
> Adapting to these new ways of life after the colorful and simple quality of Tibet, where people were so in touch with their natural environment, has been truly a great adventure. It has been made possible by the continually active presence of Jamgön Kongtrul of Sechen and Khenpo Gangshar, my teachers. They taught me about a basic sanity that has nothing to do with time and place. They taught about the neurotic aspects of the mind and the confusion in political, social and other structures of life, which are universal. I have seen many fellow Tibetans as well as Westerners drawn into these problems.[7]

So in fact, I realize that it's very important to remember what happened in the last days at Samye Ling, because it was such an important lesson. It is a constant reminder to me of the pitfalls of spiritual practice.

Six

Although we hadn't managed to get into the United States, we were excited about arriving in North America. Leaving the Toronto airport in a taxi, we noticed immediately that it was completely different from Great Britain. I was in awe of the place. The highways were huge, the cars were huge, everything seemed speeded up and larger than life. The taxi drove us to a seedy hotel, which was all we could afford, where we spent the night. The next morning we wanted something to eat, so we went out to find a market. We found our way to a supermarket, and we were completely overwhelmed by the place. They didn't have stores like this in England. The employees in the store seemed so nice. They said things like, "Hello, can I help you?" "Did you find everything you were looking for?" and "Have a nice day." This approach seemed superficial to me. This would never have happened in England. I was amazed by the hugeness and the slickness of everything in the store. There were rows and rows of vegetables, frozen foods, cookies, and toilet paper, and in the meat section there were enormous cuts of beef and pork. Rinpoche picked out a big raw steak, and I got a frozen cake with lots of frosting. We took our purchases back to the hotel, and we sat on our bed eating these huge, rich pieces of food.

The next day Rinpoche contacted a local Buddhist organization in Toronto. He explained that he was a Tibetan lama who had arrived in Toronto with nowhere to live. Originally, we had hoped to stay with Karma Thinley, a Tibetan teacher who had been living in Canada for several years. He had visited Rinpoche in Scotland, and they were quite friendly. However, he was away at the time.

We had no place to live, and we couldn't afford to continue staying in hotels. We phoned Fran Lewis and Kesang, two of Rinpoche's students who were now living in Vermont, for advice. They had recently found a piece of land that was going to be Rinpoche's first meditation center in the United States. They suggested we go to Montreal, which was only a few hours' drive from Vermont. It would be much easier for them to come up and visit us there. They were already looking for an immigration lawyer to work on our case and hoped that it would only be a few weeks before we could enter the United States.

We had barely enough money to purchase train tickets, and we took a night train to Montreal. When we got there, the Buddhist Society put us in touch with a Korean monk, Samu Kim, who invited us to stay with him and his wife. She was a Westerner, but she was an excellent Korean cook, and we had some great meals with them. They had a little baby boy named Maji, which I believe means "offering to the Buddha" in Korean. At first, we got along quite well with them. Then, one night Rinpoche and Samu stayed up drinking, and the next day, Samu asked us to leave. I don't know exactly what happened. Samu said to Rinpoche, "You look like a buddha, but you're just an ordinary man. You look the story, you walk the story, but you're not the real thing. You can't stay here any longer." It felt like a hangover from the energy in Scotland.

The situation with Buddhism in Canada was similar to what we would find in the United States. There were a number of well-established Mahayana Buddhist communities in the major cities, but most of them were made up of Asian Americans and Asian Canadians originally from China, Japan, and Korea, for whom Buddhism was the dominant religion and the culture they had grown up with. It was quite a conservative scene, not one that Rinpoche was attracted to. Perhaps it was not so surprising that our first encounter ended on a sour note.

After we left Samu's house, we found a small furnished studio apartment for twenty-four dollars a week and another three dollars a week for the television. To come up with the first week's rent, I went through the pockets of Rinpoche's suits, and we paid most of the rent in change.

Eventually, we started to receive some support from Rinpoche's students in the United States, but in the beginning we were very poor and living mainly on rice. We had a big rice pot, and sometimes we would have enough money to buy a little meat or chicken to add to the rice. One day I spent seven dollars on food at the grocery store, and Rinpoche was upset that I'd spent so much money. Another day I went out to a market in Montreal to buy meat for dinner. I walked past a stall where they sold live pigeons to take home for dinner. They would kill the bird for you on the spot. There was only one left that day, and I felt so sorry for the poor thing that I spent all our money to buy it. When I got home, Rinpoche said, "What's for dinner?" And I said, "Well, I spent all our money on this pigeon." He was very nice about it. We put the pigeon out the window, and we just had rice for dinner that night.

Sometimes we walked around Montreal. However, Rinpoche was still using a walking stick and it was difficult for him to get around. So I used to do most of the food shopping, and we stayed in the apartment a lot. Rinpoche and I slept on a big foldout couch, and we watched a lot of television. We watched *Pajama Party* and *Alfred Hitchcock Presents.* Our apartment was above a bakery, and Rinpoche would go down and visit with the French baker in the basement. He and Rinpoche liked each other a lot, and they used to drink whiskey together. Sometimes, the baker would give us a loaf of bread. We were so poor that this was really a treat.

There was a gay couple in the building who we used to hang out with sometimes. They took a lot of mescaline, and occasionally we would trip with them. I don't remember this as very significant. Later, Rinpoche became adamantly opposed to the recreational use of drugs, but at this point, he seemed to enjoy experimenting.

For the first time in my life—because I had led such a sheltered life growing up—I had to do laundry. Early on, not knowing any better, I put Rinpoche's cashmere sweater and silk shirts in the washer and dryer. Everything shrank terribly, and he was unable to wear them after that, but he was so sweet about it. When I brought his sweater back, he said, "That's all right, sweetheart. We'll save it for our first child."

As soon as we got our apartment in Montreal, Rinpoche cheered up. There was much more openness in the atmosphere, and he seemed inspired. Michael Aronowitz, a high-powered immigration lawyer in New York, was working on our case, and we were confident that we were going to be able to get into the United States. It was just a question of going through the red tape to get the visas. Rinpoche was optimistic about the future. In Montreal, we bought some 3-D postcards that were popular at that time. When you moved them back and forth, the scenes on the cards would change, and Rinpoche said, "One day we're going to be able to afford our own house, and we'll have one whole wall wall-papered in this 3-D stuff!"

His students started to come up and visit us from Vermont. Kesang and Fran came almost every week, and they often brought us some money to get by on. Joanne Newman, a new student who generously helped to finance the land for the meditation center, also came up to meet Rinpoche. They gave us news of how the center was coming along. They had decided to throw the I Ching to find a name for it. The I Ching talked about treading on the tail of the tiger, so with Rinpoche's blessing, they gave the center the name "Tail of the Tiger." Rinpoche was very excited to hear all the developments at "Tail," as we called it.

We also met Cyrus Crane in Montreal. He was about seventy at the time, one of Rinpoche's oldest students, chronologically speaking. He was a wonderful old man with long white hair. During his first meditation interview, he said, "Rinpoche, I need some advice. First, I did the Mahamudra and then I did the *maha ati* [advanced practices that take years to accomplish]. Now that I've done both of those, what should I do next?" Rinpoche told him, "I'm going to teach you to meditate."

While we were in Montreal, Rinpoche gave several public talks at Concordia University. We connected with a few people there. I remember meeting Judy Gault, who remains a very committed Buddhist. She and several other women started to hang around with us. We were also introduced in Montreal to Tindale Martin, a Western Zen teacher who had a small Zen center. He had spent time in Japan and was rather arrogant, but he was quite nice to us. His wife, Gisela, was a belly dancer. She supported the family with her exotic dancing, and we went to the club to see her dance once. The next year, Tindale invited Rinpoche to teach a weekend program at his center.

In the United States, Rinpoche would encounter other Western teachers like Tindale, people with some exposure to a genuine Buddhist tradition but lacking in their training or understanding. In fact, there were a number of rather odd misconceptions about Buddhism that were being fostered. There was a certain kind of Zen that was popular at this time—well intentioned but often quite conceptual, not grounded in enough practice or experience. One of the problems was that there were so few Asian teachers able to comprehend Western culture and able to transmit their understanding to Westerners. In some sense, it was similar to the obstacles we had already encountered in Great Britain. Many Asian teachers were intimidated by Western students. The cultural barrier seemed so high that the teacher and the students couldn't cross that divide. In America, however, the situation was ripe for a breakthrough, and indeed we were to discover that some teachers—such as Suzuki Roshi in California—were already pioneering a new approach, one based on eye-level communication.

At the end of April, we received word that our visas were coming. Kesang drove up from Vermont to pick us up. We packed up our belongings, which were few at that time, and on May 1, 1970, we crossed into the United States. A whole new future was opening for us, and when we hit the United States, there was not even a hint of the bleakness or depression that had dominated our lives for so many months. It was like a huge wind of fresh air was dispelling the last few clouds in the sky.

Tail of the Tiger was an old farmhouse with a barn next to it, located on more than four hundred acres of land in northern Vermont near Barnet, which is close to St. Johnsbury. Kesang and Fran were living there, as well as Joanne Newman and Richard Arthure. He was another of Rinpoche's close students from England and the editor of *Meditation in Action*. The day we arrived at Tail there were just a few people there, but the scene grew quickly as people from all over the East Coast started coming up to visit. At that time Tail of the Tiger was unique; there were no comparable Buddhist centers in New England.

The main house at Tail was small, with a living room and kitchen on the main floor and several tiny bedrooms. Upstairs, on the third floor, a somewhat larger room was turned into a meditation hall. Rinpoche and I were given one of the rooms on the main floor as our bedroom, in the back. Our bed was just a mattress on the floor. Most of the people who came around in that era, both men and women, had long hair and were sort of grungy. I continued to wear the hippie caftans I had brought from England, but I added peasant blouses, flowing skirts, and the occasional short skirt to my attire. At the beginning, Rinpoche's dress was noticeably more conservative than his students'. He liked to wear an ascot with a silk shirt, for example. After a little while, however, he changed his dress a bit to go along with what other people were wearing. A few weeks after we arrived in America, we were on the West Coast and spent a day in Mexico. Rinpoche bought some embroidered Mexican shirts, and he used to wear those. He also got into a flannel shirt phase for a while.

There was group sitting meditation in the shrine room upstairs every morning. I often sat with people, although some mornings I would sleep in with Rinpoche. There were a lot of late nights. In the evenings, people would gather in the living room, and Rinpoche and I would hang out with people for hours. Sometimes he would just talk with people; sometimes he would give a short lecture in the evening. The activity would go on late into the night. Up to this point, to some extent, I had had Rinpoche to myself, and I had done everything for him—cooking his meals, washing his clothes, making appointments for him, and so forth. It was an adjustment to have so many people around all the time and to have to share him with everyone.

One night I was tired of the group scene, and I decided to retire early. I thought Rinpoche should come with me. I tried to convince him to come to bed. He was in the living room talking to people about Padmasambhava bringing the teachings to Tibet. I said, "You've got to stop teaching. Please come to bed." He responded, "I'll be right there, sweetheart." I don't know how many times we must have repeated that exchange over the years! Of course, it was hours before he went to sleep. Although I sometimes missed the time we had had alone together, I was fundamentally very happy to be there—with him and everybody else— and delighted to see him able to expand and relax so much. He was really launching his campaign on the American soil.

Rinpoche was so inspired. Everyone we met in America had such open minds in those days, and they were eager to learn. Because of the openness and inquisitiveness of the new students, I think that Rinpoche felt that he could truly communicate with people. There was an immediate magnetism between him and the people who came to Tail. He didn't sit around spouting things he knew; his way of teaching was to connect on a heartfelt level with everybody in the room, whatever their state of mind was. That started from the very early times. People felt immediately drawn in and connected to him, and he felt the same way about them. He was extremely perceptive about where people were at. Some years later, he addressed a group of his students, reflecting back on these early days. He said:

> As we all remember, each one of you had a chance to come to the dharma in your own various ways. In many cases, before we began working together, your situations were rather desperate. Some of you were struggling more than others, or suffering more than others, but each of you had your own style of manifesting your struggle and your pain. You each manifested your own kind of contortions, hunched-over-ness and jumpiness.[1]

You actually could see all of this manifested in the shrine room. Rinpoche didn't give people much direction in their meditation practice at that time. I think he wanted to let people hang out in the space a little bit. He realized that you couldn't take people from the extreme of casualness they were familiar with to a perfect situation of discipline without allowing some transitional space in the middle. In England, he had seen that when you try to impose discipline on people who have no background in the tradition, a lot of people end up imitating the discipline and confusing rigid behavior with meditative accomplishment. He was not interested in making that mistake twice.

So he just told people to sit, with no agenda whatsoever. Because he gave so little direction, the scene in the shrine room sometimes appeared quite sloppy and contorted to an external observer. People would begin their hour of sitting meditation with upright posture and legs carefully crossed. As the hour progressed, they would begin to squirm, hunch over, and change position. Some would get sleepy and fold up their knees so that they could put their head on their knees and sleep. The occasional person would actually lie down in the shrine room. Yet, behind all that disarray, people's minds and hearts were being brought to the cushion, brought to the dharma—and that was what Rinpoche was going for at that time. He wanted to tap the brilliant minds he was encountering, and later, he knew that he would be able to straighten out their bodies—literally.

Often, Rinpoche also worked with people through his sense of humor, which was quite boyish at times, almost what you would call childish, but very magnetic. Once, during morning meditation practice at Tail, he came into the room and walked up to the front, where he sat facing people for several minutes. He was carrying a small paper bag, which he set down next to himself. It began to vibrate and emit strange clicking sounds. These continued for a while and then came to a stop. Rinpoche exited from the shrine hall, leaving the bag behind. After he departed, of course, people couldn't resist opening the sack. Inside there was a child's windup toy, a set of chattering teeth. It was such a perfect image of how the mind chatters on while you are meditating. At the same time, it was purely a joke, something that made people laugh and delighted them. This was characteristic of how he worked with people: the double entendre that might have been coincidence—or was it?

The first few weeks after our arrival in America is a blur of people, activity, and energy in my mind. However, I have one extremely vivid, rather peculiar memory. I was in bed with Rinpoche, and light was streaming into our room. He often used to sleep late in the morning. I was lying next to him, looking at him. I noticed that he had one single hair in the middle of his chest, which was quite long. I lay there looking and looking at this hair, and finally, I thought, "I've got to pull it out." I reached over and yanked the hair out of his chest. From a dead sleep, he woke up and tried to punch me in the face. Then we both collapsed in laughter.

Another time, when we were alone in bed, I was feeling romantic, and I said to him, "I love you more than anyone in the whole world!" He replied, proudly, "I really love you too. I love you second best of anything in the world." I said, "What do you mean, 'second best'?" Then he replied, "First I love my guru, and my guru is the buddhadharma. I'll always love the dharma more than anything else. But you'll always be the thing I love second best. My first commitment isn't to being a family man, but to propagating the Buddhist teachings. This is the point of my life. Hopefully the two things can work together." Even in matters of the heart, he was uncompromisingly honest.

One of the themes that arises from this early period is seeing how much a person may have to give up, in terms of personal happiness or fulfillment, when one's life is dedicated to helping others on such a big scale. Many people contributed to bringing Buddhism to America, and many of them made enormous personal sacrifices in order for Buddhism to take root as a genuine practice lineage in this country. When Rinpoche said that his first commitment was not to our relationship or to his family, I don't think he was being melodramatic. Essentially, he was describing what was a choiceless situation for him. At that point, I think that I already understood this, although it wasn't always easy to accept. Sometimes I just wanted to be with him and, beginning in this era, often it wasn't possible. At times, there was definitely a conflict between my desire to have some domestic privacy and his desire to be available to people twenty-four hours a day.

While we were staying at Tail of the Tiger, I had my own domestic drama. Very unexpectedly, my mother showed up in Barnet for a visit. Richard Arthure came and informed me, "Your mother is staying at an inn in Barnet, and she wants to see you." She refused to come to Tail of the Tiger because she still had not accepted my marriage to Rinpoche and wouldn't have anything to do with him. Rinpoche was worried that she would try to abduct me. However, I felt that I must go to see her. It was the first time I'd seen my mother since my marriage to Rinpoche. We'd had hysterical phone calls in Scotland, but she had refused to visit me at Samye Ling.

That evening Richard drove me to the inn. Rinpoche wanted him to stay with me. My mother was ranting and raving, and she said to Richard, "I want to know why my daughter has run away with this half-Indian, half-Chinese, half-Tibetan." Richard replied in his most proper English voice, "I can assure you, Mrs. Pybus, he's full-blooded Tibetan." This did not seem to help.

My mother insisted that I spend the night at the inn with her. I finally agreed, so Richard left me there with her. I asked him to tell Rinpoche not to worry, that I'd be back in the morning. My mother and I really had nothing civil to say to one another at this time, so shortly after Richard left, we went to sleep. Mother was in a room with two double beds. She said that there was no bedding for the second mattress and that I would have to sleep in the bed with her. I remember lying there awake and absolutely frozen in the bed. I slipped out around 5:30

in the morning and walked back to Tail of the Tiger. As I came around the bend in the road that led up to the farmhouse at Tail, I could see Rinpoche sitting in a rocking chair on the porch. He was so worried that he'd stayed up all night waiting for me. After that my mother left. Next she was going to northern India, where a private detective had tracked my sister. Tessa was living at this time in a hill station in the mountains as a hippie. (Tessa told me later how Mother hiked into the mountains to find her, carrying a bag full of bras to give my sister.) My mother had lost both of her daughters within one year. It was quite sad, but I didn't feel anything for her at the time. She was unable to appreciate anything about my life, and I didn't want to have anything to do with her.

Although we had been forced to leave the seals of the Trungpas in Scotland, Rinpoche had been able to bring a number of his paintings with him. In their own way, these were also treasures. They were done in the style of Tibetan *thangka* paintings, but like so many things that he did, they were both traditional and unusual. One of them was a painting of an important female protector of the Buddhist teachings, Ekajati, from the Nyingma tradition. It was a painting just of her head, which is what made it so unusual. Ekajati is a fierce protector with one eye, one fang, and one breast. Otherwise she is anatomically like a human being: two arms, two legs, and so forth. According to the traditional belief, she is the leader or chief of the *mamos,* who are a band of wrathful female spirits or energies who control the forces of war and peace, sickness and health. She is an extremely powerful lady. When I first spent time with Rinpoche, he was writing poetry to her, and he had this painting on the wall of his bedroom at Garwald House. He felt that in part it was invoking her energy that helped him to survive those dark times. When we moved to Colorado a few months later, Rinpoche decided to leave the painting of Ekajati at Tail of the Tiger and to make her the protector of the center. He wrote a chant to Ekajati, which he asked the practitioners there to recite at the end of their evening meditation practice. Rinpoche also left his painting of Padmasambhava at Tail of the Tiger. In this way, he began to plant the energy of his heritage in the American soil.

Even though this early time was quite formless and the atmosphere at Tail was almost like a hippie commune, Rinpoche was already subtly beginning to mold the situation. Over a relatively short period of time, perhaps a year, the atmosphere changed radically, and more discipline was introduced. Things began to tighten up. In the long run, Tail of the Tiger took on the feeling of a lay monastery where the residents were expected to follow a strict discipline of practice and study. But there were just the barest hints of this during the early days.

At the end of May, Rinpoche and I left on his first teaching tour in America. The people at Tail were putting together a series of summer seminars to begin in mid-July. We had about six weeks before the seminars would start, so we set out to see part of the country. Our first stop was New York City. We stayed with Jean-Claude van Itallie, a playwright best known at that time for his hit play *America Hurrah*. He was a friend of Kesang's who had first met Rinpoche at Samye Ling. Jean-Claude arranged for Rinpoche to give a talk at the Actors Workshop, where many avant-garde theater people congregated.

New York was amazing for us. It was so different from the European cities we both knew. We had a fabulous time touring around the city and meeting all kinds of people whom Jean-Claude introduced us to. This was the beginning of Rinpoche's very fertile relationship with Jean-Claude and more generally with Western artists. He was very taken with the experimental theater scene in New York. Rinpoche told Jean-Claude about his training in monastic dance in Tibet, and they began discussing ways that they could work together in the area of theater. Soon after this, Rinpoche began writing plays, a number of which were later staged in Boulder, Colorado, and other locations.

While we were in New York, Mary—whom Rinpoche had called the morning after we were married—came to visit for a few days. I don't know where she and Rinpoche met, but they remained friends over many years, and he corresponded with her until his death. She lived in Wales with her husband and a number of children, and she was quite settled compared to most people we knew at that time. I related to her a bit like an aunt or another mother. While she was visiting, she gave me cooking lessons. I was trying to make meals for everyone at the apartment in New York, but I found it overwhelming to cook for a group. The only training I had in cooking came from occasionally helping Mrs. Wills make a cake when I was six years old. After Mary arrived and saw the trouble I was having, she walked me through the steps of how you make a meal and how you get it out on the table. I remember telling her that I didn't know how to cope with all the chaos in the kitchen. Her help was invaluable.

From New York, we flew to San Francisco, where Sam and Hazel Bercholz met us at the airport. Sam had recently started Shambhala Publications, and the first book he had published was the American edition of *Meditation in Action*. While he was still in Great Britain, Rinpoche had been fascinated to learn that someone in America had a company named after the kingdom of Shambhala, and he was delighted that this company wanted to publish an edition of his book. Shambhala is an ancient mythical kingdom in Asia, with which the advanced Vajrayana Buddhist teachings of the Kalachakra Tantra are associated. Rinpoche had received many teachings on Shambhala in Tibet. In fact, when he was escaping from the country, he had been writing a book about Shambhala, which unfortunately was lost during the journey. Meeting his publisher was high on Rinpoche's list of things to do in America. For his part, Mr. Bercholz was quite anxious to meet the Tibetan lama whose book he had published.

Sam had a large presence and a warmth that we immediately connected with. His wife, Hazel, had been a dancer and was now the main graphic designer for the publishing company. They were absolutely welcoming of us, and in fact, Sam had arranged for Rinpoche to give several public talks and meet with interested students while we were in the Bay Area. Sam had cofounded Shambhala Publications with Michael Fagan, a rather tall, angular, and very intelligent man, and we stayed in Oakland with Michael and his wife Joanne during this visit.

One afternoon, we were taking an afternoon rest, and we made love in our bedroom at the Fagans'. The room had a sort of Elizabethan feeling, with a large purple wall hanging. We were not planning to have a child at that time. However, we were only using the rhythm method for birth control, and as we were making love, I had a definite feeling of someone else being in the room with us. I believe we conceived our first son, Taggie, that afternoon.

After spending a week in northern California, we flew to Los Angeles where Rinpoche had a speaking engagement arranged by students of J. Krishnamurti. The sponsors of the talk, I believe, had been members of the Theosophical Society but had now formed their own organization. The Theosophical Society was founded in New York at the end of the nineteenth century by Madame Blavatsky and Colonel Olcott. It fostered a great deal of public awareness of Buddhism in the West, but it also gave rise to many misconceptions, especially about the nature of Tibetan Buddhism, in particular due to Madame Blavatsky's spiritualist "communiqués" from supposed Indian and Tibetan Masters. Members of the Society discovered Krishnamurti when he was a young man in India and tried to raise him as their great find, a great *mahatma* or spiritual master. Krishnamurti reacted against the mysteries of the Theosophists and began promoting a much more genuine investigation of spirituality and how to lead a sane life.

Krishnamurti was not in favor of organized religion, and he was quite an anti-teacher or anti-guru, calling on people instead to rely purely on themselves and to separate wisdom from the trappings of any tradition. Although Rinpoche respected many of Krishnamurti's ideas, he felt that Krishnamurti's rejection of the role of the teacher was too extreme. Rinpoche himself spoke out against charlatan teachers, but he believed in the importance of a genuine student-teacher relationship as the basis for developing non-ego and compassion on the Buddhist path. Rinpoche told me that he thought that perhaps Krishnamurti never met his teacher. He liked the man very much. A few years after this trip to Los Angeles, Rinpoche and Krishnamurti lectured together and had a dialogue at some event. Rinpoche commented that Krishnamurti's presence on stage was very dramatic and contrasted noticeably with his shy off-stage presence. In Rinpoche's case, there was no difference between being on- and off-stage.

The afternoon we arrived in Los Angeles, we were taken somewhere outside the city to a motel along a river. After we checked in, we had several hours to relax before Rinpoche was to give his talk to Krishnamurti's students. Rinpoche got completely drunk in the motel room, and I was freaking out because I couldn't imagine how he was going to give a lecture in a few hours. Somehow, he often managed to get drunk—almost strategically it seemed—when he had to talk to a group of people who were tripped out or who had extreme expectations. These people definitely fell into that category, beyond anything else we experienced in California.

I managed to get him on his feet and into the car, and I sat with him on the stage at the lecture hall. He was really four sheets to the wind.

Some of the people in the audience seemed to have the Theosophical fascination with the magic and mystery of Tibet, while others seemed preoccupied with debunking any guru who might address them. People asked Rinpoche why he ate meat, why he didn't wear robes, and if he was a Buddhist. It seemed a bit ridiculous to ask a Tibetan teacher if he was a Buddhist. I felt that they were quite rude. They also wanted to know about things like psychic visions, ghosts, and astral projection. In general, they seemed extremely preoccupied with exotica and with external norms of behavior and not that interested in anything as mundane as the practice of meditation. These were exactly the kinds of misconceptions about spirituality that Rinpoche was trying to expose, so it was rather predictable that he would disappoint them and confound them with his behavior.

In fact, Rinpoche didn't respond to people, so I started answering questions for him. A woman in the audience started complaining that I shouldn't speak for him. In fact, as disciples of Krishnamurti, they didn't believe in gurus, so in a sense Rinpoche was responding to their beliefs by manifesting as the "anti-guru." They didn't seem to like this, however!

I felt that the whole thing didn't go well. At the end of the evening, the organizers gave us an envelope containing an honorarium and sent us on our way. When we opened the envelope in the taxi, we realized that it wasn't enough to cover even our lodging. There had been hundreds of people at the talk. I said to Rinpoche, "We've got to go back and ask for some money for the motel." Interestingly enough, he had sobered up completely as soon as we left the talk. He said no, we absolutely couldn't do that.

After the disastrous talk, we had a free day before flying back to San Francisco, so we took a bus into Mexico, where Rinpoche bought his Mexican shirts. The next day we returned to northern California for several more weeks. I think that Rinpoche accomplished a lot of important research on this trip. We encountered many spiritual seekers who he described as "free-style people indulging themselves in confused spiritual pursuits." In California, he witnessed some of the most extreme manifestations of the American counterculture at this time. There were hippies and Hare Krishnas roaming around Haight-Ashbury like strange lost tribes, political dissidents protesting in Berkeley and San Francisco, people at every talk who were into every imaginable spiritual trip. The scene in California was looser yet more extreme than on the East Coast, where there was still a hard edge of intellect. That was much harder to find in the West. In California, everything was "groovy, man." I think that it was while we were in the Bay Area that Rinpoche coined the phrase "cutting through spiritual materialism," which became the title of his best-selling book published in 1973. If he didn't use the phrase then, at least he was formulating the idea behind it. As he said sometime later: "Coming to this country was an interesting encounter.... A lot of people had already become professional spiritual supermarket shoppers, and some were still trying to become so."[2] At the same time, in general, he didn't seem too put off or upset by most of the people he met. In fact, he felt that people's fascination was ripe to be punctured and that there were possibilities for authentic spirituality to flourish in America, even in California!

We spent several days with Tarthang Tulku, another Tibetan teacher, who had been in the United States for about a year. He had a small house in Berkeley where he lived and conducted sessions with his students. Eventually, he purchased a center in a beautiful area of Berkeley Hills. Tarthang and Rinpoche were quite friendly, and in later years, they talked about going on vacation together in Mexico, although that never happened. Tarthang was beginning to think about bringing Western psychology into his presentation of the Buddhist teachings. That was very interesting for Rinpoche, since he too had begun to use some of the language and ideas from Western psychology to present teachings on the nature of mind and development of ego. Their approaches were quite distinct, but there was some common understanding. Tarthang extended a great deal of hospitality to Rinpoche and me at this time, and we were grateful for his generosity. We stayed with him several times when we made visits to the Bay Area.

While we were in California, Rinpoche also had a remarkable visit with Shunryu Suzuki Roshi, the founder of San Francisco Zen Center. Suzuki Roshi had been in America for more than ten years, and a large community of practitioners had grown up around him. He had an extraordinary effect on Buddhism in America. One would have to call him the true grandfather of the Practice Lineage in this country.

Sam Bercholz arranged for us to travel to Tassajara Zen Mountain Center, Roshi's rural practice center near Big Sur. We spent several days there. There was an instant connection between Rinpoche and Suzuki Roshi. Roshi toured us around Tassajara, which he was justly proud of. It was a magnificent setting, with cabins set into the hillside, a beautiful shrine room, and wonderful hot springs that we enjoyed during our stay. In meeting Roshi, Rinpoche said that he had met his first real spiritual friend in America. He asked Roshi how he taught meditation practice to his students, and Roshi said that he had decided to have all of his students count their breaths during meditation, which he described as "Bodhidharma style." Bodhidharma is considered to be the father of Zen in China. Like Padmasambhava in Tibet, he was unconventional and could be very wrathful.

Rinpoche was quite affected by seeing how Roshi was teaching meditation, especially the emphasis on group practice at Tassajara. As I've mentioned, Rinpoche was already presenting the discipline of sitting meditation as the main practice for his students. From his experiences in England, he had realized the danger of Westerners getting tripped out and confused by the tantric practices in Tibetan Buddhism. He had encouraged some students in England to do prostrations, the traditional entrance to Buddhist practice in Tibet. As soon as we came to America, however, he stopped giving that practice. Later he asked almost all of his students from England to repeat their prostrations, after they were well grounded in meditation.

The instruction Rinpoche had been giving since we arrived in America was telling people to sit without much technique at all. He felt, initially at least, that any technique could be perverted or misunderstood, especially in the Western culture with its fascinations. At the beginning, he said: Just sit, don't count your breaths, don't label your thoughts, don't do anything. Just sit. Later he began to refine the technique.[3] His discussions with Roshi about sitting practice and his observation of the environment at Tassajara played an important part in how his presentation of meditation evolved. Soon after our first visit, Rinpoche arranged for some of his senior students to practice at San Francisco Zen Center and Tassajara Zen Mountain Center so that they would have an appreciation for the approach to sitting meditation that Roshi stressed. Several students from the Zen center were also invited to conduct the first meditation intensives at Tail of the Tiger, daylong sittings that Rinpoche called *nyinthuns*.

Rinpoche was also quite taken by certain aspects of the Japanese aesthetic. In later years, when other Tibetan teachers taught at our centers, they often commented that the meditation hall had a Japanese feeling. The colors Rinpoche used were definitely Tibetan: Chinese vermilion red, bright yellow and orange, intense blues, and gold. However, the shrines he designed for his centers were quite unlike those in a Tibetan shrine hall. Traditionally, Tibetan shrines have many offerings and other objects on them, and there are lots of statues and paintings around them. From some point of view, you might almost say they're cluttered. Rinpoche designed a very simple shrine on which there were seven offering bowls filled with pure water. In the center of the shrine a crystal ball was placed, representing the open nature of mind.

Rinpoche also became fond of Japanese incense, and it was used exclusively in his centers for many years. It has a much more subtle scent than Tibetan incense. He also used Japanese gongs in the meditation hall to signal the beginning and the end of practice sessions. In addition to the sitting practice of meditation, Rinpoche introduced walking meditation, and some aspects of that practice I believe he took from the Zen model.

However, what was most important about this first meeting was the heart connection between Rinpoche and Roshi. After we left, Rinpoche said that Suzuki Roshi was the first person he met in America who reminded him of his own teacher, Jamgön Kongtrul. Rinpoche had Roshi's picture put on the shrines at all of his centers in America, along with the photograph of Jamgön Kongtrul, representing the Tibetan lineage. In this way, he honored Roshi as one of the lineage fathers in America. We would see more of him in future visits to California, although, tragically, he died from liver cancer in December of 1971, soon after we met him. In the short time they knew one another, he and Rinpoche made grand plans. It was partially Suzuki Roshi's inspiration that led in 1974 to the foundation of the Naropa Institute, a university based on the Buddhist contemplative traditions and Western scholarship as well. Rinpoche's work with psychology also went in new directions due to his conversations with Suzuki Roshi about the need for a Buddhist-inspired therapeutic community.

In addition to his publishing company, Sam Bercholz had started a metaphysical bookstore on Telegraph Avenue in Berkeley. We visited there several times during the month we were in California. Rinpoche was impressed with all the scholarly Buddhist books that Sam had there, as well as more popular titles. The bookstore was a hangout for anyone involved with the spiritual scene, and we saw posters advertising Rinpoche's public talks on the bulletin board there. Sam and Rinpoche began planning many new books, and Shambhala Publications became Rinpoche's exclusive publisher in America. Over the course of the visit, we became close friends with Sam and Hazel. The Bercholzes introduced us to many people during our stay, a number of whom became Rinpoche's students. By the time we left, a *sangha,* or Buddhist community, was beginning to form in northern California, and Rinpoche promised to return soon and to send some of his senior students from Tail to teach in Berkeley and San Francisco.

Before we left California, I went to have a pregnancy test because I had missed my period. Rinpoche took me to see an obstetrician on Market Street in San Francisco. After the doctor read the results of the test, he called Rinpoche and me into his office and told us that it was positive. Rinpoche looked shell-shocked when he heard the news. I was also somewhat overwhelmed, being only sixteen at the time. Later, when he reflected back on this moment, he said, "It felt very clean-cut to fall in love and be with my wife. But then, when I first heard a San Francisco doctor say, 'Congratulations. The test is positive,' I didn't know what to think. I felt that I'd been pulled down, made into a part of the world in an entirely new way, that the ship had dropped its anchor."[4] In the hippie era, we used to talk about being brought down, or things being "a downer, man." Rinpoche, however, talked about being brought down to earth, or being grounded, as a very positive thing. I think he related to our marriage in that way.

I asked the obstetrician if it would be okay for me to ride horses during the pregnancy, as this had been an important discipline in my life and I was hoping to start riding again soon. The doctor said, "If you couldn't ride when you were pregnant, you would look outside the window and see women riding all up and down Market Street"—implying that riding would have been used as a method to end unwanted pregnancies.

On our way back to Tail we stopped off in New York for the weekend. Rinpoche gave several public talks, one entitled "Meditation in Action" and another called "Tibetan Alchemy." It was now early July, and his seminars at Tail of the Tiger were due to start in another week. Even now, a mere two months after arriving in the United States, everywhere Rinpoche went he attracted new students. When we came back through New York, there were many more people around all the time. An important and absolutely chance meeting was running into the poet Allen Ginsberg. Allen was with his father, who was quite old and in poor health, and they were trying to hail a taxicab, the same cab we thought we were hailing. We were with someone, perhaps Richard Arthure, who introduced us to Allen. When he learned who Rinpoche was, Allen held his hands in *anjali* (hands at the heart in a gesture of respect or reverence), bowed, and said "OM VAJRA GURU PADMA SIDDHI HUM," which is the mantra of Padmasambhava, the syllables that invoke the essence of his energy. We all decided to share the cab. After dropping off Allen's father, we went to Allen's place, where he and Rinpoche talked for hours about poetry, Buddhism, politics, sex—everything. They wrote poetry together that night, and it was the beginning of a deep dharmic and poetic friendship. Later, when they knew each other better, Allen asked Rinpoche what he thought of being greeted by Padmasambhava's mantra. Rinpoche told him that at the time he had wondered whether Allen understood what he was saying.

Rinpoche had started writing poetry in English while he was in England. He had studied English poetry at Oxford, and his early poems tended to be more formal, with allusions to Christian themes and Greek mythology as well as to Buddhist deities. He also had encountered Japanese haiku in India, which had given him a different idea, a sense of how one might compose poetry that was a more direct reflection of the mind. This was similar to the training he had received from his guru in Tibet in composing *dohas,* or spontaneous songs of spiritual realization. Allen introduced Rinpoche to the possibility of even greater freedom of expression and a kind of poetry that was as fresh, wild, and evocative as our experience of America. It was the first chapter in a long and important association with American poets and poetics, which had its intense ups and downs.

Interestingly enough, this was not the first time that Rinpoche and Allen had met. After Rinpoche's death, while going through photographs from a visit to India in the early sixties, Allen saw a picture of himself taken at the Young Lamas Home School in Dalhousie. A young monk was showing him around. He looked closely at the photograph and realized that it was Rinpoche who had taken him on that tour, ten years before they met in New York. Neither one of them realized this when they ran across each other in America.

After our weekend in New York, we headed back to Tail of the Tiger, where more and more students were arriving every day. John Baker and Marvin Casper showed up around this time. They became close friends of ours and close students of Rinpoche's. They ended up living in our house when we moved to Colorado later that year. Later, they became the editors of *Cutting Through Spiritual Materialism* and the *Myth of Freedom*. Students from cities and universities all over the East Coast began appearing at Tail. There was, for example, a group from Brandeis University who started coming to Tail for seminars.

Rinpoche was scheduled to teach a long seminar on the *Jewel Ornament of Liberation,* an important book by Gampopa, one of the forefathers of Rinpoche's Tibetan lineage, and then he was to give another long seminar on the life and teachings of Milarepa. The people at Tail were expecting a hundred or more participants. I was looking forward to these seminars, which were to take place outdoors in a big white tent in a field behind the barn at Tail. I was experiencing morning sickness, but other than that, I was feeling well, and I was quite happy to be pregnant.

Just a day or two before the first seminar was scheduled to begin, I dreamt that Rinpoche's son, Ösel, was being held captive in England by Christopher Woodman and his wife Pamela. In the dream, Ösel was trapped there, and they wouldn't let him go. In fact, we knew that Ösel had been staying with the Woodmans. Akong had gone on a trip to India, and he thought that while he was away, they could provide a better environment for Ösel than he would have staying at Samye Ling. He had asked the Woodmans to take care of Ösel without asking our permission first. Given the dreadful relationship that we had with Christopher and Pamela, this made us very nervous, but there was nothing we could do. As far as we knew, everything was all right. We had been making plans to bring Ösel over as soon as things felt settled, perhaps at the end of the summer.

When I woke up, I told Rinpoche about the dream, and he was quite alarmed. He said, "You have to get on a plane right away and go get him." I said, "Oh, I think it's nothing," but he said, "No, you have to go today." Rinpoche trusted my dream life, and in fact, all my life I've had dreams that turn out to be significant. He had me phone the Woodmans to tell them that I was coming to get Ösel, and they seemed to be fine with it. Then, he booked a ticket for me from Boston to Glasgow. He couldn't accompany me because he had to teach. I was going to stay a night or two in Scotland, and then Ösel and I would travel back to be with Rinpoche at Tail of the Tiger.

I flew overnight to Prestwick Airport in Scotland, the same airport from which we'd left Scotland in early March. It wasn't very pleasant to go back there. I took a taxi from Prestwick to the Woodmans' place, Garwald House. I arrived in Glasgow early in the morning, and it was overcast, cold, and misty. The drive south toward Samye Ling was surrealistic. There were wisps of curling mist, and it was so foggy that you could hardly see the road ahead. After we had gone through Lockerbie, about two hours south of Glasgow, as we got closer to Garwald it got darker and more overcast, and there started to be dead animals on the road. First, it was just a dead little bird. Further on, I saw a dead cat. Then there was a dead dog in the road. After we came through Eskdalemuir—which is quite close to Garwald—there was a dead sheep. I know this stretches the imagination, but it actually happened. There was this roadkill gradually progressing in size between Lockerbie and Garwald House, and toward the end of the drive, both the cabbie and I were getting spooked. Just before the turnoff to Garwald House, there was a dead cow on the road. The whole scene was like a cross between Stephen King and Monty Python, and quite creepy. Somehow with the combination of the dream and all of these dead animals, I began to feel very strange. However, there was nothing to be done about it, so we continued down the long driveway to Garwald House.

Because the relationship with the Woodmans had turned so negative in the last months that we were in Britain, I was apprehensive about how they might greet me. I asked the taxi to wait while I went in. I only expected to be there for a short time. Sitting in the living room and drinking tea with the Woodmans, everything seemed very friendly and nice, and I thought, "I'm being ridiculous. Everything's fine. I've cranked up this whole thing." Ösel came in and he looked good, very relaxed and healthy. He seemed well cared for and he looked like he was enjoying himself there. I gave him a big hug and then told him, "We're going to

America to see Daddy." He seemed quite excited. After maybe half an hour, we got ready to leave.

I gathered up Ösel's things, we said goodbye to the Woodmans, and we started to get in the taxi. Before the door closed, unexpectedly, Pamela ran over to the cab, sobbing. Her whole face had changed radically. It was contorted by what seemed to me a combination of rage and pain. She leapt into the car and physically wrenched Ösel out, saying, "You can't have him." He looked completely overwhelmed and panicked. I can't imagine what this conflict was like for him.

She took Ösel back into the house. I went in to reason with her, and I said, "This is terrible. You have to let him go. You aren't his guardians. His father wants Ösel to come to America." But she was adamant, saying, "I can't let you have him. You haven't made enough of a relationship with him. He should stay here longer. I'm not going to let him go." She was crying, completely upset and unmoving.

I took the taxi back to Lockerbie and checked into a hotel there. I phoned Rinpoche, and he told me to contact a lawyer. To tell you the truth, he didn't seem that surprised that this had happened. I phoned a lawyer in Glasgow by the name of Maurice Maurissey, who agreed to help us. The next day, I met with him and we went to Social Services to get things sorted out. We discovered that the Woodmans had also been there. From what we could tell, they seemed to have painted a picture of Rinpoche as some kind of demonic person. They said that he drank too much, which may have been true, but in other respects the characterization was unrecognizable to me. It was like a replay of the earlier visa problems with Christopher. If the Woodmans couldn't have Rinpoche in England with them anymore, it seemed that they were going to hold onto his son. The people at Social Services told me that Ösel wouldn't be released to us until there had been a home study in the United States. It was quite a mess.

I ended up staying in England for many months trying to get the whole thing sorted out. I kept thinking that it would just be a few more days, a few more weeks, and then Ösel would be able to be with us. I had to go through several hearings with Maurice, trying to arrange to have Ösel released to me. Eventually, we arranged for him to leave the Woodmans and go to the Pestalozzi Village in the south of England. We knew that Ösel would be in a good setting there while we worked out the legal problems.

The Pestalozzi Village was established after World War II to care for orphans and refugees displaced by the war. In the 1960s, they began taking in Tibetan refugees, followed by refugees from other Asian and African nations. The first Pestalozzi Village was in Switzerland. The one in England was established somewhat later. They had different houses where residents of a particular nationality lived, and they provided an excellent education and loving care for the children there. There was a housemother and housefather for every residence. Ösel was able to be with other Tibetans where he could speak his own language. Tibetan was still his main language at that time. Once Ösel moved to the Pestalozzi Village, I was able to visit him regularly, and I would go down to see him as often as I could.

It took months to make these arrangements, and I stayed most of the time in London in Beauchamp Place with Francesca Fremantle, who generously shared her flat with me. She was a close student of Rinpoche's from Samye Ling who later spent time in the United States and taught at the University of Colorado and Naropa Institute. She and Rinpoche worked together on the translation of the *Tibetan Book of the Dead*. She's quite a brilliant scholar. She was incredibly kind to me during this difficult period.

Early in the fall, after his seminars were done at Tail of the Tiger, Rinpoche flew over for about a week. I was so glad to see him. He sometimes liked to cook, often quite unusual creations, and he cooked dinner one night at Francesca's. His peanut butter and lemonade soup would be a good example of his unconventional cuisine. In London, he cooked roast chicken basted in liquid vitamins for Francesca and me. I told him this was disgusting; he said I was too conservative in my thinking and simply needed to open my mind.

We visited Ösel together at the Pestalozzi Village while Rinpoche was in England. The Woodmans had told Ösel frightful stories about Rinpoche, so at that time, Ösel was quite afraid of his father. It was heartbreaking. At the end of the week, Rinpoche flew directly from London to Denver, Colorado. He was moving to Boulder to begin teaching at the University of Colorado, and I was to join him as soon as

I was able. We still hoped that I would be bringing Ösel with me. Rin-poche was quite worried about his son, and he was very grateful that I was willing to stay and work on the situation. This was another example of how he sacrificed the concerns of his personal life for his commit-ment to presenting Buddhism in America. It was truly difficult for him to leave with nothing resolved, but he felt that he had to honor his teaching commitments.

While I was in London, I was often worried that I would bump into my mother on the streets. I was showing quite pregnant by this time, and I knew she would disapprove. I had had no communication with her since she had surprised me at Tail of the Tiger in May. Francesca lived not far from Harrods, and I frequently thought about going there. They sold a game pie in the food halls there that I had a craving for. Finally, I de-cided to go and buy one. My mother often shopped at Harrods, so when I went in, I looked all over to be sure she wasn't there, and I got a sort of adrenaline rush.

Eventually, somebody told my mother I was in London, and she phoned me at Francesca's. I had just this one phone call with her, in which she said to me, "Diana, I hope the child in your womb does not do to you what you have done to me," and she hung up the phone. That was the sum total of our communication.

Finally, around the end of December, it became clear that I wasn't going to be able to bring Ösel back to the United States with me. I was now more than six months' pregnant and wouldn't be allowed to travel on an airplane that much longer. I wanted to be with Rinpoche in Col-orado to have the baby. I left England with a heavy sense of regret at leaving Ösel and took a flight to Denver. It was not until 1972 that he was able to join us in America.

SEVEN

When Rinpoche arrived in Colorado in the fall, his students rented a small cabin for him in the mountains above Boulder, near an old mining town called Gold Hill. It was quite spartan, almost what you would call a stone hut. There was no indoor plumbing, just an outhouse. Rinpoche hadn't lived in a place like this since he'd left Tibet more than ten years ago. People may have thought a Tibetan lama would be more comfortable in a simple mountain setting. This might have been more a reflection of his students' hippie aspirations than an accurate reading of who he was at this point. On the other hand, it was by no means a hovel, and he told me that he enjoyed himself there. The house was on a beautiful piece of property, with a view of the Continental Divide in the distance. It was owned by a family that had spent years in the foreign service in Asia. This was their summerhouse, which they named Gunung Mas, which is Burmese, I believe.

Before I joined Rinpoche, he moved into a larger house much closer to town. It was still a little ways into the mountains, about a ten-minute drive out of Boulder, in Four Mile Canyon. With the baby coming, he felt that we needed a better house for the family.

Rinpoche was quite proud that he was providing a home for us. Before I got there, John Baker and Marvin Casper took the train from Vermont to Boulder with all our belongings. Everything we owned fit in the allowed baggage on the train. In a phone call with John, I insisted that he take my pet goldfish on the train with him. In some areas, I behaved just like a spoiled teenager in those days. After all, I was barely seventeen. John always swore that he took the fish with him and that it died on the train, but I had my doubts.

When I arrived in Denver, Karl Usow picked me up at the airport in a Volkswagen bus. Karl was a professor of mathematics at the University of Colorado; he, along with another professor, John Visvader, had sent the postcard to Scotland inviting Rinpoche to teach at the university. He had a big moustache, and his hair was over his ears, which was actually short for those days.

Colorado was in the heart of the West, with its rough and rugged frontier feeling. I saw people with cowboy hats and boots in the airport while I was waiting to get my luggage. It was certainly a different atmosphere from either the East or the West Coast. Coming to Colorado was the beginning of another whole adventure—one that would leave a huge mark on our lives.

I was excited to be in Boulder and to have my own house. The new house was a large, two-story, fairly modern structure, what is called a "raised ranch." It was set slightly below the road that wound up the canyon, and Four Mile Creek ran in front of the house. There were poplar trees and evergreens growing around the property. Rinpoche and I had a sitting room and bedroom on the first floor, while John and Marvin lived upstairs. The living room, which was also upstairs, had been transformed into a shrine room where the community gathered to practice meditation.

Rinpoche had designed raised platforms for people to sit on. Several students built the wooden frames to hold single-bed mattresses. The frames were painted orange with gold leafing on them and were raised a few inches off the ground. Then Tibetan carpets were placed on top of the mattresses, and people sat on those. This was before Rinpoche adopted the use of meditation cushions, *zafus* and *zabutons,* from the Japanese Zen tradition. Rinpoche often sat and meditated with people in the evening.

By the time I arrived, a substantial scene had developed around Rinpoche in Boulder. Most of these people were not from Colorado. They were arriving from the East and West coasts, as well as from the Midwest. Some people flew in, but in those days, it was more than likely that someone would arrive in an old car with belongings strapped to the roof. Some people hitchhiked into town. Some took the bus. All of them seemed to converge on our house. There were people there morning, noon, and night.

People would often crash in our sitting room, which was all right with me if it was just for a night or two. Then one of Rinpoche's students brought his sleeping bag and stayed for a couple of weeks, and then his wife and children arrived and they were all camping out there. Finally I told him that they had to move out and get their own place. This wasn't the only time I felt the need for more privacy and kicked people out. When this happened, people often had very little sympathy for me. They related to me like I was this terrible woman that the guru just happened to be married to. It didn't seem to occur to people that this house was also our home and that there might be boundaries to how much we—or at least I—wanted to share the space with people.

In this instance, Rinpoche's student had a complete freak-out. He told me that I had no understanding of Buddhism, that the guru's house was his house too, and that he was always welcome in the guru's house. I told him, "Well, you can think what you want about your religion, but I'm calling the police if you're not out in twenty-four hours." The whole family left, obviously.

Even our bedroom was not always off-limits to people. There was a woman who liked to meditate in the room when we were sleeping. She would sneak in during the night, and when we woke up, she would be there on a cushion meditating in the corner. Rinpoche would lean over in bed and whisper to me, "She's in here again. Get her out of here."

God, those were really the days. It was a wonderful era, though. Anything seemed possible. It was around this time that it dawned on me that Rinpoche was going to create something magnificent. All of us, I think, began to realize that his influence was going to be enormous, on a grand scale. It seemed unstoppable. He was so much vaster than anybody else I have ever met. I began to see Rinpoche as a *mahasiddha,* someone who outwardly may live an ordinary, secular life but whose every action is an expression of ultimate sanity, or wakefulness, and compassion. I don't even think it had to do with him *choosing* to live his life this way. The essence of his being was on a different plane than most other human beings, including most of the other Tibetan teachers. There were absolutely no boundaries to his compassion and his desire to present the teachings. His passion and his role in this lifetime were to present Buddhism in the West, and he put up no barriers between himself and others. He didn't keep any little dim corner for himself at all. Many people give of themselves, but almost all of us reserve a pocket of privacy, some part of our personal life that we don't want to share. Rinpoche kept nothing for himself.

People freely flowed through the house. Even though the scene was sometimes crazy and intense, I enjoyed it most of the time, especially in the two months before our child was born. In the evenings, the house would fill up with people, and I would sometimes cook dinner for everyone. There might be twenty or thirty people for dinner. I would make a big roast or a pot of stew, and we would all sit around and eat together in the kitchen.

During this time, Rinpoche's relationships with people were so immediate and informal that his students had the sense that they could hang out with him all the time. To some extent that was true. Just before our son was born, one student who was at the house a lot asked to speak privately with Rinpoche, and she was really concerned. She said to him, "Now you're going to have a child, and you're not going to love us anymore." He reassured her that this was not the case.

A group of people who called themselves the Pygmies discovered Rinpoche and started to hang out at the house. They had a commune east of Boulder, and their motto was, "We're bodhisattvas, and we live on East Arapahoe." They were long-haired and unkempt, and they lived in tents most of the year, which wasn't all *that* unusual for those times. There were a lot of people living pseudo-tribal lifestyles in those days. I don't know how the Pygmies lived in the winter, but they seemed quite cheerful in all kinds of weather. Some of them pitched their tents around the house for a while, as I remember. I became good friends with a number of them.

People indulged in some interesting eccentricities in those days. Marvin Casper, who was living in the house, went through a phase where he didn't like to shower. Marvin had a theory that Westerners bathed too much. Marvin was a bit odd but very lovable. He liked to eat Wheatena and peas with mayonnaise on them. He often didn't wash the bowls he ate out of, putting them back in the cupboard dirty. When I inquired about this, he said that there was no reason to wash his dishes because he was just going to use them again. From this time onward, there were always people living with us who helped Rinpoche with his work. In that era, it was Marvin and John, but it was a lot of different people over the years.

Rinpoche did business at the house, as he had no outside office in those early days. He was making plans to write books, make movies, open meditation centers. He was writing poetry, writing plays, taking photographs, giving a talk every other night of the week. He was planning to go back and forth from Boulder to Vermont several times a year, and there were requests from people all over the country for him to come and teach. There was endless activity, and he involved his students in every aspect of making and carrying out these plans.

When you think about the raw material that he had, it's quite amazing that he trusted these people—all of us—to help him spread the buddhadharma in America. In fact, this was a very important way that he worked with people and trained them. I say that from my own experience. I learned so much from him, from everything he did and everything we did together. He gave me such confidence about who I was and what I could do. At the same time that he would build you up, he would also call forth the most genuine part of yourself, and he wore down the problematic parts. But he never did this by belittling you. He was very skillful that way. The only problem was that sometimes people lost track of the fact that they still had a lot of work to do on themselves. Living in his world, you sometimes felt that you had accomplished the whole thing on the spot. From some point of view, you had, but then there's always the path. We all have that to work on.

Rinpoche would give private meditation interviews in a little room on the top floor of the house. Later, it became my son's bedroom. There were two chairs and a side table in the room. Although there were many informal scenes and a lot of hanging out around the house, Rinpoche always stressed the importance of these formal meetings with students, to discuss their meditation practice and their lives. I think that all of his students had private interviews with him during the first few years he taught in America. In the interview situation, at least in terms of my own experience, Rinpoche completely connected with the other person in a way that was frighteningly direct. Anyone who expected the interview to be an extension of the informal space around the house was in for a big surprise. One felt absolutely on the spot. His ability to connect with the deepest part of a person was uncanny.

Rinpoche had several people who helped him schedule his meetings and interviews. I had done a lot of this in Scotland, but in general I was no longer involved once we arrived in the United States. Kesang, Fran, Marvin, and John all helped out, and as more and more people came, Rinpoche asked other students—new faces in Boulder—to participate in this way.

Many people who came for interviews were members of the Buddhist community that was forming in Boulder. Others were spiritual seekers passing through town or students of other teachers who had heard about the Tibetan in the mountains outside of Boulder. Two long-haired American Hindu guys, Krishna and Narayana, came for interviews during this period. They were close students of Swami Satchidananda in Los Angeles, although originally they were from the East Coast. After Narayana's initial interview, he wrote to Rinpoche,

> I have met many saints and teachers, but only one had the ability to change my state to a noticeable degree just through *darshan* [being in the teacher's presence]. Swami Satchidananda was the one, but now you are the other. I am telling you this because I realize that it was a significant encounter and one that may have bearing on how I approach life and spirituality.[1]

You never knew in those days who someone might become. Years later, in 1976, Rinpoche would appoint Narayana (also known as Thomas Rich) as his Vajra Regent, his dharma heir. Long-haired Hindus might transform into Buddhist businessmen; hippie girls might become university professors.

For many of those meeting Rinpoche for the first time, their initial interview brought a shocking realization, not unlike what Narayana described. Many, many people felt drawn to him in a way they could not explain. During these early years, he was gathering many heart disciples, people with a deep karmic connection who would remain with him throughout his life. They somehow found their way to him and he to them. It was an amazing process, an amazing time.

It was not, however, an overly solemn period. Rinpoche remained impish and always ready for a good joke. Bhagwan Dass, an American who fashioned himself as a Hindu yogi or *sadhu,* showed up at the house one day. He had spent a long time in India with Ram Dass, also known as Richard Alpert, the Harvard professor who was converted by psychedelic experiences to the life of a Hindu *sannyasin* and who wrote the classic *Be Here Now.* (At this time, we had not yet met Ram Dass.) I was sitting in the kitchen at Four Mile Canyon, and in walked Bhagwan Dass, this tall person with unbelievably long matted hair, dressed entirely in white. He said to me, "Where's the guru? I want to meet the guru. I have an interview with the guru."

I said, "Well, he's upstairs."

He responded, "I was just up there, and that fellow sent me back down here."

I asked him, "Did he, by any chance, have suspenders and a shirt on?"

"Yes," he said. I suggested that he go back up there. Apparently he had wandered upstairs and asked Rinpoche "Where's the guru?" and Rinpoche had replied, "I don't know."

In addition to all the other activities at the house, we sometimes had parties, some of which got pretty wild. I think that Rinpoche found it interesting to socialize with people in this way. During this period, Rinpoche was on a steep learning curve. It was often a wild ride for him and everyone else. He liked to get right out on the edge with people and see what would happen. It was a very creative space for him. I think he regarded it as a kind of research. Although the whole scene may sometimes have seemed merely chaotic and totally unplanned, Rinpoche was not just hanging out with people in a random fashion. As he said later,

> On my arrival in the United States of America, I was met by lots of psychologists and students of psychology, ex-Hindus, ex-Christians and ex-Americans of all kinds. . . . At the beginning, when I first arrived in the U.S.A., I was trying to find students' so-called trips and trying to push a little bit of salt and pepper into

their lives and see how they handled that. They handled that little dash of salt and pepper okay. They understood it, but they would still maintain their particular trips. So then I put more of a dash of salt and pepper into their lives and further spice . . . experimenting with how to bring up so-called American students. It's quite interesting, almost scientific. You bring up your rat in your cage and you feed it with corn or rice or oats and you give it a little bit of drugs and maybe occasionally you inject it and see how it reacts, how it works with it. I'm sorry, maybe this is not the best way of describing this—but it was some kind of experimentation as to how those particular animals called Americans and this particular animal called a Tibetan Buddhist can actually work together. And it worked fine; it worked beautifully.[2]

Rinpoche also saw himself as part of the experiment, as part of what was being worked on. Throughout this whole period, what I think drove much of the activity was a kind of electric passion or connection between Rinpoche and his students.

Soon after I arrived in Boulder, in February of 1971, there was a party to celebrate Rinpoche's birthday. Rinpoche wore his black high-necked *chuba,* which had gold piping on the collar and Tibetan buttons. He looked quite handsome in it. There was a snowstorm that night, and people came in and left their jackets and boots on the floor just outside the kitchen. At some point in the evening, Rinpoche was in the kitchen showing off all the gadgets we had. He was very proud of the sprayer that was attached to the sink. It was on a long flexible black pipe that pulled out of the sink, and we used it to spray the dishes and clean the sink. He said, "Look, I have all these modern conveniences for my family now."

I was a few weeks away from giving birth, so I went to bed quite early. Apparently, a while later, Rinpoche turned on the water in the sink and starting experimenting with the sprayer. He started with cups and glasses on the counter; then he moved on to the people around him in the kitchen. First, it was just a playful burst of water that caught someone on the shoulder, then someone else in the face. Then, he turned the water on full force and began directing the sprayer at everything within his reach. By the end, everybody's coats and boots were soaked from all the water, which spread out across the kitchen floor into the entryway. Finally, Rinpoche himself became a victim of his own prank. As the floor became slippery, he fell down in a puddle at his feet, which delighted him as much as anything else.

Although I missed most of the action that evening, I was certainly privy to similar occasions throughout the years. Sometimes these situations would remind me of the scenes in movies that turn into food fights or brawls. There's something both repulsive and attractive about those scenes. I remember a movie where a man and woman start feeding each other food out of the refrigerator, and they end up on the floor in front of the icebox, with their clothes off smearing food on one another's bodies. Most of us are willing voyeurs for such an outrageous scene in a film, but we are less ready to pursue such activities in real life. Yet there's a kind of longing for that freedom. Rinpoche had an amazing ability to take an individual or an entire group of people into those spaces, and not just as an opportunity to indulge in some fantasy. There was a way in which he invited you to unleash who you really are—and then to see the utter transparency and ordinariness of that. It didn't have to be as literal or crude as a water fight—although it *could* be. But it might also be inviting you to compose poetry with him, or cooking dinner for him, or just what you felt from a touch of his hand on your shoulder. It could be funny or very sad. It was like going through a mirror into your own mind.

When I arrived in Boulder, Rinpoche was lecturing several nights a week at the Wesley Foundation, a church on Twenty-Eighth Street and Folsom. His evening talks were in addition to classes that he was teaching once or twice a week at the University of Colorado. About a hundred people would usually attend the evening talks, although the crowd grew as the weeks went on. Around this time, some students rented a house, where a number of them lived. It had a little shrine hall in the garage, and many people started practicing there, instead of in our living room. Rinpoche did a shrine blessing there and named the house Anitya Bhavan, "house of impermanence." I think he knew the scene was going to quickly outgrow that space.

Indeed, the scene was growing exponentially, new people arriving every week from all parts of the United States. Before and after his talks, there would be people milling around outside the hall where the lectures took place. On the one hand, Rinpoche wanted people to meditate before his talks began, but on the other hand, he and his students were building a Buddhist culture. I think he knew that this social scene was an important part of building that world. Also, he did not want to always be at the center of the scene. He talked about the importance of a teacher being slightly eccentric, in the sense of off center, saying that an overly centralized situation would not encourage the students to develop their own strength and understanding.

After some period of hanging out, people would slowly filter into the room and find a place to sit on the floor. Finally, Rinpoche would arrive and slowly make his way along the edge of the audience to the stage. The Wesley Foundation was a modern building, and it had two walls of stained glass, which met at an angle in the middle. From the outside, this looked something like a bird's open beak. Inside, Rinpoche sat in front of the walls of stained glass.

Many of these talks were incorporated into his first genuinely American book, *Cutting Through Spiritual Materialism,* which was published in 1973. I was so impressed by how spacious yet charged the atmosphere was at these talks and how delighted and relaxed Rinpoche seemed to be. There was a sense that he had really arrived. He was home. After the main part of the talk, there was always a long question-and-answer period, and many of the exchanges were both brilliant and intimate. There was still the occasional off-the-wall question, usually from a newcomer, about whether the Tibetans were related to the people who built Stonehenge, or something like that. By and large, however, students were sharpening and focusing their minds, and the discussions that took place were part of that process of developing intellect. People may have looked a bit ragged at that time, but you could tell that they were jewels in the rough. All of this was going on during the last two months of my pregnancy. In fact, Rinpoche gave a talk the night before I gave birth, and he gave another in this series just a few days after our son was born.

To prepare for the birth of our child, just like any other young couple, Rinpoche and I went to Denver together to take birthing classes. Rinpoche was very supportive and involved. He came to almost all the classes. We had decided that we wanted to use natural childbirth, which was a relatively new, progressive trend in those days. Dr. Robert Bradley, who founded the Bradley method of natural childbirth, was in Denver, so we signed up for his course. Dr. Bradley preached that childbirth should be painless. He said that if you had the proper training, you wouldn't have any pain at all. Rinpoche and I were convinced that this must be true.

My son was due at the end of February, but he came almost two weeks late. On the night of March 8, Rinpoche returned after giving a lecture at the Wesley Foundation, and we both went to bed. I was awakened by pain, and after lying in bed awake for some time, I woke Rinpoche up and I said, "There's something wrong with me. I'm having a lot of pains. Do you think I'm in labor?" He responded, "Oh no, Dr. Bradley said that childbirth isn't painful. I'm sure it will pass." I sat up for a while waiting for the pains to subside, but in fact they were growing more and more intense. For some reason, we were convinced that I wasn't in labor. We were both so naive about this, Rinpoche with his monastic background and me with my alienated English upbringing. Finally, I got into a hot bath, which I thought might alleviate the pain. I never drank at this point in my life, but I had a couple of shots of Johnnie Walker that night, hoping it might help.

Very early in the morning, around six o'clock, I went upstairs to John Baker's room and knocked on his door. I said, "John, I think there's something wrong with me. I think something's terribly the matter." He said, "What do you mean?" I said, "Well I'm getting these pains, and they're coming every five minutes." Within three minutes, I would say, he was up and had his clothes on and the car keys in his hand, and he told me, "Okay, we're going to the hospital." He drove me as fast as he could to Dr. Bradley's office in Denver. I was already six centimeters dilated at that point. They took me over to Porter Memorial Hospital, which was a Seventh-day Adventist hospital, and put me in the labor room there. After John got me checked in, he phoned the house and asked someone to bring Rinpoche down right away. While I was lying there alone, I remember feeling quite afraid. During the latter phases of my pregnancy, it had been haunting me that I had no idea what to do with a baby. There was a forty-year-old woman in one of my childbirth classes who was having her fifth child. I asked her, "What do you do with a baby?" She answered, "Oh, you just change them when they're dirty, feed them when they're hungry, and hold them when they cry."

I was somewhat overwhelmed by the prospect of motherhood. I was so young and I had no helpful reference points from my past to prepare me for motherhood. I had never been around infants, and the only sort of mothering I'd known was my own mother's. I knew that I didn't want to repeat what she'd done. I was afraid that I would be an inadequate parent. There were very few women who had children in the Buddhist sangha at that time, so I didn't know who to turn to. All those anxieties came up as I was lying there alone in labor.

When Rinpoche arrived, I was well into transition. Dr. Bradley soon came into the room. When I was ten centimeters dilated, I wanted to push the baby out, and I felt that the best way to do this was to put my feet up on the end of the bed and push. Dr. Bradley told me that this was not the proper thing to do. He said that I should squat down and grab my knees and push the baby out in that position. He had been studying how some aboriginal tribes gave birth, I think. I tried to do this, but I felt that I couldn't get any leverage. He stood there in the room and wouldn't let me do what I wanted. This must have gone on for an hour and a half. Finally, he stepped out, at which point, I immediately climbed back onto the bed, put my feet up against the end of the bed and pushed. The baby crowned, I was taken to the delivery room, and my son was born shortly thereafter.

Rinpoche was surprised that our first child was a son. There's a rather chauvinistic Tibetan tradition that if a lama marries and the first child is a daughter, this proves that he made a mistake in disrobing. If the first child is a son, it was the right decision. Rinpoche was convinced we were having a daughter. He didn't think our marriage was a mistake, but he didn't expect to get any breaks, as far as these beliefs were concerned. We hadn't even picked out a name for a boy. We were going to call our daughter Dechen, which means "Great Bliss." However, Rinpoche quickly came up with a name for our son. At Rinpoche's suggestion, we named him Tagtrug, which means "tiger cub." The next week, Rinpoche wrote to the Dalai Lama and asked His Holiness for a name for our son. The Dalai Lama named him Tendzin Lhawang, which means "holder of the teachings, divine Lord." So his legal name was Tendzin Lhawang Tagtrug David Mukpo. We called him simply Taggie.

Taggie was born around seven in the evening. He was quite gray when he came out, and I wondered if that was because it took so long to push him out. After the birth, Dr. Bradley—who was very interested in Rinpoche because he was a Tibetan lama—wanted to talk to him about reincarnation, but Rinpoche wouldn't engage in the conversation. He felt that the doctor had mistreated me, and he was not enchanted with his personality.

A while later, the nurses took Taggie to the nursery. At that time, they didn't let the baby stay in the room with the mother that much. Then, at some point, Rinpoche went home so that I could get some rest. In the middle of the night, they brought Taggie to me to nurse. I remember being overwhelmed by the beauty of this child. I picked up the telephone to call Rinpoche to tell him how wonderful our child was. Rinpoche told me that he too was very excited about the birth of our son, and he read me a poem he'd written that night:

> There was a crescendo of energy at the birth of Tagtrug.
> Vajrapani flies in the space—
> The action of tiger's leap bridges the valley.[3]

While we were on the phone, the nurse came running in and took Taggie away from me. She said that I couldn't be on the phone when the baby was in the room. She said he could pick up bacteria from the telephone. This was ridiculous, but I didn't know enough at the time to argue with her. I went to sleep missing my child. The next morning I got up and went to look at Taggie in the nursery. I felt such a maternal instinct that I decided I wanted to take him home immediately. I phoned Rinpoche and John and asked them to pick me up. When they arrived, I discharged myself from the hospital, and we took Taggie home.

Back at Four Mile Canyon, the situation was chaotic. Sam Bercholz was there visiting from California, and Kesang and other people were in the kitchen. They popped open a bottle of champagne to celebrate the birth of the baby. Unfortunately, the cork almost hit him in the head. After a little while, I decided to retire with Taggie to the bedroom.

Rinpoche was having more and more intense sessions with his students in the evenings. While earlier I would have joined him in these sessions, as my pregnancy advanced, my interest in the group scene decreased, especially late at night. Now, with my newborn son, I had less than no interest. This particularly didn't seem like the night for it, as far as I was concerned. I would have liked to have time alone with Rinpoche and the baby, and I felt incredibly invaded with all the people in the house. These scenes continued almost every night after Taggie and I came home. I found that I couldn't get enough sleep because there was so much noise. The baby was being woken up many extra times a night.

A few nights after Taggie was born, Rinpoche was sitting around the kitchen table with some students listening to reel-to-reel tapes of his talks, which they were discussing. At this time Sam Bercholz had already been talking with Rinpoche about editing his talks into a book, and Rinpoche and some of his close students were starting to go through the talks to determine what material might work in a book. The volume on the tape recorder was turned up quite loud, and they weren't being very quiet themselves. I couldn't sleep and I kept going in and saying, "Please try to be a little bit quieter. Please try to be quieter." It would quiet down a little bit, but then it would start up again. Finally, I marched into the room and snapped the tape reel in two with my bare hands. That put an end to it, at least for that night.

There were many times that I would complain to Rinpoche that I wanted more time alone with him. He would say to me, "Don't you like people?" And I would answer him, "Well, yes, I like people, but not as much as you do." When I complained to him that we didn't have enough time together, he would say to me, "Do you want to have a suburb-ian marriage? That would be terrible!" Well, there was no chance of that.

Sometimes during this era I would take drastic measures to get time with him. On Easter Sunday, I announced to everyone at the house that I had prepared an egg hunt in the yard, and they all went outside to look for the eggs. Then I locked the doors and the windows, so that no one could get back in. Rinpoche asked me what was going on, and I just said, "Now you're mine!"

To me, one particular occasion marks the change in my life that came with the birth of my first child. When Taggie was only two weeks old, Rinpoche left for several days to investigate buying a piece of land in the mountains above Fort Collins. Before this, I almost always accompanied him when he traveled, and it was quite a shock when I realized that I was going to stay behind. Rinpoche would have welcomed my company, but tramping around in the snow in the Rocky Mountains in March with an infant made no sense. So I decided to stay home with Taggie. However, I felt abandoned and somewhat afraid of being home alone with the baby. When Rinpoche left, I was crying, sobbing actually. The house had been full of people ever since I'd arrived in Boulder. Now, for the first time, it was empty. A few people came by to visit and help out, but I was alone most of the time.

When Rinpoche came back, he said, "We're going to buy some land," and he was really happy about it. I was really happy to see him. I had no idea how significant it was that Rinpoche had located this land. The land he had discovered became the future home of the Rocky Mountain Dharma Center, now renamed Shambhala Mountain Center. In his mind, establishing a rural practice center in Colorado was a crucial step. He wanted a place in the western United States, similar to Tail of the Tiger in the east, where he could teach intensive seminars outside of the speed and confusion of the city. He also wanted a center with a lot of land where his students could do intensive group practice as well as solitary retreats. Later, he talked about the establishment of Rocky Mountain Dharma Center as the key to making meditation the foundation of his students' experience.

Rinpoche had great faith in the students from those early days. He always saw their workability. He invited the Pygmies to move to RMDC and help settle the land, because he could see their strength and their resilience. They were used to difficult living situations without many amenities, so they took to the land quite easily. They built a number of houses there, some of them quite strange, idiosyncratic constructions that are still there. They weren't great meditators at that time, but many of them have become so. In part, this is because he believed in them. He saw so much potential in everyone.

Finding the land for RMDC in my mind marks the end of our first year in North America, the first of seventeen years we spent together on this continent. In 1969, while still in England, Rinpoche wrote a poem, "In the North of the Sky," that expresses what coming to America was all about for him. As he said about himself there, "Here comes Chögyam disguised as a hailstorm." Indeed, our first year in America was a whirlwind, a kind of spiritual storm that was gathering energy as it moved across the country. Like so many things I experienced in my life with him, it was a time that was both magnificent and sometimes lonely. I felt part of his world, absolutely, but I also had to begin to come to terms with my life separate from him. It was not always easy to be the guru's wife. But I must say, it was rarely boring.

EIGHT

Taggie was a very easy baby. In fact, had he not been my first child, I think I might have worried because he so rarely cried. You could do almost anything with him, take him anywhere, and he didn't complain unless he was hungry. He would go right back to sleep after I fed him or rest passively in his crib. Later, when we discovered that he had so many problems, I wished I had known what to look for earlier.

When the baby was around two months old, in May of 1971, we all went to California together. We visited Suzuki Roshi again, this time at San Francisco Zen Center on Page Street. We had tea with Roshi and his wife Okusan in the garden at SFZC, and Roshi did a special ceremony for Taggie. He bestowed on him the Japanese name Toronoko-san, which means "tiger cub" in Japanese. During our second visit to California, we also met Alan Watts, and Rinpoche gave a seminar on Alan's houseboat in Sausalito. Alan had converted part of the boat into a shrine hall where his students came to meditate. He would sit up in front in brown robes while people chanted, and then he would give his talk. The scene there felt strange to me, somewhat of a Westerner's kooky approach to Buddhism. Rinpoche, however, was quite fond of Alan and appreciated him for having laid the ground for the further introduction of Buddhism in America by popularizing Zen during the sixties.

John Baker came on the trip to California with us. One day John was driving us somewhere in Oakland, and he said to Rinpoche, "Could you tell me something about mindfulness in the Hinayana?" He said that right as he drove through a red light, and we had a car accident. Rinpoche ended up with a few broken ribs, but fortunately no one was seriously hurt.

When we left the Bay Area, we drove down the coast to spend several days at Tassajara, where we had had such a lovely visit with Roshi the year before. While we were there, Rinpoche received a letter, hand delivered by one of his students, from His Holiness the Gyalwa Karmapa, the head of Rinpoche's lineage. His Holiness said that he had recognized Taggie as a *tulku,* the reincarnation of one of his own teachers, Surmang Tenga Rinpoche. The night the letter arrived, Taggie cried all night, which was very, very unusual for him.

It was a great honor that our child was being recognized as an important Buddhist teacher. This announcement signaled some measure of acceptance from the head of the lineage—who had not been especially happy when Rinpoche gave up his robes and married me. Still, we knew that this appointment would bring with it a heavy burden of expectation from the Tibetan hierarchy. Earlier, I described Rinpoche's education and upbringing in Tibet. This was the normally accepted pattern for raising a young *tulku.* Although everything in Tibet had been disrupted by the Chinese occupation, many of the Tibetan teachers who succeeded in escaping were establishing monasteries in India and other countries bordering Tibet. As much as they could, they were reinstating the traditional approach to educating young lamas. In fact, His Holiness Karmapa had established his monastery in Sikkim and was training many young teachers there. There would be pressure on Rinpoche and me to send Taggie over to be educated, as soon as he was old enough to go. The Tibetans believe that if a *tulku* is not recognized, enthroned, and properly educated, he will develop mental illness, a kind of *tulku's* disease, because he is not fulfilling the role that is intended for him and for which he presumably came back and took rebirth.

Rinpoche didn't want to send Taggie back to India for training. Because he felt so strongly that the future of Buddhism lay in the West, he thought it would be better if his children were educated here. From his own experience at Oxford, he had tremendous respect and appreciation for the Western educational system. He also didn't want to recreate the loneliness of his monastic childhood for his own children. As well, he wanted to play a personal role in their upbringing, not only as the children's father, but by providing whatever spiritual guidance his children might need. So he wanted Taggie to remain with us. Then, at a later date his son could receive further training in Asia. As Taggie's mother, I naturally wanted him to stay at home with us. With all of these issues and feelings, it's no wonder that Taggie cried all night after we received the letter!

From Tassajara, we continued down the coast to Los Angeles, where Rinpoche taught a seminar entitled the "Battle of Ego." He began to attract committed students in L.A. We spent time with Baird Bryant and Johanna Demetrakas, two filmmakers with whom Rinpoche made a close connection. Rinpoche was in the early stages of making a film about the life of Milarepa, in which he wanted to try out an approach to filmmaking that involved applying concepts from the tantric or Vajrayana school of Buddhism in which he was trained. He was interested in applying a tantric framework called the Five Buddha Families to making a film.

The Five Buddha Families—buddha, *vajra,* karma, *padma,* and *ratna*—refer to five distinct styles of both enlightened and confused behavior. Each "family" has both a sane and a neurotic manifestation.[1] During the early seventies, Rinpoche used this paradigm in much of his work, not only as it applied to art but also in understanding human psychology. In terms of filmmaking, he felt that how a scene is shot can capture or convey the energy of any of the five families. The camera could look at the same situation from five different angles and convey five different interpretations or insights. The idea of working with the qualities of the buddha families in their art was intriguing to Johanna and Baird, as it was to many other artists Rinpoche would meet.

In 1973 Johanna and Baird would travel with Rinpoche to Stockholm, Sweden, to film some magnificent *thangkas* of Milarepa's life housed in the Museum Ethnographia. He intended to use the footage of these *thangkas* in his film, but because of a problem with the camera lens, the footage they shot was out of focus, and largely due to this obstacle, the movie was never completed.

While we were in Los Angeles, we were invited to have dinner with Krishna and Narayana at the Integral Yoga Institute, or the IYI as they called it, which was Swami Satchidananda's center. Rinpoche was excited about going to the IYI for dinner because he liked Indian food so much. They served us an excellent Indian vegetarian meal. After meeting Krishna and Narayana in Boulder earlier that year, Rinpoche had become interested in getting to know them better, particularly Narayana. Narayana came to dinner in a red velvet shirt. I was impressed by his charisma. He was warm and outgoing and seemed quite intelligent. Shortly after our visit, Narayana and his girlfriend, Lila, along with Krishna and his new girlfriend, Helen, joined our community. Rinpoche asked them to move to Tail of the Tiger, which they did that summer. On their way there, they drove through New York to get Swamiji's blessing, which was freely given, and headed on up to Tail. They got a house in Kirby, Vermont, where they started the Trikaya Bakery. Lila was pregnant at the time with their first child. She and Narayana were married at Tail.

Now that I had the responsibilities of motherhood, I stayed home more of the time when Rinpoche traveled. Over the next few years, he crisscrossed America I don't know how many times. I can't count the number of days a year he was on the road traveling and teaching. When he was in Boulder, there was still a beehive of activity at the Four Mile Canyon house. In spite of the chaos that was a feature of our lives, this was a truly magical time in my life and marriage with Rinpoche. We were very close during these years. It was a time full of hope and promise, and I remember this as a particularly happy chapter in our life together.

There was something energizing about the chaos, in fact. Rinpoche was so expansive in its midst, and we had a lot of fun together during this era. In spite of all the people around all the time, it was quite intimate in a way. The community was still small, relatively speaking, and I rather liked it that so much occurred at our house. I enjoyed having Rinpoche at home a lot, even though he brought so much activity in his wake. I could always go to bed when I got sick of it. There were obvious frustrations—the house was a mess and we had almost no privacy—but it was a very relaxed time. I was experiencing my own sense of exhilaration and relief that I'd gotten out of the English situation and away from my mother. I was riding on the freedom high and the fact that I had this wonderful relationship, a wonderful life. Having a child was also fulfilling for me. We had left behind the black era completely. I couldn't imagine my life being any other way.

In tantric Buddhism, there is a whole pantheon of deities that practitioners visualize as part of their meditation practice. Some of these have a rather normal anthropomorphic form: two arms and legs, one head, two eyes, two ears, and so forth. However, some of the Vajrayana deities have multiple arms and legs, a number of heads, and many eyes that see in all directions. This is connected with the accomplishment of compassion or the bodhisattva's skillful means. Avalokiteshvara, for example, the buddha of compassion, is sometimes depicted as having a thousand arms and a thousand eyes, to convey his untiring and remarkable efforts to alleviate the suffering of beings. Beginning in this era, Rinpoche seemed to take on this quality of all-accomplishing, all-seeing superhuman activity. The multifaceted way he worked with people was remarkable. He seemed to have hundreds of conversations about all kinds of things going on with all kinds of people all the time. If I tried to describe all of these relationships to you or tried to tell you about everything he was doing, even in one month, it would take up hundreds of pages. At the same time, being with him, it often seemed as though nothing was happening. There was a way in which he was absolutely open and spacious in the midst of all of this activity, and you never felt that he was distracted when he was with you. When he was talking to you, you always felt that you had his complete attention. I think that is one reason that I was able to tolerate the chaos and all these people so intimately involved in our life. I didn't feel that they were stealing him away from me. He was very much there for me, when he was there!

On the other hand, we both began to acknowledge that if we wanted to have time alone together, it was not going to happen at our house in Boulder or on his teaching tours. So we began to take vacations, or holidays, as Rinpoche preferred to call them, which was time set aside for the family. Occasionally, someone would come along to help out, but in the early days, it would just be Rinpoche, me, and our child, or our children, as it became quite soon.

The first vacation I can remember us taking was to New Mexico in 1971 when Taggie was an infant. I now had a driver's license and I drove

the three of us to Santa Fe. On the way down, we spent the night somewhere in the mountains of southern Colorado in a motel. We went to a
cowboy café for breakfast, and Rinpoche wore his Stetson hat. Then we
drove on into New Mexico. We had rented a small trailer, which was
located in the landlord's backyard behind the main house. Rinpoche
helped out a lot with Taggie while we were there. He used to put Taggie in bed with us, and he was very sweet with him. He would watch
him when I had a bath and call me if he cried. One time, I left Rinpoche
alone with Taggie to go to the grocery store, and he figured out how to
change diapers with one hand, but he got irritated that Taggie would
squirm. Rinpoche also tried out his theories of insect control in New
Mexico. He didn't want to kill the ants that invaded our trailer, so he put
little lines of Ajax cleanser in front of the glasses and the plates, because
he thought the ants wouldn't cross the Ajax. Actually, it did work.

We liked to walk around the plaza in downtown Santa Fe and look at
the things for sale. Most of the vendors were Native Americans who had
pottery, jewelry, and other items laid out on blankets or a table on the
wide sidewalks along the sides of the square. Rinpoche bought me some
silver and turquoise jewelry while we were there. He commented that
the Native Americans looked a lot like Tibetans, and we talked about the
magic in the Native American culture and his appreciation for that. We
visited a number of pueblos in the surrounding area during our visit.

We both loved the spicy Mexican food in Santa Fe. One night we
wanted to eat in an expensive restaurant in Santa Fe, which was still
something quite rare for us because we didn't have very much money.
Rinpoche insisted that we splurge. We dressed nicely and made a late
reservation for a romantic dinner. The restaurant was completely done
up in red velvet, and it seemed to be a very exclusive place, a place of fine
dining. We were served an elegant meal, and everything was beautifully
presented. In the middle of the meal, Rinpoche picked up his baked potato in his hand and bit into it. I said, "What are you doing? This is really,
really embarrassing." He replied offhandedly, "Oh, Prince Philip would
do something like this."

Altogether, he felt very connected with the land in the Santa Fe area
and the Native American traditions. We enjoyed ourselves immensely,
and we planned to return the next year. On the drive home, Rinpoche
commented that we should have named our first son "Gesar," after the

Tibetan warrior king. I told him not to worry, that we could give that name to our next son.

After we got back to Boulder, Rinpoche took off on another teaching tour, and I was left at home. John Baker went with Rinpoche, and Marvin Casper was away somewhere else. At this time, P.D., another senior student, was also staying in the house with us. While Rinpoche was away, P.D. started to lose touch with reality and ultimately had a psychotic episode, which I had to deal with on my own.

When the two of us went to the supermarket together, P.D. picked out a huge raw ham and an industrial-sized package of coffee filters. Nobody in the household drank coffee, so I found this odd, but I didn't think too much about it. That night, after I went to bed, P.D. came into my bedroom in a manic state. I felt threatened by his tone of voice and his erratic movements and comments. I had the baby and I didn't want him in my room, so I got him to leave, and then I put the dresser in front of my bedroom door. He banged on the door for a while and tried to push his way in. This went on for a few nights. Every night he would try to break into the bedroom, and I kept myself barricaded in. Then, one morning when I got up and moved the dresser, I looked around the house but P.D. was nowhere around. I got the baby up and dressed to go out shopping. When I went out to the car, I found P.D. walking naked down the road in front of our house at Four Mile Canyon. I convinced him to come back inside and get some clothes on.

At that point, I phoned Rinpoche and told him that we had to deal with this issue as soon as possible. The night that Rinpoche got home, there was a party at the house to welcome him back. As always, a lot of people showed up to hang out with Rinpoche. During the evening, P.D.'s behavior disintegrated, and it was obvious that he needed help. After observing him for a while, Rinpoche said, "I think we have to take him down to the hospital." So John Baker took our disturbed friend in one car, and I drove Rinpoche in the other. We went down the canyon to Boulder Memorial Hospital at the end of Mapleton Avenue. At this point, it was about two in the morning.

P.D. and John Baker had arrived ahead of us, and we joined them in the waiting room. The psychiatrist on duty came over to where we were all sitting, and before anyone could say anything, P.D. announced, "Here is Mr. Mukpo. I've come to commit him." Rinpoche replied, "Actually,

P.D., I've come to commit you." Confusion ensued, with P.D. insisting that Rinpoche was the prospective patient. Finally, the psychiatrist said, "I want everybody to be quiet. I'm going to ask a third party who has come to commit whom." Shortly thereafter, P.D. was admitted to the hospital. There were a lot of wild times, but this one stands out for me because I had to deal with much of the situation alone. To me, it signified how vulnerable and somewhat abandoned I felt at times when Rinpoche was away.

That summer, we went to Allen's Park, which is a small town near Rocky Mountain National Park, about an hour north of Boulder. Rinpoche conducted a major seminar there on the six states of *bardo,* teachings connected with the *Tibetan Book of the Dead.* We stayed in a small log cabin next to the main lodge at the conference facility in Allen's Park, and Rinpoche taught in an outdoor tent. By now, there were around three hundred students attending his major seminars in Colorado. The tent was packed.

Rinpoche explained to me that his lineage and his monastery in Tibet were particularly associated with practicing and propagating the *bardo* teachings, and during 1971 he gave three seminars on material related to this. Although he had people practicing a basic form of sitting meditation, his lectures in these early years imparted some of the most advanced teachings from his lineage. I think that most of us understood about 2 percent of what he was presenting at that time. Some of the material was incorporated over the next few years into the study material for students interested in Buddhist psychology, and some of it was used in Rinpoche's commentary on the *Tibetan Book of the Dead,* which he translated with Francesca Fremantle. However, a great deal of it was simply being planted in people's subconscious, I think, so that much later they would come back to these lectures and begin to unravel the profundity of what he was presenting. After he died, the talks from this program were incorporated in a posthumous book, *Transcending Madness: The Experience of the Six Bardos,* edited by one of his senior students and primary editors, Judith Lief.

At the end of the summer, we went out to Tail for a month. We rented a house near Harvey's Lake, a five-minute drive from Tail of the Tiger, and Francesca Fremantle stayed there with us. Rinpoche taught a seminar entitled "Work, Sex, and Money," and then he gave another lecture series on the *Tibetan Book of the Dead*, which he and Francesca were just starting to translate. She edited much of the material from his talks at Tail for the commentary in that book.

There was a huge group scene at Tail, but at the house we could get away from it and have time together as a family. Rinpoche was drinking a lot at the talks. One would have to say that his drinking was a regular feature of our lives. At that time, I didn't see it as a problem. Had Rinpoche remained in Tibet or the Tibetan diaspora in India, the ground would have been laid for him to present the Buddhist teachings. There was a traditional format there and a basic understanding to accommodate whatever he might want to present. Instead, he struck out into completely foreign territory. I feel that in presenting the Buddhist teachings in the West, alcohol was one of the vehicles that he employed. He told me that it helped to ground him and allowed him to communicate. Without it, I don't know if he would have taught with such outrageous directness and expansiveness. In tantric Buddhism, *amrita,* or blessed alcohol, represents turning poison into nectar or inspiration. It is the idea that you do not reject any situation or state of mind in your life, but you use the most extreme or negative things as fuel to transform the ignorance of ego into wakefulness. I think Rinpoche did use his drinking in that way, which I know is a controversial thing to say.[2] On the other hand, I certainly acknowledge that, over time, alcohol was very destructive to his body. But that was not a question at that time, and in those days I didn't have an issue with his drinking.

I was often Rinpoche's chauffeur to and from his talks. One night, he was quite drunk by the time we got into the car at Tail to come home. I parked in front of the house at Harvey's Lake, and he opened his door, stepped out, and just disappeared. When I got out, I realized that I had parked right next to a ditch on the property. Rinpoche was completely relaxed because of how much he had drunk, so luckily he was uninjured. I helped him scramble out of the ditch.

Another time at Harvey's Lake, one night after dinner, he drank until he sort of passed out on the hardwood floor in the living room. I didn't want to leave him there for the night, and I didn't want to sleep by myself, so I tried to figure out how to get him to bed. I found a large Indian blanket, I rolled him onto it, and I dragged him on the blanket down the hardwood corridor. He was quite heavy, so this wasn't all that easy to do.

When I got to the bedroom, just when I was trying to figure out how to get him from the blanket to the bed, he started laughing, got up, and walked really fast back into the living room, where he lay back down and appeared to pass out again.

We often ate with people at Tail, but sometimes we would have a family dinner at the house. Rinpoche always liked meat for dinner. One night I worked really hard preparing a leg of lamb. He got impatient waiting for dinner to be served, and he said to me, "This is ridiculous. This whole cooking and eating thing doesn't make sense. You spend so much time cooking dinner, when it takes so little time to eat it." I went out into the garden to pick some vegetables to go with dinner. When I came back, the leg of lamb—which had been sitting on the table ready to carve—had bite marks where big chunks of meat had been taken out of it. Rinpoche had just picked it up and eaten his dinner off the bone.

That summer, we spent time with Narayana, Lila, Krishna, and Helen at their house in Kirby, just outside of Barnet. Lila went into labor in September while we were staying at Harvey's Lake, and we went over to the house to witness the birth. Narayana was going to deliver the baby himself, but Lila had a terrible labor and ended up being driven to the hospital in St. Johnsbury, where she gave birth to their son Vajra. After that, Lila and I used to spend time together with our children. Rinpoche did a child blessing ceremony at Tail, and I remember Lila bringing Vajra to be blessed when he was just a tiny baby.

That fall when we left Vermont, I went with Taggie to England to visit Ösel at the Pestalozzi Village. We were still waiting for the home visit from the Social Services people in Boulder. We didn't seem to be able to speed things up at all, which was quite frustrating. While I was in England, Rinpoche traveled to Canada to teach. I believe it was the first time he'd been back since arriving in the United States. He was scheduled to give seminars in both Montreal and Toronto. He kept phoning me in England to ask about Ösel and to say how much he missed me. In Toronto, he gave a seminar at the home of one of his students, Beverly Webster, a very elegant woman who later became his executive secretary. While he was there, he met with Kalu Rinpoche, a venerable Tibetan teacher then in his mid-sixties, whom Rinpoche admired very much.

Suzuki Roshi had been quite ill and jaundiced that fall, but the cause of his symptoms had not been diagnosed. Rinpoche always wanted to have news of what was happening with Roshi. One of Rinpoche's close students at this time, Bob Halpern, had been a student at San Francisco Zen Center for a long time before he joined us in Boulder. Bob went with Rinpoche on the trip to Canada, and Fran and Kesang also traveled with him. The night that Kalu Rinpoche visited, after he left, Kesang came to Rinpoche with the news that Roshi had been diagnosed with liver cancer, which was a terminal condition.

Before she finished telling him the news, he started weeping. Later, Bob told me that Rinpoche was screaming in agony, as though he were in the midst of death throes. Bob said that his tears actually turned red with blood, which fell on Beverly's snow-white carpet. After a long time, when he finally stopped, he said to Bob, "Go out first thing in the morning. I'll be there in a few days." He had his last visit with Roshi at San Francisco Zen Center a short time before Roshi's death. Rinpoche returned there for Roshi's funeral in December. During the ceremony, he went up to offer a *khata,* a Tibetan ceremonial white scarf. With one hand, he unfurled the scarf and it hung in the air and then draped perfectly, beautifully, over the casket at the same time that he uttered a piercing cry. After the funeral, he was asked to give a talk to everyone assembled at the Zen center, and during his remarks, he broke down in tears. Some people said that it helped them to recognize and express their own grief.

Rinpoche was so moved by Roshi's life and example and so saddened by his death. I believe that it spurred him on to implement the plans that they had made. He pushed forward the Maitri Project, which involved starting a therapeutic community for people with mental problems. Maitri means "loving kindness" in Sanskrit. The Maitri facility opened in Elizabethtown, New York, in the fall of 1973, and moved to land in Wingdale, New York, donated by Lex and Sheila Hixon in early 1974. The Naropa Institute, based on another of their joint inspirations, was inaugurated in the summer of 1974.

The end of 1971 was also an important time for another dharmic relationship in Rinpoche's life. In December, he spent another week at Tail teaching while I remained in Boulder. At that time, he met privately with Narayana and asked him to become his Vajra Regent and dharma heir, the primary inheritor of his spiritual lineage. In Rinpoche's tradition, the continuity of the teachings from one generation to the next is expressed through the teacher's handing down the oral teachings and the responsibility for maintaining the purity of the teachings to one or more dharma heirs. There is usually a primary dharma heir, as well as potentially many secondary heirs. In some situations, usually when a teacher has an established organization, he gives the position of regent to one student, who is expected to act on behalf of the teacher and the lineage after the teacher's death, until, in the case of many *tulku* lineages in Tibet, the teacher's next incarnation is old enough to assume his or her position. This idea of a regent who assumes power between one generation and the next has also been used in many monarchies, so regency is not purely an Asian concept.

For Rinpoche, it was extremely important to give the complete teachings of his lineage to a Westerner. In fact, I think he felt that he was giving many unique transmissions to his Western students, and he did not want them to feel that they were playing second fiddle to the Tibetans. So this appointment was a very important step. It showed that a Westerner could be trusted with the complete teachings and with the responsibility for the future of those teachings.

Rinpoche told Narayana to make plans to move to Boulder, so that Rinpoche could work closely with him, observing him and giving him proper training. Rinpoche had already told me that he was planning to do this. He often shared these kinds of plans and decisions with me. He would say, "This is a great person. I've brought him (or her) in. This is what he can do, and this is where we're going with it." Rinpoche asked Narayana to keep this future appointment secret for the time being. Rinpoche did not feel it was time yet to make this appointment public. With Rinpoche's permission, however, Narayana told his wife, his heart friend Krishna, and Helen. Indeed, this choice would have many implications for the future. I felt that Narayana was an excellent choice, although I didn't have Rinpoche's insight into his character. I thought he was quite charismatic and he had a special quality, a kind of intensity and brightness that were unique.

Our life was affected directly in another way by Rinpoche's visit to Tail that December. Another child came into our lives at this time. One of Rinpoche's students living on the East Coast, Eileen, was having serious psychological problems. She was a friend as well as a member of the *sangha*. She was so affected by her own psychological crisis that she couldn't care properly for her daughter Felicity, who was around seven. Felicity had been in a boarding school in New England, but she was very unhappy there. Eileen came to Tail of the Tiger with Felicity in tow when Rinpoche was there. She said that she couldn't handle her child any longer, and she was looking for someone to take her for a while. Rinpoche called and told me that he felt terrible about the situation. I suggested that we take Felicity, but he thought it would be too much for us to handle. Then Felicity gave Rinpoche a drawing she had made for him, and he was so touched by the gesture that he decided to bring her home with him. She joined our household for about a year.

During Taggie's first year, he was extremely uncomplicated. His motor development was quite advanced. He was sitting up and rolling over on his own at four months old. All the physical milestones were early, in fact. He was running around on his first birthday, in March 1972. However, I felt some concern when I talked with George Marshall, a student of Rinpoche's, when Taggie was fifteen months old. Adam, George's son, was the same age, and George told me how well Adam could talk. I thought to myself, "Oh, my child is a little slow in his speech development." Taggie did develop some speech, but often he just repeated what you said to him. He rarely vocalized anything on his own. He would repeat "doggie-dog" after me, for example, but he rarely would point at a dog and say, "doggie-dog" without prompting. However, he was my first child and I didn't know what to expect, so I didn't worry that much.

In the summer of 1972, Rinpoche and I went to Rocky Mountain Dharma Center for several weeks. It was to be the first time Rinpoche would teach a seminar there. For the summer, campgrounds were established for people attending the program, and a large tent was erected in a field, where Rinpoche would give his talks. I drove us up to "the Land," as we called it then. We had a Volkswagen Carmen Ghia at that time. As we were driving through the mountains, Rinpoche said to me, "Very soon we're going to be driving here in a Mercedes." I responded, "You know, you always have these terribly big plans." I wasn't convinced much would come of this. Sure enough, within a few years, we were driving to RMDC in a Mercedes, and Rinpoche reminded me about that conversation, as if to say, "See!"

As time progressed, our family finances became more stable. Rinpoche was able to take a salary for his work, and most of the time—but not always—he got paid. Our living situation remained modest for a number of years, and when we began to live in a more ostentatious way, it actually was not that we were spending huge amounts of money, but that we were using our rather modest means and those of the organization to create an apparent manifestation of wealth. I am not saying that we remained terribly poor, by any means, but we were really living with what would be a comfortable middle-class income, most of the time. Sometimes, throughout our life together and up until the very end, there was no money and we were scrounging for the money to buy groceries. Most of the time, we were fine. On an inner—nonmaterialistically based—level, Rinpoche was the wealthiest person I have ever known, but he wasn't the richest, in terms of financial assets. So, for example, when we got a Mercedes it was a used car. We never had a fleet of Mercedes or anything like that. We managed to keep up one slightly tattered vehicle for him at a time.

That summer we stayed in a little A-frame called Aloka, which means "light" in Sanskrit. Earlier that year, while we were at Tail, I had had a dream in which a being appeared to me and said, "Please give me a place in your body." I replied, "Yes, I will." While we were at RMDC, I conceived our second son, Gesar. He was the only one of my children who was planned, so to speak.

While I was pregnant with Gesar and we had both Taggie and Felicity at home with us, we received word that there would finally be a visit from Social Services in Boulder to establish whether we had a fit home for Ösel. I had the house spotlessly clean when a man came to do the evaluation. He was a bit taken aback by how young I was, and when he saw that there were already two children in the home and that I was pregnant with a third, he questioned whether we could really handle another child. I was indignant. "Do my children look dirty? Do they look uncared for?" I guess that in the end we impressed him as being suitable parents for Ösel, because not long after this we heard that Ösel could come and live with us. Once again, Rinpoche's teaching schedule made it impossible for him to travel to England at the specified time, so once again I made the journey in the middle of a pregnancy to bring Ösel home. This time, the outcome was as we had hoped. I picked him and his belongings up at the Pestalozzi Village, and we drove to London where we spent the night before flying to Denver.

To celebrate Ösel's arrival and to help with his process of acclimatizing to family life and life in America altogether, Rinpoche and I decided to take another vacation to New Mexico before starting Ösel in school. We decided to leave Felicity with friends in Boulder, and the four of us—Rinpoche, Ösel, Taggie, and I—headed off to Santa Fe. For a few days, we stayed in the little trailer we'd had the year before, and then we moved in with Allen Ginsberg and a friend of his.

Just a few years ago, Ösel—who is now known as Sakyong Mipham Rinpoche, the head of the Shambhala network of meditation centers—shared with me jokingly how he felt as a child during this period. Apparently, when I told him we were going to take a family vacation alone, he was struck by anxiety. He thought to himself, "Oh no, nobody else is coming?" Rinpoche and I may have been somewhat overwhelming for him, and our unconventional, albeit cheerful, life was something he was not yet fully accustomed to. We thought it was so generous of us to take this trip, a great idea, at the time! He was probably relieved when we decided to stay with other people.

Allen Ginsberg suggested that we join him at David Padua's house, a friend in Santa Fe who had an adobe home near the Sangre de Cristo mountain range. Allen was staying there with his boyfriend Peter Orlovsky. During this vacation, it was pretty clear to me that Allen had a big crush on Rinpoche, and that he was a little jealous of me. When I went horseback riding with him one day, he made a number of sarcastic remarks that seemed out of place. I was surprised that he was mean to me. Allen probably imagined that, as Rinpoche's wife, I stood in the way of his having a relationship with the guru. Rinpoche was a beautiful young man at that time, just Allen's type. However, Rinpoche was not interested in men in that way. On the other hand, he and Allen had a lot to discuss in other areas. They were already making plans to launch a poetry school as part of the much bigger plans that Rinpoche had in mind for a Buddhist university.

Earlier that year, Allen had invited several poets to Boulder for a poetry reading. Gary Snyder, Robert Bly, and Nanao Sasaki were invited to read poetry with Allen Ginsberg and Rinpoche. In addition to his own poetry, Allen read some of Rinpoche's poems from a recently published book, *Mudra*, which included many of the early poems Rinpoche had written in England in the sixties. The evening ended rather disastrously after Rinpoche put a large Japanese gong over his head while Robert Bly was reading a serious and significant poem. Rinpoche did a number of things to disrupt Bly's reading, actually. Gary Snyder and Robert Bly interpreted Rinpoche's behavior as rude and drunken. I guess it was, but from his point of view, their behavior was arrogant and bombastic, and he felt that humor was needed to lighten up the space. Allen took this controversy remarkably in stride, and managed to remain friends with all involved. Snyder and Bly, however, wanted nothing further to do with Rinpoche, and as far as I know, he had no regrets on his side.

Allen was an amazing human being in that way. As outrageous as he was and as much as he flaunted his sexuality and his politics, he was also a peacemaker and, except when he viewed me as a rival that one time, he was one of the most gentle, kind people I have ever known. It seemed to me that, sexual politics aside, he loved Rinpoche without hesitation, and as a student he was very devoted. He never seemed to doubt that what Rinpoche was doing was for the good of everyone involved—even when it created difficulties for Allen in his relationships with other poets. He saw Rinpoche as a complete representative of the crazy wisdom lineage, and he took the crazy with the wisdom, with no questions asked.

While we were in New Mexico, Rinpoche killed a scorpion that we found in the boys' bedroom. It was the only time I ever saw Rinpoche kill anything. Rinpoche squashed it and flushed it down the sink. He felt badly about this, but he didn't want the boys to get bitten. While we were there, we also got our first big message that something was not right with Taggie. One morning, Taggie woke up early. He came and climbed into bed with me and put his hands on my chest. As I started to wake up, I saw that my chest was covered in blood. I soon realized that Taggie had cuts all over his hands. Somewhere in the house, he had found pieces of broken glass and had been playing with them. I completely freaked out, but Rinpoche's response was very practical. He said that we should clean up his cuts and put socks on his hands. We did that, and he was okay. But it was very unsettling. Taggie's relationship with pain was never like a normal child's. A normal kid would cut himself once and cry, but Taggie kept playing with the glass. But we still weren't sure what it meant at this time.

When we got back to Boulder, we settled into a kind of routine, to the extent that our lives were ever routine, with me taking care of the three children in the household, and Rinpoche putting most of his time into teaching and the many other projects he had going. He lectured at the University of Colorado several times a week, and he traveled to both coasts to teach, as well as making side trips to many new places like Minneapolis and Topeka, Kansas. He also gave a number of seminars in Boulder over the next six months, and he had special meetings and led workshops for people involved in psychology, film, and theater. In the spring of 1973, he and his students in Boulder were going to host a seminar on the Milarepa film project, as well as two other weeklong conferences, one on the Maitri approach to psychology (involving the Five Buddha Families and other concepts) and a ten-day conference sponsored by the Mudra theater group, which was working with exercises that Rinpoche was developing out of his own experiences with monastic dance in Tibet. The theater conference was being partially funded by a grant from the National Endowment for the Arts, which Jean-Claude van Itallie had obtained. He invited a number of prominent theater people to the conference in Boulder, including Robert Wilson, the eminent American artist and playwright, and his group of actors, as well as many others. There was a tremendous amount of work to prepare for all of this. And these are just a few highlights of what Rinpoche was doing at this time, just the tip of the iceberg.

Rinpoche was incorporating facets of the Tibetan Vajrayana tradition into his presentation of secular disciplines such as film, theater, and psychology; later he would expand into many other areas as well. This weaving together of the secular and the sacred was characteristic of how he taught. Even in Great Britain he had had this tendency. In the 1960s he had already recognized that he was going to work with both the secular and the spiritual as indivisible aspects of his teaching. In the diary that he kept at that time, he wrote:

> There are many people who are more learned than I and more elevated in their wisdom. However, I have never made a separation between the spiritual and the worldly. If you understand the ultimate aspect of the dharma, this is the ultimate aspect of the world. And if you should cultivate the ultimate aspect of the world, this should be in harmony with the dharma. I am alone in presenting the tradition of thinking this way.[3]

In December 1972, Rinpoche spent ten days in Jackson Hole, Wyoming, near Yellowstone National Park, teaching a seminar on crazy wisdom. Several of his students had bought a hotel there and were renovating it, planning to operate it as a tourist hotel called the Snow Lion Inn. In his seminar he presented an in-depth examination of the life of Padmasambhava and how his teachings and many manifestations were applicable to the present day as well as to the Tibetan medieval world of the eighth century. We all went to Tail of the Tiger for the Christmas holidays that year, where Rinpoche gave another crazy wisdom seminar. The teachings were magnificent, very much the heart's blood of his lineage. He had been waiting so long to present this material. After his death, these two seminars were edited into the book *Crazy Wisdom*.

Although I supported Rinpoche in whatever he felt he needed to do at this time, his lack of everyday involvement in our household was not ideal for our young family. When you have young children, I think almost everyone goes through a period that seems completely insane, and this was the era we were in during the early seventies, especially since we had so many children join our family so quickly. At this time, I was not even twenty years old. We didn't have much money for babysitters, and Rinpoche thought it was odd and somewhat degrading to hire people as domestic help. In Tibet, people served a teacher out of devotion rather than for money. It wasn't that Rinpoche was miserly, but he really felt that this kind of master-servant relationship was not healthy when it was purely a financial deal. He hoped that his students would help us out, and many of them did. I found, however, that by and large people didn't appreciate the difficulties of our domestic situation. Nevertheless, we made do as best we could.

Ösel was trying to adjust to life in America and found school very challenging. Felicity was spaced out and often depressed and needing cheering up, and Taggie was becoming a real handful. I would get phone calls from the neighbors at five in the morning to tell me that Taggie was running around somewhere. While the rest of the household was still sleeping, Taggie would get out of his crib and go off for an adventure by himself in the neighborhood. One time, I found him playing on the roof of the garage of the Four Mile Canyon house. I remember trying to lure him away from the edge with jelly beans, holding them in my open palm and saying, "Candies, candies." Eventually I realized that I had to put an intercom in his room, and later I had to put a hook on the outside of the door. I felt terrible about locking him into his bedroom at night, but it seemed to be the only way to keep him safe. Once, when I was quite pregnant with Gesar, he slipped out of the house when I had taken my eyes off him for just a minute. I turned around and he was gone. He had on a little yellow, black, and red striped sweater, and I rushed frantically out of the house to see if I could spot him in the yard. Finally, I spied him in his bright-colored sweater across the highway halfway up a mountain. I had to climb the mountain in my pregnant state and carry him down. He was becoming difficult to care for.

Ösel came into an already chaotic home situation, and in retrospect I feel that I was not a very good mother to him during these years. He was trying to adjust to America and to learn English, and on top of that, we found out later that he had a learning disability that exacerbated his problems. It took years to sort all of this out. When Ösel was having trouble with math in school, for example, I would review his multiplication tables with him over and over. The next day, he would fail his math test, and I would become quite exasperated. He was incredibly shy, which made it more difficult for me to communicate with him. I was only nineteen at this point, and coping with three children—each of whom had unique difficulties that needed attending to—proved difficult. I was often frustrated.

Rinpoche was away a great deal of the time, and when he was in town he had so much going on that he was rarely home. There was still a lot of activity at the house, but in late 1971 we had acquired space for a meditation center in downtown Boulder, at 1111 Pearl Street, on what would later become the Boulder Mall. There was a meditation hall that could hold about a hundred people, several meeting rooms, and a suite of offices. Rinpoche gave the name Karma Dzong to the new center, which means "fortress of action," or it could also mean "fortress of the Karma Kagyü lineage." Rinpoche's students paid membership dues to cover the rent on this space. Although the hordes would still descend on the house from time to time, now much of the community activity was centered around Karma Dzong. So I was frequently home alone with the kids, even when Rinpoche was in town. Although this was a difficult adjustment, I also found that I enjoyed the space. I began to have more sense of my own life, apart from the scene that surrounded our life together.

However, I didn't have enough help with the children. Rinpoche and I talked about all this many times, and he tried to help find solutions. He continued to ask some of his students to provide assistance at the house. However, they were much more interested in being with him than in spending time with the children and me. Also, there weren't many people in our community at that time who had children. Rinpoche's students, many of them young people in their twenties, couldn't relate to what I was going through at all. There were a few mothers who were sympathetic, but they had their own families to care for. A few other people stepped forward and offered to help. However, sometimes, if I asked for someone's help, he or she would criticize me, saying that I should be doing a better job on my own. This didn't help the situation at all.

I wished that Rinpoche had more time for the family, and I think that he would have liked that too. He enjoyed those times that we were together as a family, on our vacations and such. But in general he was not that involved day to day. He had warned me this would be the case when we were first at Tail of the Tiger. Everything else came second to the dharma in his life. His mission, as I guess you might call it, was to bring the Buddhist teachings to America and to make sure that they flourished here, and he sacrificed much personal happiness for that. Unfortunately, his family suffered as well. On the other hand, he loved all of us tremendously, and he tried to be there for us as much as he could be. Whenever anyone in the family was having an acute problem, he would make time to attend to that. However, he couldn't do much to improve the overall quality of our family life during this era.

In the very early days, when we were still at Samye Ling, he once said to me, "I wish I were someone like Einstein." I asked him, "What do you mean?" He said, "Well, I wish I was one of those people who was so into something that I would get up in the morning and I would have a mission, something to do that was really driving me." Well, as they say, you should be careful what you wish for! He certainly became one of those people.

Luckily, with everything else that was going on, I had a very straightforward pregnancy with Gesar. I hardly had morning sickness or nausea throughout the pregnancy, which was good, because I didn't have time for it. By the time I was eight-and-a-half months pregnant, I was ready for this pregnancy to end. I wanted to get on with it. Hoping to induce labor, I went riding when I was enormous. When that didn't jump-start my labor, I came home and drank a glass of castor oil mixed in orange juice. (Somehow I knew that castor oil can cause contractions of the uterus.) Undoubtedly, it was an irresponsible thing to do. My water broke soon after that. I was admitted to Community Hospital in Boulder, and my doctor, Dr. Brown, was quite upset when I told him what I had done.

Although my water had broken, my labor didn't progress. They held me in the hospital, and after twenty-four hours, they began to administer Pitocin to induce labor. Dr. Brown had to leave unexpectedly, and I was left with another doctor. After I had contractions for twelve hours, he told me that he had surgery at 7 A.M., which was a few hours away, and that if I hadn't had the baby by 5 A.M., he was going to do a C-section.

Quite a large group of *sangha* members was hanging out in Community Hospital, camped out in the waiting room, waiting for the child to be born. They were calculating the baby's astrological aspects while I was having contractions. Different people kept coming into my labor room, saying, "If you hold off just another half hour, the moon will be in the tenth house" and things like that. When Gesar was finally born, he was a triple Taurus. Rinpoche was with me the whole time. I was in an enormous amount of pain, the kind of pain where you don't know where the center or the focus of the pain is. They tried to give me a spinal injection of anesthesia, but it didn't work. The pain just kept going and going and going. Rinpoche was a fabulous labor coach, it turned out. He seemed to know exactly how I was experiencing the pain, and he advised me on how to get through each contraction.

Gesar was finally born early in the morning on April 26. He came out with a full head of black hair and long fingernails. When they opened his mouth to suction him, I said to the doctor, "He has teeth!" The doctor said, "No, he doesn't have teeth." The doctor was fed up with me at that point because the whole thing had gone on forever. He said, "He doesn't have teeth. I've delivered thousands of babies, and babies aren't born with teeth." I started to have a panic attack, because I thought that if he had teeth, he might have a deformity. So I insisted, "No, he has teeth!" He said, "Listen, you need a cup of tea. You're English, and that will help. I'm going to show you the baby now, and the baby doesn't have teeth." Then he exclaimed, "Wait a minute. He's got teeth!" He had two pointed teeth that looked like fangs.

Gesar emerged as a strong personality in all respects. We gave him the name Gesar Tsewang Arthur Mukpo. According to Rinpoche, King Gesar of Tibet was the first Mukpo, and he is regarded as a great warrior-protector of the Tibetan people. Tsewang means "lord of life." We added Arthur for King Arthur, another regal warrior king. Gesar was a little dynamo from the beginning. They removed his teeth in the hospital, because they were loose. Two months later he was teething again. He grew several teeth on the bottom, and they were also an odd set of teeth, so he was in the dentist's chair at two months old. Then, he didn't have center teeth on the bottom until his permanent teeth came in. The dentist put in a spacer to hold his back teeth in the proper position and prevent them from filling in the front. As a toddler, Gesar used to bite other kids sometimes, and you could always tell if it was Gesar because you could see the mark of the spacer.

When Gesar was an infant, we were still living at Four Mile Canyon. When he was just a few days old and we were just back from the hospital, I put him in his bassinette and went to take a hot bath. Taggie came into the bathroom while I was in the tub, and I asked him, "How is Gesar?" And Taggie said, "Gesar is good. He's eating candies." I jumped out of the bath and ran into the other room. Taggie had stuffed lots of candies into Gesar's mouth, which I had to fish out. Another time, Taggie fed Gesar a container of blue shoe polish with a spoon. I became a rather frequent visitor to the emergency room.

As a baby, Gesar slept in the room with us. Rinpoche said that Tibetans would never have a separate bed for the baby, but I always thought we should have the baby in a bassinette or a crib. When Gesar was just a few days old, I put him to bed in his crib with a windup mobile. Whenever the mobile stopped moving, Gesar would start screaming. This continued until around two A.M., when Rinpoche insisted that we put him in bed with us. He said that if Gesar were in the middle, between us, he would be content and fall asleep. I told Rinpoche that I was afraid one of us would roll over on him in our sleep. Rinpoche said, "A father's instinct would never allow this." I gave in. About two hours later, I awoke to small muffled cries. In his sleep, Rinpoche had rolled on top of Gesar and was basically suffocating him. I started screaming to wake Rinpoche up, "Get off him! Get off him!" After that, if I put Gesar in bed with us, he slept on my side of the bed.

Gesar took to solid food very early, around three or four months old. At one point, I told Rinpoche that I didn't know when to stop feeding him, because Gesar would take everything I gave him. He never closed his mouth to refuse food, like Taggie did. So Rinpoche suggested, "Let's stage an experiment. Let's feed him and see how much he'll eat." Gesar sat in his infant chair, and Rinpoche and I fed him two bananas, a bowl of yogurt, and two pots of meat. We kept feeding him, and he ate until he threw up!

Gesar walked when he was eight months old, and he was an extremely active little boy. I remember thinking of him as a mindless body that destroyed my house. At age three and a half, Taggie began having seizures, but before that point, Taggie was actually much more in touch with the things around him than he was later, and he did talk a little bit. He was very fond of his brother and liked to take care of him. When Gesar was one and Taggie was three, they accidentally walked in on us making love. They stood at the door for a while staring at us, hand in hand. At a certain point, Taggie said, "Gesar, you can't be here. Go back to bed."

Two weeks after Gesar was born, Rinpoche and I took the two youngest boys with us to California. We stayed in the Bay Area for several weeks while Rinpoche taught a seminar on "The Nine Yanas of Tibetan Buddhism," which was the basis for a book entitled the *Lion's Roar*, published in 1992. Rinpoche was preparing to teach the first Vajradhatu Seminary in the fall of 1973, a three-month intensive program, during which he was going to make a formal transmission of the Vajrayana teachings to his most senior students. He saw this as a crucial step in the full transmission of Buddhism to the West, and he was thinking a great deal about the proper way to introduce this material. It was not just going to be an intellectual presentation, but he wanted to enter his students into the full practice and study of Vajrayana, which brings with it a heavy burden of responsibility for both the students and the teacher. He was acutely aware that if this were not properly done, if he failed to plant the true heart of Vajrayana in his students, it would be catastrophic for the future of his work altogether.

In preparation for the presentation at the seminary in the fall, he had decided to teach a more in-depth public seminar on the different stages of the Buddhist path. This was the "Nine Yanas" lecture series given in

May 1973 in San Francisco. Rinpoche's students rented a small bungalow for us in a modest neighborhood in Berkeley, across the bay from
San Francisco. I tried to attend most of the talks, but much of my time
was consumed with caring for Taggie and the baby.

In early 1973, Krishna and his family had made the move to Boulder
at Rinpoche's request. At that time, Rinpoche established Vajradhatu,
which means "indestructible space," as the umbrella organization for all
of his meditation centers and his work in the United States. He appointed
a board of directors that included Marvin Casper, Fran Lewis, Krishna
(also known as Ken Green), and several others. Rinpoche wanted to
overcome territorial struggles between the two power centers of his
work: Tail of the Tiger in Vermont and Karma Dzong in Boulder. Not
long after this, Narayana (who was now going by his given name, Thomas
Rich) also moved to Boulder and joined the board. Rinpoche wanted to
make Boulder the national headquarters of what he envisioned would
become a large organization made up of many centers around the country. Vajradhatu and its board were set up to oversee the activities of all of
the centers and the expansion of the spiritual empire, of sorts, that Rinpoche was creating. *Cutting Through Spiritual Materialism* was published in
1973, and sales of the book were taking off. It came onto the spiritual
scene in America at just the right time to spark tremendous interest. It
sold more than a hundred thousand copies in the first two years, which
was a lot of books for that time. It spoke to the counterculture of that era
in a direct, intimate way. More and more people came to hear Rinpoche
speak. When Rinpoche gave a public talk in San Francisco during our
visit in 1973, more than five hundred people attended. Within a year,
there would be more like fifteen hundred in the audience.

Once again, all of these developments brought energy and chaos into
our domestic life. Rinpoche had invited several members of the board to
come to California with him, including Marvin, Tom, and Ken. A quo-
rum of the board of directors was having spontaneous meetings in our
dining room in Berkeley every other day and night, and the house was
filled with a kind of backroom, smoky, corporate power-politics energy.
The scene during this era was a bit like our version of scenes from the
reality show *The Apprentice.* All of these guys—and it was definitely a
huge preponderance of male energy—were learning how to be spiritual
corporate types under Rinpoche's tutelage.

Starting around this time, Rinpoche began to experiment with the corporate model to see if it could be adapted as the framework for organizing the Buddhist world in America. This energy was certainly an antidote to the energy of hippiedom. Rinpoche had already put forward the idea to his students that they should view themselves as yogi householders rather than as monks and nuns. He definitely felt that a secular model was the way to go in America. Beyond that, he needed a structure for what was emerging as a large and complex spiritual organism with many arms and legs. As he brought new people onto the board, each one was given areas of responsibility. The growing staff at Karma Dzong was organized into departments, with each employee reporting to a department head who reported to a member of the board. Some of the plans for this structure were hatched in our little house in Berkeley. The group literally met around the dining room table a lot of the time. I found that I didn't want or need a seat at that table, and I watched this emerging organization with interest and some bemusement. Energy was really high during this visit.

Before going back to Boulder, we passed through Los Angeles, where Rinpoche gave a weekend seminar, and then we headed down to Acapulco for a few weeks of vacation. Gesar was only about six weeks old at this time, so it was quite adventurous of us. My sister, Tessa, was now living in Boulder, and she came along on the trip. We were invited to Mexico by Marty Franco, a student from Mexico, who paid all the expenses. She had a mariachi band meet us at the airport, and she arranged for us to stay in a diplomat's apartment, which came with maids. The maids cooked three meals a day for us. The first night they served us a cold beetroot soup, which no one liked except Rinpoche. He drank everybody's soup, and the next day his bowel movement was absolutely red and he was afraid that he had blood in his stool. I don't think he'd ever eaten beets before. The maids decided we really liked the soup, so they started making it every other night for dinner, and every time it was served, Rinpoche would drink all the soup. After a few of these meals, he finally said, "I can't drink this stuff anymore." There was a potted palm tree in the hall, planted in a hollowed-out elephant's foot, and we decided to pour the soup in the soil. Rinpoche didn't want to hurt the maids' feelings. However, they came in to clear the soup bowls just as we were pouring it out; we were never given that soup again.

There was a swimming pool in the apartment complex, and I gave Rinpoche swimming lessons while we were there. He was absolutely terrified of water. (Tibetans have no tradition of swimming at all. However, it distressed him that he couldn't swim, and he wanted to overcome his fear.) So every day we'd go into the pool together. I would hold his neck while trying to teach him to float on his back. I would tell him to relax, because he would completely tense up in the water. If I let go of his neck, suddenly he would sink. Finally, we got him a huge inner tube, so that he could enjoy being in the water and maneuver around the pool.

Our apartment had a balcony with a narrow railing that looked out over the pool. At night, Rinpoche liked to sit on the balcony and try to hit the swimming pool with melons from the fruit bowl. He usually missed, so in the morning there would be squashed melons around the sides of the pool as well as floating in the water. Eventually, the superintendent figured out who was doing this. They didn't kick us out; they just told us that we couldn't throw melons anymore.

Rinpoche also went parasailing in Acapulco. You are taken out on the ocean in a speedboat, with a parachute strapped to your body, and as the boat speeds up you're lifted into the air. I was so frightened for him that I couldn't watch. With his paralysis, I thought this was an absolutely insane thing to do. A week before a tourist had been killed parasailing. I went into the bedroom and closed all the curtains so I wouldn't catch sight of him. Apparently, when the sail brought him down in the water, he started to sink, so all these people had to swim out and save him from drowning.

While we were in Acapulco, Rinpoche wanted to take me to a tailor to have a suit made. The dress code was beginning to change in that era, and my hippie clothes no longer fit the visualization. Rinpoche thought that we should get a pale blue suit made for me, like the one that the Pan Am stewardesses wore. He thought that would be the perfect outfit for me.

Some days, we would sit and watch the cliff divers at the beach. We spent a lot of time at the beach, and Rinpoche got a dark tan. One day, when we were walking around town, an American woman came up and started talking to him in broken Spanish. He let her go on for a while, but eventually he said, "Madam, you can speak English if you want." I think she was taken aback by his proper English accent. Rinpoche also liked to go to the local market where you could bargain over the price of things. While we were in Acapulco, we took a side trip up to Tasco, where all the Mexican silver was made. It was quite a nice trip for all of us.

That summer there were further seminars at Rocky Mountain Dharma Center (RMDC). He gave another seminar on the *Tibetan Book of the Dead,* which was attended by about four hundred students. His second seminar there that summer was entitled "The Energy of Discipline," again perhaps in preparation for the seminary. At RMDC, they had purchased a small used trailer for Rinpoche to live in. They put it on a hillside that overlooked the tent where he gave his talks. It was a tiny place with a cramped living room and kitchen combined and a small bedroom in the back, barely big enough to fit our bed. It got quite hot in there in the summer, but Rinpoche loved it. They built a deck out the front door where he could sit and look at the mountains in the distance, and he also liked to sit out back behind the trailer, under some small pine trees. He was still waking up in the middle of the night and asking for a snack, and during this era he became fond of cold Spam and tomatoes on French bread. He called this "food-o," a pun on the Japanese bodhisattva, Fudo.

That year a house was purchased for us in Vermont, about ten minutes from Tail, and we went out to stay there for two weeks at the end of the summer. Rinpoche gave it the name Bhumipali Bhavan, which means the "place of the female earth protector." Rinpoche told me that it was named for me and was to be my house, and I have always thought of it that way. It was an old Vermont farmhouse with a spacious kitchen, dining room, and large living room on the main floor and four bedrooms upstairs. There was plenty of room for the whole family there. Rinpoche taught a seminar on "The True Nature of Devotion," and a second one entitled "The Question of Reality," in which he compared the Buddhist teachings to the teachings of Don Juan, which were popularized by Carlos Castaneda in that era. Some of his students were interested in the Don Juan books, and Rinpoche indicated that there was some sanity in them, along with a lot of confused ideas. Ram Dass attended this seminar, having connected with Rinpoche in Boulder earlier that year. Rinpoche teased him a lot during the talks. At one point during a talk, he had Ram Dass sit at his feet, and he dropped the ashes from his cigarette onto his head. Ram Dass was quite into the outer purity approach: wearing

white, eating special food, and doing purifications of the body. So perhaps Rinpoche was making a statement to him about innate purity. In
any case, their interactions were quite playful and fun to observe. Ram
Dass was taken with Rinpoche in that era, and they were making plans
to teach together. His long-haired Hindu persona was a contrast to the
approach now developing within the community. We were starting to
wear more conservative dress at that time, not yet suits and ties, but the
bare-chested men were putting on shirts, and the madras and paisley
were disappearing.

At the end of September, Rinpoche went off to Jackson Hole,
Wyoming, where the first seminary was being held at the Snow Lion Inn.
There were less than one hundred students accepted for the seminary, because Rinpoche wanted to be sure that he had a small group to whom he
could impart these teachings very intimately the first time. There were
many qualified people, but he took less than half of those who applied. It
was important to him to have the right group and the right chemistry
among the students and with him. Everybody lived in the lodge, and
there was a schedule for everybody to help with cooking, cleaning, and
other chores. The program was divided into three sections: Hinayana,
Mahayana, and Vajrayana. Each section was further subdivided into a
practice period and a period of study, during which the students attended
discussion groups and took courses from student-instructors during the
day and attended Rinpoche's talks in the late afternoon or evening.

The seminary began with a week of sitting meditation. Everyone was
expected to sit from seven A.M. until eight or nine o'clock at night, with
breaks for meals and chores. Rinpoche gave one orientation talk, and
then left for the week while people meditated. He went right back out
on the road and gave talks in Boston while people were practicing at the
seminary. He wanted them to really clear the decks, so to speak, by sitting for a week before study commenced.

When the seminary started, I was left back in Boulder with Ösel,
Taggie, and Gesar. Felicity had gone to live with her grandmother by
this time. I was going for the Vajrayana portion of the program at the end
of November, but I just couldn't take the children there for the whole
three months. I celebrated my twentieth birthday on October 8, and I
felt so lonely. This was the first time Rinpoche had been away for my
birthday since we were married. He had celebrated my birthday each

year with a special dinner, a gift, or a small party, which was really important to me, especially after the way my mother often ignored these events during my childhood. Some friends organized a small party, but I was still missing him. I went to my birthday party telling myself that I would have a good time. After everyone arrived, the host said that Rinpoche had sent a present for me and that it was in the closet. With much urging, I opened the closet door, and out he came. He had come back for my birthday.

He stayed a night or two and then went back to the seminary. I joined him there with the two youngest boys about a month later, just before he began presenting the Vajrayana teachings. This was such a significant event for Rinpoche. There were many reasons why he might not have gone ahead with this. For one thing, although there was a great deal of interest in Eastern religion at this time, there was also tremendous naïveté and spiritual materialism in the United States. Many people saw Tibetan Buddhism as a set of magical and esoteric teachings and as a way to gain instant—or at least quick—enlightenment. There was much misunderstanding about what genuine spirituality is in the Buddhist tradition. Teachers like Suzuki Roshi had laid the ground for a true understanding of Mahayana Buddhism and had begun to teach the importance of practicing the teachings through meditation and applying them through the discipline of everyday life. However, there were still huge areas of misunderstanding.

Rinpoche had been working extremely hard to plow what he saw as fertile but confused ground, planting the genuine seeds of dharma in the American soil. During the three years that he had been in the country—and it had only been three years—his students had transformed themselves in many ways. He always attracted an incredibly intelligent bunch, and he nurtured that intelligence and encouraged a degree of cynicism and doubt to cut through the fascination with spirituality as a gadget or a toy. However, he also had to work with the ingrained individualism of the culture, which was both a strength and an obstacle to understanding the nature of a real devotional relationship between teacher and student. There has to be a degree of giving in or surrendering one's hard edge of egotism; otherwise, the Vajrayana teachings in particular can be perverted into egomania or misconstrued as purely an intellectual, or mind, game.

When people see photographs or videos from the very early days, what they are shocked by is how disheveled, underdressed, and hairy everybody was. In fact, that was a relatively small obstacle. The real question was whether Rinpoche could actually penetrate past the shell, the veneer, that people were presenting. Could he get to the heart of the matter with them? It was still an open question for him after all this time.

He gave twenty talks in the first part of the seminary, in which he presented the Hinayana and the Mahayana aspects of the Buddhist path. People weren't sitting as much as he would have liked; they were partying a bit too much, but generally he was pleased with people's attitude and openness. He felt that people were ready and receptive for him to launch into the presentation of Vajrayana. This was a detailed but also very deep presentation of the path of tantra. He was pouring information into people, but much more than that, he was pouring his heart and the heart of his tradition into the minds and hearts of the students. Once he started, he was so inspired that his talks grew longer and longer. He himself was studying the teachings of Jamgön Kongtrul the Great, his root teacher's predecessor, as the basis for his presentation, and he was so animated and excited to be able to share this material with people.

About halfway through the Vajrayana section of the seminary, just as he was reaching a crescendo in the presentation of the material, as he began to describe the parts of the path that were central to the practices that his students would soon begin to practice—just at that point, there was a disastrous incident. One afternoon, Rinpoche was so inspired that he talked for several hours without giving us any kind of a break. He seemed ready to continue lecturing on into the night. People began to get restless and fidgety. Usually the talks took place before dinner, and people were getting hungry. Their appetite for Rinpoche and the teachings, which had seemed insatiable for so long, was now overridden by their appetite for dinner. People were, I think, a bit overwhelmed by what Rinpoche was presenting, so their restlessness in part reflected their inability to take it all in. He went beyond anyone's idea of what was acceptable, conventional, in terms of how long he talked. Finally, someone suggested taking a break and continuing the next day. Then one of Rinpoche's closest students, who was a member of the board and someone we were very close to, suggested to Rinpoche that they vote on whether to continue or to stop for the night.

He could not have made a worse suggestion. The idea that the timing of the inaugural presentation in America of the essence of Rinpoche's lineage was going to be decided by a vote, by democratic process, was antithetical to the understanding of devotion that Rinpoche had been trying to foster in his students. It suggested to him that perhaps they hadn't heard a word he had said. When the students applied and were accepted to the seminary, it was like becoming engaged, in a spiritual sense. It wasn't a casual invitation. Presenting the Vajrayana teachings was, for Rinpoche, like getting married to these students. They were mutually about to embark on a relationship that would last throughout the rest of their lives and hopefully one that would be transformative for everyone involved. Essentially, he and the students were at the altar, in the middle of a wedding ceremony. When they decided to take a vote, he was about to present the ring, kiss the bride, and say, "I do." They were asking him to stop the ceremony in midstream.

He asked them to repeat what had been said. Someone else said, "Let's vote." He threw down the microphone and walked out of the hall. As he strode out, someone said, "Rinpoche, come back. He doesn't speak for all of us." It was too late. The air was black. He was never coming back. People sensed that immediately.

Rinpoche had been waiting ever since he came to the West to make this presentation. America had been waiting centuries for these teachings. But the students couldn't wait to have their dinner. It was over.

It seemed that way for several days. I have never seen him angrier. People were devastated. A huge black space hung over the seminary. Slowly, there was an outpouring of people's love and dedication to what was happening there. The students supplicated Rinpoche to continue. In the end, he saw, I guess, that there was ground to go forward, without compromise. Four days later he started to teach again, and this time, people were ready to hear what he was presenting, with no strings attached, no boundaries. He went forward and completed the presentation, and it was beyond magnificent. These were really unspeakably brilliant teachings.

What was so interesting was that when he got over his anger, he was completely over it. There was no hangover. Of course, people never forgot that lesson, and news of what had happened spread throughout the *sangha*. In a way, it completely changed the tenor of the space in which he taught from then on. It wasn't a game. It wasn't a party. This was real.

During the last days of the seminary, we received the sad news that Alan Watts had died suddenly of a heart attack in California. The next day Rinpoche and I were alone, sitting together in our room. We both turned to each other at the same time and said, "Alan Watts." We felt him go through the room at the same instant. I'm sure his consciousness passed through.

At the end of the seminary, just a day or so before we were preparing to return to Boulder, Rinpoche said to me, "You know, I might die soon." I said to him, "What do you mean?" He responded, "Well, now that I've finished the seminary, I've taught everything I have to teach. There's nothing left for me to present. So I might die soon." He'd been in the United States for just three years. Now, he was saying that he'd done all he could. I told him, "That can't possibly be true. There must be something more." He paused for a minute, and then he said, "Yes, well, I have been having dreams about being a general. I had one last night. I was a general and I was leading the troops in battle. That was fantastic." Then he said, "I'd love to be a general." Finally, he said, "I guess if I could become a king and rule a nation, then I would have something to live for!"

This was one of those times when I realized that I did not know at all what to expect from Rinpoche. Ultimately, I don't think anybody did. You could never apply the same logic to Rinpoche that you could to other human beings. When you're very close to somebody, you presume that when a situation comes up, you can predict how this person is going to react. With Rinpoche, you never really knew, because he was operating in such a vast space compared to ordinary people. I wondered what to expect from him in the future. Clearly, it would be something out of the ordinary.

NINE

E arly in 1974, we moved into a two-story raised-ranch-style home
in Boulder Heights, an area in the foothills north of Boulder. It
was on the outskirts of town, much closer to Karma Dzong.
There was a stable on the property where we kept a pony for Ösel to
ride, and the house had a comfortable feeling. Although some people
thought it was too casual for Rinpoche, I felt it was a good family home,
which accommodated more warmth and relaxation in our lives. It had a
sunken living room and a big stone fireplace that I liked.

Even though Felicity had gone back to her grandmother, I still had
my hands full with the three boys. During this era, Marty Franco sent
Mexican maids to live with us and help out on the domestic front. Rinpoche was upset that we had live-in hired help, which he didn't approve
of, but I was relieved, frankly, to have assistance with the children and the
house. Rinpoche tried to get one of his students to marry the first maid
so she could stay in the United States, but it never worked out. As an infant, Gesar started speaking Spanish because the second maid, Ensanada,
spoke to him in Spanish all the time. At times, I had to speak to him in
my broken Spanish so that he would understand me.

Rinpoche did a lot of traveling at the beginning of that year. In part due to the huge success of *Cutting Through*, he now drew audiences of more than a thousand people almost anywhere he gave a public talk. In January he taught at Tail; in San Antonio and Houston, Texas; and in Boulder. In February, he lectured in Chicago, New York, and Boston, flew back to teach in Boulder, and went on to San Francisco. So I was left on my own with the kids more and more.

I weaned Gesar when he was about eight months old, and soon after that I got my first period since he'd been born. I bled so heavily that I was almost hemorrhaging. We still had very little money in those days, and on this occasion our bank account was overdrawn. I had no money to buy groceries, there was nothing to eat in the house, and I needed to see a doctor about my bleeding. Rinpoche was on the road teaching. I phoned him to tell him all these developments, and he said that he was going to wire money to Western Union. I was losing a lot of blood, but I decided that I was going to pick up the cash on my way to the hospital. While I was standing in line at Western Union, I was bleeding on the floor. After I finally got the money, I drove myself straight to the hospital where I was admitted to have a D & C (dilation and curettage, a procedure that involves scraping the uterus). Those were challenging times.

My sister had settled in Boulder, and she lived with us in the house at Boulder Heights for a while. That spring, my mother decided to make a visit to Boulder to see both of her daughters. I hadn't seen her in four years. She timed her trip so that Rinpoche was out of town, and she stayed with me at the house. At that time, Ösel was in boarding school in Ojai, California. We thought that an intense residential situation might help overcome his difficulties learning to read and write in English.

This was the first time that my mother met her grandchildren. I found her incredibly judgmental, going out of her way to tell me all the things I was doing wrong. She criticized everything about the way I fed and dressed my children. When I cooked baby food for Gesar, for example, she criticized me if I fed him the same meal twice. One day I left her at the house to do errands in town. When I came back, she had re-arranged the furniture.

Most of my life, I had felt intimidated by my mother, so I had never confronted her directly, although obviously I hadn't gone along with her ideas about how I should live my life. This visit was a pivotal one, because I finally stood up to her. After she'd been at the house for several days, we decided to put the boys in the car and go for a drive. The two boys were in the backseat, and Mother and I were in the front. She asked me, "Are you planning to have any more children?" She had obviously been waiting to ask this question. I replied, "Yes, we're thinking about it." She became completely unraveled, and she started ranting, "You know, that man wants to keep you barefoot and pregnant. That's all he wants." Then she got more and more hysterical. Taggie leaned over and touched her from the backseat, as though he were trying to comfort her. She slapped his hand away and screamed at him, "Don't touch me. You're black."

I didn't say anything. I turned the car around, and I drove back up to the house. I asked her to get out in the garage. I backed out, closed the garage door, drove back down to Boulder, and went to a friend's house. I phoned my mother from there and told her, "I'm not coming back to my house until you've left. You can find a way to get yourself to the airport and back to England. I don't care what you do, but I want you out of my house." I think that this completely shocked her, because I'd never said anything like that to her before. I thought that I might never see my mother again.

That spring, the graduates of the first Vajradhatu Seminary were beginning their *ngöndro,* the preliminary meditation practices that prepare you for more advanced Vajrayana practice. Rinpoche did these practices in Tibet at the age of nine. As I described earlier, they include a hundred thousand full prostrations that are made while visualizing the Buddhist lineage in front of you and reciting the refuge vow. Then one completes the recitation of a hundred thousand mantras connected with purifying one's neurotic upheavals, followed by a hundred thousand offerings of a mandala that one represents symbolically by arranging heaps of rice. These offerings signify the surrender of ego, offering up one's neurosis as a gift to the Buddhist lineage. Finally, the student completes a million recitations of a short chant calling on the teachers of the lineage, which is connected with further surrender and the development of authentic devotion. This is not hero worship but invoking the indestructible qualities of sanity over and over, as represented in the teacher.

In Rinpoche's relationship with his students, if the seminary had been like the wedding, then *ngöndro* was like the first year of marriage. Before beginning their prostrations, the students received a formal mind transmission from Rinpoche, which communicates the very heart of Vajrayana, stipped bare. In this transmission, the mind of the teacher meets the mind of the student, and it might be described as the spiritual equivalent of a honeymoon. In contrast, practicing the Vajrayana preliminaries is quite difficult and demanding, nothing like you might have expected when you said, "I do." About fifty students in Boulder had completed the seminary and were now tantra students, or *tantrikas.* The tantra group met with Rinpoche almost every month, sometimes several times a month. Many of these gatherings took place at our house. We talked about the teachings we had received, how these were affecting people's experience, and the practice we were doing. Many people experienced intense ups and downs and a great deal of emotionality when they started prostrations—as well as excitement and a feeling of being energized. Rinpoche felt committed to being there for people and seeing that they didn't go off the rails, so to speak.

Rinpoche understood that this was a critical time in the introduction of Vajrayana Buddhism in America. Altogether, he saw this as a dramatic era in Western history, when the pith of Buddhism was being introduced to Westerners for the first time ever. Since Western society is quite distinct from the world he grew up in, he also was constantly evaluating how best to present Vajrayana to us. Nevertheless, he felt that people had the desire and the capacity to absorb the teachings, and ultimately the fact that we were Westerners was not a barrier. Although Rinpoche had to overcome the obstacles I described earlier before presenting Vajrayana at the seminary, he trusted his students 100 percent. Why should Tibetans be able to practice and to understand better than Western students? To some extent, Rinpoche felt that corruption had occurred in certain quarters in Tibet, which had weakened the way the dharma was practiced and taught there. So he welcomed America as new ground to be able to teach the essence of dharma without preconceptions. "Buddhadharma without credentials" was a phrase he often used in this era.

Although I received Vajrayana transmission after the seminary, I wasn't trying to do my *ngöndro* practice. When I would ask Rinpoche about going on practice retreats, he never encouraged me. I felt that my practice at this time was being with him and with the children. I also saw horseback riding as a contemplative practice for me because it demanded mindfulness and tremendous discipline. For the first time since marrying Rinpoche, I had resumed riding regularly a few months after Gesar was born. For me, it was a bright spot in my demanding life.

During this period, Rinpoche was quite consumed with preparations for the inaugural summer of the Naropa Institute. Rinpoche's vision for Naropa, which he had been refining for a number of years, was to create a university that would revitalize the connection to spiritual and intellectual traditions, whether of the East or the West. He felt that a contemplative approach to education, combining rigorous intellectual studies with the direct investigation of mind through meditation and other disciplines, would be a great addition to higher education in America. He had experienced the best of Western education, in his opinion, at Oxford, and while he had tremendous appreciation for the approach there, he felt that it lacked a connection to direct experience. He wanted to create a learning environment that would encourage both students and faculty to join together intellect and intuition.

As the months progressed, there were constant phone calls and innumerable planning meetings. Before the summer got underway, Rinpoche and I decided that we should take the children on another family holiday. Since Ösel was away at school, it was just going to be the four of us.

During this era, Marvin and John no longer lived with us. They were both involved in preparations for opening the institute, and they were working on editing a sequel to *Cutting Through Spiritual Materialism,* which was to be called the *Myth of Freedom.* Two other people had largely replaced the role that John and Marvin had played earlier. One was David Rome, who played a pivotal role in my husband's work for many years. The other was Landon Mallery, who was also a dedicated student. They drove Rinpoche to and from the office, helped schedule his appointments, and assisted him in many other ways. They didn't live with us, but they were around the house almost every day. Landy's parents owned a house in Eleuthera in the Bahamas, and he offered us the use of the house for our holiday, which sounded great.

Unfortunately, when we got there, we didn't enjoy ourselves at all. We were bitten by sand fleas on the beach, and it was alternately rainy and cold or hot and humid. No one wanted to go swimming in the ocean or lie on the beach, and there was really nothing else to do. The

kids were bored and not having a good time, which made it more difficult for everyone. On top of that, Rinpoche was constantly getting calls
from people in Boulder, phoning about this or that issue related to
Naropa starting up. It was hardly a vacation.

We finally decided to leave the Bahamas early, and the two of us
would go somewhere else to have time by ourselves. I don't know how
long it had been since we had spent time alone like that. Rinpoche suggested we go to the south of France. We arranged for someone to fly
down and pick up the kids, and we went to Nice. Nobody could reach
us there, so we actually had uninterrupted time to ourselves, which was
delightful. We spent about ten days staying in a tiny bed and breakfast.
Rinpoche loved the brioche and the croissants and the café au lait they
served us for breakfast.

While we were there, I wanted to gamble, so we went to a casino.
I played roulette while Rinpoche sat by himself at the bar, grumbling
about what a waste of time and money this was. Finally, I took a break
and joined him at the bar, which was on the second floor looking down
on the gaming tables. Rinpoche was in a foul mood, feeling moralistic
about how degraded it was to gamble. Then, he noticed some Japanese
businessmen in silk suits approach a roulette table and start playing. He
was intrigued by them, and his attitude changed completely. He said,
"Okay! Let's gamble." So we went downstairs and sat at the roulette table
together. He put one hundred dollars on red and one hundred dollars on
black. Rinpoche kept playing red and black, red and black. The croupier
was rolling his eyes. Eventually zero came up, and Rinpoche lost his two
hundred dollars, much to his shock. He was beside himself, "I want my
money back. I'm going to stay and gamble till it comes back!" I said, "No
you're not. We're going home." That was the end of our gambling experience in Nice.

We enjoyed wandering through the Moroccan district in Nice,
shopping and looking for places to eat. Rinpoche had a theory that the
smallest restaurants would definitely have the best food. He found a tiny
restaurant that had a beaded curtain across the front entrance. You went
down a long corridor into the restaurant. There was no menu. You sat
down, and they put food in front of you. They served us each a plate of
ravioli. I bit into mine and found it rather disgusting. I asked the waiter
to come over, and I asked, "What is this?" He said, "Madame, c'est ravioli

sang de cheval," which means ravioli filled with horse's blood. I didn't finish my food, but of course Rinpoche finished his and ate mine, too. There was a mirror on the wall of the restaurant that Rinpoche liked, and he convinced them to sell it to him. We bought a few other things at antique shops while we were there. I still have a gold clock that we bought on the trip to Nice, which I keep on my mantel.

In the last weeks before Naropa started, Rinpoche was extremely busy getting ready for the institute's inaugural summer session. When everything finally came together, it was an unbelievable success. We had been hoping that maybe four or five hundred students would enroll for the summer. The opening ceremonies were held in a large auditorium in Boulder on June 10, 1974, and as the president of the Naropa Institute, Rinpoche made welcoming remarks to an audience of more than twenty-five hundred which included the faculty, interested members of the public, and many of the two thousand students who attended the institute that summer.

Originally, Rinpoche thought about naming this new university Nalanda, which was the name of a renowned university in India. It was the greatest ancient center of Buddhist learning. Founded in the fifth century by the Gupta emperors, it remained an important institution until it was destroyed in the twelfth century by Muslim invaders. Some of Rinpoche's students thought that this name was too bold or perhaps too arrogant for a little institute in Boulder, Colorado, so Rinpoche decided on the name Naropa Institute. Naropa was a great Buddhist scholar who taught at Nalanda in the eleventh century. He left the university to find his teacher when he realized that he understood the words of the teachings but not the real sense or meaning behind them. He is one of the forefathers in Rinpoche's lineage, so this was a particularly appropriate name.

Rinpoche wanted Naropa to be known as the premier place for Buddhist studies in North America, but he also wanted to encourage other religious and spiritual traditions to find a home there. Thus, a few years later, he inaugurated a Christian-Buddhist contemplative conference that has sponsored an interfaith dialogue for many years now. Rinpoche also envisioned the visual arts, music, theater, writing, and poetry being part of the curriculum at Naropa. It was a home for many avant-garde artists in the seventies and has become quite well known for the

Jack Kerouac School of Disembodied Poetics, which was founded by Allen Ginsberg and Anne Waldman.

That first summer the faculty included a diverse and rather stellar lineup. Ram Dass drew about eight hundred devotees to the first session, many of whom had never met him but had read *Be Here Now.* He taught an evening course, which alternated with Rinpoche's evening lectures. The eminent anthropologist Gregory Bateson came and taught for one session. Jack Kornfield, who was not well known at that time, came for half the summer. He and other founding members of the Insight Meditation movement, including Joseph Goldstein and Sharon Salzberg, were also there. Allen Ginsberg was teaching poetry, as were Anne Waldman and many other American poets. The composer John Cage came for a weekend. You could study *thangka* painting or Japanese tea ceremony. Rinpoche taught two evening courses the first session, and one the second. One of his plays, *Prajna,* was performed at Naropa by members of Mudra Theater during the summer. There was a great deal of theater, art, and music going on. Naropa was very much the happening thing.

Some nights I would go to Rinpoche's talk and if it went on too late, I'd send Taggie up to the stage in his pajamas to get a good-night kiss from his daddy before taking him home and putting him to bed. There were dinners and cocktail parties that we hosted and attended. I wasn't able to attend as many events as I would have liked since I was busy with the children. Rinpoche had meetings at all hours throughout the summer. He was thrilled to see the situation take shape and to have the opportunity to work with all of these people.

A group of Rinpoche's students had been working tirelessly, and largely without pay, for the past year to organize and prepare for the opening of the institute. Marty Janowitz, who is still a member of the Naropa board, was very involved. Rinpoche's students constituted the core of the administration. John Baker and Marvin Casper played key roles, with John acting as Chief Executive Officer. He introduced Rinpoche at the opening of the institute, along with Jeremy Hayward, an English physicist who worked closely with Naropa in the early years and later joined the board of directors of Vajradhatu.[1] The mayor of Boulder was also onstage for the opening of the institute. Rinpoche's students were there at Naropa in force as managers, conference organizers, teachers, and jacks-of-all-trades. Without the intense involvement of many of Rinpoche's senior students, Naropa could never have come into being. At the same time, this was a training ground for them, and they emerged from the experience with confidence and skills to apply in many other areas of their lives.

As the summer progressed, Rinpoche began to focus on the next big event. He had invited the head of his lineage, His Holiness the Karmapa, to come to America in the fall to visit Rinpoche, to see his students, and to make his first teaching tour in America. His Holiness was due to arrive in September. They had not seen each other since 1968, when Rinpoche briefly visited His Holiness's monastery in Sikkim. Rinpoche was nervous about the visit because he knew that His Holiness had heard stories about what Rinpoche was up to, and the version he had been told had been heavy on the outrageous, wild side and light on the "working for the dharma" side. Rinpoche did not know whether His Holiness would fully appreciate what he was trying to do in America.

Lecturing to more than a thousand scantily garbed hippies at Naropa that summer gave him pause as to how to present his students to His Holiness. Rinpoche might be able to see past the long beards, cutoff jeans, and tank tops, but this was not the image he wanted to present to his lineage. He wanted His Holiness to be able to appreciate the mind and heart connection he had made with all these Westerners. He feared that His Holiness would think that Rinpoche was consorting with barbarians, somewhat like having moved into the zoo with a bunch of jungle animals. Sometimes, if you looked around the room when Rinpoche was lecturing that first summer at Naropa, especially with the influx of Ramdassians at the beginning, you would see a menagerie of topless men with matted hair and long beards and long-haired girls sporting white robes or showing lots of cleavage. What to do?

In addition to concerns about their appearance, Rinpoche was faced with the challenge of introducing decorum to his students, in terms of how they would behave around the Karmapa. When Rinpoche first came to America, he was careful not to create a barrier between himself and others. He wanted to experience fully the world he was entering and meet people at eye level. He gave up his robes because he did not want to create an exotic impression where people would indulge their fantasies about him. He wanted them to see him not as a mystery man from Tibet but as a human being.

Rinpoche had grown up with attendants who treated him as a spiritual prince, but when he came to the West, he let all of that go. He didn't demand or expect special treatment. For one thing, there was no cultural reference point for the Western students to provide service to him. However, what he accepted for himself was not what he wanted to present to His Holiness. In preparation for His Holiness's visit, Rinpoche made it clear to his students how he himself wanted to receive the Karmapa and how he expected them to treat His Holiness as well. He described this later as follows:

> In 1974, His Holiness the 16th Gyalwa Karmapa, the head of the Karma Kagyü lineage of Buddhism to which I belong, was to arrive for his first visit to North America. A group of us had a meeting, and we talked about protocol and other arrangements. Quite a number of people said, "Couldn't we just take His Holiness to a disco and feed him a steak? Do we really have to vacuum the floor? Maybe he should sleep on a waterbed. Couldn't he just come along and see what America is like?" In the end, that wasn't the approach we decided to take! ... That approach is bloated with arrogance.[2]

The previous year, Karma Dzong had moved into a much larger shrine room in the back of the building at 1111 Pearl Street in Boulder. The new meditation hall was a large room with a balcony above the main floor and could hold up to three hundred people. For His Holiness's visit, the room was completely redone. At Rinpoche's direction, walls were painted, floors were sanded, windows scrubbed spotless. Around the edges of the room, Rinpoche had the students paint the mantra from the *Heart Sutra* (one of the essential teachings of the Buddha) in gold letters. Rinpoche insisted that they build traditional Tibetan thrones, covered in brocade, for His Holiness to use when he presented teachings or held audiences, whether in the main shrine hall or at his residence. At the house rented for His Holiness in Boulder, Rinpoche had the walls draped in satin and brocade. For weeks before His Holiness arrived, he stayed up all night. He actually didn't sleep for days at a time because he wouldn't stop working on the preparations. Everyone was going full-out, turning themselves into seamstresses, carpenters, secretaries, housekeepers, cooks, administrators—he pushed people as far as they could possibly go. He asked Tom Rich and Ken Green (aka Narayana and Krishna) to take charge of the visit preparations along with Karl Springer, another student from the early days at Tail, and they worked around the clock as he did, both in Boulder and also traveling as the advance parties to both the East and the West coasts, wherever His Holiness would be traveling. Rinpoche asked all of his male students to wear a suit jacket and a tie during the visit, and women wore conservative skirts and blouses or suits.

Rinpoche also emphasized the style in which His Holiness should be served, explaining that the Karmapa was truly a spiritual monarch and that by treating him as such, the students would be able to appreciate the depth of the wisdom he embodied. People learned how to serve in both the Western and the Tibetan style. It was a crash course in table manners and etiquette for all of us. For some, it was reminding us of what we knew from our upbringing. For others, it was a completely new experience.

Rinpoche asked another group of his students to accompany His Holiness wherever he traveled, providing security and logistical support for the visit. The Karmapa arrived first in New York. He was given diplomatic status by the State Department in the United States. Therefore, he received police escorts in major cities and was accorded official recognition in other ways. Rinpoche's students organized a motorcade in every major city His Holiness visited, which included advance cars, a limousine for His Holiness, and vans following behind for the other members of his party, including the translator and the monks. The students who trained to be the drivers for His Holiness and his party also worked with local law enforcement wherever he went. They provided security for the high-profile parts of the visit.

At the household, a group of senior male students was trained to be personal attendants to His Holiness, in somewhat traditional Tibetan style. Because His Holiness was very strict about his monastic vows, he would not allow women attendants in his personal quarters. However, women were involved in many other aspects of the tour and the household.

While His Holiness was in Boulder, Rinpoche invited him to have tea at our home in Pine Brook Hills. While he was at the house, I noticed that the Karmapa wouldn't make eye contact with me. I felt badly about this, and later I asked Rinpoche why His Holiness wouldn't look at me. Rinpoche said, "He's very uncomfortable around you." And I said, "Why on earth would that be?" He said, "Because if you had the power to se-duce me, you must be a very dangerous woman." After the first time he came to the house, Rinpoche talked with him about our marriage, and explained that I was not a seductress. Then, His Holiness seemed more comfortable around me, and in fact we had a very close, wonderful rela-tionship. But that first encounter was very disconcerting.

Rinpoche also asked me to take a drive around Boulder with His Holiness and show him various local landmarks. Rinpoche instructed me that whenever His Holiness admired a building or noted that it was impressive or anything like that, I was to tell the Karmapa that the build-ing belonged to us. I thought this was ridiculous, but Rinpoche insisted. I suppose it was some sort of macho Tibetan thing. His Holiness and I drove all over town, with me telling him that every large building in town, including the Harvest House Hotel and the entire University of Colorado, belonged to Rinpoche and his students. I'm sure His Holiness checked later and learned that we had considerably fewer real estate holdings than I had suggested.

While he was in Boulder, the Karmapa especially wanted to spend time with Taggie, who was the reincarnation of one of His Holiness's own teachers in Tibet. He brought a number of gifts for Taggie, pre-cious items that had belonged to the former Tenga Rinpoche. It was now obvious to everyone who spent time around Taggie that he was not developing normally. His Holiness felt that this was because Taggie needed to be raised in a monastic situation. He suggested that we send Taggie to Sikkim as soon as possible to study and receive training from His Holiness and to have a formal enthronement ceremony there. We took this under advisement, but Rinpoche still did not want to give in to this traditional approach. He felt that we should work with Taggie at home and also begin to investigate what Western doctors would say about his condition.

Traditionally, the veneration or respect that one shows a teacher is con-sidered part of making an offering in order to receive the teachings. In medieval Tibetan times, students would travel to India to study with the great Buddhist teachers there. It was a long and truly perilous journey, not unlike the one my husband made when he escaped from Tibet in 1959. Practitioners traveling to India would amass a quantity of gold, which they used to cover their expenses, with the remainder being offered to the teachers they studied with. On the one hand, this was simply tuition. On another level, the point of the teaching gift was to give or surrender something in appreciation of the value of the teaching. It wasn't that the teachers wanted to get rich.

There is a well-known story about one figure in my husband's lineage, Marpa, who gathered together a great deal of gold dust to finance his three trips to India. Marpa later became Milarepa's root guru, or main teacher. When Marpa made his second trip to India, he returned there to study with Naropa, the great Indian teacher who was one of his main gurus, his root guru in fact. Marpa offered Naropa a portion of his gold but held some back for the trip home. Naropa demanded that Marpa give him all the gold. Marpa hesitated but Naropa insisted, saying, "Do you think you can buy my teaching with your deception?" When Marpa finally gave in, Naropa threw the gold dust into the air, scattering it everywhere, crying, "Gold, gold. What is gold to me? All the world is gold to me."

The visit of the Karmapa awakened Rinpoche's students to the traditional approach to devotion, which is exemplified by this story of Marpa. The teacher doesn't want your wealth for his personal gain. Rather, one has to surrender one's comfortable world. Rinpoche's students began to understand this through Rinpoche's own example of devotion to His Holiness.

The preparations and formality surrounding the visit of the Karmapa allowed hundreds of students in different parts of the country to be an intimate part of the visit. People lined up to serve in his household. It was hardly possible to accommodate them all, so more and more positions were added. Kitchen assistants, gardeners, housekeepers, shrine keepers, tea makers, and all sorts of positions were created or multiplied so that everyone could be included. This became an important way for people to spend time with His Holiness, because the Karmapa rarely gave lectures or invited dialogue in the way that Rinpoche did.

Instead, His Holiness conducted traditional ceremonies, which are considered to convey what is called *adhishthana,* or a blessing, to people.

Mostly, these empowerments were conducted in Tibetan, so although a summary of the ceremony and the text was given to people in English, the audience often had very little idea what was going on. It was not so much what His Holiness said but rather his way of being that struck people and communicated to them. Being in his presence was quite an overwhelming experience. He radiated loving kindness and compassion and a warmth that was almost palpable.

During this visit, His Holiness performed the Vajra Crown ceremony in locations across the country. It is said that during this event His Holiness fully manifests as the buddha of compassion, Avalokiteshvara, and that anyone who sees this ceremony will be freed from rebirth in the lower realms (the realms of hell, hungry ghosts, or animals). When the Fifth Karmapa, Teshin Shekpa, visited the court of the emperor of China in the fifteenth century, the emperor had a vision in which he saw a black vajra crown hovering over the head of the Karmapa. The emperor became a deeply devoted disciple of the Karmapa, and he had a replica of this crown made and presented to Teshin Shekpa. From this time forward, all of the Karmapas have conducted a ceremony in which His Holiness places this crown on his head and radiates a state of compassion and enlightenment. More than three thousand people came to the Vajra Crown ceremony in San Francisco, and there was similar attendance at ceremonies held in Boulder, Boston, New York, and other North American cities.

While in Boulder, His Holiness also performed a special ceremony in the newly renovated shrine hall at Karma Dzong, officially acknowledging Rinpoche's work to plant the Buddhist teachings in America and encouraging him as a vajra master to go further, especially in presenting the Vajrayana tradition. From this time forward, Rinpoche was known by the titles Vajracharya, or "holder of the Vajrayana teachings," and later as Vidyadhara, or "holder of wisdom." The Karmapa thus made a public statement of his appreciation for Rinpoche's efforts and achievements, and he wrote a special proclamation to this effect. I think everyone in His Holiness's party was amazed by what Rinpoche had accomplished, especially in light of how little time had passed since Rinpoche had arrived in America.

His Holiness also visited the land centers, the rural retreat centers Rinpoche had established: Rocky Mountain Dharma Center in Colorado, Tail of the Tiger in Vermont, and the newly acquired Padma Jong in northern California. (This center was to focus on presenting programs combining meditation and the arts; after several years, it was sold.) Rinpoche asked His Holiness to rename Tail, and the Karmapa gave the center the name Karme Chöling, the "place of the teachings of the Karma Kagyü lineage." It is still known by that name today. His Holiness also traveled to the second seminary, which was being held in Snowmass, Colorado, and performed the Vajra Crown ceremony for the participants there.

His Holiness's visit reinvigorated Rinpoche and gave him a sense of further direction in his work. Reestablishing his direct connection with the head of the lineage inspired him. He was so pleased to actually be able to bring together the old and new worlds. After His Holiness left, in late November, Rinpoche gave a seminar on his own teacher, Jamgön Kongtrül of Sechen, in which he talked about his upbringing and his relationship with his teacher in a very personal manner, beyond anything he had transmitted before. It was as though the visit of the Karmapa had forged a link to the lineage in a way that allowed Rinpoche to go deeper into the wisdom of that tradition and to share that with his students. In the past, he had given seminars on early teachers of the lineage, but now he was talking more about his own, intimate, direct heritage.

The Jamgön Kongtrül seminar coincided with the first Dharmadhatu Conference, which brought representatives from every major meditation center, or dharmadhatu (which means "space of dharma") to Boulder to meet with one another and to confer with the members of the Vajradhatu board of directors and with Rinpoche himself. This was a further step in creating the institutions that Rinpoche hoped would carry the teachings forward into the future. Tables were arranged in a huge rectangle in the large meeting room at Karma Dzong so the representatives from each dharmadhatu could sit together at the table, sharing information and making their reports. Rinpoche and the board of directors were seated at the head of the room, which was equipped with flip charts, markers, and pointers. Dharmadhatu members reported to the entire group on their activities, and key Vajradhatu staff people and members of the board of Vajradhatu made presentations to the assembled group. As Rinpoche began to understand more fully the energy of America, he began to create more of these situations that could harness the power of the corporate world—which generally is a vehicle for materialism. However, he also saw the potential to adopt this model to promote the energy of enlightenment in America. Later, he perceived its limitations and the toll the corporate approach can take on people. For now, however, this was a skilful framework to employ. It encouraged Rinpoche's students to engage a bigger world and to feel that they were part of an exciting and expansive project. It also gave them familiar reference points from within their own culture for this expansion. At this time, you might say that Vajradhatu and the scene in Boulder were manifesting like the Wall Street of Buddhism in America (a phrase that a columnist in the *Village Voice* used around this time to describe Vajradhatu).

During this era, Rinpoche was also beginning to hand over more responsibility to his students for teaching meditation to others. In December, at Karme Chöling, he conducted the first formal training for about fifty meditation instructors, and he held another training in Boulder in April 1975. Previously, he had authorized a few individuals as instructors, but this was the first time he gave this training to a group of his students. The sitting practice of meditation was always the bedrock of practice in our community. Starting in 1973, Rinpoche had instituted monthlong periods of meditation, called *dathuns,* which all students were encouraged to complete, and attending a *dathun* became a requirement for being accepted to the seminary starting in 1975.

At the end of April 1975, Rinpoche and I went on a trip to Europe with the two older boys, Taggie and Ösel, leaving Gesar in the care of friends. This was partially to be our vacation, but we were also traveling to Samye Ling to retrieve the official seals of office of the Trungpas, which were still in Akong's possession. With the recent recognition of Rinpoche's achievements by His Holiness the Karmapa, Akong could hardly justify keeping them any longer.

Rinpoche wrote ahead, informing Akong that we would be coming. Rinpoche asked Karl Springer, who had been instrumental in all of the arrangements for His Holiness the Karmapa's visit, to accompany us on this trip. Karl was becoming very adept at dealing with Tibetan politics. Later, as a member of the board of directors, he became the head of the department of external affairs, which handled all of the visits of Tibetan teachers to our community.

For the meeting with Akong, we all dressed in our best business suits, even the children. Akong was very polite; there was no outward sign of conflict. After a long preamble, in which Rinpoche talked about his work in America and his family and inquired about Akong's work and his family, he told Akong that he had come to get his seals back, as well as other treasures that belonged to him from Tibet. Rinpoche was no longer somebody that Akong could mistreat. Within a few short years in America, Rinpoche was already much more influential than Akong would ever be. Rinpoche manifested that confidence and power, yet without any bravado. He demanded what was rightfully his.

Without hesitation, Akong returned everything, and we brought the seals back with us to the United States. From this time forward, wherever Rinpoche traveled, he kept his seals with him. They traveled in a special briefcase designed to hold them, and they came in the car or on the plane with him whenever he went somewhere to teach. In Boulder, or anywhere else where he resided for a period of time, the seals were always kept with him at his residence. Rinpoche barely let them out of his sight.

After we got home, Rinpoche wrote to Akong and thanked him for the return of the seals and told him how good it had been to see him again. However, he also said in this letter that he felt that the rupture in their connection was one that would not be repaired for many lifetimes.

From Samye Ling, we went down to London. To celebrate our victory, Rinpoche wanted to stay at one of the most posh, old-fashioned hotels in London, the Ritz in Piccadilly. Our room was beautifully appointed, with exquisite pink silk linens and bedspreads. Taggie proceeded to have diarrhea all over the bedspread, which I found beyond embarrassing. Later, when we went down to the Palm Court to have tea, Taggie was completely out of control, racing down the corridors. We had dressed him in a beautiful outfit, but this little child was a whirling dervish flying around the tearoom. He was becoming more and more hyperactive, which was especially apparent in this situation.

While we were in London, Rinpoche enjoyed shopping for clothes. He wanted to get a Jaeger suit for each of us, and he also bought himself a nice suit at Harrods. In later years, when we had more income, Rinpoche would get his clothes hand-tailored on Savile Row. Rinpoche had always enjoyed shopping for ties. During this era, he liked striped ties a lot. Later he had quite a collection of Japanese brocade ties. In general, he was rather conservative in his clothing tastes. He often wore pinstriped suits, and he also built up a collection of sports jackets. He especially liked French cuffs on his shirts, and he bought a number of pairs of cuff links while we were in London.

We had so much extra clothing that it wouldn't fit in our luggage. Instead of buying another suitcase, I simply took a garbage bag and put our dirty laundry and casual clothing in it. When we checked out, the uniformed doorman at the Ritz pushed the trolley containing our luggage out to the street, where we were going to hail a cab to the airport. The garbage bag was sitting on top of the luggage. As we approached the curb, the bag was jostled and a pair of my underwear fell out onto the street. I was mortified. The doorman, however, didn't skip a beat. He leaned over, picked up my underwear with his white-gloved hands, and put it back in the bag. That was our departure from the Ritz.

From London we flew to Nice for several days of holiday. Having had such a lovely time the year before, we both wanted to return. While we were in France, I convinced Rinpoche that we should go to Vienna so that I could visit the Spanish Riding School. Now that I was riding regularly again, I had started to develop a great interest in the discipline of dressage, a classic form of horsemanship whose pinnacle was achieved at the school.

We visited a number of places in Vienna, including Schönbrunn Palace. Rinpoche liked to spend long hours in the restaurants in Vienna, and Taggie was very difficult to manage throughout all of this.

Luckily, we were able to obtain tickets for one of the dressage performances at the Spanish Riding School, known as "the Spanish." The day of the performance, we stood outside the Winter Palace in Vienna, where the Spanish is located. We waited in line a long time to get in to see the performance. When they finally opened the doors, people started pushing and shoving all around us. We finally made our way through the crowd and into the building. To get to our seats, we had to walk up a narrow flight of wooden stairs to the balcony overlooking the arena. The hall is magnificent, with enormous crystal chandeliers hanging from the ceiling. The arena can hold several thousand spectators. It's an extraordinary environment.

We settled ourselves in our seats, and then classical music began to play over the speakers, signaling the beginning of the performance. In rode the most majestic white horses in formation, their bridles inlaid with gold and the saddle pads trimmed in gold braid. The riders rode impeccably in their brown uniforms and bicorne hats. It was like watching a completely synchronized ballet performed by horses and riders. Five or ten minutes into the performance, Rinpoche started sobbing. I couldn't imagine why, and I said to him, "What's the matter with you? Is something wrong?" He answered, "There's nothing wrong. It's so beautiful. It's a magnificent expression of windhorse." (Windhorse is the uplifted expression of dignity that is described in the Shambhala teachings.) Rinpoche wept throughout the performance. I also was moved by this display of horse and rider so nobly joined in the art of dressage.

Afterward, when we discussed our experience, I told Rinpoche that the fulfillment of my dreams as a rider would be to study the classical approach to dressage with one of the teachers from the Spanish Riding School. Although I was still very new to this discipline, Rinpoche took me quite seriously. He said to me, "You know, it's too soon right now, but I would imagine that within a couple of years you're going to find a way to come here and study."

When we came home, Ösel went back to school, Rinpoche went back on the road to teach, and I was left alone in the house with Taggie and Gesar. They slept in a bedroom together, and they were a handful. Although Gesar was two, he still had a crib. Taggie slept in the four-poster bed that had been mine when I was a child. The two of them together could be absolutely dreadful. After I put them to bed for the night, they sometimes would get up and play and totally destroy any order in the room.

When His Holiness had been in Boulder the year before, one of his gifts to Taggie was a small but exquisite *rupa,* or statue of the Buddha. His Holiness told me that in the Karma Kagyü lineage there were seven very special Buddha *rupas* made from the body relics of important teachers, and that he was presenting one of these to Taggie. We were proud that Taggie had been given one of these statues, and we put Taggie's Buddha on a special shrine in his bedroom. One morning when I went into their bedroom to get the boys up, my eyes turned to the shrine. The Buddha had been decapitated. I called out, "Oh, my god, oh my god. What happened to the Buddha?" Taggie said, "Gesar was hungry." Gesar ate the head of the Buddha. You could see the tell-tale teeth marks.

Although Gesar was active and often quite naughty, he was a normal, exuberant two-year-old. Unfortunately, this was not the case with Taggie. There were now many signs of his developmental problems. Earlier that year, we had put Taggie in preschool several mornings a week. One morning after we returned from Europe, his teacher called me from school and said that Taggie had collapsed and been taken to Boulder Community Hospital. By the time I got to the hospital, he seemed fine, and he was released without any recommendations for follow-up. Later, we realized that this was the first of many epileptic seizures.

Shortly thereafter, I was awakened by a wild noise at about 5:30 in the morning. When I came downstairs, I saw that Taggie had turned the blender onto high speed. In his right hand he had a bag of rice; in his left hand, he had a container of small silver balls that are used as decorations for cookies. He was pouring the rice and the balls into the blender and watching the whole mixture fly all over the kitchen. Lots of small children might do something like this if they had the opportunity. But Taggie seemed completely unaware that I was in the room with him, and he couldn't comprehend that he had done anything naughty. The quality of Taggie's behavior was abnormally distant and detached. What speech he had developed was deteriorating, and he was becoming more and more out of touch with ordinary life.

Taggie also became more agitated and out of control at this point. After a number of incidents, I called Rinpoche—who was out of town at the time—completely freaking out. I felt that I needed help. Rinpoche phoned one of his students, someone who worked closely with him, to see if we could get more help taking care of Taggie. I received a phone call from this man, whom I considered a close personal friend, and he said to me, "I don't know why you can't take care of Taggie. He's your child." It was, I guess, the typical male reaction, especially in those days, from someone who doesn't have any children. He was absolutely clueless what was happening and did nothing to help.

When Taggie's condition seemed to deteriorate, Rinpoche and I decided to take Taggie to a neurologist in Boulder. We explained to the doctor that our child had been more normal earlier on but that he was now getting both more out of touch and more hyperactive. After the doctor examined him, he said that we had to consider the possibility that Taggie might have a brain tumor. We were shocked and very distressed. The doctor recommended that we do a whole battery of tests, including a pneumoencephalogram, in which they put air between the brain and the skull so that they can obtain an image of the brain. This procedure is supposed to be unbelievably painful. Now they have less invasive and less painful methods, but this was what they used in that era. Taggie had the test, but he never reacted as though he had any pain at all. He was supposed to have splitting headaches afterward, but he was up bouncing around on his bed shortly after the test was done. The results did not show a problem, but a subsequent electroencephalogram, or EEG, showed that Taggie's brain waves were abnormal. This set off another round of doctors' appointments and tests.

We took Taggie to a whole slew of specialists, none of whom could tell us exactly what was wrong with him. There was some dysfunction in his cortex, the doctors said, but we were told that he didn't fit the classical diagnosis of autism, so his condition was somewhat of a mystery.

I began to think that I had done something terribly wrong in the past. I felt responsible. I thought back to every accident Taggie had as a young child. I remembered the time he fell off of his changing table as an infant. He seemed fine, but I wondered: Did something happen then? Once as a young boy he fell and hit his head in a sausage shop in Boulder. I thought to myself, "That time he fell on his head, I took him to the doctor immediately and he was completely fine afterward." It seemed to me that if an accident had caused these problems when he was little, there should have been ramifications soon after the event. I remembered that Taggie had a bad reaction to a pertussis vaccination when he was quite young, including a prolonged, high fever. Could this be the cause of his behavioral problems?

In fact, I don't think we will never know what caused Taggie's problems. That was the most frustrating thing for us at that time: being unable to find out what was the matter with him and what was the cause. The doctors could point to certain things, but they never gave us a label for what was wrong with Taggie, no definite answers, diagnosis, prognosis, or indication of what we should do. Clearly, he had autistic-like behavior, but no one called it autism at that time. Things might be quite different today.

Even to this day, to a certain extent, I keep trying to find the cause of Taggie's problems. I say to myself, "Did he have an accident? Did something happen to him?" But I can't put my finger on anything specific. Sometimes I wonder if the problems date back to his birth, when it took so long for him to be born and he came out all gray and oxygen-deprived. Sometimes I think there was a genetic problem. I wonder sometimes if there was a genetic mutation due to Rinpoche's heavy drinking. I was so young when Taggie was conceived: could this have made a genetic problem more likely? In my more rational moments, I realize that none of these theories are that relevant. I don't think I'm ever going to know what happened to Taggie.

The last time the doctor met with me, he said that they could describe what was wrong, but there was no name for it. He couldn't recommend treatment because there was really no diagnosis. I felt that I had to accept that we would never have a diagnosis for what was wrong with our child.

I began to feel that Rinpoche and I couldn't provide the proper care for our son and that we needed to do more to help him. It was terrible to feel so inadequate. Around this time, Taggie developed fears that he hadn't had before. We had several Tibetan paintings of wrathful deities, called *mahakalas,* at the house. Now, every time Taggie saw one of these pictures, he would go crazy, screaming and sobbing and running away. He had always been a happy child, so this change seemed strange and out of character.

In Tibetan monasteries, the main *mahakala* images traditionally are kept in a separate building, where practitioners conduct particular practices related to working with this wrathful energy. There are special rules about how certain *mahakala* paintings and sculptures are to be handled, when they are to be viewed, and other things like that. One of the earlier Tenga Rinpoches, one of Taggie's predecessors, is said to have made a fatal error in relating to the *mahakala* shrines at his monastery. Against the advice of senior monks, he ignored the regulations and decided to uncover the painting of a particular deity at a time that was forbidden. After that, he apparently went mad. Taggie's fears and our knowledge of this history in Taggie's spiritual background tended to reinforce the theory that his problems were spiritual rather than physical or genetic. In any case, Taggie became extremely afraid of the wrathful deities, and we thought perhaps it was related to the *tulku* disease that His Holiness was telling us was a product of not allowing him to be brought up in the monastery.

That fall while Rinpoche was away, after one particularly difficult week, I phoned him to ask again for his help. He was at the 1975 seminary in Snowmass, Colorado, a program that lasted three months, and wouldn't be back for at least another month. The seminary that year in Snowmass ended up being quite difficult in certain respects. Against his better judgment, Rinpoche had allowed the American poet W. S. Merwin, who had spent the summer at Naropa, and his girlfriend, Dana, to attend the seminary, although they were extremely new to our community. As the Vajrayana section of the seminary approached, Bill (Merwin) and Dana remained isolated from the rest of the participants, and Rinpoche felt they weren't connecting with him or with what he was trying to teach.

On Halloween things turned ugly. There was a costume party that night, which Bill and Dana tried to duck out of. From what I heard, the situation got quite extreme. Rinpoche had suggested that rather than using costumes to disguise themselves, people should unmask and expose themselves. He told people that they should literally unmask by taking their clothes off. Everybody got naked. Rinpoche noticed that Bill and Dana weren't there. He insisted that they should come to the party too and sent students to rouse them from their room at the hotel. When they didn't answer the door, the messengers broke in through the balcony. Bill became alarmed and fearful, and he cut one of them with a jagged piece of broken glass. He and Dana were eventually brought down to the ballroom, where they were stripped of their clothing. It was pretty shocking.

A day or two later, Rinpoche told Merwin and Dana, as well as all the other participants, that they could leave the seminary or they could stay. They remained, but after the program ended, they left for good. The story filtered out of the seminary—in fact, nobody was trying to hide what had happened. Investigating the incident actually became a class project in the poetics department at Naropa Institute a year or two later, and the story made its way into an article in *Harper's* magazine in 1979.

Although I wasn't there when these events transpired, I was with Rinpoche in situations that were probably as extreme as that. If he felt that the elements of a situation were ripe to puncture delusion or self-deception, he never held back—though I don't expect people to understand or accept this at face value.

In some way, this incident was tied in for me to what was happening with Taggie. This was such a difficult time in our lives. In a certain sense, Rinpoche was dealing with extreme and seemingly unworkable energy at the seminary, while I was driving into a high wall of insanity (his phrase) in terms of Taggie and our family life. In fact, in a scenario that is unrelated yet strangely in keeping with the dark energies I've described, a child died at the very end of the 1975 seminary from complications of asthma while sleeping in the room at the hotel that Merwin and Dana had stayed in. (Although they stayed for the final talk of the seminary, they had left a bit earlier than others.)

Before this tragic event, I phoned Rinpoche at the seminary. I was just beside myself about Taggie. After listening to me describe the situation at home, finally, he said, "We should send Taggie to Karme Chöling. It's a more monastic environment there, and there are people there who I can ask to help take care of him. He can stay there for a few years, and then we may have to send him to His Holiness. I don't see an alternative. I don't think we should wait any longer." Rinpoche said that he would talk to one of his close students, David Nudell, about becoming Taggie's main attendant at Karme Chöling.

Some part of me was relieved. I remember Rinpoche saying, "There are a lot of people with a lot of sanity at Karme Chöling. They are going to be able to look after him. You have to begin to let go."

I felt that Rinpoche was making the right decision for Taggie, based on what we knew at the time. We couldn't continue to care for him. He was not getting what he needed. That was very clear. Although I felt that we were making the right decision, it was an unbelievably painful prospect. Taggie was just four years old. I was losing my firstborn son.

We all have hopes and dreams for our children. In our case, we expected our first son to grow up and become a great Tibetan teacher. At the very least, we expected him to grow up and lead a healthy life. It wasn't like he was born with an obvious condition, such as Down syndrome, where we'd been told from the beginning that he would never be "normal." That must also be incredibly difficult for a parent, but sometimes it seemed that it would have been easier for me to accept Taggie's disabilities if I had known about them from the beginning. Perhaps we could have adjusted our expectations much earlier, understanding that he was going to have many mental challenges. Ours was the difficulty of not knowing. We had the excruciatingly slow realization that Taggie was not all right. Coming to this realization was heart-wrenching.

Rinpoche also found the whole process very painful, although he didn't talk about it much. A few months earlier, in July 1975, he wrote a poem which began with a reference to the situation with Taggie:

Wounded son—
How sad.
Never expected this.
Oily seagulls
Crippled jackal
Complaining flower—
Very sad.
Is it?[3]

Beyond the need to let go of the hopes that I had for my child's future, now I also had to figure out how to physically let him go out of my life. That was the most difficult part of all for me. In the years after he went to Karme Chöling, I was able to process some of this. But at this particular time, I found the prospect inconceivably painful.

While Rinpoche was still away at the seminary, I received a phone call from someone at Karme Chöling saying that a member of the *sangha,* Tom Ryken, was on his way from Boulder to Karme Chöling in a few days and could take Taggie with him. At that point, I phoned Rinpoche, pretty much in hysterics. Rinpoche said firmly, "Drop him off at Tom's house. He'll take Taggie to Karme Chöling. Let him go." I was devastated. I felt absolutely alone. I couldn't even call anyone to help me because I couldn't stand to verbalize what was happening. Although I accepted that this was the right thing to do, it was unbearable.

I packed up Taggie's things, and on the appointed day I drove him over to Tom's house. I deposited him on the porch with his suitcase, rang the doorbell, and left. I didn't want to see anyone, and I just couldn't bear to say good-bye. It was awful. Clearly I didn't handle this well, but I couldn't do any better at that point. I felt that I had to let my child go, and this was the only way I could do it.

I suffered over this decision for a long time after that. For years, I had dreams where I was searching for Taggie.

TEN

During most of my childhood and early adolescence in England, I had been a rider. From the first moment I got on a pony as a small child, I felt deeply connected to horses and to horsemanship. My early training was in jumping and cross-country riding. When I was in boarding school, we were also allowed to go out on fox hunts. I never went to the kill, but I would go out in the early part of the hunt with my pony, Blaze. Later on I did "eventing," which involves competitions or events in three phases, consisting of a simple dressage test, a cross-country test, and a jumping competition. As a teenager, I always hated the dressage component. I found it boring. In England in those years there was very little interest in dressage, so I had little exposure and no real feeling for it.

After my first two years at Benenden, I sold my pony. I didn't ride at all at Kirby Lodge. In fact, I didn't take up riding again until Rinpoche and I moved to Colorado. When Taggie was a baby, I would sometimes go riding at a local stable for an hour or so. I broached the subject with Rinpoche of whether I could buy my own horse. At that time he said that he didn't think it would be a good idea. It might make us look wealthy, which we certainly were not, and people might think that we

were throwing money around. He was afraid that people would disapprove of him as a spiritual teacher if they thought that we were living a
wealthy, aristocratic sort of life. He asked me to wait. I let the idea go for
the time being, although I continued to ride occasionally.

During my pregnancy with Gesar, as I've mentioned, I rode from
time to time. When Gesar was a few months old, Rinpoche told me that
it would be all right for me to buy a horse. At that time, I had started taking riding lessons with Haze Kennedy, an Australian woman who taught
at a stable north of Boulder called Hidden Valley Ranch. From our house
in Boulder Heights it was a short drive to the stables. There was a young
thoroughbred mare available for purchase and I found her particularly
appealing. She was a light bay by the name of Fleur. Rinpoche renamed
her Mirage.

I did some jumping competitions with Mirage, and I rode her in
some hunter classes. After a few months, my riding instructor approached me with a proposal. She had a slightly older horse that was a
more experienced jumper and had some training in dressage, and she
herself wanted a young prospect. She asked me if I would be interested
in a trade. Her horse was a saddle-bred–thoroughbred cross by the name
of Mr. Chips. I agreed to make the trade because I thought it would be
helpful for my education as a rider. I felt that I could learn from a horse
that knew more than I did.

Mr. Chips was large, a sixteen three hand liver chestnut, a big horse
with a wonderful temperament.[1] He was sensitive and responsive and
willing to work. Rinpoche began calling me Mrs. Chips because I
started spending so much time at the barn. I competed Chips in some
jumper competitions, and I did quite well in the lower jumper classes
with him. Then I decided to ride him in a three-phase novice event in
Colorado. I scored well on the cross-country and the stadium jumping,
but I did poorly in dressage.

In order to improve as an all-around rider, I decided to take time off
from jumping and concentrate on learning more about dressage. In
fact, I decided to devote a year to it. At the end of that year, I fully intended to go back to jumping as my main riding discipline. I began by
taking dressage lessons from Haze Kennedy on a regular basis, three
times a week. She had some elementary dressage training and was a
good instructor. I found that I looked forward to my time at the barn as

a break from the hectic, chaotic life that I had with Rinpoche and the children.

At that time, a Hungarian rider by the name of Charles de Kunffy was coming to Colorado on a regular basis to teach dressage clinics. He had been a member of the Hungarian three-event team. I took several of his clinics and then started to show my horse in lower-level dressage events. In a short time, I discovered that I was becoming absolutely fascinated by the art of dressage.

Dressage itself is a French word that simply means "training." The origin of classical horsemanship goes back more than two thousand years. Greek warriors trained their horses so that they would be supple and maneuverable in battle. The earliest surviving treatises on dressage were written by Xenophon, a great Greek general who employed what we would now call dressage training techniques to improve the performance of his horses in battle.

There is no exact equivalent for the word *dressage* in the English language. Dressage is the deliberate, gymnastic training of the horse over a long period of time, making use of the horse's natural movements and gaits, so that the horse becomes highly trained, agile, and extremely strong while still maintaining the beauty and flexibility that one sees in the natural movements of animals loose in the field. Dressage is a joining together of horse and rider. It is not just that horse and rider work together physically, but a meeting of minds must take place if the training is to be successful. Part of the attraction of dressage is that it produces and depends on such intimate and thorough communication between horse and rider.

The Romans did not have much use for this approach to horsemanship, and during the Dark Ages, the art of dressage was almost completely lost. The armor worn by knights was so heavy that it was impossible for the horses to maneuver with agility. What was needed for medieval battles were sturdy horses that could move in a straight line carrying their knights into combat. The subtlety of dressage was useless in these situations.

During the Renaissance, beginning in the fifteenth century, dressage flourished once again. It was rediscovered in Italy, where the first riding academy in Europe dedicated to the classical art of horsemanship was opened in 1532 in Naples. Noblemen came from all over the continent to learn the discipline of riding, and it soon spread to France, Spain, Germany, and England. It became the fashion to have a small dressage arena attached to all the major courts and noble households of Europe. The Spanish Riding School in Vienna, which Rinpoche and I had visited together in 1975, is the premier example of the classical approach to dressage that developed during the Renaissance. It was built in 1735 as the manège, or arena, attached to the Hapsburg Palace in Vienna, but the school itself predates the building by almost two hundred years, making it the oldest school of dressage still functioning today. Archduke Maximilian, son of emperor Ferdinand I, introduced Spanish horses in Austria in the sixteenth century. The first Spanish horses were given to the Hapsburg family as part of a dowry. They were interbred with local horses at Lippiza, producing the distinct Lippizan breed. It is the stallions from this breed that are used exclusively in the Spanish Riding School.

As I pursued my novice training and learned more about the history of dressage, I felt that I was making a link to a noble discipline, which I wanted to thoroughly explore and master. At a time in my life that was difficult, with the painful realization of the situation with Taggie, it was extremely helpful to have this growing connection to something so uplifted and profound.

Around this time, I purchased a thoroughbred stallion, which we named Vajra Dance. He was from the bloodlines of a famous racehorse named Native Dancer. Vajra Dance had apparently been purchased by a syndicate for a large amount of money. He was competed on the racetrack circuit, but he turned out to be very slow. Then he fractured his sesamoid bone in his left front leg and had to be retired from racing. He was sold for very little to a gentleman living in Sonoma County, California, who gave the horse some training, and the horse had shown an aptitude for dressage. I purchased him to upgrade to a better mount, one that would be more appropriate for dressage competition. I brought the horse back to Colorado, and working with Haze and in clinics with Charles, I learned to ride many dressage movements on him.

When Rinpoche and I visited the Spanish Riding School in Vienna, it spurred me on to involve myself more deeply in my training. Around this time, Charles de Kunffy told me that he felt that I had natural talent and feel for the horse, and I began to sense that this might be the case. I became increasingly committed to fully pursuing the discipline of dressage.

After Taggie left for Karme Chöling, I looked into spending an extended period of time studying with Charles. He was headquartered in northern California, where he had been teaching riding at a school for gifted children, and he invited me to come out and work with him. At that point I felt it was impossible for my riding to progress beyond a certain point with the limited resources in Colorado. I discussed this with Rinpoche, telling him that I felt that I was not going to be able to get fully trained riding three times a week at Hidden Valley Ranch. Rinpoche was quite encouraging. He was traveling a great deal and understood that I needed to pursue my own discipline. He supported my need to develop myself in this way.

Dressage was just starting to be appreciated and practiced in the United States at this time, so it was difficult to find a qualified teacher. I went out for two months to train with Charles. Initially, I brought Gesar with me, but the child-care arrangements were very complicated there, so after a few weeks, I sent him back to Boulder. We arranged for a nanny to help care for him in Boulder while I was gone.

I dove into the riding situation in California, and it was a very healing time for me. I spent all day at the barn, and with Charles giving me instruction, I was able to make quite good progress in my riding.

At the end of the two months, I returned home and continued riding on my own. In late February 1976, Rinpoche and I went to Mexico on holiday, accompanied by John and Karen Roper. John was a lawyer and a member of the Vajradhatu board of directors. This time, we went to the village of Pátzcuaro, a charming town on the edge of Lake Pátzcuaro, several hours south of Guadalajara. Louise and Roger Randolph, students of Rinpoche's from Oklahoma, owned a small vacation house there, with a beautiful walled garden and several other cottages on the property. They were very generous to Rinpoche and me—and to the Buddhist community as a whole. Earlier, Roger had donated a large parcel of land in southern Colorado to be used as a retreat center. Rinpoche named it Dorje Khyung Dzong, after the retreat center at his monastery in Tibet where he had spent so much time as a young man.

Roger and Louise gave us the use of their house in Mexico many times. On this, our first trip there, we had a delightful holiday. Rinpoche liked to go to the open market in Pátzcuaro to buy food for dinner. You also could bargain for beautiful copper plates and bowls there, which were locally made. We sometimes went to a hotel on the main square for dinner. They served a soup there that Rinpoche loved, called Sopa Tarasca, named I believe after the Tarascan Indians whose capital was located on the shores of Lake Pátzcuaro. Apparently the recipe was created originally around 1960 by one of the chefs in the area. The tomato broth has a dark chili added to it that gives it a smoky flavor, and pieces of tortilla are broken up and put into the broth.

I brought along my saddle from home, thinking that I would be able to go riding in the village. John Roper thought this was ludicrous and that it was a complete waste of energy to haul the saddle around with us. However, I found a stable near the house and was indeed able to ride almost every day.

When we returned from Mexico, Rinpoche jumped back into teaching and traveling. He was also busy making preparations for the arrival later that spring of His Holiness Dilgo Khyentse Rinpoche, with whom he had a heart connection from their time together in Tibet and later in India.[2]

Back in Boulder, I found myself unsatisfied with my riding regimen. I wanted to devote myself to dressage and training myself as a rider during this period of my life, in addition to being a mother and wife. I told Rinpoche that I was interested in moving to California to study with Charles for a year or two. I could take Gesar with me, and we could come home for extended visits as often as possible. Initially, Rinpoche was a bit shocked, and he seemed conflicted about whether it was a good idea, as was I in some respects. It was not common for a woman with young children to do something like this in this era. Perhaps it would not seem so extreme today. However, I felt it was the right thing for me to do. Rinpoche said, "I'm going to lose my wife if you do this." I replied, "No, it's not a question of you losing your wife. I just want to get proper training. You're traveling so much these days that I don't need to stay here all the time. I need an opportunity to realize *my* discipline to the fullest potential." I told him that if I wasn't able to pursue the discipline 100 percent, I was going to give it up. I wasn't going to do this unless I could do it properly and completely. After we discussed the situation for a while, he said, "Sweetheart, if this is what you need to do, it's fine. Go ahead." From that time onward, he was completely supportive.

Within quite a short period of time, I had rented a house in Lafayette, California, near Walnut Creek, and Gesar and I moved there. He went to preschool in the neighborhood, and I found a stable near the house where I could keep Vajra Dance. Charles came several times a week to give me riding lessons, and I was able to work with the horse myself on the other days.

Somewhat to my surprise, although I missed Rinpoche, I felt very satisfied having my own life and my own household in California. In a certain way, it felt as though a cloud had been lifted in my life. I didn't feel that there was a problem in my marriage or my relationship with Rinpoche, but I did feel that it was almost impossible for me to have any kind of settled life in Boulder. It was so difficult to raise a family in the midst of everything that was happening there, and it was even more difficult when nobody outside of the family seemed to appreciate how hard it was.

In that era in Boulder I did have some close friends as well as my relationship with Rinpoche to sustain me, but that was not always enough. There was another side to my relationship with people in the Buddhist community. At times, there was an element of jealousy toward me on the part of some of Rinpoche's students. I was married to him, and in some ways, as his wife, I was the closest person to him. People were extremely hungry for the teachings, and sometimes I appeared to stand in the way of their unfettered access to my husband. I was often complacent about this because I felt content in my life with Rinpoche, so I was able to relax, have my family, and ignore a lot of things. The early seventies was my time to have my family and my children with him. At the same time, there was a growing dichotomy between Rinpoche's role as a teacher and his role as my husband and the father of our children. This became most apparent at the time that Taggie left our household. I wanted something, a commitment of time, from Rinpoche in the domestic realm, and I could have almost nothing. This was frustrating.

But, at the same time, I didn't develop my riding career out of a conscious desire to get away. I simply became fascinated by dressage and I loved horses. But studying dressage did allow me to develop my own space and my own life. I think, to tell you the truth, that pursuing my own profession was the only way that our marriage was able to survive. On the one hand, there was the unconditional nature of our love and our relationship. On the other hand, to a very great extent, Rinpoche belonged to his students. He belonged to the dharma. There was never a question about that. I had to make peace with it.

Once Rinpoche understood the genuine nature of my commitment to riding, he encouraged my independence and helped me to grow with my own discipline. He was incredibly supportive, and he never complained again about my being away because of my riding career. He didn't seem threatened by it or concerned. His encouragement helped me to find the sense of freedom and enjoyment at this time in my life. I was still so, so sad about Taggie. I dreamed about him a great deal. But I began to move forward and to put my life back together.

I was barely settled in the house in Lafayette when Khyentse Rinpoche arrived at the end of April for a two-week visit to the Bay Area. He had already been in New York and was going on to Boulder after he left California. Rinpoche had told me stories about him for many years, and I was aware that he held him in the highest esteem. I would say that Rinpoche had a bit of a spiritual love affair with Khyentse Rinpoche. When you saw the two of them together, they seemed extremely close.

Interestingly, His Holiness Khyentse Rinpoche and his party arrived in Berkeley before Rinpoche did. He had already greeted His Holiness in New York and spent time with him there, and he was committed to teaching a seminar at Karme Chöling before coming out to Berkeley. I think it was very telling that he let other people do the advance work for His Holiness's visit. Rinpoche felt that his students could greet Khyentse Rinpoche and host him properly until he arrived. This was a measure of how much trust he put in his students and how far he felt they had come in just a few years.

After the Karmapa's visit in 1974, Rinpoche kept certain organizational features of that visit intact. For one thing, he felt that the students who had provided security for the Karmapa's visit and had been his drivers were both benefiting from this discipline and also creating a strong container in which the teachings of the Buddha could be presented with proper respect for and recognition of their power. Rinpoche originally gave the name Dorje Kusung, or "*vajra* body protectors," to this group. Later, they became known as the Dorje Kasung, which means the "protectors or guardians of the command or the sacred word"—

which refers to the Buddhist teachings. He asked several people to assume leadership roles within this new organization in Boulder, and he charged them with protecting the physical space at Dorje Dzong (the name he gave our national headquarters in Boulder) and with protecting and serving himself and his family, as well as visiting teachers. He also began to develop local chapters of the Dorje Kasung in other centers. Wherever Rinpoche taught, after His Holiness Karmapa's visit, members of the Dorje Kasung were present as his personal guards, or guardians, and they also created a sense of boundary when he taught, positioning themselves in various parts of the shrine room where he was speaking. Some people found the presence of the Dorje Kasung threatening, and they mistakenly thought that either these people were armed, which was ridiculous, or that they were trained to be aggressors. In fact, their function was much more as peacekeepers. There would be more developments in this realm as time went along.

In 1976, when Dilgo Khyentse Rinpoche arrived, members of the Dorje Kasung provided service to him and his party and also to Rinpoche and our family. Once again, they put together the motorcades for the visit, as they had done for the Karmapa, and they were on duty in His Holiness's household as well as at Rinpoche's house. When His Holiness was scheduled to be at the center in Berkeley or San Francisco, the Dorje Kasung would drive him there, greet him at the door, and provide an unobtrusive presence in the hall where he spoke or conducted a ceremony.

To prepare for Khyentse Rinpoche's visit, Rinpoche sent out several students as an advance team, including Michael Root and Tom Rich. At this time, Rinpoche had made an announcement to the Vajradhatu staff in Boulder that Tom Rich would be empowered in the summer of 1976 as his regent. This was still supposed to be a secret, but gossip has always traveled fast in our community, and most people were aware that Tom Rich was going to play a very important role in the future of Rinpoche's teaching.

My house was about a thirty-minute drive from the Berkeley dharmadhatu, where Khyentse Rinpoche would be teaching. It was not feasible for Rinpoche to stay with me throughout the whole visit since he had many events to attend or conduct in Berkeley and San Francisco. The members of the dharmadhatu rented a nice house for him in the

Berkeley Hills. I sometimes stayed with him there, and he spent time at my house in Lafayette.

Part of the preparations centered on transforming the home of Sam and Hazel Bercholz into a residence for Khyentse Rinpoche. They had generously offered the use of their house for this purpose. Once again, as had been done for His Holiness the Karmapa, walls were covered in satin, brocades put on chairs and made into bedspreads, shrines constructed and installed. People were now becoming a little more familiar with this approach to hosting a Tibetan teacher, and although it was a huge undertaking, it went fairly smoothly. Once Khyentse Rinpoche arrived, Ani Pema Chödrön (now the resident teacher at Gampo Abbey and the best-selling author of many books on Buddhism) was among a group of students who often served at His Holiness's residence in Berkeley Hills. She had taken her ordination as a novice nun in 1974 and was one of very few Western monastics in our community at this time. She was very cheerful and always willing to help with things around the house. This is the first time I that I can remember meeting Pema.

There were also many preparations at the Berkeley dharmadhatu. More shocking to people was that Michael and Tom also wanted Rinpoche's rented house to be dolled up a great deal.

It was one thing to make all this fuss for His Holiness Dilgo Khyentse Rinpoche, but why did my husband need such fancy accommodations? No one suggested satin, but Michael and Tom made it clear that the house's weary couches and slightly broken-down, overstuffed chairs wouldn't do, nor would it work to use its Indian bedspreads on either the bed or the walls. Furniture was borrowed and rented, floors scrubbed, art borrowed and hung on the walls, and the house was transformed from a middle-class intellectual's frumpy home to something of another order.

The idea was also introduced that Rinpoche would be dining more formally, and that good china, silver, and crystal were needed for his household. Jacquie Giorgi, a woman in the dharmadhatu, had been given Lenox china and silver as wedding gifts, and she agreed to loan everything. Inexpensive crystal glasses were purchased, along with a set of Oriental dishes for Japanese and Chinese food service. People were invited to sign up to serve meals at Rinpoche's residence and to help out around the house in other ways.

I myself was a bit surprised by all this, watching it at a distance, since

Rinpoche and I had never lived this way in Boulder. Apparently this experiment had gotten under way in New York the previous month when Rinpoche was there to teach several seminars and host His Holiness. Rinpoche stayed in an elegant apartment in Manhattan, and his household had been much more elaborate than anyone remembered from the past. Rinpoche seemed to be taking another leap or embarking on yet another path, putting together the beginnings of what would soon become the Kalapa Court, as our home was known from the summer of 1976 on.

As the date for Khyentse Rinpoche's arrival loomed, it was clear that His Holiness's household would not be ready in time. I volunteered to have him stay at my house for several days while the transformation of his residence was completed. On the day of Khyentse Rinpoche's arrival, Gesar and I drove with people from the dharmadhatu to the airport. Sam and Hazel were in the welcoming party from the dharmadhatu, along with Tom Rich, David Rome, Michael Root, and others representing Vajradhatu. We all greeted His Holiness as he stepped off the plane at the San Francisco airport. A tall, stately gentleman with penetrating eyes and a huge smile, Khyentse Rinpoche traveled in robes, but they were layman's robes since he was a married lama. His wife had stayed behind in Bhutan. He was accompanied by his daughter, Chime Wangmo, his grandson Rapjam Rinpoche, and several other attendants. His bearing and presence were noble. He beamed, and people melted around him. I felt immediately drawn to him.

After a welcoming ceremony at the Berkeley dharmadhatu, His Holiness was driven to my house in Lafayette. I gave him Gesar's bedroom, and Gesar and I slept together in my bedroom across the hall. His daughter and grandson were put up somewhere else, as my house was simply too small for all of them. With Khyentse Rinpoche came an entourage of drivers, attendants, cooks, and other dharmadhatu members. I made *momos* for His Holiness, which are Tibetan dumplings that Rinpoche had taught me how to prepare. They are a great favorite with Tibetans and quite delicious. The newly trained servers brought the food out to us with shaking hands. His Holiness took it all in stride. I think he would have been happy with a simple family-style meal, but he graciously accepted the awkward pomp and circumstance that was offered.

For the remainder of the time that he stayed with me, the hordes were banished. His Holiness had his translator, Tulku Pema Wangyal Rinpoche, stay with him so that he could communicate with me. We provided a single Dorje Kasung member and driver to help out at the house. Everyone else cleared out, so it was a quiet and delightful time for me being in the presence of this greatly accomplished teacher.

The day after Khyentse Rinpoche arrived, I invited him to come to the stables with me, and he spent several hours watching me ride. He loved the horses, and seemed to enjoy himself. He came out to the stables several times. When I think about it now, realizing what a truly great man His Holiness was, I marvel how I took the whole situation for granted.

One morning while he was staying in the house, I came out of my bedroom, and His Holiness and his attendant were sitting cross-legged on the floor in the narrow corridor between the two bedrooms. He motioned me to sit down across from him. I came and sat down on the floor near him. He was sitting in front of a little heating grate. I sat on the other side of the grate. After a little while, through his translator he said to me, "I'm sorry. I have to give you some difficult news." I inquired, "What is it?" He said, "I had a dream last night. Your son Gesar is the incarnation of Sechen Kongtrul." Then he said, "I know this may be very difficult for you, but this is my dream, and we should enthrone him right away."

I have to say I was somewhat shocked. He was telling me that Gesar was the reincarnation of my husband's own teacher, Jamgön Kongtrül of Sechen, who had died in prison in Tibet around 1960. Somehow, being in Khyentse Rinpoche's presence, I was able to accept what he was saying and to take it in stride. Like Rinpoche, he commanded the space in such a way that you felt completely at ease and able to set aside normal, habitual patterns and reactions to things, at least for a while. So I just took this in, and we proceeded to talk about the plans for how to accomplish the enthronement ceremony in Berkeley.

As soon as I could, I excused myself and phoned Rinpoche with this news. He also seemed to take it as somewhat matter-of-fact, and he seemed quite pleased and excited. We talked about having the enthronement ceremony as soon as possible, within the next few days, as soon as possible after Rinpoche's arrival from the East Coast.

Then, of course, I had to break the news to Gesar. He also seemed to think it was a fine idea, although I wasn't sure if he understood what I was telling him. He was barely three at the time. Much later, he told me that as a child he had many memories of life in Tibet, so I think he had always sensed something and now it was making sense to him why he had these sorts of flashbacks.

One thing that was curious was that Rinpoche had scheduled a public seminar to be held in Berkeley on the weekend right after His Holiness left for Boulder. It had been entitled—months in advance— "Empowerment." This seemed remarkably synchronistic.

A date for Gesar's enthronement was set, and the next day His Holiness moved to his own residence in Berkeley, where he was joined by his daughter Chime and his grandson Rapjam Rinpoche. His Holiness was already scheduled to conduct several public ceremonies for the members of the dharmadhatu. It was decided that a few days following those ceremonies, he would enthrone Gesar as Jamgön Kongtrül of Sechen.

About a year earlier, the dharmadhatu had moved into the second floor of an office building in downtown Berkeley that was owned by the Odd Fellows of Berkeley, a group somewhat like the Freemasons. In fact, it was their headquarters. They still kept one or two offices and a large hall for their own ceremonies, but they leased us a smaller hall, which held about 150 people. The Berkeley center is still in that space today.

Throughout Khyentse Rinpoche's visit, I was trying to juggle my commitments in the riding world with the events in the Buddhist world. One day I drove up to Santa Rosa, which was about two hours north, to look at a horse that I was interested in buying. I had to speed back to get to the dharmadhatu in time for a ceremony that afternoon. I have always been an absolutely wild driver. I was driving my truck, a silver Dodge Ram Charger, and going at least ninety miles per hour. Suddenly I saw lights flashing in my rearview mirror, and I realized that I was about to get pulled over by the police. I was afraid that I would get a big ticket and certainly be very late for the events in Berkeley. So I started braking and putting my other foot on the gas at the same time, to make the truck's movements look very erratic. Then I leaned down and pulled off the gas pedal.

In that truck there were two buttons that attached the pedal to the base. It had come loose before, so I knew about this. Then I pulled over and stopped, obtrusively holding the pedal in one hand. When the state trooper approached the car, he looked quite stern. I pretended to be completely hysterical. I told him the gas pedal had jammed, so that the only way I could stop the truck was to pull it off. I kept saying, "I thought I was going to die! I thought I was going to die!" I threw myself on the steering wheel. The trooper was quite concerned, and he was incredibly nice to me. He said, "Please calm down. Everything's going to be okay. Don't worry. I'm going to help you." Then he asked me if I thought I could drive, and I told him I thought I'd be okay. I didn't want him to see how easy it would be to reconnect the gas pedal, so we tried controlling the gas pedal by pushing on the little metal thing on the end, and it seemed to work okay. He said, "Okay, I'll lead you to the nearest gas station, and they can help you there." When we got to a gas station, I waited for him to leave, and then I put the gas pedal back on and took off. I arrived just in time for the beginning of the event.

To prepare for Gesar's enthronement ceremony, some women in the dharmadhatu who had experience sewing had made him a tiny set of Tibetan monastic robes to wear. A small throne was hastily constructed for the ceremony, from plywood covered in cotton batting, topped with satin and brocades.

Gesar had to have his hair cut short for the ceremony. Rinpoche told me that I didn't have to shave his head, but I made such a mess of his hair when I tried to cut it that we ended up shaving it anyway. When he returned to preschool after this event, some of the children teased him about his bald head, but he didn't take much notice.

I might have worried that something terrible would happen to Gesar, based on the experience with Taggie, but I didn't really believe that *tulku* disease was the source of Taggie's problems. I knew that Gesar was a strong individual who could handle whatever came along. Rinpoche and I both felt that he would be fine. When Rinpoche got to town, he stayed out at the house in Lafayette with us for several nights so that we could all be together and adjust to His Holiness's recognition of our second son as a *tulku*. While Rinpoche was there, he came to the stables, where he met Charles de Kunffy for the first time. He had wanted to meet the man for whom I had moved to California. Charles was completely taken with Rinpoche and wanted to visit him in Berkeley at the first opportunity.

The day of his enthronement, Gesar and I were driven by members of the Dorje Kasung to the dharmadhatu in Berkeley. He was dressed in his little monks' robes, and he looked adorable, I must say. He was beaming the entire time. When we got there, His Holiness was on a throne in the shrine hall, already making preparations. Rinpoche had also arrived ahead of us, having come from his house in Berkeley. There were several hundred members of the dharmadhatu assembled in the shrine room. When we got to the entrance of the meditation hall, everyone stood up and Gesar walked in, very much a little gentleman, with me right behind him. He sat on his little throne and I sat in a chair next to him for most of the ceremony. At one point when he became restless, I had to sit up on the throne and he sat on my lap. Rinpoche was seated on a chair next to the thrones for His Holiness and Gesar. Rinpoche looked incredibly happy throughout the whole thing. Ösel was also there to witness the enthronement. He was in boarding school at the Ojai Valley School near Santa Barbara at this time, a school founded on the teachings of Krishnamurti and Rudolf Steiner. He was maturing into a much more confident and outgoing young man.

The enthronement of a reincarnate teacher is a traditional ceremony. His Holiness performed the liturgy in Tibetan, with a translator explaining to all of us what Khyentse Rinpoche was doing and saying. He presented Gesar with certain ritual objects, and he gave him a series of blessings and empowerments. To keep him quiet during the whole thing, His Holiness would lean over and feed Gesar candies. He had quite a supply with him to dole out! I also had a stash of sweets in case more were needed. His Holiness also gave a talk about the relationship between the Kongtrüls and the Trungpa *tulkus* and how they had been close during each generation, with one being the teacher to the next, and vice versa, as new generations were born. At the end of the ceremony, everyone was invited to come up and present a white scarf to His Holiness and another to Gesar as an offering, and Gesar blessed everyone by putting his hand on their heads, which is also traditional. Rinpoche and I were the first ones to offer scarves and receive our son's blessing. Then everyone else filed up. Gesar behaved magnificently during all of these proceedings, and he seemed to take to the whole situation quite naturally. Of course, children love attention, and he was definitely the center of attention that day!

The day after the enthronement, Khyentse Rinpoche departed from the San Francisco airport. Everyone had been deeply affected by his visit and by his extraordinary presence, so it was a touchingly sad good-bye for us all. We felt that in meeting him we were meeting the heart of the Tibetan tradition in which Rinpoche had been raised, and to have that coming so personally into our lives was very moving.

For the next several weeks, Rinpoche was teaching a lecture series at the Berkeley dharmadhatu. One night I went out to a club in San Francisco with Charles and Rod, a good friend of his. Around eleven o'clock I suggested that we drop in on Rinpoche. Charles was worried that Rinpoche would have already gone to sleep, but I assured him this was extremely unlikely. So we dropped by, without any notice. When we got there, Rinpoche was sitting in the living room, impeccably dressed in a suit, surrounded by a group of about a dozen students who were also very well dressed. They were having drinks before sitting down to a formal dinner. Rinpoche was delighted to see us and insisted that we stay for dinner.

We sat down to a lavish meal in the dining room. There was an exquisite linen tablecloth and beautiful linen napkins, and the food was served on the very nice Lenox china that was on loan. In the middle of the table was a large ornate silver candelabra. There were five or six servers, who served each course, kept the wine flowing, and cleared our plates from one course to the next. Charles couldn't believe that Rinpoche ate like this every night. I couldn't believe it either, but I didn't let on that this was any different than a typical night in our household had ever been.

Charles was enchanted. As the evening progressed, I could see that Rinpoche had a few designs on Charles. He wanted to know everything about Charles's riding background. Rinpoche also started to intimate that Charles might make a very successful career in Colorado by starting a school there with me. I realized that he had my interests at heart—wanting to see my career go forward and wanting me to connect with powerful people in the dressage world—and also that he might have an idea about how to bring his wife back to Colorado at some time in the future!

Throughout the month, Rinpoche continued to court Charles, and Charles remained absolutely enamored of Rinpoche. At the very end of the month, just before Rinpoche went to Santa Cruz, he invited Charles, Rod, and me for a banquet at the house. During this month, Rinpoche had Max King, one of his students who was an excellent Chinese cook, preparing all of his meals. Rinpoche arranged for Max to make a roast suckling pig for the banquet. Max had never cooked a whole animal like this before, but he consulted a number of chefs and was able to make a delicious meal that was also magnificently presented at the dinner table. Charles was absolutely beside himself. He was a pretty sybaritic individual, and Rinpoche really got to him with the roast suckling pig. It was beyond the beyond of what he could imagine someone doing in their own home. I must say it was quite a tour de force on Rinpoche's part.

At the end of the month Rinpoche returned to Boulder, and I stayed on in Lafayette. Around this time, Pat Cate joined our household as Gesar's nanny. She was the mother of Kelsey, the child who had tragically died at the 1975 seminary. Kelsey had been her only child, and she was still very much in mourning for him. I saw her at one of the events at the dharmadhatu in Berkeley, and I could feel her pain. My heart went out to her. I particularly sympathized with her because of my feelings for Taggie. Rinpoche and I talked about it, and he thought it would be a good thing for her to be part of a family and to have some positive contact with a young child. I invited her to live with me and help with Gesar. She stayed with us on and off for a number of years. When she remarried, her husband, Tom Adducci, also joined the household.

Pat became quite involved in our life day to day. I remember that once she had to break up a terrible fight between Gesar and me. I put him to bed at the end of a particularly trying day, but he absolutely would not stay down. He kept getting up while Pat and I were trying to have dinner. Finally, I said, "If you get up one more time, I'm going to spank you." He got up again, and I swatted him. Gesar being Gesar, he hit me back. He was absolutely indomitable, even at that age. He was just three years old, and I couldn't control him at all, even with physical force. We really started going at it, and Pat had to separate us. She put Gesar to bed, and I stayed out of it.

Gesar was strong willed from day one, and becoming a *tulku* didn't put a dent in that. He could be quite naughty at times. Gesar was terribly cute, but he was a wild man at that age. At the house in Lafayette, I received a new checkbook in the mail one day. Gesar woke up in the wee hours of the morning and ripped all the checks out and laid them on the living room floor. He then took paints from his room and proceeded to paint not only the checks but the whole carpet in the living room of our rental house. Perhaps this was the first sign that he had inherited some of his father's artistic talent, but I didn't appreciate what he had done at all.

During the summer, I took Gesar to Boulder with me to see Rinpoche for a few weeks. While I was home, Rinpoche invited Charles to come for a visit as well. Rinpoche definitely was still courting Charles and pushing the idea that he should start a dressage academy in Boulder. Charles, however, resisted. He wanted to remain in California and wasn't ready to make such a big move. He had just invested in property in southern California, where he hoped to have a successful training school. I also think he was a little intimidated by Rinpoche and the scene around him, and not sure what he would be getting into if he moved to Colorado.

At the end of the summer, when I went back to California to continue my dressage training, Gesar and I moved down to Charles's property in Hesperia, which was in the high desert in southern California. Charles had recently opened his school there, where he felt he could do more intensive training of both horses and riders. I only stayed for a short period of time, a matter of months, because I was becoming increasingly frustrated with my riding. I was training intensely, but I wasn't getting the scores that I wanted in competition. I began to feel that there were major holes in my training. I was already competing Vajra Dance at the upper or international levels of dressage, having worked very hard on his training. Still, although the horse was showing at these levels, I didn't feel that my own training was anywhere near complete. Charles would tell me that I shouldn't be so fixated on my scores. However, I felt that they were reflective of my ability and knowledge.

I knew that something was missing. On an ongoing basis I was not scoring nearly as high as I should, based on the time and effort I was putting in and the feedback I was getting from Charles. When I didn't do well in an event and was upset, Charles would just say to me, "Well, a lady would come back after not doing well at a show, have a glass of sherry, and forget about it."

Over time, considerable tension developed between Charles and me about my training. Nevertheless, I enjoyed spending time with him, and I valued his help. I also felt obligated to help him build up his school. He became concerned about being able to make the mortgage payments on the property because it turned out that not enough people were willing to study with him in that remote desert location. He became very stressed out and developed high blood pressure. We continued to have serious disagreements. Finally, I reached a decision that I couldn't get the training that I needed in this situation. I decided to return home to Boulder for a while until I could sort out what the next step for my dressage career might be.

ELEVEN

In the Summer of 1976, Gesar and I returned to Boulder to visit Rinpoche, who had just moved into town from Boulder Heights. Later that year, we would move into our new home on Mapleton Hill. While the new house was being renovated, Rinpoche was living in a rental at the corner of Seventh Street and Aurora, in an area of Boulder called "the Hill." The house had been owned by Scott Carpenter, who made the second manned spaceflight orbiting the earth in 1962. He named his spacecraft Aurora 7—based on the address of his house in Boulder. Rinpoche referred to the house as Aurora 7 in several poems that he wrote that summer.

Rinpoche had asked one of his students, John Perks, to help him put together a household at Aurora 7 modeled, somewhat loosely, on an English court or perhaps the house of an English lord. John himself was English, and he had been a footman and a bar boy in England, so he had a background in English service. More than that, however, he had a great flair for the theatrical and for large, somewhat ostentatious undertakings. He had also worked in several alternative schools in America and taught experiential education at Naropa Institute in 1974 and 1975. John was a colorful character and the perfect person to help

Rinpoche create the Kalapa Court. For the next five years, John was intimately involved in Rinpoche's life and in the life of our family. He was immensely helpful and loyal. However, in the 1980s, around the time that His Holiness the Karmapa passed away, John found it difficult to continue working with Rinpoche at the Court. Problems developed, and finally Rinpoche had to ask John to stop teaching and doing certain other things, which had gotten out of hand, and Johnnie moved away from Boulder and psychologically distanced himself from us.

In this era, however, he was very much in tune with what Rinpoche wanted to do. Together they were creating an uplifted household atmosphere where many of Rinpoche's students could have direct contact with him by being involved in various areas of our domestic life. John became Rinpoche's butler and the head of his household. Now that I was not planning to live in Boulder year-round, Rinpoche had the freedom to expand the household and to invite more and more people in. He didn't have to worry as much about my reaction to all of that, and frankly, for short periods of time, I found it quite bearable, enjoyable, and often entertaining. It was theater and pageantry, and I could also see that it was good training in mindfulness and devotion for Rinpoche's students.

The Court approach was certainly influenced by the success of the households that were organized for His Holiness the Karmapa, Dilgo Khyentse Rinpoche, and other major Tibetan teachers. Rinpoche's students loved having this kind of intimate contact with a teacher's everyday life, and it was quite natural to begin to extend that model to Rinpoche. He still was working with somewhat of a corporate model in terms of his office and office staff, but on the home front, the nearest Western model on which to base a Shambhala household seemed to be the courts of European monarchs, with a touch of Asia thrown in the mix. I suppose that if he wanted a more homegrown approach, Rinpoche could have suggested organizing his life around the model of the American White House, which is really another take on a European court, but he was not attracted to this bastion of democracy as a role model for himself or his students.

The situation at the Aurora 7 house was a bit toned down from the more elaborate scenes that would develop at the Court on Mapleton Avenue in the fall. Rinpoche and John were still experimenting with how to set the whole thing up. Rinpoche had asked Max King to come out from California and be his cook. I think Max was the first full-time cook we had. During the month he spent in California, Rinpoche had been very impressed with Max's talent as a chef and had started calling him "Cookie Divine." Cookie Divine was also a graduate student getting his Ph.D. in psychology, but he put that aspect of his life aside to move to Boulder to cook for Rinpoche.

With Max able to cook almost any meal from the Oriental or Western repertoire that Rinpoche might desire, it was a small step to organizing many dinner parties and setting up a rota for kitchen assistants, servers, and dishwashers. People signed up for these jobs because they got to hang out at the house and witness what unfolded, and on many occasions, Rinpoche would draw them into the action in some way or other. When he met somebody, he instantly connected with them, and he never forgot a face. This I think was because he wasn't just superficially getting to know people, but instantaneously he could see into the deepest parts of a person. A server at the house might have just a small exchange with him while putting a potato on his plate, but it meant a tremendous amount to him or her. The scene was often playful and magical, I must say.

There were dinners in the backyard served by candlelight. John Perks would direct people to move the dining room table and chairs, plus candelabras and good china, and set a beautiful table on the back patio. Sometimes, Rinpoche would have a bed made up in the backyard and he would sleep out there. Ösel was home for the summer, and he remembers sleeping under the stars in the backyard with his father.

Earlier in the summer, Rinpoche had invited David Rome, who was now his secretary, to move into the house. David had at first resisted the idea. In response, Rinpoche asked some people to go over to David's house while he was out and turn all the furniture in the whole house upside down. When David came home, he could only think of one person who would pull this practical joke, and he took it as a message that he should agree to live in Rinpoche's house.

Starting in New York earlier in the year, Rinpoche had developed some spontaneous theater, shall we say, in connection with taking his evening pill to control his blood pressure. (He had developed high blood pressure in the early 1970s.) This ritual reached new heights that summer. At the end of an evening at Aurora 7, whoever was there when

Rinpoche was getting ready to retire, which often included the servers, would be invited into the living room to witness a spontaneous play. The drama always revolved around Rinpoche taking his medicine. He would speak in what sounded like Japanese, although he didn't know Japanese, and David would tell the audience what he was supposedly saying. The point of the play was that, when Rinpoche would swallow the pill, it was supposed to be committing *seppuku,* or ritual suicide, as in the Japanese samurai films. Instead of using a sword, Rinpoche would die by the pill. When he actually swallowed the pill, he would fall down on the floor, writhing in what seemed like genuine agony, and sometimes a little saliva would leak out of the corner of his mouth. Then he would fall silent, his eyes would roll up in his head, and frankly, he looked like he was dead. Then he would revive himself and laugh heartily about the whole thing. The first time I witnessed this, I thought we should call an ambulance.

This was the kind of thing that went on at the house, and the excitement around such everyday events was why many people wanted to serve at the house. It is a bit like people signing up to usher at the theater so that they can see the show.

I had witnessed early on in our married life that Rinpoche did not like having paid servants, which he considered demeaning to both them and him. He was never comfortable with the hired help that Marty Franco provided to us. The situation at the emerging Court was quite different. Being around Rinpoche in this intimate, everyday environment was really part of what I would call the love affair that so many of his students had with him. It was mutual: Rinpoche loved his students tremendously, each one of them, and he wanted to spend time with so many people up close. Being at the Court was a learning experience for people and a way to express their devotion.

That summer, after Ösel came home from school in Ojai, we decided that he should stay in Boulder permanently with his father and me, when I was there. He had really gotten all that he needed out of the boarding school situation, and Rinpoche wanted to spend time with him and also let him spend more time with friends in Boulder. A few years later, some of Rinpoche's students started a private day school called Vidya School in Boulder, which aimed to provide both a good Western education and an education in Buddhism and meditation for the students. Ösel went to Vidya for several years while he also was pursuing meditation and Buddhist studies directly with his father.

I don't think I realized at this time how far Rinpoche would go with the whole Court idea. In some ways, it was more organized and less chaotic at the Aurora 7 house than our family life had been before. John was extremely sweet and helpful during this era, and there was a measure of privacy for us at this time. David Rome had almost been a member of our family for years anyway, since he had been helping at the house at Boulder Heights and driving Rinpoche to the office and doing all manner of things for him since late 1973. I suppose I also wasn't so heavily invested in the household being a certain way, because I was just visiting with Gesar that summer. At the end of the summer, I was going to be on my way back to California to continue working with Charles.

Naropa Institute was into its third summer, and Rinpoche taught two major seminars there that year. In June, at the first session, Rinpoche taught a seminar on "Viewing and Working With the Phenomenal World," which was an overview of the Buddhist path, and during the second session he taught a seminar on the "Yogic Songs of Milarepa." There were plans to have Naropa expand from a summer institute into a year-round program, offering degree programs in psychology, Buddhist studies, poetry, and other disciplines. Several times a week, Rinpoche taught in the evenings there, and throughout the summer, he was involved in meetings to discuss the expansion of the institute.

One of the reasons that I came back to spend time in Boulder that summer was that my sister Tessa was getting married at the end of July. She was marrying Douglas Penick, who was a delightful man whom Rinpoche and I were both very fond of. She had had a few difficult and unsuccessful relationships, so we were both very happy about her marriage to Douglas. That summer Rinpoche presided over the weddings of many of his oldest and closest students. There must have been a wedding a week. The ceremonies were held in the shrine room at 1111 Pearl Street, and then most of the receptions were in someone's backyard. This was an era in which many people were settling down into long-term relationships and thinking about starting families. Over the next few years, many children were born into the Buddhist community, which is one reason that Vidya School got started. There was also a lot of interest in starting a preschool, and in 1976 Alaya Preschool, started by community members, opened in north Boulder.

A major event that summer was the empowerment of Thomas Rich as the Vajra Regent Ösel Tendzin. The ceremony took place at the end of August in the main shrine room at 1111 Pearl Street, and the hall was packed beyond capacity. More than six hundred people attended. It was a landmark event in the community. Rinpoche decided to hold the Regent's empowerment at the end of a gathering of Vajrayana students, which he called a Vajra Assembly. Students came from all over North America to practice together and to hear Rinpoche lecture on the principles of lineage. The last night, the Regent's empowerment was held. As I mentioned earlier, it was very important to Rinpoche to be able to fully transmit the teachings of his lineage to Westerners. Having a Western regent and dharma heir to preserve his teachings was crucial in his mind. He wanted as many people as possible to witness this event. Everyone had great hopes for the Regent. As part of the ceremony, the Regent took an oath to uphold the Kagyü lineage and the teachings of Buddhism, and he drank what is called oath water, or *samaya* water, to mark taking this oath. This is a common feature of taking on commitments in the Vajrayana path of Buddhism. According to the tradition, if you uphold your oath, the water you drink will be an aid and act almost like a magic potion to enhance your accomplishment. If you break the oath, it is said that the water will turn to molten lead in your veins and destroy you. It is a heavy-handed commitment, to say the least.

Rinpoche was well aware that the Regent needed training and mentoring over a long period of time if he was going to fully step into the role for which he was being groomed. Rinpoche had already been working with the Regent for a number of years, but they both knew that much more was needed. So while Rinpoche expressed his appreciation for what the Regent had already accomplished, Rinpoche also put a great deal of thought into how to work further with his educational process. Rinpoche told me that he wanted Ösel Tendzin and his family to move into the house with us on Mapleton Avenue, the future home of the Kalapa Court. He wanted to have intimate, day-to-day contact with the Regent as part of their work together.

The Regent and Lila had their second son, Anthony, earlier that summer. Rinpoche and I were both at the hospital the night he was born. We were in the waiting room when the Regent came out to say that they had another son and that it had been a difficult birth. The four Riches—the Regent, Lila, Vajra, and Anthony—would be joining Rinpoche, Ösel, Gesar, and me at the Kalapa Court on Mapleton. I didn't see this as a problem at that time. Again, I was planning to be away a fair amount of time each year until my dressage training was completed. I realized that making the decision to pursue my own career was good not only for my discipline, but for my greater sanity, given the expansion of our personal life into a bigger and bigger scene.

Rinpoche also let people know that summer that he was planning to take almost the entire next year, 1977, as a year of retreat. He was going to spend the year in a house near Charlemont, Massachusetts, where he had done other short retreats in the early seventies. Jean-Claude van Itallie, the playwright, had offered Rinpoche the use of the house. Rinpoche was going to take John Perks and Max King into retreat as his staff, and various people would visit throughout the year. However, he would not be teaching at Naropa the following summer, and he was going to turn over the running of the administration to Ösel Tendzin. Rinpoche said, among other things, that by leaving for a year both he and his students would get a much better idea of what had actually been transmitted and where further work was needed. While he was away from Boulder, I didn't expect to spend that much time in town, so for that reason also I was not worried about having other people living in our home. In fact, I thought it would be a good idea if the house were not left empty with both of us away.

At the end of the summer, Rinpoche went to Rocky Mountain Dharma Center and I headed to Charles's new location in southern California. The fourth Vajradhatu Seminary took place that fall in Land O'Lakes, Wisconsin, at the King's Gate Hotel. This year there were close to two hundred students attending the seminary. Rinpoche had a suite of rooms in the hotel that he lived in toward the end of the seminary, but which he initially used mainly to hold meetings and to prepare his talks. His actual residence was a tiny little trailer on a lake about a half-hour's drive from the hotel. Max went to the seminary as Rinpoche's cook and lived in the second bedroom in the trailer. Various people from the seminary would come over to help with the cooking, cleaning, and driving, but Rinpoche had a very modest domestic situation, almost retreatlike in its simplicity.

This seminary was notable in that Rinpoche began to present the Shambhala teachings on warriorship and enlightened society while he was there. During the Vajrayana section of that seminary, he gave a number of teachings about the meaning of Shambhala and its importance for the modern age. Since he had left Tibet in 1959, the only *terma* teaching that he had received was the *Sadhana of Mahamudra,* which he discovered when he did his retreat in Bhutan in 1969. He had found a number of *terma* in Tibet as a young man, but he hadn't received anything else since the experience in Bhutan. At Land O' Lakes, he received the first Shambhala *terma* that he discovered in the West, and this was really a turning point in both the content and the style of his teaching in America.

While he was at Land O' Lakes, Rinpoche first received a symbol of the Shambhala teachings as *terma,* rather than a written teaching. While he was staying in that tiny cabin on the lake, one night he stayed up all night after giving a talk, and sometime before dawn, he started doing calligraphy with large Japanese brushes, using *sumi* ink on white paper. He kept doing the same calligraphy stroke over and over. It didn't have a name, but Rinpoche felt that it meant something important. He shared it with David Rome, who was teaching a course at the seminary, and with a few other students, but he didn't want it generally distributed to anyone. A few days later, a Shambhala text, called the *Golden Sun of the Great East,* arose in his mind. It described the stroke and its significance and gave it a name: the stroke of Ashe. The text talked about how to overcome the spiritual, psychological, and political obstacles and the degeneration of the current era by connecting with human dignity and manifesting the confidence and strength embodied in the Ashe symbol.

About a week later, Rinpoche left the seminary to teach a course at Karme Chöling, and while he was there, he wrote a long commentary on the text he had received. Together, these writings constitute what I would call almost a manual of political and psychological strategy for working with conflict and aggression. This text is often referred to as the "root text," because it is the root of so many Shambhala teachings that Rinpoche transmitted. He felt that only a few of his students were ready to receive these teachings directly at that point, and he and David worked together to decide how to share this material. A few days after

Rinpoche received the stroke of Ashe and the root text, the Vajra Regent visited the seminary, and Rinpoche gave him and a few other people transmission in doing this calligraphy stroke as a practice.

A program of study eventually was developed, called Shambhala Education, to present the groundwork to people so they could understand and apply the teachings in the text. Further Shambhala texts unfolded over the next two years, a whole cycle of Shambhala *terma,* which Rinpoche said came not directly from Padmasambhava, but from Padmasambhava as he manifested in the form of King Gesar of Ling and from the mind of the Rigden kings, the rulers of the Shambhala kingdom. These discoveries would have a huge and intimate effect on our lives, perhaps not so much immediately, but more and more as time went on. The Shambhala teachings became the driving force for Rinpoche in the last ten years of his life.

One of the correlations between the teachings and our personal lives was that this text and all the subsequent texts used the language and the symbolism of monarchy and a royal existence. This is also very much the language that is often used in the Vajrayana Buddhist tradition. Rinpoche talked a great deal about ruling your life as part of the Shambhala teachings. In *Great Eastern Sun: The Wisdom of Shambhala,* he said:

> Royalty in the Shambhala world is not based on creating a Shambhala elite or a class system. In that case, I wouldn't share the Shambhala vision with everybody. I wouldn't be telling you about this at all. I would probably have selected ten or twenty people to hear about the universal monarch who joins heaven and earth rather than discussing this openly. Why should I tell you these things? One of our topics, gentleness and opening up, has something to do with it. Every one of you can join heaven and earth. You could be a king or queen—every one of you. That's the switcheroo, the great switcheroo. That's why the entire vision is shared with everyone. That is a very important point. [1]

He was not referring here to some system of building up confidence in yourself in, say, the fashion of self-improvement or the human potential movement, which he really detested because he felt these approaches make false promises and do not address the fundamental, underlying issues. He was talking about a much more complete process of transformation, by seeing your life as a whole and realizing that you can conquer the obstacles you encounter, not through aggression or bravado but through the application of gentleness, intelligence, and fearlessness—the fundamental qualities of the Shambhala warrior. He truly believed that every human being could do this.

He also felt that the teacher in this situation has to set the example for the students, as is true throughout the Buddhist teachings. In presenting the Shambhala teachings of enlightened society, he felt that his own life should be an example, his life should be an open book, or an open court, I guess. In some way, this had always been true, but clearly this was moving to another level.

As mentioned earlier, in Tibet Rinpoche's teacher Jamgön Kongtrül talked to him about how a monk might have to become a king for the teachings of the Buddha to survive in the modern world. At first, Rinpoche seemed to think that this mainly meant that the presentation of Buddhism in the West would need to be more secular, less monastic. Beginning in this era, however, he began to see this as more literal advice. I think he felt that he was to be a messenger for the Rigden kings as well as their servant; he felt that he had to embody the enlightened energy of Shambhala as best as he could. And the model for that, in terms of everyday life, was the court of the king and queen. Voilà the Kalapa Court. Voilà its occupants: Rinpoche and me.

Previously I mentioned that, around 1974, the people at Karme Chöling had purchased an old farmhouse about a ten-minute drive from the main building for Rinpoche and our family. The name he gave it, Bhumipali Bhavan, means "the dwelling place of the female earth protector." The Sanskrit word *Bhumipali* in Tibetan is *Sakyong Wangmo*. At the 1976 seminary, Rinpoche gave a talk about Bhumipala, the male earth protector, as the guardian of the dharma. He assumed the title of Sakyong, the Tibetan for Bhumipala, within the year. In Tibetan mythology, the Sakyong is the messenger or the representative of the Rigden kings on earth, since they are now supposed to be in a celestial realm. A few years later, Rinpoche and I would both take a formal empowerment as Sakyong and Sakyong Wangmo, or Bhumipala and Bhumipali, depending on whether you use the Tibetan or the Sanskrit. His Holiness Dilgo Khyentse Rinpoche conferred this empowerment on us. But back in 1974, when we were just at the end of living a semihippie life, Rinpoche already was employing the term Bhumipali to refer to me.

He also referred to me as the Sakyong Wangmo in a poem he wrote while I was home in the summer of 1976. He wrote: "She is the only Sakyong Wangmo / . . . She deserves to be coronated in the midst of Shambhala kingdom as the only monarch who exists as Vajra queen." At the time, I didn't pay much attention to these references. Little did I know what was in store for me.

I returned to Boulder in early December 1976, somewhat uncertain about the future of my riding career now that things had fallen apart with Charles. I came home to move into our new home with Rinpoche et al, to spend the holidays together as a family and to give Gesar and myself some time with Rinpoche before he left for his long retreat.

I knew that our new home was to be called the Kalapa Court and I knew that Rinpoche was moving in the direction of a much grander lifestyle that would include many more people being and working in our home, but I wasn't prepared for what I encountered. While Rinpoche was concluding the seminary that fall, John had been busy creating a rather over-the-top courtlike situation to receive him. The house had been furnished in the style of an upper-class English manor house, not unlike what the Ham Manor of my childhood had been like, but with the addition of a lot more brocade. Additionally, there was the influence of an Oriental and often specifically Japanese aesthetic, at this point more in the little touches than in the furniture or layout as a whole. In consultation with Rinpoche, John had arranged for a young couple to join the household staff: Bob Vogler and his fiancée Shari. They had been living at Karme Chöling but moved to Boulder to live and work at the Court. Bob was to be the butler working under John, and Shari was in charge of housekeeping and worked in the kitchen under Max. While Rinpoche was away in 1977, they would be the main staff for the Regent and his family. John also had assembled a cadre of volunteers to serve at the house, and he had created uniforms for them. The women who worked in the kitchen wore red aprons; those serving in the rest of the house wore white aprons with very ostentatious white shoulders over a black dress. We began referring to them as "the penguins." There were people arranging flowers, polishing brass doorknobs, greeting you at the door, taking your coat, bringing you something to drink, setting the table, and performing all manner of household functions.

John, Shari, and Bob all lived in rooms in the basement. On the main floor, there was a library off the large entry hall as well as a living room with a large mantle and fireplace, behind which was the formal dining room. There was a lot of dark wood paneling in this house. The kitchen was also on the main floor. Rinpoche and I had a bedroom with a sitting room upstairs, and Ösel's room was on the second floor. Gesar lived on the top floor with Pat Adducci. It was very good for him that he had the continuity of his relationship with Pat throughout all the changes in our life at this time. The Regent, Lila, and their children had their rooms on the second floor as well. The so-called servants could be found on all floors at all hours of the day and night performing all manner of tasks.

When Rinpoche arrived, he was delighted by the Court, and he immediately began to have receptions, dinners, and other social gatherings at the house, inviting as many members of the *sangha* as he could into our home. You might be invited as a guest one night and return as a servant the next. People were anxious to be around the house as much as possible since this was where people felt it was all "happening" at this time. The word spread that casual dress was out. Men came to dinner in suits and ties; women in cocktail dresses and high heels. The dress code had been changing for some time, but many still looked uncomfortable in their new apparel, with the men's hair shortened, the ladies' carefully coiffed. People also began to practice their table manners before going to dinner at the Court. There were, in fact, classes on both serving and proper guest etiquette offered to members of the *sangha*.

During this period, I had to buy a lot of clothes. I was trying to find a happy medium between frumpy and fashionable, and I bought a black jacket that I thought was attractive. Rinpoche told me, "It's not tailored that well for you." It was the first time that Rinpoche had been critical of my dress. So then I said to John Perks, "Well, don't you think that this looks good?" John replied, "Well, madam, although anything you wear looks wonderful on you, I think that you could have a more tailored jacket." I believe I dumped the jacket and bought something else.

The evening gatherings at the Mapleton Court often led to sessions of calligraphy practice late at night, usually held in the entryway, where Rinpoche would demonstrate the new Shambhala practice and initiate students on the spot. These proceedings usually were accompanied by readings from the new Shambhala text. There were rumors about all this flying throughout the community, and there was tremendous curiosity about the Shambhala teachings that Rinpoche had received and was now beginning to present. In fact, people's curiosity and desire to be included were whetted by the fact that the whole thing was supposed to be a big secret, but everyone had heard something about it.

Rinpoche was, at this stage, introducing people to this new material in small informal gatherings. Within a few months, classes and study groups were organized at Karma Dzong, but for now, most of the transmissions took place at our home. Many nights that December and January, if you drove down Mapleton Avenue, you would see lights blazing at number 550. From the street, you might see a throng of people at three A.M. congregated in the front hallway. I'm sure our neighbors wondered what we were up to. The guests were usually either practicing calligraphy or watching others. As part of this practice, at one point, the person performing the stroke touches the brush to the tip of the tongue. Frequently, especially in the early days, people overdid this part of the practice and ended up with a quantity of black *sumi* ink on their tongue and teeth. Later, if someone smiled at you, he or she often revealed a distinct black stain on the inside of the mouth. It could be a bit ghoulish.

A week before Christmas, the community held the official opening of Dorje Dzong, which means "indestructible fortress." This event marked the community's move into a new building at 1345 Spruce Street, which remains the headquarters in Boulder today. The new location was a three-story stone office building. It was acquired early in 1976, and throughout most of the year, renovations had been going on. The top floor was turned into a beautiful shrine room, with twenty-foot ceilings. The room could hold many more people than the old location, which we had completely outgrown at this point. The *thangka* of the Buddha, which the queen of Bhutan had given to Rinpoche so many years ago, was installed as the centerpiece of the new shrine. On either side of it were banners designed by Rinpoche bearing the logos for Vajradhatu that he had created. A few years later, Rinpoche would invite Sherab Palden Beru to come over from Scotland to paint a huge new *thangka* of the Buddha Vajradhara especially for the shrine room. During his last visit to America, His Holiness the Karmapa placed his handprint in ink on the back of this *thangka* to consecrate this beautiful and powerful image.

On the second floor of the new building, Rinpoche had a suite of offices, called "A Suite," and the Regent was given a suite on the other end of the floor, called "B Suite." Classrooms and other offices were located mainly in the basement and on the main floor. Almost the entire Boulder community attended the opening of the building, which was held in the shrine room. The room was packed. The ceremony was very similar to one held in 1972 to mark the opening of 1111 Pearl Street: Rinpoche lit the candles on the main shrine and then, from one of those candles, he lit another candle which he passed to the Regent, who lit his candle, and then the light was passed from one person to another. Each person was holding a candle, so that by the end, there were close to a thousand lights glimmering in the room.

In late December, at our house, we were preparing to celebrate Christmas. I had always enjoyed this holiday: I loved to have a tree and exchange gifts. Rinpoche was not so keen on Christmas because of its obvious Christian connotations. (Two years later he inaugurated the celebration of Children's Day on the winter solstice as an alternative festival.) However, this year he didn't object to my decorating the house and buying gifts for the children, and we planned to have a nice family Christmas dinner together in our new home.

I had not seen my mother since the day she had recoiled from touching her grandchildren. I had heard stories from my sister that Mother was spending what was left of her funds on private detectives to keep tabs on me. At one point, earlier this year, a story had spread that my mother had taken out a contract on Rinpoche's life. This probably wasn't true, but the danger seemed very real at the time. At one point, the *vajra* guards, the Dorje Kasung, were told to be on alert against this possibility. Frankly, I think Rinpoche probably enjoyed having a threat like this to heighten the awareness of the Dorje Kasung.

In any case, I thought that I might never see my mother again. I certainly had no plans to reconcile with her, especially now that she seemed to be trying to get my husband killed! She had somewhat made peace with Tessa, and to my great surprise, she decided to come to Boulder to have Christmas with Tessa and Douglas. We knew that she was in town, but I planned to ignore her completely.

Then, seemingly out of the blue and certainly not to my liking, Rinpoche announced on Christmas Day that he would like to invite my mother to dinner with Douglas and Tessa. I was astounded. I thought that there was not a chance that she would accept. So I said, "Go ahead."

Rinpoche asked his *kasung* to drive the Mercedes over to Tessa's house, which was only about a five-minute drive from our home. He asked the *kasung* to deliver an invitation to Mrs. Pybus, my mother, to come for Christmas dinner. The *kasung* dutifully went with the invitation, but returned empty-handed. Mrs. Pybus had replied that she would only accept the invitation if Rinpoche would come himself and beg her forgiveness on bended knee for having stolen her daughter away.

Rinpoche was so excited. He was already dressed to the nines for dinner, and he immediately asked for his coat and hat and went off with the driver. He went to Tessa's house, where he went down on his knees and apologized to Mrs. Pybus for taking her daughter and invited her back to Christmas dinner. She was, I think, completely disarmed by his willingness to humble himself in this manner. She accepted the invitation.

They arrived back at the house together, with Tessa and Douglas in tow as well. I was somewhat in shock. Rinpoche, however, was beaming. As you can imagine, my mother was thoroughly impressed with the house, the dinner, the service—the whole thing. It was quite different from our lifestyle a few years earlier. In addition to our family, the Regent and Lila and their family joined us for dinner, and I believe there were several other guests, nicely dressed and on their very best behavior. My mother made charming chitchat with people, and she herself was clearly charmed. She and Rinpoche had a long conversation about the history of European architecture over drinks. By the end of the evening, she was completely won over. Rinpoche sent his car to take her home, the perfect crowning touch.

We saw her almost every day during the rest of her visit in Boulder. She couldn't get enough of Rinpoche or the Court. A few days later, Rinpoche arranged to have a formal reception for her at the fanciest hotel in Boulder, which at this time was the Harvest House. He rented the largest ballroom there, and told all his students to wear formal attire. Women came in long dresses and white gloves; men rented tuxedos. Handel's *Water Music,* which Rinpoche loved, was playing over the sound system as people arrived and were introduced. There was a receiving line where each person was formally presented to Mrs. Pybus, who was clearly being showcased as something equivalent to the Queen Mother in our world. If there was a contract out on Rinpoche, my mother certainly cancelled it at that point. She was utterly enthralled at this point with her son-in-law and the world in which he was living, as well as her potential position in that world.

Rinpoche was enormously pleased with himself for having won her over. That first evening, after she went home from Christmas dinner, we sat up for awhile in the living room talking about what had happened. At one point, he turned to me with a huge smile on his face and said, "If I can conquer your mother, I can conquer the whole world!" At that moment, I had to agree with him. The next day he wrote a poem to celebrate his victory:

The Kalapa Court: Conquering the Pybuses

Big mountains don't apologize to other mountains
All oceans are big oceans
Big mind sweeps away the little chitchat
Genuine surprise disperses dark corners
Proclamation of the lion's roar is different from the mouse's squeak
Seeing through, conquering, accomplishing beyond two nervous
    daughters and their neurosis
Eat big meal
Drink large sake
And solve enormous problem
In the name of the tiger lion *garuda* dragon dignity
My love and gratitude to David Humphrey Pybus

(BOULDER, COLORADO, DECEMBER 26, 1976)[2]

TWELVE

My mother never again complained about my marriage to Rinpoche. He very quickly gave her a sense of position and belonging within the Shambhala world that he was creating. In some sense, it fulfilled her long-held desire to be an important person in society, although not in the society in which she had tried for so long to be accepted. She became very fond of her grandchildren, and seemingly forgot that they were less than lily white. Within a year, she closed up her household in England and moved to Boulder. She remained there until a few years after Rinpoche's death, when she returned to England to receive health care during her final years. Although she and I remained somewhat cool to one another, outwardly we had a fairly good mother-daughter relationship. It was amazing what a complete transformation she underwent. She became a beloved adviser and mentor to many people in the Buddhist community, who looked to her for advice on everything from etiquette to conducting their romantic relationships.

While she was still in Boulder, following her conversion experience over Christmas, Rinpoche invited her to attend the first Shambhala empowerment ceremony that he conducted. This took place at the

Kalapa Court on January 1, 1977. Rinpoche wanted to create a complete court situation, or mandala, and to place his most trusted students in positions of authority within the Shambhala world, not just to hold the seat of the ruler himself. His first court appointment was installing David Rome as the Dorje Kasung, the "indestructible command protector" of Shambhala. I believe that, in making this and other Shambhala appointments, Rinpoche was trying to formulate and put into effect the principles that are important in governing one's life and a society as a whole. The principle of command protector has to do with maintaining order. David used to joke that he was the Sakyong's "top cop." (David used this phrase quite humorously, in a way that made it sound like something from Gilbert and Sullivan.) In his presentation of the Shambhala teachings, Rinpoche said that law and order have to do with the natural hierarchy that exists in the world. He used the four seasons as a good example of this nonvertical sense of order and predictability in life. Rinpoche felt that society should have a similar sense of orderly flow. David's real role was, I think, to point out how to live one's life in accordance with that fundamental order, rather than to police our Shambhala society.

The ceremony was held in the dining room of the Court, which had been completely emptied of its usual furniture. A shrine was set up along one wall of the room and there were meditation cushions on the floor to accommodate the fifty or so guests who were invited to witness the ceremony. Rinpoche and I sat in chairs on either side of the shrine, while David kneeled on a cushion facing us and the shrine. David was asked questions about his understanding of the teachings contained in the *Golden Sun of the Great East* text. Then, as part of the ceremony, he was asked to perform the stroke of Ashe on the spot. As he made the calligraphy stroke, all of those assembled loudly chanted the warrior's victory cry: KI KI SO SO ASHE LHA GYAL LO TAK SENG KHYUNG DRUK DI YAR KYE. This chant invokes the energy of Shambhala and the supreme confidence of the warrior. As part of the ceremony, Rinpoche appointed David to the Order of the Dragon of Shambhala, which Rinpoche created on the spot. The Shambhala text that he was teaching from at this time talks a great deal about the enlightened qualities of the warrior in terms of the tiger, the lion, the *garuda* (a mythical bird like the phoenix), and the dragon. Later, Rinpoche also wrote about these aspects of the Shambhala teachings in *Shambhala: The Sacred Path of the Warrior*. The dragon is associated with inscrutability, which in the Shambhala teachings refers to mind beyond mind, mind that is completely fearless, open, and fathomless rather than the normal connotation of some kind of reticence or sneakiness. Around David's neck, during the ceremony Rinpoche placed a medal he himself was given many years previously, when he received the Order of Bhutan from the Bhutanese royal family. It was not a permanent gift to David. Rinpoche used it during the ceremony in place of the real Order of the Dragon medal that did not yet exist. Rinpoche expected to design and have many Shambhala medals executed in the future. (In fact, some were designed during his retreat in the coming year, and a few were manufactured in England. He designed others that were never actually crafted, including the Order of the Dragon.)

Around this time, Rinpoche had also asked David Rome to assume the leadership of the *vajra* guards. I believe that he chose David for this role in part because he was such a thoroughly gentle person. David abhorred pretense and violence, so I think that Rinpoche felt that David would safeguard the Dorje Kasung situation and ensure that it did not become some sort of paramilitary joke. On the contrary, Rinpoche wanted it to be a vehicle to conquer aggression. I think David was quite challenged by being asked to take on a leadership role in this aspect of Rinpoche's world. But he really did have the strength of mind to be a great general, and he was well respected for his integrity and honesty. In one of several poems that Rinpoche composed to mark this occasion, he wrote:

> Dorje Kasung is genuine general
> He respects the grand lady and her husband
> In brief, Dorje Kasung is the razor knife
> With rubber handle
> Because he is tough and soft at once
> May such Dorje Kasungship expand in our kingdom. . . .
> Long live the Order of the Dragon,
> Inscrutability[1]

On January 3, 1977, we celebrated our seventh wedding anniversary. It seemed that so much had happened in such a short span of years! That day, Rinpoche conducted another ceremony, this one from the Vajrayana Buddhist tradition. The first group of about forty students had completed all of the *ngöndro,* the preliminary practices first introduced following the 1973 seminary. This represented about one-third of the students who had attended the first seminary. It was quite impressive that such a high percentage of the students finished in this period of time. Following the completion of these preliminaries, a student may request that the teacher enter him or her into the practice and the mandala, or the world, of a Vajrayana deity, or *yidam.* In this case, a *yidam* represents binding one's mind to the Vajrayana practice and understanding of wakefulness. It has nothing to do with an outside entity. If the teacher accepts the student, he or she receives *abhisheka,* a Sanskrit word that translates as "initiation" or "empowerment." The word in Tibetan, *wangkur,* literally means a "field of power." On this day, Rinpoche gave the Vajrayogini *abhisheka* to these students plus a few other senior students, including David Rome and the Vajra Regent, who hadn't finished the preliminaries but whom he decided to include anyway. (I did not receive this empowerment until 1984.)

The principle of Vajrayogini is depicted as a sixteen-year-old, very beautiful, and somewhat threatening, maiden. She is red in color and represents, among other things, the wisdom of complete non-thought, or wisdom that cuts through all conceptions. She is often the first *yidam* that is given to students, and I think that Rinpoche felt that the simplicity and power of the practice would be particularly appropriate for Western students. The *abhisheka* is quite a long and involved ceremony, taking most of a day to complete. Rinpoche had been working for several years on the translation of the text, or the *sadhana,* that students would practice after receiving this empowerment. He felt that it was absolutely necessary that students practice this liturgy in English so they would know what they were chanting, what they were visualizing, and why. The group that worked with him on this translation, the Nalanda Translation Committee, has continued on—having completed many important translation projects. Rinpoche always enjoyed his meetings with the translators, and he put a great deal of time into working with them.

Altogether, it felt like a great achievement to reach this stage in the presentation of Vajrayana in America. During Rinpoche's lifetime, he conducted this *abhisheka* ten times, and more than one thousand students received this initiation from him. From small gestures in Rinpoche's life, big things would often come!

Shortly after he finished the *abhisheka* program, which included not only the ceremony itself but also a number of training sessions, Rinpoche jumped right back into furthering the Shambhala world. This time, he held a joint ceremony for the Vajra Regent Ösel Tendzin and myself. He appointed Ösel Tendzin as the Katham Sikyong or the "keeper of the command seal of Shambhala," which was equivalent, according to Rinpoche, to being the Lord Chancellor of Shambhala. His role was to take the visionary aspect of the Shambhala teachings, as presented by Rinpoche, and to communicate it and execute its vision in terms of practicality. It was also to be his role to understand the needs and wishes of community members and communicate those to Rinpoche, so that there would be a sense of heaven—the Sakyong's vision—and earth—the needs of the people—being joined.

I was formally appointed as the Sakyong Wangmo during this ceremony. In some ways, my role as described by Rinpoche was similar to the Regent's, in that he saw it as my responsibility to encourage communication in all forms within the Shambhala world. He also talked about the Sakyong Wangmo principle in terms of creating harmony and a sense of elegance.

The Regent received the Order of the Great Eastern Sun, and I was given the Order of the Rigden. Again, these awards were created on the spot. Rinpoche did not say a great deal about the meaning of our awards, but I believe that the Order of the Great Eastern Sun has to do with connecting with the overall brilliance and wakefulness of Shambhala, while the Order of the Rigden was given to me to signify my connection to the principle of rulership within Shambhala. The setting was similar to the ceremony for David Rome: the guests assembled in the dining room on cushions; the Regent and I were seated facing Rinpoche and the shrine. We were questioned on our understanding of Shambhala principles, and we performed the stroke of Ashe. To seal our appointments, we took an oath, which David had also taken, in which we offered our eyes, tongue, and heart—symbolically—to furthering the sanity of the kingdom of Shambhala. This is very similar to the Vajrayana oaths that students take. Essentially, because the energies are so powerful and somewhat dangerous, the commitment that is required is also very heavy. It is not so much that someone is going to come and throw you in jail if you violate your oath or your position; the idea is more that you will destroy yourself if you become an egomaniac rather than becoming more gentle and exposed. Of course, there is a lot of middle ground—but the idea is that one should not take on this kind of commitment casually. In fact, it felt as though we were assuming quite a serious responsibility to assist in safeguarding and furthering the sanity and wakefulness of the Shambhala world.

When I look back, I think that Rinpoche's decision to give the two of us this Shambhala empowerment together was quite a deliberate, strategic move. In part, I think that Rinpoche saw our roles as complementary, and he always hoped that we would see that commonality of purpose and find ways to work together. But I also think that Rinpoche was trying to address the interpersonal tension between Ösel Tendzin and me by putting us together for this empowerment.

You see, from the time the Regent moved into the Court, he and I did not get along too well. From this time onward, although I tried to connect with the Regent, the chemistry between us was not very compatible. In the beginning, the very early years, I was quite fond of him. Later, when he lived with us, I had a harder time with him. I felt that he ignored other people's feelings to a certain extent and that there was a certain lack of identification with others. Rinpoche was raised almost from birth in a position of responsibility and rulership. His teachers in Tibet had hammered into him the need to behave properly, with gentleness, and not to mistake his position as an opportunity to lord it over others. But for the Regent, and all of us in the West, we were entering into uncharted territory and assuming leadership positions with no prior experience and few sane reference points. We were walking into a minefield where our lack of training and our insecurities were liable to explode into arrogance.

None of us were angels at that point. We all had our own neuroses, which were quite full blown in that era. Nevertheless, I perceived a lack

of empathy in the Regent that used to trouble me. I always could connect with Lila a lot more. I felt that she had more sympathy for other
people. It used to scare me sometimes how the Regent treated people
because it was so different from how Rinpoche treated people. I had a
basic mistrust of the Regent for a long time. I know this bothered Rinpoche, and he periodically tried to push me together with the Regent.
He wanted the communication to be more workable between us. In the
end, though, the Regent had very little respect for me, and I had not
very much for him. I objected to his ostentatious, slightly Americanized
style. I also questioned his personal discipline. He seemed self-indulgent,
and he could get really carried away with himself. On the other hand,
I'm sure he was struggling with who and what he was supposed to be as
the Regent. I was young and quite unreasonable at times too. We just
didn't hit it off.

After our joint Shambhala empowerment, Rinpoche wrote poems
about each of us, in which he talked about our neurotic and our enlightened qualities. He also said in each poem something to the effect that
Diana was the Regent and the Regent was Diana. I think that he was
hoping that we would find a mutual working basis, a meeting of minds,
and that we would come to appreciate one another. I'm afraid that in the
long run it didn't do much to affect our relationship. We both tried over
the years, but we were never overly fond of one another.

These poems, which appear at the end of this chapter, reveal how
Rinpoche saw his students' potential. The working basis that he had with
all of us was rooted in acknowledging the diversity and complexity of
our basic being. He always saw both the potentially enlightened aspect
of someone as well as the confused, neurotic side. Given the problems
that developed later with Ösel Tendzin, people have often asked both
why Rinpoche chose Ösel Tendzin to be his Regent and whether Rinpoche made a fundamental mistake in doing so. I don't think so. I believe
that he perceived genuine brilliance in his dharma heir, which all of us
could see, as well as the Regent's potential for compassion and for
greatly benefiting others.

Rinpoche also saw the other side: all the issues that could become
problematic in the future. However, he did not believe that some people
are good and others bad. He thought that everyone was workable and

that the raw material of ego could be hammered into the gold of genuine spiritual realization. So here, in these poems, Rinpoche is pointing out all the qualities in the Regent and in myself that could lead to problems, and at the same time, he was saying: you are actually Tiger; you are actually Lion; you are actually Garuda; you are actually Dragon—you are actually the embodiment of the sanity or the potential achievements of the Shambhala world. Click into that. Be that. Rinpoche was astute. He knew, with both of us and with all of his students, that there was the potential to miss the point completely. I think we—the Regent, myself, and Rinpoche's students in general—understood that the greater the responsibility that we accepted in his world, the greater the potential for failure—as well as for success—and the greater the penalties for failing.

Rinpoche's approach was always twofold: first, seeing and believing in the inseparability of neurosis and sanity, samsara and nirvana, and second, applying the skillful means to bring that potential to fruition and thus to produce realization in one lifetime for a human being. That is the unique insight of the Vajrayana teachings altogether and a hallmark of Rinpoche's teaching in the West. I think this is something that distinguishes him from other teachers and has made his teaching the basis of genuine dharma taking root in the West. He actually applied this insight in his work with his students. It wasn't just theoretical. He trusted that realization was possible, intensification of one's path was required, and he put people into situations that would cause that to happen.

Toward the end of January, His Holiness the Karmapa arrived for his second visit in North America. There were thousands of people in North America who wanted to meet His Holiness and receive his blessings. In Boulder a large white mansion on Mapleton Hill, about six blocks from our house, was rented for him. We nicknamed it the Wedding Cake House because it had so many columns and the exterior was so ornate. Once again, there were armies of attendants, drivers, cooks, and members of the Dorje Kasung to help with the visit. Rinpoche was to depart for Charlemont to begin his retreat in late February, but before his departure, he took time to travel to San Francisco with the Karmapa as well as to receive him in Boulder.

In San Francisco, His Holiness performed the Vajra Crown ceremony for several thousand followers of EST, or Erhard Seminar Training, which was popular in this era. EST was started by Werner Erhard, who was quite enamored of His Holiness and asked him to do the Vajra Crown ceremony for his students. Rinpoche thought that Erhard was something of a charlatan, although he also seemed to find him interesting, or perhaps amusing would be a better word. Before the Vajra Crown ceremony itself, His Holiness asked Rinpoche to make remarks to the assembled students explaining what would happen. Rinpoche told the crowd to keep their shirts on—metaphorically speaking. It was a bit cryptic, but it seemed to be addressing their tendency to bliss out, or indulge in the energy.

While he was in San Francisco, Rinpoche also celebrated the Shambhala New Year with His Holiness. (The celebration of the new year in Tibet is based on the lunar calendar and usually occurs in late January or February.) Rinpoche arranged for these celebrations to take place at the Karmapa's mansion in San Francisco. The day included three banquets: an Indian breakfast, a Tibetan lunch, and a Chinese dinner. Rinpoche had invited my mother to go along on this trip. She was completely overwhelmed by the Karmapa. Apparently, when my mother had an audience with him, she proposed marriage to him. She said to him, "This would be very convenient. It would be all in the family. My daughter is married to Trungpa Rinpoche so maybe you should marry me." His Holiness was very kind to her. He said that, if he were the marrying sort of person, he would definitely consider marrying her. Since he was the Karmapa, however, he had to remain a monk and unfortunately couldn't accept her proposal.

So our family journey and the larger journey continued. At the end of February, Rinpoche was off to Charlemont for what I hoped would be a much-needed rest for him. Little did I know that Rinpoche's idea of "retreat" was what most people would consider formulating a campaign. I was soon to be off to Europe to continue my training in dressage. From rebellious English teenager, to young mother, to Queen of Shambhala—the transformations were somewhat overwhelming. Essentially, I felt that I was just a young woman embarking on my life, with so much to learn. I still did not fully understand what it meant to be the guru's wife, let alone to be a king's consort! And really it was only beginning.

Katham Sikyong: Lord Chancellor and Keeper of the Command Seal,
Prodigy of the Sakyong

He is called after my son's name
He is a funny man because he is almost lady dragon
He is obviously inscrutable; he possesses many faces
He was a Hindu rat; he was a stapling machine; he was a sandal
Before I met him he was a creep; when I met him he was decent
When I told him he cried
He is a very intriguing young gentleman
He is nobody, somebody
I was shocked when he shaved his beard because he looked too
    ingratiating
Then he was a director administrator fighter commander
For the first time he was a tiger cub: He learned to lick himself
    and clean up just like a cat
Then he was a jaguar: He began to eat raw meat
When he began to suck my own milk from my tit, the Vajra Master
    amrita potion, he began to become dangerously dangerous:
    he wouldn't smile
He still didn't have good posture, however
He was willing to fight the heretics with claw and teeth
He met his grandfather, he learned how to behave, then he began
    to see the Great Eastern Sun: he became chic
He was being molded by the Kingdom; finally he became civilized
My Lord Chancellor, today you have assumed the second-
    generation project
Now you are *vajra* and *ghanta* with Ashe on it
O Lord Chancellor, please sit on Shambhala rug
However, the Lord Chancellor's tree had a tractor, telephone,
    machine gun, central heating in the oriental sneak
You are protection cord, you are band-aid, you are aspirin, you are
    Dettol, you are Marmite
You are Mercedes, you are Rolls Royce
You are actually Diana Judith
You are actually Tiger, you are actually Lion, you are actually
    Garuda, you are actually Dragon

You are what you are in the name of the Great Eastern Sun
In brief, you are the genuine Kiku Masamune of the Discoverer's
    Selection
Glory be to the Holder of the Order of the Great Eastern Sun.[2]

Sakyong Wangmo: The Grand Lady of the Realm, the Lady of the
    Razor Knife

She she she she: She is the she
She is the first lady of she, the youngest oldest lady of she
When she is she, she is ideal Ashe: Tough lady good lady gentle lady
    but nevertheless she is she
When she begins to become her we have problems
However, when her becomes she, she is majestically the Grand Lady
    of the Realm
She is thread, she is threat, she is beautiful, she is confusing, she is
    genuine, she is red, she is purple
She is Vajrayogini
She deceives us sometimes: She pretends to be the occidental sun
She is a brook, she is a river, she is a confidante, she is the ocean
When she is her: Hers is very expensive, hers spends a lot of money,
    hers is impulsive, hers is not so good
Hers is a bad cook, hers is a bad driver, hers is a bad society lady
However, hers is she
When she realizes she is the lady, she is no longer her
She loves me, she loves her world, she loves a horse
She loves the Chancellor, she loves she, she loves the Grand
    Duchess
She is inscrutable, she is meek, she is perky, she is outrageous
When she is not her, she is glorious
When her is her, wretched
When she is she: such power and dignity in her
She is truly what she is
She certainly does make love to the first dot of Ashe when she is
    she
She is black lady of black and gold

She is tiger lady, manifestations of all facets in her
She is garuda lady, she flies high and low
She is lion lady, she dives in the ocean of snow
She is dragon lady, she proclaims the dragon's roar
She is sometimes also the Chancellor, she shares her vision, she is
    Thomas Rich
She joins family affair: She is all.[3]

The Pybus family, Thorney Court, London, circa 1962.
(Diana is seated on the rug.) Photographer unknown.

Chögyam Trungpa (*center front*) at Samye Ling Meditation Center in Scotland, circa 1967. Shown here with Akong Rinpoche (*right*), Sherab Palden Beru (*left*), and a number of early Western students. Photographer unknown.

Schoolgirl bride Diana and her groom after yesterday's ceremony.

Diana, 16, runs away to marry a monk

Sunday Mirror Reporter

SCHOOLGIRL Diana Pybus, 16, shocked her mother yesterday by marrying 30-year-old Buddhist monk Chogyan Mukpu after a secret romance lasting a year.

Diana's mother, Mrs. Elizabeth Pybus, said last night: "I shall try to get the marriage dis-

solved." At her home in Gloucester - road, South Kensington, she said: "I thought she was staying with a girl friend.

"I had not the slightest suspicion she was thinking of marry-ing this man. How

could she do such a thing?

"He was crippled after a car accident and I believe Diana feels sorry for him."

Mrs. Pybus said that Diana, who is studying for her "A" levels, turned to Buddhism three years ago when her father died in a fire.

Romance blossomed after she went to one of Chogyan's religious lec-tures in London.

Yesterday the couple married at an Edinburgh register office immedi-ately after being granted a special licence at the city's Sheriff's Court.

Afterwards Chogyan, a former head of the Tibetan Centre in Dum-fries, sat with his bride at their honeymoon hotel.

Diana said: "All I want to do now is go wherever Chogyan goes."

150 SOCCER FANS IN STREET CLASH

Police were called to a fight between about 150 Southampton and Newcastle football fans in Southampton's main shop-ping centre. A number were injured in the clash, which started in a restaurant.

Printed and Published by DAILY MIRROR NEWSPAPERS, Ltd. (01-353 0246) at, and for I P C New

News clipping from the *Sunday Mirror,* January 4, 1970.

Rinpoche and Diana, soon after their arrival in the United States.
Photographer unknown.

Rinpoche meditating with students in the living room at
Four Mile Canyon, 1971. Photo by Blair Hansen.

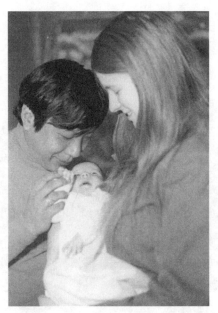

Rinpoche and Diana with Taggie as a
newborn, 1971. Photo by Blair Hansen.

Diana, Gesar, and Khyentse Rinpoche during Gesar's enthronement as
Jamgön Kongtrul. Berkeley, California, 1976. Photo by George Holmes.
Private collection.

Khyentse Rinpoche and Trungpa Rinpoche, 1976.
Photograph by Ray Ellis.

Left to right: The Vajra Regent Ösel Tendzin; the Vidyadhara the Venerable Chögyam Trungpa Rinpoche; His Holiness the Sixteenth Gyalwa Karmapa; and His Eminence Jamgön Kongtrul Rinpoche. Japan Center, San Francisco, January 1977. Photograph by Tharpa Chotron.

Reception at the first Kalapa Court, Boulder, circa 1978.
Elizabeth Pybus with Rinpoche and Diana. The family dog,
Ganesh, is at their feet. Photographer unknown.

Diana at the Spanish Riding School, 1979.
Reprinted by permission of the Spanish Riding School.

Rinpoche on his horse, Drala, at the Magyel Pomra
Encampment, 1980. Photo by Andrea Roth.

Rinpoche and Diana lead the procession on horseback at a
Midsummer's Day Celebration outside of Boulder, 1981.
Photo by Andrea Roth.

The Mukpo Family at the Kalapa Court, Boulder, 1982.
Front row: Rinpoche, Diana, and baby Ashoka (on Diana's lap).
Back row, left to right: Ösel, Taggie, and Gesar. An enlarged reproduction
of the Order of Ashe hangs on the wall behind them.
Photo by Blair Hansen and George Holmes.

The funeral procession at the cremation ceremony for Rinpoche,
May 1987, at Karme Chöling. Photo by Andrea Roth.

Mukpo family portrait, Tibet, Summer 2002. *Standing, left to right:* Rolpe Dorje Rinpoche, Tulku A, Karma Senge Rinpoche, Khenpo Tsering, Gesar Mukpo, Diana Mukpo, Ashoka Mukpo, Surmang Garwang Rinpoche, Mitchell Levy. *Kneeling:* Chandali Mukpo and David Mukpo. Photo by Jane Carpenter.

Diana Mukpo, Khamnyön Rinpoche (Ashoka), and Sechen Kongtrül Rinpoche (Gesar) giving blessings at Sechen Monastery, Tibet, 2002. Photo by Jane Carpenter.

Diana and Mitchell, New York, 2002.
Photo by Gracie Atherton.

THIRTEEN

I n the months before Rinpoche left for retreat, I was making my own
plans for the coming year. I began to turn my mind to going to Europe to further my dressage training. Since Rinpoche and I had been
deeply impressed with the Spanish Riding School when we visited Vienna in 1975, it was natural to think about studying with someone from
the Spanish as the next step in my education. At that time, I did not think
it would actually be possible for me to study in the school itself; it was
an all-male institution, and, as far as I knew, they only accepted Austrian
nationals as riders in the school.

When we watched the performance there, one rider in particular
had impressed me, Ernst Bachinger. I wrote a letter to him in early 1977
telling him that I would like to come and study with him. He replied
that he had just left the school and was in a time of personal transition,
so he was not accepting new students. He recommended that I train
with Arthur Kottas, who had his own training facility near Vienna. I
wrote to Kottas and asked him if he would accept me as a student.
Within a month, he wrote back saying that I could come that summer.

Rinpoche was tremendously supportive of my going to Vienna, much
more so than he had been about California. He felt that the classical

tradition practiced in Austria was the real McCoy, so to speak. When I received the letter of acceptance from Kottas, we were both overjoyed.

After Rinpoche left for Charlemont, I stayed on in Boulder for several months, preparing for my trip. I took German lessons from the Berlitz Institute in Denver so I would be able to communicate a little bit in German with my teachers and fellow riders. I also sold Vajra Dance before leaving. I knew that I would need a better horse in Vienna.

Rinpoche had been thinking for some time about establishing Vajradhatu in Europe. There was already a meditation group in England, but he felt it was time to start something on the continent. He also wanted me to have support, being a bit worried about me going over to Vienna alone. He asked one of his close students, Michael Kohn, if he and his family would move to Vienna to start the Vienna dharmadhatu, to get things rolling in Europe. Michael was to be the Vajradhatu ambassador to Europe. Michael was a very literate person who had worked on a number of Rinpoche's early books and other editorial projects, and he had a facility with foreign languages. He was very devoted to Rinpoche and had been trained by him as a meditation instructor and teacher, and for all these reasons Rinpoche thought he would be an excellent person for the job. The plan was that Michael would be based in Vienna and would travel and teach in a number of locations throughout western Europe. Michael, his wife Judy, and their daughter (a second child was born in Europe) relocated to Vienna around the same time that I did. The Vienna dharmadhatu has continued to this day, although after I left, Michael and his family relocated to Amsterdam and then finally established the headquarters of Vajradhatu Europe in Marburg, Germany.

Rinpoche also wanted me to have someone to help out at the house, and this was the beginning, really, of my having personal attendants. Rinpoche asked Jeanine Wieder, a French woman in the *sangha,* if she would accompany me. During this era, Rinpoche was trying to include the family and me much more as part of the environment of the teachings that should be respected. I think that he may have realized that there was a problem with the large discrepancy in how students treated him— almost like a god—and how we were treated—often like unwelcome interlopers in his life. With the emphasis on a Court mandala in his presentation of the Shambhala teachings, it made sense that the entire household had to be included and regarded as part of the sacredness of his world. As well, the message he was trying to communicate to all of his students was that every part of one's life is part of one's practice. You don't just meditate in the midst of your dirty pots and pans, ignoring your spouse and children. Given the hippie roots of many of his students, there was sometimes this tendency to ignore the basic details and fabric of everyday life. In fact, this was one reason that some of Rinpoche's students were resistant to his presentation of the Shambhala teachings. They didn't want to have to clean up their act. They liked the smelly nest, which Rinpoche referred to in his Shambhala presentations as "the cocoon."

My mother wrote an amusing letter to Rinpoche during the first month of his retreat, March 1977, about her view of hippie society in Boulder and why Rinpoche would want to get away from it for awhile. She wrote, "I can understand that you might want to escape the trivia that populate Boulder with its various cafés and stores. Most of these people appear to lack all idea of personal grooming and one cannot begin to imagine whether anything exists within the cerebral cranium. It is a horrifying aspect of an ignorance bordering on barbarity."[1] Rinpoche I think shared her view that people looked worse than unkempt on the outside, but he saw the intelligence behind the "barbarous" exterior.

At this time, Rinpoche was beginning to work much more with promoting feminine energy, not just in the abstract—which is certainly an important part of the Vajrayana Buddhist teachings—but the energy of women in the community. I think it's interesting that this coincided with his presentation of the Vajrayogini *abhisheka*. Vajrayogini is the personification of wisdom and represents the feminine principle. But interestingly, at the same time that he started giving this practice to people, he also began to appoint many more women to important leadership roles, and he suggested that I should also have such a role within the Shambhala world. Rinpoche's contact with and understanding of Western women had been growing exponentially since he came to North America and since we married. I think he got to know "woman" on an intimate, day-to-day basis in part through our marriage, as well as through other relationships with Western women students. Just as he broke through so many other cultural divides, his chauvinism began to wear out in a fundamental way, and he started to feel that women could play very important roles. Here again, we take these things for granted now, but in that era, leadership was not as open for women as it is now.

In any case, during this period, one of the changes that he instituted involved elevating my status, which was often uncomfortable for me. I don't think I always handled it well, especially in the beginning. At the seminary the previous fall, Rinpoche had floated his idea with some senior students that perhaps I should now be addressed as Her Highness Lady Diana Mukpo. He said that he wanted me to have a title that was commensurate with him being referred to as the Vajracharya or the Sakyong. David Rome, among others, tried to talk him out of this, as did I initially, but he would not be dissuaded, no matter how ridiculous people told him it was. I reluctantly came to the conclusion that, if we were going to live in a Shambhala Court, it would not be completely inappropriate for me to be a lady. Within a few months, I became used to people calling me "Your Highness" within the Buddhist community. I still found it awkward when this title was used in the larger world by well-intentioned but—from my point of view—naive community members.

I think that one reason that students were willing to "attend" me was because of all this energy that Rinpoche was putting into expanding the Shambhala world and extending that into our home. Jeanine referred to me at home as "Lady Diana." Unfortunately, she also called me that frequently when I was riding at Kottas's barn, no matter how many times I asked her to just call me Diana when we were there. On some level, I didn't find it that bizarre, but I was trying to keep these two worlds separate. When Jeanine called me Lady Diana at the barn, I cringed. I wanted to be ordinary in that situation, get my work done, and focus purely on my riding.

For my first day at Kottas's school, I drove through the Vienna Woods and turned off onto a small driveway that led to his barn. The barn was in a large clearing, and there were about twenty-five horses stabled there. There was a well-appointed indoor arena, as well as paths on the property where you could ride your horse through the forest.

I was dressed in my best riding clothes, and I was quite excited. I thought I was pretty hot stuff, and I imagined that I would impress Herr Kottas. He greeted me and told me that he had a nice horse for me to ride. He said, "Let me see what you can do." The horse was the current Austrian champion. I realized almost immediately that I was in trouble.

I couldn't make the horse do anything. Obviously, the way I had been trained to ride in the United States was completely different from what they expected in Vienna. I felt humiliated. Afterward, I went out for coffee with Kottas, and he said to me, "If you don't improve greatly within the next three months, you'll have to leave. I'm represented by my students. If you don't get better, you'll go. That's that."

He told me that if I wanted to stay and train with him, first I would have to go to his barn every morning while he was away riding at the Spanish. I would report to his assistant, and she would longe me. *Longeing* is a means to teach the rider to sit correctly on the horse. The instructor has the horse on a long line called a longe line. You sit on the horse without reins or stirrups, and you learn how to balance and keep your body in exactly the correct position. Kottas wanted me to return to this absolutely basic training before going any further.

I agreed to his terms, and starting the next day, I reported every morning to his assistant, a German woman named Jutta. Every morning, I was given the same horse to be longed on, a seventeen-hand Bavarian warmblood by the name of Donald. Donald had a terrible habit of bucking, and he bucked me off almost every day. It was a good day if I hadn't fallen off him. I spent my first three months sitting on this horse and ending up in the dirt on an ongoing basis. Fortunately, I was never seriously hurt, but it wasn't a pleasant experience. When I fell off, Jutta would say to me, "Get up. Get back on." She never said, "Are you okay?" The custom at the barn was that you were expected to buy a liter of wine for people every time you fell off a horse. At one point, I bought eighteen liters of wine. I invited everyone; I put the wine out for them and said "Drink up!" It was a miserable time.

After about a month of this, I became discouraged and convinced that I was never going to make any progress. I felt ready to pack up and go back to the United States. I missed everyone terribly, especially Gesar, and I thought that at the end of the year I would go home. I called Rinpoche a number of times to discuss all this. I was looking for understanding and sympathy somewhere in my life. Altogether, I felt discouraged and inadequate.

In mid-September Rinpoche wrote me a letter. To me, it exemplifies how he worked with all of his students. He was immensely kind and loving, but he expected a lot from everyone—especially his wife, as I realized when I read what he had written. It was somewhat shocking, because he was so honest and unguarded and offered such direct advice. He wrote:

My darling,

Isn't it magnificent that I am writing a letter to you? We have never communicated with each other in this way before. Usually we use a telephone or mutual mind contact. But I hope that what I have to say in this letter won't shock you too much.

I have never met a human being like you. You are so extraordinary, outrageous, and intrinsically good. I miss you a lot, but sometimes I feel for your future. I want you to be the world's most outstanding dressage rider. This is not just because I am going along with your schemes or your plans, but I want you really to become a truly good equestrian. Therefore I would like to push you in your discipline.

Thank you, by the way, for your letter and your phone calls. I understand how you feel about all of this, the riding and your disappointment in the Spanish Court Riding School. But I would like to encourage you as your husband and your good friend. I do not want you to chicken out. I want you to know that my pride is not purely invested in you as my famous wife. But I certainly do feel that it is my role and my delightful duty to push you to become the top rider in the dressage world. Therefore I would like you to stay longer with Kottas and study with him. Any financial or moral support, whatever is needed, I obviously volunteer. Of course, it is my duty.

Sometimes you feel disappointed because of your impatience. Sometimes you feel disappointed because of what you expected from the best system of dressage in the world. If you could stay beyond Christmas and at least spend next year with Kottas, I would feel more proud of you. You might find it strange that my urge to push you becomes greater. As far as I am concerned, it is my pride in you and in me. I hope you will never give up all this. Please consider: patience is great. . . . I want you to stay with the discipline of the Spanish Court Riding School. If this seems unreasonable, let us talk about it when we are together—but I want you to stay in this school.

You said the European championship was so materialistic. Sometimes it is necessary to give in to people's trips; otherwise there is no working basis. As long as you are not hypocritical to yourself, that is the key to remaining genuine.

There is something to the Spanish Court Riding School. It is internationally acceptable, and moreover it has a great lineage which has been handed down from generation to generation. You can't find that kind of inspiration from individual practice alone. I know that; I have done it myself. If you try to do your own trip and practice riding by yourself independent of any tradition, you are going to become the Ram Dass of the dressage tradition.

You might want to do it on your own terms, but self-styled disciplines are dubious. Only the Americans do things that way because they don't like the discipline of the forefathers of whatever lineage they might have belonged to. Instead, they prefer to give up any pain they feel and try to insert their own pleasure by manufacturing their own discipline. Darling, I don't want you to become Americanized. It is silly and ridiculous.

Sweetheart, I don't want to push you, but I feel if you trust me, my judgment is right. I know it is painful and uncomfortable not being with our people, but our people will appreciate you more if you come back victorious and good. I really insist on this, you know. Please think it over. We can discuss it when we are together.

The main point is that you realize that no discipline will come along with hospitality. Exertion and diligence beyond physical discomfort are the key.

Your most loving Sakyong and husband writes this letter remembering you with tremendous love and longing. Sweetheart, I remain your most obedient husband, the Sakyong. . . .

I love you CT²

I couldn't ignore a message like this. It was really the heart advice that I would have given myself, had I been able to transcend my own doubt and see things from a bigger perspective. Rinpoche told me things that at some level I already knew and believed. I had to admit that he was right. From that point on, my attitude changed. I gave up any thought of leaving, and I started to work really hard. Between that and my change of attitude, I made quite a lot of progress.

In his letter, when Rinpoche told me that he didn't want me to be-come "Americanized" in my approach to riding, he was appealing to my English chauvinism. From the time we arrived in the United States, al-though we both appreciated the fresh, unbridled quality of the Ameri-can spirit, we were also both aware of what we perceived as a lack of discipline and a rejection of tradition. As much as I rebelled against my upbringing, there was much that I appreciated about the British mental-ity. It was part of me. There was a stuffiness and close-mindedness that I reacted against, but I also learned about genuine discipline from grow-ing up in England. I also appreciated that Rinpoche had this connection to discipline from his own education and upbringing, so I knew that he spoke from firsthand experience.

In terms of my education as a rider, before coming over to Europe, I had realized that there was something missing in my training in Amer-ica. I had seemed to make extremely rapid progress there, but the foun-dation of the discipline was not well established, and a certain attention to the basics was missing. Having to start over from the ground up was not just helpful but essential to my progress as a rider.

In dressage, the first objective for the rider should be to learn to fol-low the horse's movements and to be able to stay in balance with the horse, without hanging onto the reins or squeezing with your legs. First, you have to learn to harmonize with the horse's movement, and this process can take a long time. If riders don't have correct training on the seat position early on, it's going to show up later in their riding because there will be always be some degree of inability to harmonize with the horse. And if the rider can't harmonize with the horse, then the horse's movements can't be graceful or beautiful.

When dressage is performed at the highest levels, with a skilled rider and a well-trained horse, the communication between the horse and the rider should be almost indiscernible. This certainly doesn't mean that the rider is not doing anything. The rider may be doing quite a bit, giving the horse various aids or instructions. This is done through leg move-ments, how you hold the reins, and how you sit in the saddle, but all of this should be so extremely well-timed and subtle that the casual ob-server may notice nothing but the unity of horse and rider. It takes a minimum of five years to train a dressage horse to the highest level. Throughout that process you refine the aids. When you see a completely finished horse, when you watch him going through all the highest movements of dressage, the rider's influence should be almost imperceptible. Horse and rider should look as if they're moving as one.

It was this basic connection to the horse that I was gaining through my work on the longe line. Rinpoche was absolutely correct about the training in Europe. Especially in Vienna, where they follow this classical approach, training is not based on immediate gratification. New riders always spend a long time on the longe line. When you longe a horse, it is controlled by the instructor on the ground, and the horse walks, trots, and canters on command, in a circle around the instructor. The student's only objective is to learn how to sit, and how to synchronize and to follow along with the horse's movements. I was told that in the Spanish Riding School, the young apprentices would often longe for six months before they're ever given the stirrups or the reins. In the end, I was grateful to have had a similar experience.

Several weeks after he sent me the letter, Rinpoche came over to Vienna. I guess you could say that he took a kind of vacation from his retreat! He traveled with a group of his students to see me and to check in on how Michael Kohn was doing setting up the European branch of Vajradhatu. I was delighted to see him.

Kottas's training facility was near a small village called Tulbinger-kogel. There was a very nice hotel in the village, the Berghotel Tulbingerkogel, a few minutes up the road, owned by the Blauel family. Rinpoche and his party stayed there. (Interestingly enough, one of the sons in the Blauel family later became a member of the Buddhist community.) John Perks accompanied Rinpoche, as did Sam Bercholz. The party also included Jim Gimian, who Rinpoche was about to appoint to an important post within the *vajra* guards. Jim's rank was to be just below David Rome. Rinpoche had decided to create two divisions within the guards. Jim was to be the *dapon,* or chief, of the *kasung* division providing the outer protection for Rinpoche and his world, while John Perks was being appointed as the *dapon* of the *kusung* division, which included the personal attendants, or the inner service, to Rinpoche, myself, the Regent, and a few others. Jim, a very warm man with a great sense of humor, was also the associate publisher at Shambhala Publications.

Rinpoche had also invited Sara Kapp to accompany him, a runway model well known in both New York and Europe. Sara was famous for having pioneered a certain look on the runway, and she became the model for mannequins at Saks Fifth Avenue in the eighties. Later, she was the first "Princess Borghese," the face of the Borghese line of cosmetics. In short, she was a very elegant woman, and she was one of Rinpoche's close friends, girlfriends, at the time. Several famous Italian and French designers had loaned Sara evening gowns to wear on this tour of Europe. Every evening, she would appear for dinner in yet another extraordinary outfit. I was by this time in our married life quite accustomed to Rinpoche having relationships with other women. In general, for whatever reasons, I did not find them threatening or degrading. Many of these women were my friends. We shared the appreciation of Rinpoche as an extraordinary human being, someone who no one person could possess in the traditional sense. I did find it difficult if a woman spending time with Rinpoche did not have some respect for my position as his wife. This was rare, luckily. In Sara's case, we were old friends, and I was happy to see her.

Rinpoche, as I mentioned earlier, had always made an effort to celebrate my birthday with me, and this year was no exception. I turned twenty-four while he was in Vienna. Throughout the visit, John Perks shaved his moustache to look "Hitlerian," and Rinpoche kept saying "Fetus" to people instead of "Auf Wiedersehen," which means good-bye in German. No one seemed to notice. I'm sure they just thought he couldn't speak the language. Rinpoche and John were often making fun of Austria's Nazi past in the most tasteless fashion. (Rinpoche could make fun of almost anything.)

For my birthday, Rinpoche reserved a private room at the hotel and ordered a whole wild boar to be roasted and served at the table. It cheered me up a lot to have him and his crazy, loving world there for a few days. During his visit, we ate a lot of Sacher torte for dessert, which Rinpoche was very fond of.

While he was there, Rinpoche and I talked further about my riding. I told him that I was going to stick it out and also that I had heard that the Spanish Riding School was now accepting a few foreign students. It was my extraordinary good fortune to be there during this era. I told Rinpoche that it was my greatest desire to work hard and progress so that I would be able to apply. I understood at this point that it was only by following the approach he was suggesting that I would ever master the discipline to the point that I might be accepted.

Rinpoche came out to Kottas's barn to meet him and to see me ride, and he really loved it there. He had ridden in Tibet, and from that he had a great appreciation for riding, as well as an intuitive feeling for it. I also took him and his party to the Spanish Riding School. Since I was now studying under one of the riders at the school, I was able to arrange for Rinpoche and his party to watch the morning lessons and to have a private tour of the facilities, rather than having to attend a performance with a huge crowd of people. I was so sad to see him leave, but altogether, his visit gave me the further encouragement I needed.

For the next year, I continued my training with Arthur Kottas. At the end of Rinpoche's retreat, December 1977, I traveled back to Boulder to spend time with him. Throughout 1978, I made several visits to the United States to participate in various activities in the Buddhist community, but for most of this time I was based in Vienna.

A few months after I settled in Vienna, Taggie came through on his way to His Holiness's monastery in Rumtek, Sikkim, chaperoned by Karl Springer. When His Holiness had made his second visit to America, he saw Taggie at Karme Chöling. He strongly suggested to Rinpoche and me that we allow Taggie to go to Rumtek, where he would be formally enthroned as Tenga Rinpoche. His Holiness thought this might help Taggie. I had visited my son at Karme Chöling several times, and during that period I continued to hold out hope that he was going to somehow become a more normal child. When I saw him in Vienna, however, it was absolutely clear that he was not normal, and I began to give up any expectation. At this point, although he was my child and always will be, I became more disconnected from him. I didn't know what else to do. His life was out of my control now. Rinpoche had agreed with His Holiness and made the decision to send Taggie to Rumtek. I couldn't care for him. When he came through, it was very difficult for me because I felt our connection dissolving. I felt the hopelessness of it all. I remained skeptical that Taggie's condition was *tulku* disease.

Perhaps in part in reaction to the pain of seeing Taggie, I threw myself even more into my riding after his visit. At a certain point, when I began to feel that I was making adequate progress, and taking to heart Rinpoche's offer of financial support, I decided to purchase a horse for myself.

I wanted a horse that was already trained to the medium level in Europe. (This is roughly the equivalent of the fourth, or highest, national level in the United States. After that there are four international levels, which are the same throughout the world.) Kottas was kind enough to accompany me to Munich to look at a Hungarian horse that was owned by a woman by the name of Katrina Hilger Henkel (of the Henkel family who produces a popular sparkling wine in Germany). Her stable was near Munich, where she had competed him through the medium level of dressage. When I rode the horse, I instantly felt a connection and felt he suited me well. He was a chestnut horse, maybe sixteen one hands, not very big, but very pleasant to ride.

There are certain guidelines one uses in picking a horse for dressage. When you evaluate a young untrained horse as a dressage prospect, you are looking for a very sensitive horse. When he's young, he might misbehave sometimes, but you want that sort of hot temperament, because that shows you that he's sensitive and energetic. If a dressage horse were a person, he would not be a couch potato. Dressage becomes very taxing physiologically as the training goes on, so you need a horse that is a natural athlete. That's one thing to look for: the athletic ability of the horses, as well as their desire to do the work. You want a horse with plenty of energy when it's young.

Male horses are generally better for dressage. There are very few mares in competition, although there are some very good ones at the top of our sport. At the Spanish Riding School, only stallions are used. However, the vast majority of dressage horses in competition are geldings, castrated males. The problem with the stallions is that they often have other things on their mind than dressage and therefore need a very experienced rider.

When I was at the Henkel barn, I saw another horse that absolutely wowed me. He was my ideal of a dressage horse at the time, a sixteen two hand liver chestnut Hanoverian who exhibited tremendous energy and supple movements. I asked Katrina Hilger Henkel if that horse was for sale, but she was not willing to sell him. We ended up buying the Hungarian. I brought him back to Vienna and named him Shambhala. Two weeks later, I got a phone call from Katrina, telling me that the other horse was now available. Without much hesitation, I agreed to buy him as well, much to the understandable consternation of the financial people in Vajradhatu to whom Rinpoche turned to finance the purchase. In Vienna, I was surrounded by wealthy people, many of whom had a number of expensive horses, and I think I lost my perspective a bit.

There was one person within Vajradhatu in charge of our family finances, Chuck Lief, a student of Rinpoche's since 1970. Chuck was quite upset, and I don't really blame him; I had just gone ahead without thinking, saying, "Fine, we'll have the second horse as well"—and they certainly were not inexpensive. Over the years, Chuck had a lot of hand-wringing to do in connection with my dressage horses.

Nevertheless, both purchases went ahead, and within a few weeks, I ended up with two very interesting horses to ride and compete. I named the second horse Warrior. In 1978, I began competing Shambhala in Austria. The first year, I didn't do dismally, but I was not tremendously successful. However, by the second year, I did very well with Shambhala, winning a number of tests at the medium level. Toward the end of my time in Vienna, I started competing both horses in the first international level, the Prix St. Georges.

Studying with Arthur Kottas, I was learning how to be a good rider. Kottas's approach was very demanding; it was very tough training for me, but it was necessary to go through this process. I was also beginning to learn how to train my horses. I began to realize that, as a rider, you are like the personal trainer of the horse. It's very much a mutual relationship; the rider also has to learn to listen to the horse. If you're a really good rider, you're going to discover how your horse wants to be ridden. You have to learn to adjust to the needs of each horse. Every horse is different, and the hallmark of a good rider is that he can get on many different horses and quickly figure out where the problems are. To begin with, the horse always has to be obedient to the rider and has to follow the direction of the rider. On the other hand, the rider has to be able to communicate to the horse in a precise manner what he wants the horse to do. So dressage involves two-way communication.

If you look at dressage training in terms of the alphabet, when you ride a very young horse, you only teach him the letters A and B. A is that he must go forward, and B is that he has to stop. Ultimately, when your horse is at the Grand Prix level, he should know all twenty-six letters, so to speak, and you should be able to make words with them. How does the communication take place? It has to be accomplished through subtle movements, by closing your leg, by bracing your back, by putting pressure on your seat bones or closing your fist on the reins. As a result of training, all those little things mean something to the horse, and eventually the different combinations of those aids will also mean something to him.

Dressage is a bit like ballet. In the early training, you concentrate on basic movements. The basic elements eventually are put together into complex movements that look somewhat like dance. On the other hand, it's quite different than becoming a dancer in that you are trying to train not just your own mind and body, but also the mind and body of another being, a huge, twelve-hundred-pound animal. You are trying to harness and direct the energy of this being, and beyond that, you are trying to connect with the animal in the most fundamental way, so that at times, there is no division between you and the horse. You feel that you are completely in sync, physically, mentally, and one might almost say spiritually, or at least energetically.

In the Shambhala teachings that Rinpoche began presenting in this era, there is extensive discussion of the principle of windhorse, or *lungta* in Tibetan. This term refers to raising or harnessing your energy. Rinpoche described *lungta* as follows:

> When we pay attention to everything around us, the overall effect is upliftedness. The Shambhalian term for that is *windhorse*. The *wind* principle is very airy and powerful. *Horse* means that the energy is ridable. That particular airy and sophisticated energy, so clean and full of decency, can be ridden. You don't just have a bird flying by itself in the sky, but you have something to ride on. Such energy is fresh and exuberant but, at the same time, ridable. Therefore, it is known as windhorse.[3]

This is parallel to what you are doing in dressage. I found that the Shambhala teachings altogether were often applicable to my experience as a dressage rider. In the Shambhala teachings, one of the factors in raising windhorse is that the uplifted quality of *lungta* arises from applying mindfulness and awareness in everyday life. This lofty quality rests on the foundation of paying attention to every aspect of your life. That is exactly the same as in dressage, and that is what I was learning in such great detail during that early phase in Vienna. I already had some intuitive sense of the possible grandeur and magnificence and power of dressage, but I needed to concentrate on the essentials.

It's beyond the scope of this book to go into detail about every aspect of dressage, but I would like to explain some basic principles, which are relevant to training in other disciplines as well. All the movements in dressage are natural movements of the horse. You just harness them. Everything that you see someone do on a dressage horse, with perhaps one exception, the horse will naturally do in the field. For example, horses in a field outdoors will canter a lot and change which leg they are leading with. When you train a horse, you are putting the natural movement in a context, while building up the horse's strength and his ability to understand and move in unity with the rider. If you train your horse incorrectly, which means using undue force, the horse may cease to enjoy his work. He has to be a willing partner. As soon as the horse stops enjoying what he's doing, it becomes very evident: the movement is no longer beautiful. So there's a real psychological aspect to this work. You work with your horse so that his body's fit for what he's doing and also so that he feels good in his mind about it. When those things work together, then you can have a beautiful and harmonious picture. This is, in fact, similar to the principles that one applies in meditation. Meditation works with the natural qualities and habits of mind, gradually building on the student's natural capacity for wakefulness.

In dressage, one of the key principles that you work on developing is collection. Collection is when the horse's energy is gradually controlled without being reduced. A young horse will trot and canter forward with very long strides, and his balance will be a little bit on his forelegs. When you train the horse, you teach him to take more weight on the hindquarters, and the center of gravity will gradually shift backward. Over years, this allows him to have what we call lightness of the forehand. You gradually teach the horse to channel the energy upward and his movement becomes more elevated.

Midway through my training with Kottas, His Holiness the Karmapa visited Vienna. He came to the dharmadhatu to perform the Vajra

Crown ceremony while he was in Europe. It was a big to-do. I had a white Mercedes at the time, which I loaned to the dharmadhatu for His Holiness's use during the visit. While His Holiness was visiting, I arranged for him to attend a performance at the Spanish Riding School. I was able to get seats for his party in the Royal Box, which is reserved for special guests. Located underneath the portrait of the Austrian emperor, the Royal Box has upholstered chairs and is the only heated part of the arena. Among all of us in the dharmadhatu, we only had one decent car, the Mercedes, so His Holiness and I both rode in it. Generally, he never rode in a car with a woman because of his monastic vows. However, because I was Rinpoche's wife, he made an exception. (I had already ridden with him in Boulder once before, as he may have remembered.)

I had a mink stole that I was very proud of, and I wore it to the Spanish with an evening gown. We sat together in the Royal Box and watched the performance, which never failed to move me. At one point, His Holiness pointed at my stole and, through his translator, said to me, "So many rabbits died to make that!" I turned to the translator and I said, "Please tell His Holiness, actually it was so many minks." Then His Holiness wanted to know how much it would cost to buy one of the Lipizzaners, the rare breed of horse ridden at the Spanish. I told him it would be about $100,000, and he was somewhat shocked by that.

He enjoyed watching the performance for awhile, but then toward the end, he realized it was time to do his evening meditation, which included a number of chants. It was cold in the box, even with the heat, so he decided that he would also do a meditation practice called *tummo,* which among other things generates warmth in your body. I was paralyzed with embarrassment as he started to do his evening practice right there during the performance. Everyone in the arena could hear him chanting. Later, Rinpoche told me I could have told the Karmapa that the program would be over soon and that he could go home and do his practice there. Instead I just sat there, quietly freaking out. At one point, when he was doing his *tummo* practice, he held my hand for a moment, and his body really was hot, which was kind of amazing. Once again, it was strange to see these worlds of mine coming together, but I survived and in the end, I was delighted that His Holiness had come to the Spanish.

FOURTEEN

While I was riding with Arthur Kottas, I learned more about the program for foreign students at the Spanish Riding School. Based on passing an entrance examination, both men and women could be accepted at the school for a three-month period. They were taking one or two foreign students at a time. I aspired to become one of those students.

I talked to Kottas about this after I had been training with him for some months. At that time, he told me that I would need at least another year before he would feel comfortable allowing me to take the entrance examination. I continued training with him throughout 1978. The training program was demanding. As a student, you were rarely praised. The feedback was almost always negative, and the constant criticism served as the encouragement to improve.

In addition to taking lessons at Kottas's barn, his students were allowed to watch the morning classes at the Spanish Riding School. At least three or four days a week, I would go to the school in the early morning. I never tired of watching the riders.

When I first arrived in Vienna, I had left Gesar in Boulder. He stayed at the Court with Pat because I didn't know if my living situation in

Europe was going to be stable enough for him. It was difficult for him to be separated from me. He used to ask Pat to call me so that we could talk on the phone. He was quite concerned about when he could join me. After about six months, I found a nice house to rent, with a garden with plum trees and a beautiful lawn.

When I moved into my little house in Vienna, on Roterdestrasse, I arranged for Pat to bring Gesar over to live with me. (By this time Jeanine had returned to the United States.) Pat and her new husband, Tom Adducci, both lived in the house with us. Soon after Gesar arrived, I took him to a performance at the Spanish Riding School, which he loved. It gave him some idea of what his mother was doing all this time in Vienna.

When he was four-and-a-half, Gesar enrolled in kindergarten at the British Diplomatic School in Grinzing, a very nice area of Vienna. Although his school was conducted in English, he also learned German during his time in Vienna. I think this was a positive time in Gesar's life. He found it exciting to live in Europe. However, the other children sometimes teased Gesar on the bus to school. They called him Quasar, and then they called him *Gay*-sar. For the winter, I bought him a Russian-style fur hat, and he looked very cute in it. The kids would steal his hat and throw it around the bus.

As the end of 1978 approached, Kottas and I agreed that I was ready to take the entrance examination to become a foreign student at the Spanish Riding School. I was both terrified and excited by the prospect that I might actually be riding there in the new year. I wrote a letter to the director of the Spanish Riding School, Colonel Albrecht, requesting that I be allowed to take the entrance examination. My test was scheduled for the middle of December.

The day of the examination arrived. Afterward, I wrote to Rinpoche, describing my experience:

> The whole thing was quite fantastic. It should have been a time to be most paranoid, because I was being judged by the best school in the world. Strangely, I felt very at home. I arrived at the Spanish Riding School twenty minutes before the test and was very nervous. I roused my sense of confidence.
>
> As I set foot into the sand of the arena, I was overwhelmed

with the feeling that it was sacred ground. Siglavy Beja, the riding master's star horse, was led out. He was wearing a bridle inlaid with gold. The groom held him as I mounted and then I put all four reins in one hand (left) and dropped my right hand and as I walked past the portrait of Emperor Karl, I saluted. I then proceeded to ride. The reins are held in the traditional manner with three in the left and one only in the right to leave room for the sword.

The commands were called and as I started to ride, I realized that I felt completely at home. The horse was the most wonderful one I have ever ridden. He is a Lipizzaner stallion, like the old sculptures with a baroque neck. He felt so strong and energetic. There was never speed, but only rhythm and power.

At some point I was told to stop. I dismounted and saluted. The director came and shook my hand and told me that I had passed. I am very grateful to my teacher for his support throughout the test.

Riding in such a beautiful environment on such a magnificent horse, I was totally carried away. The environment had its own magical wholesomeness, and I lost all awareness of myself. Only afterward did I realize that it had been like a dream with only impressions of color and energy. It was very brilliant. I hope I don't sound overdramatic, because I feel very grounded. It was the most intense experience of my life. I now understand what you mean when you talk about 100 percent lack of doubt.

You know, without your teaching, I never could have appreciated the experience. Thank you.

Even now, when I look back on the entrance examination, I remember how awe-inspiring it was to ride in that hall for the first time. The manège, or the arena, itself is huge: fifty-five meters long, eighteen meters wide, and seventeen meters high. Forty-six columns support the gallery. The interior is entirely painted in white and bathed in light, which comes both from the windows in the hall as well as the magnificent chandeliers that hang from the ceiling. It felt like such a gift to be able to ride in these circumstances. During the test I remember thinking, "Even if I don't pass this examination, at least I've ridden in this hall."

As Christmas 1978 approached, I felt a quality of joy and celebration in my life. It had been a long and difficult journey with many ups and downs, but I felt now a sense of satisfaction that I had accomplished a cherished goal: to be accepted as a student in the Spanish Riding School. I looked forward to beginning my studies there in the new year.

On December 24, 1978, I rode in a Christmas quadrille at Kottas's barn. A quadrille is when a number of riders execute all of the same dressage movements in formation together. It is quite beautiful and requires a great deal of harmony and communication among all of the riders and their horses. After the quadrille, we had a party where a hot alcoholic punch was served. I had invited Gesar, Pat, and Tom to come and watch the quadrille and stay for the party. Pat had driven her car to the barn, and she took Gesar home early in the evening. Tom and I stayed later, and we both got a bit intoxicated. I had just purchased a used powder-blue Mercedes. Tom volunteered to drive my car home, and I accepted. On the road from the barn going through the Vienna Woods, there were steep hairpin turns. The road was quite icy. At a certain point, as we were driving around one of these hairpin turns, Tom said to me, "Hang on." Up to that point, I hadn't realized that anything was the matter. However, the car was skidding out of control on the ice, and the road was about to go into an even sharper turn. Tom tried to drive the car off of the road between two trees so that we could come to rest in a field. However, the passenger side of the car, just behind my seat, impacted with the tree. The tree crushed my seat forward against the dashboard, and I knew immediately that I was seriously hurt. I wasn't wearing a seat belt. I think if I had been, I would have died, actually, because of the way the tree came through the back seat. The only thankful part was that Gesar had gone home earlier with Pat. If Gesar had been in the back seat, he would have been killed.

I remember knowing that I must have broken some bones, but I still wanted to get out of the car, which I probably shouldn't have. People from the barn pulled me out of the car, and I remember lying on the road. Tom was fine, but he was hysterical. He nearly got run over because he was completely panicking. A doctor who had been at the quadrille stopped to help us, but without medical equipment, he couldn't do much.

They called an ambulance, and I was taken to the hospital. I didn't have any say about where the ambulance took me. They drove me to

what they call in Germany a Gastarbeiter Krankenhaus, which is a so
of immigrant workers' hospital. Most of the patients were Turkish work
ers who didn't speak German. At the hospital, I told the staff that the
absolutely were not allowed to cut off my riding boots. It's funny th
things you fixate on in a situation like this. It turned out that I had frac
tured four ribs and that I had a fair amount of bleeding into my lung
and chest cavity.

The facilities at the hospital were primitive. The beds didn't evei
crank up and down. There was a metal bar that hung from the ceiling
and if you wanted to sit up, you had to grab hold of it and pull yoursel
up. It was Christmas Eve, so they had to get the doctor on call to com(
into the hospital from a party he was attending. A rotund, white-hairec
Austrian doctor arrived. As he leaned over me and was asking me how l
was feeling, he exhaled what seemed to be pure Schnapps. I became terrified about what might happen to me at that point. Altogether, the hospital stay was frightening and uncomfortable. The only good thing wa$
the food. However, I couldn't appreciate it that much because I was in a
considerable amount of pain and they were stingy with the pain med-
ication. My ribs weren't just cracked; they were actually severed. I had a
liter of blood in my left lung.

When word of the accident got back to Colorado, the rumor went
around that I'd been driving the car and that I shouldn't be allowed to
drive myself anywhere ever again. Actually, of course, I hadn't been driving. But we hadn't gotten insurance on the car yet, and the car was destroyed. It was a total disaster.

I remember feeling somewhat devastated while I was in the hospital.
My teacher Kottas didn't visit me once. My mother didn't call me either.
I had been fighting with my mother over the phone for a few weeks
prior to that, over petty things. But she couldn't let things go enough to
just pick up the phone and ask if I was okay. I felt abandoned by her once
again.

I talked to Rinpoche frequently by phone from the hospital. After a
few days, I told him that I wanted to come home to the United States to
recuperate, but he was concerned about my traveling when I was badly
injured and said that I would have to stay in Austria and weather it out.
In fact, I don't think they would have let me get on a plane at that point.
Mitchell Levy, Rinpoche's doctor and my very good friend, stayed in

communication with me. He explained to me that the doctors in Vienna didn't feel I was stable enough to travel. I was quite miserable. After a week in the hospital, I was allowed to return to my house in Vienna, but then I had to return to the doctor because I hadn't reabsorbed some of the blood from my chest cavity and I continued to be in a great deal of pain. The doctor decided to insert a needle in my chest to try to drain off some of the blood. Something went wrong, I became very ill again, and I had to go back into the hospital for another week. When I was finally sent home, I had to stay in bed for over a month. I was laid up altogether for seven weeks. I wasn't allowed to ride at all for several months. This was depressing to me because it delayed my entrance into the Spanish Riding School.

In May of 1979, I was finally well enough to start riding at the Spanish. I would go to the school in the morning, and then I would go back to Kottas's barn and ride there in the afternoon. It was a busy schedule.

There was a strict dress code at the school. Every day I would ride in white breeches and immaculately clean boots, and I polished my spurs every day with silver polish. I wore a white shirt with what we call a white stock tie, a black jacket, and a black derby, which is a hat somewhat like a bowler hat.

The horses live across the road from the manège in stables built for the Spanish Riding School. In the morning, they are led by the grooms under the big arches across the road, right through the traffic, and all the traffic stops for the horses. The horses are born black, and as they grow older they become first gray and then white. However, to this day, they still try to have a dark horse in the school, just one horse of a different color. Lipizzaners are not very big horses, but they're very powerful. They have short backs and strong necks, and often a baroque look to their head, somewhat like the Michelangelo paintings of horses. Some of them have a bit of a Roman nose.

I would arrive at the school at 6:30 to 6:45 every morning and pick up my plan, which would tell me which horses I would be riding and who my instructors would be. Every day began with a longe lesson, followed by two other lessons. Sometimes the head rider would be kind enough to let me ride his horse, in which case I would have a longe lesson and then be allowed to ride three other horses.

The format of the lessons was extremely formal and traditional. The

rider comes into the arena at exactly the prescribed time for the lesson. You would salute the portrait of King Karl, the founder of the Spanish Riding School, and then you would track to the right. You would perform the exercises and make corrections as dictated by the instructor. At the end of the lesson, you would line your horse up parallel to the short side of the arena. Then, you would dismount, salute your instructor, and then, if you wished, you could ask him a question. At this point, periodically the director would come out and you would face him and salute him also.

Dressage has been practiced in an unchanged form at the Spanish Riding School for the last four hundred years. The transmission of this equestrian art form is mainly an oral tradition, handed down from one rider to the next. The form that is practiced at the school is a little different than the form of dressage that's practised in competition today. Although the Lipizzaners are not used for competition, the Spanish Riding School is still to this day the holder of the classical ancient tradition of dressage, as it was practiced in the sixteenth century.

I remember my first day there vividly. My initial lesson was a longe lesson, which seemed to go fairly well. For the second lesson, they brought in a horse in with a snaffle bridle (a single set of reins with one bit), and I started to ride him around the arena. The instructor said, "Oh, you think you're so good, but you're terrible. You can't even put this horse on the bit. [This refers to the horse having the correct head positions.] You're a dreadful rider. What's more, your posture is terrible. You don't sit up straight at all. We're going to ask you to ride with a whip behind your elbows to make you sit up straight. Don't lean on it; don't apply any pressure, because this is the property of the Spanish Riding School, and we'd prefer that you don't break it."

I was in physical pain that day as I rode because my broken ribs were still healing. At a certain point, I started to sweat, and my hat started to slip. The instructor said, "Look at you. You look like you came out of the *heurigan*," which is a wine bar in Vienna. I remember thinking to myself, "I wish I had come out of the *heurigan*. This would be more pleasant if I were drunk." Then the instructor said again, "Oh look at you. You think you're so good, but you still can't put the horse on the bit." It was a dreadfully demeaning experience.

Later on, I learned that none of the riders at the school could put this horse on the bit in a snaffle bridle. They only rode it in the double bridle, which is much more refined and powerful. The instructor was just being nasty because it was my first day and this was how they treated all the new riders. As well, I think there was definitely a stigma about women and foreigners riding in this venerable Austrian institution. But fundamentally, this is just their way of teaching.

After I finished for the day, I was upset and also noticeably disoriented. Driving back to the barn to ride my horses in the afternoon, I took a wrong turn and ended up heading in the direction of Czechoslovakia. I was preoccupied by my disastrous ride that morning. When I finally got turned around and made it to the barn, I said to Kottas, "So, are they going to kick me out?" He laughed at me and said, "No, no, this is normal."

I had been waiting for so long to study at the Spanish Riding School, and after just one day, I was feeling deeply discouraged and humiliated. However, I was determined to go forward. I remember thinking, "If I want to get the training and I want to learn this properly, I am going to have to take my personal feelings out of the situation. I'm going to have to take nothing personally and try to take only the good out of this. I have to use my time to learn. I must try my best and not become upset with anything that anybody says." Amazingly, I stuck to this, and this attitude held me in good stead the entire time that I rode in the school. Rinpoche had given me the basic advice that I needed when I started riding with Kottas, and now I found that I could give myself the advice to persevere at the Spanish, knowing that this was a precious opportunity that would not come again.

There's definitely value in the approach they follow at the school. Putting intense pressure on people creates such a sharp edge that people have to push themselves very hard to absolutely do their best. On the other hand, sometimes this approach can have a demeaning and degrading aspect to it. When you are trying your best and the teacher is still relentlessly criticizing you, ultimately you may begin to loathe your instructor. In fact, I think this method encourages that. I definitely went through periods of that when I was training in the school. The mentality is that you will get good in spite of your instructor. You feel that, because they're so demeaning, you're going to show them.

When I'm working with my own students, I try not to rob them of their self-esteem. When people are learning a discipline, it's essential at times to put pressure on them. I had witnessed Rinpoche using this approach with people, including myself, many times. You have to inspire people to perform at their best. However, if you make people feel worthless, you create aggression between teacher and student. I feel that 99 percent of what I learned in the Spanish Riding School was fantastic, but 1 percent was, for me, about learning what not to do as a teacher. This is just my opinion. I don't feel qualified to pass judgment on the methods they use at the school because they've produced brilliant riders and brilliant horses. It is my personal feeling, however, that we should always work with students in an uplifted manner.

As time went on, my experience in the school became more and more enriching. I think I earned respect by sticking with the program and not being overly reactive. I was given exceptional horses to ride, and I had exceptional instructors. I also had the opportunity to broaden my knowledge about dressage and horsemanship in general by reading books in the wonderful library at the school.

At the Spanish, I also began to understand dressage in another way, as a true Shambhala discipline. The discipline of dressage is a very direct way of harnessing windhorse. At times when I was training there, my riding would completely "click." When everything clicks into place, the experience is unbelievable. You feel that nothing whatsoever is happening, in a very positive sense. How do you verbalize that? Your mind and your horse's body become as one. You experience a regal, uplifted feeling that Rinpoche would describe as the experience of the universal monarch. At times it goes beyond even that. You can have an experience of non-thought, mind beyond mind. The horse also shares some of this experience, I believe. The horses get absolutely hooked on the energy and the discipline if the rider is good.

Recently, I was listening to one of the top coaches in the United States talk to his students before they went around the ring at a horse show. He said: "Pull yourself up. Let them know that you're there. Radiate confidence when you go around the ring. Make the judges say, 'look at me.'" From my perspective, he was basically explaining in his own way how to raise windhorse. He had obviously had this experience himself, and he was trying to communicate it. I believe that the best riders all understand this.

So much of riding is working with your own state of mind. If you let your mind get in the way, you can't work with your horse. I see that in terms of my own development, and I see that in watching other riders and working with students. To be a good rider, you have to go beyond your conceptual ideas about it. You've got to constantly question yourself, to question your state of mind, to push yourself, to constantly be looking at yourself. Otherwise, you don't get any better. There's never a feeling of having mastered the discipline. You can never master dressage. Anybody who's any good is constantly learning. There's never a sense of having arrived at an ultimate destination.

Dressage also teaches you the ability to focus. If you're riding well, even at the most basic level, you don't think about anything except what you're doing. You are completely focused. You have to have control over your mind. If you can't control your mind, you definitely can't control your horse's mind. I learned this over and over again while I was training at the Spanish Riding School.

The head rider, Ignaz Lauscha, was extremely generous to me during my time at the school. He was in his sixties at that point and close to retirement. He took me under his wing, and he would sometimes let me ride his best horse, which led the quadrille at the school on a regular basis. Lauscha was a wonderful instructor, and the horse was also an amazing teacher because he was fantastically trained. With this horse, you could go from the extended trot into passage and back into the extended trot with the most delicate of aids. The extended trot is when the horse is able to trot with the farthest possible reach of the legs. Passage is a very slow, floating trot. (It covers ground, unlike the *piaffe,* which is trotting in place.) In passage the horse is able, as he trots forward, to hold a very high degree of suspension. He's able to hold himself in the air for longer periods of time, giving a very noble gait. It requires a great deal of strength. One might say it's sort of like equine push-ups. Lauscha's horse was gifted in both the passage and the extended trot, and he could move from one to the other flawlessly.

Ignaz Lauscha had the most beautiful tack on his horse, the most beautiful bridle inlaid with gold. Once when he let me ride his horse, he asked me to ride a half halt before I performed the next movement. A half halt is a rebalancing of the horse. You brace your back, you close your leg, and you push the horse more up to the bridle, so that you are encouraging the horse to shift the center of gravity more to the hind legs. It's sort of punctuation in your riding. He asked me to rebalance the horse, and he wasn't satisfied with the way I did it, so he said to me, "Come on. Half halt!" Then, I made a much bigger one, at which point his gold bridle broke into all these little pieces. I remember them falling to the ground. He said, "Well, you did what I told you, but you broke the bridle!" He was really nice about it. I'm sure it must have been already weak.

Another time I had some difficulty when the director gave me his horse for a lesson. He was well known as an international judge, but he wasn't a fantastic rider. He thought he was an excellent rider, but he had some problems. He had a stallion that he used to ride all the time, and everybody used to laugh at him when he was riding because he used to ride around the arena in a peculiar gait, which he thought was passage. He looked very snotty, with his nose and his chin held up as he rode. We would all sort of snicker at him because his horse was doing the strangest thing with only his front legs whilst the hind legs shuffled along. Then the terrible day came when he said to me, "Because you've been studying so hard, I'm going to allow you to ride my stallion." I thought, "Oh no," because I knew I could never produce passage on that horse. It was a dreadful lesson because he kept saying to me, "Ride passage, ride passage." Probably the horse was doing exactly the same thing with me that it did with him. He obviously had no idea that this was what the gait looked like when he was riding, so he could only be critical of me. Everybody was laughing while I rode.

Another movement that I worked with quite a lot at the Spanish was the flying changes of lead, when the horse changes from one leading leg at the canter to the other leading leg at the canter, without any trot or intermittent walk steps. He just reverses which leg he's leading with in midair. At Grand Prix, the highest level of dressage, a horse learns to do that on every single stride. It's a very difficult movement, because the horse is really no longer cantering at that point. According to the classical view, which is that dressage uses only the natural movements of the horse in the field, the flying change at every stride is a controversial movement because you actually have lost the gait of the horse at that point. So you're taking the training beyond what the horse would naturally do.

One day when I was riding Siglavy Dubovina, the horse of the head rider, he said to me, "All right, just canter down the center line, through the pillars, making flying changes every stride." I had no clue how to do this. (The pillars, by the way, are two posts that are two-and-a-half meters high, with one-and-a-half meters of space between them. As part of their training, the most advanced horses often stand between the pillars and do *piaffe,* the trot in place, for a long time.) Flying changes at every stride was one movement I hadn't yet ridden. As I rode past Kottas, I said to him under my breath, "How do I do this?" And he said to me, "In the Spanish Riding School we don't ask questions." So I just turned down the center line, and I gave the horse the aids that I thought would be correct for flying changes every stride. The horse was so beautifully trained that he just did it for me. I was thrilled.

There are many classical movements, classical figures, in dressage, just as there are positions in ballet. In dressage, however, many of the figures have their roots in battle movements. For example, canter pirouette was used in battle when you came with a sword toward your enemy. Then, to leave, you'd continue in the full pirouette. The canter half-pass and the trot half-pass, when you go both forward and sideward, were supposed to confuse your opponent, because he couldn't know on which line you were traveling. The flying changes of lead in the air made it possible to turn and escape quickly.

The military origins of dressage are reflected in many customs at the Spanish. For example, when you ride with a double bridle with four reins in the Spanish Riding School, you ride with three reins in the left hand and one in the right. (I mentioned this in the letter I wrote after my examination.) This tradition came about so that your right hand wouldn't be too encumbered to use a sword in battle. Normally, outside of the Spanish, we ride with two reins in each hand. Some military traditions are ubiquitous, however. For example, the main reason that one always mounted the horse from the left side was because the sword used to be on the left hip, so you didn't want the sword to hit the horse as you went over the top. That is now the universal convention. Also, in the Spanish Riding School the mane has to be on the right of the horse's neck. This was so that if you drew your sword, you wouldn't have the mane caught up with your sword.

There are also classical dressage movements that are only practiced at the Spanish. These make up what is called the "haute school," or the airs above the ground. They are not practiced in modern-day competition. However the Lipizzaners are especially talented at these movements. I had the opportunity to experience many of them while I was riding at the Spanish. When I had photos taken at the end of my time there, I did some of these movements for the photographs. I didn't do them on a daily basis, however. One, called the *levade,* is an amazing expression of collection and shifting of the center of gravity to the hindquarters. The horse actually sits down and brings the forehand completely off the ground. You see many statues in Europe in that pose. Unlike when a horse rears up, in the *levade* the horse's legs are bent. In the *pesade,* the horse also has his weight completely on the hind legs, but he is raised up even a little bit higher, but is still on flexed hind leg. This is completely different from when horses rear, which is disobedient.

Then you have the capriole, which is a battle movement in which the horse jumps off the ground and kicks out violently with both hind legs. You could unseat your opponent in that way. There is another movement called the *courbette* in which the horse comes up on his hind legs, and he jumps forward four to six strides on his hind legs. In battle, you could use that move to advance on your opponent. All in all, it must have been a beautiful war!

I remember the rich feeling of being immersed in the training at the school. Periodically my mind would just stop, and I would think, "How incredibly fortunate I am to be in such a wonderful situation as this." It was so brilliant riding on those horses in that hall, which itself was exquisite and uplifting. There is nothing I've done either before or after that matches that experience. I feel extremely fortunate to have ridden in the Spanish Riding School, and I had that sense of appreciation and almost awe during the whole time I was there.

At the end of my three-month session, I talked to the director, Colonel Albrecht. I said to him, "I know I've almost completed the session. However, I want to understand this tradition more fully, because I want to become a well-trained instructor in the future. I'd like to request that you let me stay for a further few months. In that way, I can learn even more, so that I can take some of this tradition home with me."

When the director told me that it was all right and I could stay longer, I was so happy that I gave him a huge hug. He was appalled, I think, but he said I could return.

After I received the acceptance to stay on, I went home to Colorado for a few weeks of the summer, knowing that I would be allowed to return in the fall. I began to ponder what I was going to do in terms of future training after the Spanish. I had a wonderful situation training at Kottas's barn, but after riding in the Spanish itself, I felt that my time in Vienna was drawing to an end. When I was home, Rinpoche and I discussed my future direction. At one point, he suggested to me, "The training at the Spanish Riding School is excellent classical training for you. However, from what you've told me, the competitive tradition is centered in Germany at this point, and I think you will want to understand both schools and both traditions. To complete your training properly, perhaps you should ride in Germany for a few years."

Rinpoche's instincts about my riding career were amazingly accurate. As I said earlier, he had a connection to horsemanship that went back to Tibet. Rinpoche had a white Chinese thoroughbred in Tibet which he rode from earliest childhood on. His horse could do passage, the slow, floating trot in which a horse hovers above the ground a little bit, in moments of suspension. It looks very elegant and lofty. He said that when he would travel to a new monastery, he would do passage as he entered.

Horses were part of his culture. People there still traveled everywhere on horseback; in fact, in parts of Tibet they still do. He always loved horses. But how he knew what was good for me in the Western riding world is a bit of a mystery. His advice to me at this time was instrumental in my decision to leave Austria and go to Germany. I don't think I would have gone there without his influence.

In the latter part of 1979, I wrote to Herbert Rehbein, who was the current German professional champion and legendary in terms of his ability to produce Grand Prix horses. In my letter, I asked if I could bring my horses up in late 1979 and study with him when I had finished in the Spanish. I was happy to receive a letter of acceptance, and I took my horses up to northern Germany just before Christmas in 1979.

Herr Rehbein worked for a man by the name of Otto Schulte Frohlinde, an elderly gentleman who was a patron of dressage. He had built a facility north of Hamburg, which had a stunning indoor arena, as well as beautiful stalls for the horses. It was a first-class, state-of-the-art riding facility. The floors in the barn were mosaics in brick, and everything was immaculate and magnificent. After my horses were transported up there, I had a chance to settle in over Christmas.

After the Christmas holidays, I met Herr Rehbein. I was struck by his persona from the start. He had the real air of a master. He was very genuine, a man who had a thorough mastery of his riding yet was always gentle and kind. He was someone whom Rinpoche would have said had authentic presence. He was a wonderful instructor. I remember thinking during the first few weeks that I rode with Rehbein how accurate Rinpoche had been in recommending that I go there. I had experienced some difficulties with my big Hanoverian horse, Warrior. Herr Rehbein was brilliant in helping me to sort out these problems.

When I was at Gronwohldhof, Rehbein's barn, I was also given the opportunity to ride other horses apart from my own. I had many opportunities to feel Grand Prix movements on different horses. Rinpoche termed the place a factory for producing great horses, and it was quite a marvelous environment in which people could learn. Rehbein provided a very open ground, and when you saw the people working around you, they didn't make many mistakes as riders. You found yourself going along with the program, and it worked. It was very different from Vienna. There wasn't a lot of external pressure. The approach was quite positive for everybody. Things went well for people, and so you went along.

I'd heard about Herbert Rehbein for a number of years before I began studying with him. He was known at that time to be one of the greatest dressage teachers and riders. He was quite selective about whom he would teach. He also had a reputation for ignoring people who had come to study with him. Sometimes he would say, "Good morning," and that was it. He wouldn't teach them directly at all. He was thought of as a moderately outrageous character, in his own way. This was familiar to me, so it didn't really bother me. I found that he was very helpful with my riding. Herr Rehbein taught that if you're rash and aggressive with your horse on a regular basis, this reflects a lack of knowledge. There are many different ways to communicate something to your horse, and you have to be flexible. If you try to teach your horse something, and he doesn't understand right away or doesn't respond, you don't become aggressive. You have to think, "Can I explain this a different way? Do I need to break it down? What in the communication isn't working? What do I need to establish again in terms of the basic rules?" He stressed that trainers who frequently beat their horses and are abusive to them are never going to produce a good end product.

I've seen horses that shake before their saddles are put on, and I've seen horses that, when they're taken to learn *piaffe*, will actually lie down because they're so afraid. I witnessed this during my time in Vienna— not at the Spanish, but at other barns. You need to be firm, but you never need to be abusive. Of course, if the horse is really out of control, sometimes you have to use very strong methods, but that should be rare.

Herr Rehbein had an enormous amount of experience and seemingly endless psychological resources. He was able to help me train my horses in a very kind way. I learned a great deal from him in a short time.

In this training environment, I felt a sense of genuine relaxation for the first time. In my heart, I'd always known the way that I wanted to ride my horses. When I came to Rehbein, I felt that I was given the freedom to experiment. Everything started to come together. It was a magical time; the riding became very cohesive. In terms of learning how to train horses, it was the first time I was able to trust my basic instincts thoroughly and take possession of the knowledge that I'd accumulated. I felt that he empowered me to do that. I always felt that the hallmark of Rinpoche's teaching was his ability to appreciate people's strength and then to give them the freedom to express this and to develop their own intelligence. Herbert Rehbein was that type of teacher too. Studying with him, I started to come into my own.

I remember watching Herr Rehbein doing a canter pirouette on his horse. He had a feeling of complete, total relaxation. I was watching him ride in front of the mirror, and he was looking at himself in the mirror. His horse was executing an absolutely perfect canter pirouette. I looked up and realized that Rehbein had the reins in one hand and was fumbling in his breast pocket with the other. I finally realized that he was looking for his cigarettes. He managed to pull out a Marlboro and light it, while the entire time, his horse stayed in a double or triple pirouette that was absolutely perfect, right in front of the mirror. Rehbein was really a riding genius, the likes of which the century did not see again.

After spending a few months at his facility in the beginning of 1980,

I took my horses over to England for a few months. Gesar had been enrolled in school there the previous fall. Tom and Pat had taken him over. I didn't want to keep putting him in and out of school, and I knew that—at this point in time—I could only stay at Rehbein's for a few months. We had rented a small house in England that was called the Deerkeeper's Lodge, on a large estate. You went down a long driveway to this ancient house, built in the sixteenth century.

I came over to England to have the opportunity to compete my horses there. At that time, all foreign horses in England had to go through a test at the National Riding Centre, and then you were told at which level you had to compete. But I felt that I was forced to compete at a level that was too difficult for my horses, especially for Warrior. I think the English didn't want foreigners to bring their horses into the country and then start winning in all the shows. There was a bit of a prejudice toward me, I felt, because I had trained my horses on the continent. However, all in all, I enjoyed the time I spent in England reconnecting with my English roots.

This was the end of a long period when I had quite a bit of independence in my marriage. Although I felt very committed to Rinpoche, at the same time, I was living my own life. There was an interesting tension there. I had realized years ago that I couldn't spend my life having doors slammed in my face, and there was definitely an element of that when I was around him. Everybody wanted to get to Rinpoche, and I was sort of superfluous, on some level. Once when we were on vacation in Mexico, the person helping Rinpoche opened a swinging door for Rinpoche to go in, and then just let it go in my face. At times, it was like I was invisible. I felt that I needed to pursue something for myself or I was going to get depressed. As a creative person, I couldn't play the role of his passive wife all the time. People didn't feel they could be judgmental about Rinpoche, but it was easy for people to be judgmental about me. I didn't want to get caught up in that. Instead, I concentrated on developing myself, through engaging in a discipline that I had a great passion for.

During the years that I was in Vienna, I tried to spend seven months in Europe and seven weeks back home. I had that formula in my mind, seven months and seven weeks. I made a point of coming back for things that were important to Rinpoche. I also started the Shambhala School of

Dressage in Boulder, and it continued during my absence. A student of mine and fellow rider, Mary Louise Barrett, would run the school when I was away. I would teach when I came home.

During the summer of 1981, after spending several months in England with Gesar, I decided to leave England and return to Colorado for an extended period of time. I wanted to concentrate on developing the Shambhala School of Dressage, where I was trying to introduce classical dressage training. I decided to bring one of my horses, Shambhala, home with me.

FIFTEEN

Back in late February 1977, a few months before I had first moved to Vienna to study with Arthur Kottas, Rinpoche went into his year's retreat in an old farmhouse in Rowe, Massachusetts. The property was close to Charlemont, and we always referred to the place simply as "Charlemont." Charlemont was an old house, so old in fact that there was a separate little room for the telephone. When anyone called to talk to Rinpoche, he had to go into this little booth off of the living room to speak with the caller. There was a large country kitchen and dining room on the main floor, as well as a living room and an office off of that. This was well before the era not only of cellphones but also of home computers. There was a typewriter in the office that was used for typing up the various documents and poems that he wrote throughout the year. Upstairs, there were a number of bedrooms.

According to Rinpoche, there was a ghost in the house, named Rosie, and Rinpoche was very fond of her. Once when I was visiting him, he said, "You know, I was at the top of the stairs today, and Rosie was standing there with blood pouring down her chest. We were talking about the arrangement of the furniture, and she wasn't sure if she liked the way that I'd changed the furniture around." I could sometimes feel

Rosie around Charlemont. As I was drifting off to sleep, I would feel that there was somebody else in the room. Rinpoche used to say that when someone dies, they become a ghost if they don't know that they're dead. At the right time, you can release them from being a spirit by telling them that they're no longer alive. Rinpoche never wanted to exorcise Rosie because he liked her so much.

Another time while I was visiting Rinpoche during his retreat, a local farmer dropped by the house. He had heard that a Tibetan lama was staying there. There was one area of the farmer's fields where the grass didn't grow normally. The grass lay flat in that area and it was a strange silver color, and he was having nightmares about two-headed cows being born there. He fertilized the grass and tried other things, but whatever he did, the grass wouldn't grow properly. Rinpoche said, "Fine, we'll come along. We'll see." So all of us who were there at the time went out to the field with him. From a distance you could see that the grass in that area was quite different. It looked unhealthy. Rinpoche took his walking stick with him. While he stood on the edge, he had everybody else sit in the middle of this area. We sat there and practiced meditation while he walked around with the stick tapping the ground and doing various chants. After a while, he said he had done the exorcism. He told us it was very sad, because somebody was stabbed in this place, and they were continuously reliving their death. "Now I've released him into the *bardo*," he said. We went back to the house and didn't think anything more about it. A year after Rinpoche's retreat, when the owner of the house was there, the farmer came by again, and he said he'd done some research. He had discovered that there had been a highway in the old days running through the field. Exactly in the location where the grass didn't grow, as best as the farmer could tell, a young man had been way-laid by a highwayman and stabbed. The farmer said that the grass had grown back normally the year after the exorcism was done.

As I mentioned earlier, Rinpoche took John Perks and Max King along as his staff in retreat, and throughout the year, other people were invited to visit and spend time with him there. A lot of the time that Rinpoche spent in Charlemont, it just seemed that he was hanging out and not doing very much. There was a shrine room there, and occasionally he did some formal practice, but most of the time, he sat and talked with people in the kitchen or the living room. Hanging out with Rinpoche was quite demanding, somehow. It wasn't like being entertained or anything. During one period of the retreat, Rinpoche, Max, and John all learned to catch flies that were buzzing around the kitchen with their bare hands. They would sit quietly and when the fly landed, they would swipe it up in their hand and then put it outside. That was what they did for entertainment.

Max in particular found it hard to be in this isolated situation after the first few months, and by the end of the year, he was ready to go back into "private life." Both he and John did the cooking. John got into a phase where he did a lot of Indian cooking, and he would sometimes make a great feast of Indian curries.

Rinpoche got reports about what was happening in the Buddhist community while he was away. During the first few months, his newly appointed regent made a tour of the various dharmadhatus, or meditation centers, around the United States. There were reports of Ösel Tendzin being very demanding and heavy-handed with people. People found the Regent to be an accomplished teacher, but he was also extremely critical of students at times, in ways that they found demeaning and excessively negative. I think he settled down after a couple of months, but it was in some respects a troubling sign of things to come in future years.

Later in the retreat, Rinpoche received messages expressing much more appreciation for the Regent. I heard from Rinpoche that people described the Regent as a very insightful teacher with a true grasp of the Buddhist path. I had few opportunities to hear him teach, in fact.

Occasionally, Rinpoche would leave the retreat—usually for a short jaunt to a nearby city. He would sometimes go out to dinner at a restaurant or go shopping. I think he ventured as far as Hartford, Connecticut, to buy some ties. Usually, he had a female companion staying with him in Charlemont. I was used to this arrangement by this point. I had my own life, and as far as I was concerned, he was there for me when I needed him. It really didn't bother me.

A lot of what Rinpoche was doing in retreat that year—when he wasn't catching flies—was working on various aspects of the Shambhala teachings, elaborating on the basic vision he had already conceived.

When Shakyamuni Buddha became enlightened, there were no Buddhist teachings or Buddhist texts. He had the experience of enlightenment and then gradually he began to expound the teachings, based on
what he had realized. In a similar way, when Rinpoche received the
stroke of Ashe in 1976, it was a primordial experience of the heart of
warriorship. Everything else came out of that over a long period of time.
While he was in Charlemont, he said that he could feel Padmasambhava
breathing down the back of his neck. Padmasambhava, as you may remember, was a very important figure in the transmission of Buddhism
from India to Tibet. He was an unconventional teacher who used whatever means were necessary to wake people up. Rinpoche identified with
him a great deal.

John Perks brought a record to the retreat called *Trooping the Colour,*
which is the music from the Queen's Birthday Parade, a ceremony held
each year where the Queen of England reviews the troops on horseback.
Rinpoche took one of the well-known tunes from this and wrote lyrics
for a Shambhala anthem, which was sung hundreds of times during the
Charlemont retreat and thousands of times thereafter. Over the next few
years, he wrote a number of Shambhala songs. Rinpoche did a lot of
other writing during his retreat as well, including a little unpublished volume about the Shambhala world called *Court Vision.* It has chapters in it
about the different roles that people would play in the Shambhala kingdom, including a chapter on the Sakyong Wangmo—which was me. My
role was described as the binding factor within Shambhala, harmonizing
all the energies in society. Rinpoche wrote that she should provide the
people of Shambhala "with a sense of genuine relationship to, and appreciation of, the kingdom. She must fully inspire them with a sense of loyalty and a natural sense of refinement. It is her task to harvest peace in
Shambhala, by developing sophistication and communication."[1]

I think about the kingdom of Shambhala as a way of describing how
one might relate to one's life altogether. If we live an uplifted life, with
kindness and decency, we might come to recognize that we are living in
this kingdom. All these years later, I am still working with understanding
my role as Sakyong Wangmo: what it means to me in a personal, intimate
way, how I can possibly live up to this, and how I can be helpful to others. The chapter on my role in *Court Vision* was a challenging portrait, to
say the least.

Over the years, I have come to appreciate the Sakyong Wangmo as a manifestation of the feminine principle. The Sakyong Wangmo represents the left side or the left hand of the Sakyong, who represents leadership overall in the Shambhala world. The feminine principle of the Sakyong Wangmo supports the Sakyong principle. In order to create a good society, you need to have the masculine principle of the Sakyong, which is steadfastness and action. At the same time, you also need to have the feminine principle, which is nurturing and gives birth to situations. In any society, it's very important to have both aspects of leadership.

While at Charlemont, Rinpoche also worked on the designs for Shambhala flags, pins, and the various Shambhala awards that he had created before leaving Boulder. He arranged for a number of medals to be handcrafted in England. He took the designs over with him when he came to Europe in the fall for my birthday.

Rinpoche made another long journey during the year he was in retreat. He left Charlemont in June to travel to the province of Nova Scotia on the east coast of Canada. At this time, he was already thinking about moving the headquarters of Vajradhatu to Canada, although there were very few people who knew this then. He felt that in the long run the United States would not be the best home for the Shambhala world. He sensed that in the future there would be a great deal of aggression to deal with in America; whereas he thought that in Canada the atmosphere would remain more peaceful and workable. Rinpoche was not afraid of obstacles such as aggression, which he regarded as simply the raw material of human life that we have to work with. He simply felt that certain environments were more conducive than others for the development of the Shambhala teachings and the personal development of his students.

Rinpoche had picked Nova Scotia as a possible home base from looking at it on a map of North America. He had never been there. I personally had never been to Nova Scotia either, and I couldn't quite imagine what we would do there. After his trip, he told me that the people he met there were open and kindhearted, and that something about the place reminded him of Tibet, oddly enough. He insisted on traveling with his party throughout Nova Scotia as Prince Mukpo of Tibet. I have no idea what people actually thought, but in some respects it was no stranger for the Nova Scotians than if he traveled as a high Tibetan lama. Certainly, he did not intend to enter Nova Scotia incognito. He was ready to make an impression on the place and engage the energy from the moment he set foot there.

I didn't entirely understand what he was doing with the Shambhala teachings at the time, but now when I look back on this era, I see it in terms of how I see Rinpoche altogether—as a great *mahasiddha,* someone who is presenting the essence of the teachings to people in their ordinary lives. From that perspective, I view his activity in terms of his compassion for his students and his vision for a time far into the future. It is hard to communicate just what an extraordinary and visionary person Rinpoche was. What I can communicate is simply how he manifested for me and the kind of absolute love I had for him and faith that I relied on to get through the difficult times. During 1977, sheltered as I was in Vienna with my own household and daily life, I was able to look with some equanimity on the early stirrings of Shambhala in North America.

At the end of the year, Rinpoche finished the retreat in Charlemont and visited Karme Chöling before flying to Boulder. I flew to the East Coast to meet him, and we flew back to Boulder together. It was an amazing homecoming. People had missed him so much, and he was overjoyed to see everyone. He picked up the reins and dove into his work with a great deal of renewed energy.

During the last six months that he was in Charlemont, he had asked his senior students to put together a program of meditation for non-Buddhists. We had come up with the name "Shambhala Training" for this program, and various senior students had been working in small study groups, trying to decide how best to present meditation together with the Shambhala teachings in a nonsectarian way. The various people who in Rinpoche's absence had directed the first weekends of Shambhala Training seemed to have only a vague idea what they were doing. They tended to rely on a parody of charisma, with little substance to it. So when Rinpoche returned to Boulder, he had a lot of work to do to put Shambhala Training on a genuine footing. Rinpoche began meeting with the Shambhala Training directors several times a week, introducing material on how to present the basic teachings to people in a direct, genuine fashion. After these meetings, which lasted throughout the early months of 1978, Shambhala Training took root. It became the main vehicle for Rinpoche and his students to introduce meditation and the path of the Shambhala warrior. Now, more than twenty years later, tens of thousands of people have gone through this program, and it continues to address the popular interest in meditation. I was there for a few of these early meetings, but then I was off to Vienna again, and I did not return until the fall.

There were several other Shambhala ceremonies that spring. Rinpoche empowered the members of the board of directors of Vajradhatu as ministers in the Shambhala kingdom, and he also had a ceremony jointly confirming John Perks as the Kusung Dapon and James Gimian as the Kasung Dapon of Shambhala (*dapon* means "chief" or "general" in Tibetan). I think that in essence, all of this was about making the people in his world think much bigger about their responsibilities. Rather than purely seeing themselves as administrators in a church, he wanted his senior students to view themselves as having a duty to society, a duty to help others on a big scale. There was always the danger that people would get an inflated view of themselves, and in a way he encouraged that. He would create a situation for people to expand their feeling of self-importance, and then he could prune that back, undercut it, and encourage people to develop genuine warmth and commitment.

This is not dissimilar to what occurs in a Vajrayana *abhisheka*. When students complete their preliminary practices, the empowerment they then receive is based on a sort of coronation. During the *abhisheka*, the student is presented with a crown, which symbolizes that one is the lord or lady of a particular family or energy. One is given a scepter, a bell, and other implements, and one receives a new name. The idea is that you are transforming ego into enlightened being. At the beginning, when you receive *abhisheka*, in a sense you are pretending to be something or someone. It's only through a long process of practice and surrendering that you can give up your small, ego-centered schemes. If you don't actually make that transformation, then you are just confirming your egomania. That is one reason that there are so many warnings about the Vajrayana path. The Shambhala empowerments are similar: one is assuming a new identity in the society of warrior bodhisattvas, and here too there is risk involved. However, Rinpoche was quite inspired about creating this new mandala, or Shambhala world.

Another seminary was held that spring, and there were more than

250 participants. This time, the seminary was held at the Balsams Hotel in Dixville Notch, New Hampshire. For many years, Vajradhatu arranged to rent grand old hotels that were not being used during their "down season." I don't think these hotels close up this way anymore. However, during this era, Vajradhatu was able to rent the entire hotel and take over running it for three months or more to hold these big programs. We provided our own kitchen staff, people did their own laundry and kept their rooms clean, and participants had jobs on a rota to clean the common areas. Usually, we converted a ballroom or large dining room into the meditation hall. It was like converting the hotel into a monastery for the period of the seminary. This was before we had expanded the facilities at our own centers to accommodate these large programs.

During this seminary, Rinpoche had a love affair with one of the participants, Cynde Grieve. He was quite in love, which he shared with me when we talked on the phone. This relationship went beyond what I was used to, and it was a little shocking at first. However, Rinpoche was so warm and loving with me, and so open, that I couldn't hold on to my insecurities. The reference point of a conventional monogamous marriage did not apply to our relationship, which remained very strong.

That summer, Rinpoche was scheduled, as usual, to teach a seminar at the Rocky Mountain Dharma Center. The subject of the seminar was announced as "Warriorship in the Three Yanas." *Yana* literally means "vehicle" and refers to the stages on the Buddhist path, the Hinayana, Mahayana, and Vajrayana. Several hundred people came to hear the talks. Rinpoche invited the members of the Dorje Kasung, the *vajra* guards, to set up an encampment in a field at RMDC, above the main facilities. There were about forty participants in the encampment, which was separate from the main program. Rinpoche decided that, although he was lecturing at night in a large tent down below, he would live at the encampment up above during the seminar and conduct intensive training there with the small group of Dorje Kasung.

Rinpoche lived in an L.L. Bean cabin-style tent at the encampment that first year. A few years later, he designed a white Tibetan-style tent that had a bedroom and a sitting room in it. It had beautiful embroidered patterns sewn onto it. Just below his tent there were two rows of smaller tents for the leadership of the Dorje Kasung, including David Rome (now known as the Kasung Kyi Khyap, or overall commander of the

Dorje Kasung), the two *dapons,* and other Dorje Kasung leaders. Other members of the Dorje Kasung lived in three large white tents farther down the hill. In later years, when there were up to three hundred participants, Dorje Kasung members lived in tents along the perimeter of the camp. There was also a meditation tent and a dining tent within the camp. All the *kasung* wore uniforms, which at that time consisted of khakis purchased from Army surplus. Later, we designed our own uniforms.

You couldn't just walk into this camp. There was a front gate, and you had to present yourself to the Dorje Kasung member on duty and state your business. Tent poles were erected on a parade ground, and the Shambhala flags were raised every morning and lowered in the evening, with the Dorje Kasung standing at attention and saluting. The Dorje Kasung sang the Shambhala anthem as well. The parade ground was a fairly flat area for drilling, which was a discipline that everyone learned at the encampment. From my experience of it in later years, I realize that it contains many of the same elements as dressage does, without the horses of course. At the encampment, marching was taught with tremendous emphasis on the precision of the discipline; the Dorje Kasung were learning mindfulness and awareness and invoking the energy of windhorse through the practice of drilling. It is quite an exhilarating experience to march in formation with so many other people. In a sense, everyone has to have one mind for the exercises to really work. In the discipline of the drill as it was taught at the encampment, there was an emphasis on learning to channel energy in much the same way as we teach our horses collection in dressage.

Before the encampment began, Rinpoche phoned me in Vienna to tell me how excited he was about this new program, and I received many reports about what happened there, both from him and others I was in touch with in Colorado. Many of the people down below at the seminar at RMDC didn't know what to make of the encampment. Some of them found it threatening, others just odd. All of the Dorje Kasung members would pile into a couple of old trucks to drive down to the evening talks, where there was a special section for them set aside in the tent. Rinpoche was giving a series of talks on how the Buddhist practitioner is a warrior who is rousing the energy of enlightenment. Up the hill, the Dorje Kasung were raising the warrior's cry and setting off a cannon every morning. It really pushed a lot of people's buttons.

A number of people decided to make raids on the encampment, which I think Rinpoche may have clandestinely encouraged. At night, therefore, there was a lot of activity in the camp responding to the invaders. Rinpoche would egg the whole thing on, by encouraging the camp to defend itself and suggesting that the Dorje Kasung should try to take prisoners. Then, he would do things to undercut the quality of people playing Cowboys and Indians. He started to develop various training exercises, and he introduced little twists that sharpened people's intelligence. For example, both the invaders and the defenders would use their flashlights to move around at night. Rinpoche pointed out that many flashlights have a red plastic edge to them, which makes the light glow slightly red in the dark. He told all the Dorje Kasung members to tape over the red plastic so that, if they saw a red light shining, they would know it was one of the "enemy." He also conducted exercises for the Dorje Kasung in which he taught them to lie down and be absolutely still in the dark. Later, he expanded this to show people how to "be like a rock." He had people do this for quite long periods of time, so that they began to learn how to blend into the darkness and the landscape while waiting for someone to attack. From what I heard, that first year was mind-blowing for the Dorje Kasung members who attended. It started with them being awkward and uncertain and feeling that they were pretending to be something, but by the end, people felt that they were connecting with some deep thread of warrior lore. It had a big effect on people, and Rinpoche certainly was delighted. The encampment became an annual affair.

I was not able to attend the encampment until 1980, the third year, when I actually brought horses to it and worked with a group of people there who were starting Windhorse, a division of the Dorje Kasung that we formed for people who ride. It was the Shambhala equivalent of the cavalry, I suppose—an unarmed cavalry, however.

Altogether, it seems interestingly synchronistic to me that I connected with the military tradition of the Spanish Riding School right around the time that Rinpoche began taking the Dorje Kasung much more in the direction of military discipline through the introduction of the encampment training process. What I found about the Spanish was that here was a tradition that relied so much on military discipline, yet no one uses horses in battle any longer. So it was taking the essence of the strength of that tradition and using it in an entirely different way. I suppose you could say that it is a Western martial art at this point.

Similarly, within the Dorje Kasung training, Rinpoche wanted to adopt aspects of the Western military tradition without the aggression and without the intent of killing others or causing harm. In some sense, his approach to the encampment was similar to having matches in aikido, but on a much bigger scale involving large groups of people. He was, to some extent, choreographing the whole situation so that it would allow people to uncover and work with aggression and fear. There is the appearance in the martial arts that you are working with an external enemy, but you discover that in fact the first thing you have to do is to work with your own state of mind and overcome the internal enemies. Of course, there are actual obstacles in life that one must confront. Ultimately, the Dorje Kasung discipline can prove to be a powerful ally in working with those external issues, but primarily it is a mind-training discipline that develops strength of character and teaches one to synchronize body and mind. Then it can provide the basis to work with chaos and conflict.

As well, Rinpoche always loved what he called "tent culture." In Tibet, he traveled in caravans from one monastery to the next over a period of days. The monks walked or rode on horseback and at night they camped. He loved this life. It was also how he lived for ten months when he walked out of Tibet. I think, being the person that he was, he had taken something very positive from that long, difficult journey and he wanted to share this outdoor life with his students. A great part of what he brought to the encampment was his appreciation for this. He also found that there were similarities between the military bivouac culture he created at the encampment and the monastic world that he came from. The quality of order and hierarchy applies to both. Rinpoche understood this as the ground of freedom, not the ground of aggression. I think that many of his students came to feel this quite profoundly as a result of the experiences they had at the encampment.

For me, these same years were also a time of committing myself to a discipline that had been firmly rooted for centuries in the life of the nobility in Europe. It was the kings and queens of Europe who kept dressage horses and built the great arenas for them to perform in. So, strangely enough, although I was away for much of the developing years of Rinpoche's Shambhala vision, I was also immersed in a regal training, of sorts.

In October 1978, I returned to the United States for the first Kalapa Assembly, the first large Shambhala program for the presentation of the most advanced Shambhala teachings. In this situation, as he had done in travelling through Nova Scotia, Rinpoche insisted that everything be conducted in a court mandala, with all of us living together in the Kingdom of Shambhala, but in Snowmass, Colorado! He presided over the assembly as the Sakyong, the ruling monarch of Shambhala, and I was at his side as the Sakyong Wangmo.

The first assembly was held in the same hotel in Snowmass where two of the earliest seminaries had taken place. Because the hotel could only hold about a hundred people, the assembly was divided into two two-week sessions, as there were now around two hundred people practicing the Shambhala teachings at the highest level. The whole program lasted for a month.

Rinpoche gave seventeen talks over the month, which was about one every other night. There was meditation practice during the day, people attended discussion groups, and then there were formal dinners, banquets, and a number of ceremonies. One of the highlights was a troupe of *bugaku* dancers performing an ancient repertoire of dances of the imperial court of Japan, who happened to be touring the United States at this time. Rinpoche's lectures reminded me in a way of the first seminary, in that he was giving an overview of the entire Shambhala path, and he was pouring both information and emotion into his talks. He was sharing his heart of hearts with people, trying to give us the essence of his understanding of the Shambhala teachings. That aspect I found magical and wonderful.

I was not so enamored of other things. I could see the point of Rinpoche as Sakyong; he was transmitting the wisdom of Shambhala to people, and I saw him as a unique human being. I thought that there should be an acknowledgment of his leadership and the wisdom that he embodied. Seeing him as the Sakyong, a spiritual king and protector of the earth, was not difficult for me. However, I couldn't understand why we were building up so many other people, putting them into positions that I thought were rather bogus. What was the point of having all these lords, ladies, ministers, and generals?

So at the beginning of the first assembly, I was quite uncomfortable. Actually, a lot of the participants were having quite a hard time adjusting to this new Shambhala world. I was certainly not the only one. Everybody was calling me "Your Highness." I had Dorje Kasung members accompanying me wherever I went, and Rinpoche wanted me to have my own personal attendants and all the rest of it. I found it incredibly awkward and unsettling to land in the middle of this heightened environment and to have to function in that world. I trusted him fundamentally, but I thought things had gone crazy. Actually, in some ways, from a conventional point of view, things *had* gone crazy and I was expected to uphold this crazy world! It was one thing to adjust to it, but I was actually supposed to be a spokesperson for what was happening.

I remember the day that this all came out. He and I were together in the suite at the hotel, and I broke down crying at some point. We were out on the balcony of the suite, which was on the roof of the hotel. Things were overwhelming to me. He sat down with me and started to explain his thinking. He was very sweet.

I think it was a hallmark of the way Rinpoche taught that he always appreciated something about a situation. Even in the worst of the worst conditions, he could always find wisdom. In this case, he started describing his appreciation for Mao Tse-tung. In spite of the devastation Mao had wrought in Tibet, Rinpoche admired certain aspects of his approach. Only someone with such a big mind, like Rinpoche, could appreciate someone like Mao, who had done these awful things that had destroyed Rinpoche's life in Tibet. He described to me how Mao Tse-tung proceeded when he decided he was going to conquer China. The first thing he did was to create the complete structure for the future government. Rinpoche said that Mao understood that when you attain power, there's a lot of chaos. You prepare for that future transition by having a structure in place that can function when things change. Rinpoche said that this applied to what we were creating with Shambhala; we had to plan for the chaos. If nothing else, Rinpoche had to plan for his own death. He wanted the people he was training to be prepared to go forward after his death and to have a big view of their responsibility and their duty in the future. He wanted to put them into positions of responsibility now so they would be fully trained and able to function after he was gone.

He explained to me that the future of the dharma in the West would inevitably involve pain and chaos. He thought it was quite sensible, in a strange way, to draw on Mao's approach. And you know, I actually could accept this. It made sense to me because I could see that the way he was working with people was preparing them to take on more responsibility, either within Vajradhatu or the larger society. You could see that people were becoming much more tamed and much more commanding at the same time. At that point, I was more able to relax and accept the situation.

After we talked, things seemed better to me. I decided that we weren't really nuts, although we were decidedly eccentric. What we were doing had a purpose that was founded in truth. Rinpoche also said that he was trying to provide an example for people, a structure for them to learn how to be, in ways that would be helpful to them. He talked about the importance of manifesting Shambhala society within our day-to-day lives. He was always thinking about how he could bring more people in and how he could work with people in an intimate way.

While I could accept this intellectually, it was extremely difficult for me to accept a total lack of freedom in my everyday life, which my role implied. Whenever I was living in Rinpoche's world, there was absolutely no break, no time off, so to speak. For so many years, even my bedroom wasn't my own. My attendants would come in and out of the bedroom all the time, and I was expected to be kind to them. There were constantly other people in the house. If I went into my kitchen, there were always other people there, even at three A.M. Although people were polite to me, there were people serving at the Court, especially men, who didn't understand what I needed for my children and myself. One of the reasons I was so upset, even in 1978, was that I could see that becoming the Sakyong Wangmo meant the complete relinquishment of my freedom, and that was extremely difficult for me to accept. Rinpoche was asking me to do what he had done, which was to accept having no privacy. Even now, I find this difficult. I have my own life, but when I go to programs with the Shambhala community, after three days, I think, "I'm so glad I don't live like this all the time!"

I gained some insight into how Rinpoche lived his whole life when I went to Tibet after his death. I saw that many of the teachers there live this way. They are completely accessible. People just come into a teacher's room unannounced all the time. I realized that this was how Rinpoche grew up—without any understanding of what privacy meant. He belonged to the people. Maybe it's easier if you've grown up in that environment.

It was, however, a big jump for me. Rinpoche wasn't any longer just the Buddhist teacher going into his office and giving talks. He was essentially asking me and his whole family to join him in this new teaching adventure. He was asking me to also take on a role and to train people as well as train myself. Now it wasn't just that he wanted me to put up with students being around all the time. He also wanted me to think of *myself* as a teacher or a role model in the Court. It was intense and challenging. At the same time, it was remarkable, given his upbringing and his culture, that he wanted to offer such respect and responsibility to a woman. He had developed tremendous respect for women, and proclaiming my role as the Sakyong Wangmo was a way of expressing that.

Rinpoche told me that I was him, basically, that we were one mind. He said that I was the feminine representation of the Sakyong. He told me that I had the responsibility of nurturing the feminine in our world: the cultural and enriching aspects of the kingdom. He said that we had to work together as a team and therefore that he wanted to put me on the same elevation as him. In my role as Sakyong Wangmo, I was given the responsibility to create our kingdom's culture.

That was what I was working with during the first Kalapa Assembly, and that was a huge leap for me at that point. On another very personal level, there was another big development in my life at this time. I became romantically involved with Rinpoche's doctor, Mitchell Levy, during the first assembly.

Before the assembly started, I was in Boulder with Rinpoche for a little while. It was the first time I had seen the new Kalapa Court, located at the corner of Eleventh and Cascade in Boulder. The house on Mapleton had proved too small for all of us, so we had found a new house, which was renovated over the summer of 1978. Rinpoche was able to move into the new Court a little while before the assembly started. He was anxious to share it with me. He and the Regent had worked together on the furniture and the interior decoration with various other people in the *sangha,* such as Robert Rader, a talented interior designer.

The new Court had much more light and a wonderful feeling to it, and it had more room for everyone, along with a beautiful garden. It was where we lived in Boulder until we moved to Nova Scotia in 1986, and it worked quite well for us. In the beginning, Rinpoche and I had a bedroom with a sitting room attached to it, and the Regent and Lila, who was now Lady Rich, were next door to us. Ösel also had a bedroom on the same floor upstairs. Down the hall were rooms for Vajra and Anthony, the Regent's children, and a room for Gesar. The living room downstairs had blue rugs that had dragon designs cut into them. They were custom-made for the Court, and they were supposed to be very special, but they didn't turn out so well. I used to call them the bath mats, which Rinpoche hated. All in all, however, the new house was a great improvement.

When I got home, I had a bad cough, and I was sure that I had bronchitis. I had a tendency to get respiratory infections at that time because I smoked. The night I got in from Vienna, Rinpoche and I had dinner together, and I was coughing a lot, so he suggested that I go downstairs and see his doctor, who was hanging out in the basement. The new Court had a full, finished basement on the ground floor, with quite a lot of light, so it was much improved over the old house. John Perks and his wife Jeannie lived there; Shari and Bob also lived in the basement, and soon Walter and Joanne Fordham also joined us as part of the live-in Court staff. The people who had these live-in positions were close students and friends, not servants in the traditional sense. Rinpoche's lineage is called the Trungpa lineage, and in Tibetan *trungpa* means one who is close to the teacher, which basically means "servant." It is quite a desirable thing in this lineage to serve the teacher because this is how you receive the most intimate training.

In addition to bedrooms, offices, and a staff living room in the basement, the Court also included a little carriage house where various staff people lived over the years. During certain periods, John Perks organized staff dinners, which took place in the basement either before or after the family ate. It was quite a nice setup and a lot of socializing in the house went on down there.

In any case, I went down to the basement and looked around and finally found this young Jewish gentleman, whom I'd never met before. This was Dr. Levy. He had a great deal of hair at that time; it almost looked like he had an Afro. I told him that Rinpoche had sent me to see him and that I had bronchitis. He told me, "I hate patients who diagnose themselves." Then he listened to my chest and said that he didn't think that I had bronchitis, and I was probably okay. I insisted that I had bronchitis, and he got a bit pissed off. There was chemistry between us right from the start.

I proceeded to go on up to the assembly, where I became increasingly ill. Mitchell came to see me again and realized that I actually did have bronchitis. In the course of treating my illness, we developed a liking for one another. In addition to being Rinpoche's doctor, Mitchell was also one of his main attendants, or *kusung*. Rinpoche liked having him around, so Mitchell was there a lot. He was in the suite all day. After I got to know Mitchell, I developed a real crush on him. Finally, I confessed to Rinpoche that I wanted to sleep with his doctor. Rinpoche thought that was a great idea. He told Mitchell that he should ask me out on a date. Mitchell had only been married a few months, so this idea freaked him out quite a lot at first. At the same time, he and his wife had what you would call an open relationship; but he still hesitated. Finally, he decided that he'd like to spend time with me, so he asked me out and that's how we got together.

I suppose this sounds like it was a quite casual arrangement, which might be shocking to people. At the beginning, I did think of it as a casual liaison. My husband, as many people knew, had a great number of girlfriends. It was something that I accepted, and perhaps because that was our arrangement, I also had the occasional indiscretion myself. In my case, there were not many of them, and they didn't have a great deal of meaning to me. Sleeping with somebody else had been an expression of friendship, and of course of youthful passion. I imagined that spending time with Mitchell would be the same. But that was not at all the case. From the very beginning, I had a special connection with him. At that assembly, we spent a fair amount of time together. By the end, we developed a strong bond, and I was falling in love with him. Rinpoche didn't seem to have a problem with it at all, at least not at that time. It got a little bit rockier later.

I didn't exactly think that I was having an affair. I didn't conceptualize the relationship much at that time. It was just what was happening.

Mitchell's wife, Sarah, knew what we were doing. In my mind, I figured everything was okay. I was married to Rinpoche, and Mitchell was married to Sarah. Mitchell and I had a nice relationship too, and it was going to be fine. I suppose it was a little naive on my part.

For the next two years, while I was living in Vienna, Mitchell and I saw each other whenever I was back in Boulder. When I was in town, we would spend about one night a week together. It seemed to be fine with everybody. It was, more or less, completely agreed upon. I adored Mitchell. I loved him. I found that there was great communication between us.

For me, one offshoot of the creation of the Court was that, in general, I found myself emotionally isolated from people. Having friendships with people was quite loaded in some ways. I had only a very few close friends. Other relationships seemed to be clouded by people having an agenda of personal gain. It was difficult to get away from that. I found that it was rare that I could have a relationship that didn't come with a lot of baggage.

My life was quite lonely at times. I felt a separation between me and the rest of the *sangha,* with me being the Sakyong Wangmo and being served and all of that. I imagine that my experience was somewhat like the queens of old. On some level we had recreated that culture. I felt that I had a fresh relationship with Mitchell, one completely outside of all of that. With him, I could really be who I was. I could share things with him, and I felt that he understood me better than almost anyone, except Rinpoche. My relationship with Mitchell gave me something to look forward to when I came home. As well, I could share my whole crazy life with him, without having to edit anything or hold anything back. I found that quite freeing. We shared a lot of the same perceptions, which was extremely helpful.

So this year, 1978, proved to be a watershed in our lives. After the Kalapa Assembly, I returned to Vienna. According to the Shambhala calendar, which we began to use in our community during this era, the new year usually comes in late January or February. The ten days at the end of the year are supposed to be a very tricky time, filled with obstacles. 1978 and early '79 was the Year of the Earth Horse, interesting for me because I was so involved with the horse world at this time. The very end of 1978 was when I had my automobile accident, which certainly seemed inauspicious. Because of this occurrence, I couldn't return to Boulder for the celebration of the New Year.

During the period that I was recuperating, Rinpoche phoned me several times a week to see how I was doing. In the middle of January, Rinpoche phoned me to tell me about a crisis involving the Vajra Regent. Since Rinpoche's return from Charlemont the previous year, the Regent had continued to manifest a lot of heavy-handedness and arrogance. He had moments when he really shone, and he worked extremely hard to grow into his role as Regent, but he also had a kind of street fighter's mentality that dumped a lot of aggression on others at times. More than that, he seemed to get carried away with who he was. In the fall of 1978, Rinpoche and the Regent taught several meditation programs together called "Transforming Confusion into Wisdom." They taught one in Boston and one in Los Angeles. The title of the seminar seemed to exemplify what Rinpoche was hoping could be accomplished in working with his Regent, Ösel Tendzin.

By January 1979, while I was recovering from my accident, things were getting out of hand. One night Rinpoche attended a birthday party for Ken Green, who was a member of the Vajradhatu board. During the party, several board members took Rinpoche aside and began complaining to him about the Regent's conduct and their fears that he was becoming an egomaniac. On the spot, Rinpoche called a late-night meeting of his board of directors at the Kalapa Court to discuss the issues involving the Regent and his abuse of power. All the members of the board, as well as the two *dapons,* were summoned. David Rome was the chairman of the board, in addition to his other duties, and he also attended. That night, the Regent was at a private house party for gay men across town. Even before he and Lila moved into the Court with us, I became aware that the Regent was interested in men as sexual partners. He was, at the very least, bisexual.

It's probably important to clarify that Rinpoche did not have a problem with the Regent's sexual orientation per se. He was concerned with whether the Regent treated others properly, regardless of the sexual politics. Rinpoche had himself been concerned about the Regent's arrogance for some time, and that night in January he decided that it was time to do something about the situation. He called over to the party to tell the Regent to come to the Court to join the meeting. When the Regent didn't appear, Rinpoche sent Dapon Gimian to find the Regent and tell him to return to the Court right away. The Regent didn't appear for another hour.

When the Regent finally arrived, Rinpoche tried to get the board of directors to confront the problems with the Regent. They were all gathered in the blue room, the room with the blue rugs, in the Court. Rinpoche asked various members of the board to address the Regent directly and to say what they thought the problem was. Apparently, as Rinpoche told me later, the members of the board were rather feeble in their statements. After some time, Rinpoche said good night and went upstairs. Most of the board members left, but several people stayed behind to review what had happened. At that point, nothing had been resolved. Those who remained were David Rome, the Kasung Kyi Khyap; Jim Gimian, the Kasung Dapon; Lodro Dorje, who was the head of practice and study and had the title of Dorje Loppon; and Michael Root, the Regent's chief of staff. The Regent was also there. Rinpoche sent John Perks down to ask everyone downstairs to join him.

They went upstairs to Rinpoche's sitting room, where he suggested that they all drop acid together. When Rinpoche had given bodhisattva vows earlier that month, a student had presented him with quite a large vial of LSD as a gift. As part of taking the bodhisattva vow, you give something to the teacher that symbolizes surrender to you. For this student, giving up drugs was that gesture. Rinpoche had held onto the vial of LSD, and he produced it for this occasion.

Rinpoche asked John Perks to be the attendant for the night, so John didn't take LSD. He was there to take care of everybody. As the LSD started to take effect, the Regent started to manifest more and more in a caricatured feminine way, as a woman. He was apparently quite outrageous and somewhat sleazily seductive, fawning over Rinpoche and the others. Rinpoche was trying to talk to him about the problems with his comportment as the Regent, but the Regent was quite out of it, and didn't seem able to hear what Rinpoche was saying at all.

At one point Rinpoche decided to phone me and asked me to talk to the Regent. (By the way, Rinpoche didn't change at all when he took LSD. Not one bit, although he understood completely what other people experienced on drugs.) Rinpoche said to me, "Sweetheart, I need your help. I need you to talk to the Regent. You have to bring him back. Make him understand what's happening." So Rinpoche passed the phone to the Regent and said, "Here's Diana to talk to you." For some reason, the Regent refused to believe that it was me. He kept saying, "Jane, is that you? Is that you, Jane?" I kept telling him that he should listen to what Rinpoche was saying to him, and that he should remember who he was. But he couldn't hear me at all. He passed the phone back to Rinpoche, saying, "That isn't Diana. That's Jane. I don't know what you're talking about."

After I hung up, still unable to get the Regent's attention, Rinpoche smashed his hand down on the coffee table in our sitting room at the Court and screamed "NO!!!!!!!!!!!" I heard that it was earsplitting. He put a dent in the table with his hand. Finally, he got through, and the Regent crumpled at his feet. Rinpoche placed his hands together in front of the Regent's face. He held up his two hands, cupping them as if they were holding a treasure. Indicating the space between his hands, with everyone as witnesses, he said to the Regent, "This is the dharma. This is unbelievably precious. And if you pervert the dharma, I will destroy you. You have to understand that I made you, and I can destroy you."

It was a very heavy message. After Rinpoche lowered the boom, so to speak, the Regent was a mess, and he became much more gentle and humble. He sat at Rinpoche's feet and tried to pull himself together. A few hours later, Rinpoche said that he wanted the wives of all of the people who were there to come over. Everybody phoned their spouses, who provided more witnesses to what was going on. When the ladies arrived, Rinpoche didn't say too much about what had happened. He asked everyone to join him downstairs in the front hallway of the Court. He said that he wanted to do a calligraphy to mark this occasion. He had a huge calligraphy brush that was kept on a shrine in the house. He asked for the brush to be brought into the hallway, along with a bowl of black *sumi* ink. He also asked for a long roll of paper, which was unrolled and spread out to give him room to do the calligraphy. Then, with everyone gathered around him, he made a huge slashing stroke with the brush and screamed the word NO again. Ink went everywhere. The entire hallway had to be repainted, and everyone's clothing was splattered with ink. It was a deafening message. At the end of the year, Rinpoche did another calligraphy for the Regent, which is made up of the word *no*, with the N inside of the O. At the end of 1980, Rinpoche wrote a poem about what he called the "Big No." Later, in 1982, he talked about the experience when he was conducting a Shambhala Training in Boulder. His talk was on the subject of self-deception. He said:

> The antidote to a setting-sun mentality is to be free from deception. In connection with that, I'd like to tell you about the Big No, which is different than just saying no to our little habits, such as scratching yourself like a dog. When we scratch ourselves, we try to do it in a slightly more sophisticated way. But we're still scratching, and there is a limit: we have to learn how to be human, as opposed to how to be an animal.
>
> The Big No is a whole different level of no. I think it's public knowledge; anyway, you should know that my Vajra Regent and I took LSD at the Kalapa Court, my house, some time ago. The concept of the Big No became the main point of our trip. That No is that you don't give in to things that indulge your reality. There is no special reality beyond your reality. That is the Big No, as opposed to the regular no.
>
> The ordinary Shambhala type of no applies to things like not scratching yourself or keeping your hair brushed. That no brings a sense of discipline, rather than constantly negating you. In fact, it's a *yes*, the biggest yes.
>
> When we took LSD together, the Big No came out. Everybody was indulging in their world so much. So how to say no? I had to crash my arm and fist down on my coffee table and break it. I painted a giant picture in the entrance hall of my house. **Big No**. From now onwards it's **NO**. Later on, I executed another calligraphy for the Regent as another special reminder, which he has in his office. If you want to look at it, you can. You can look at *no no*.

You cannot by any means, for any religious reasons or for any spiritual metaphysical reasons step on an ant or kill your mosquitoes—at all. That is Buddhism. That is Shambhala. You *cannot* destroy life. We have to respect everybody. You cannot make a random judgment on that at all. That is the rule of the king of Shambhala. You can't act on your desires alone. You have to think, contemplate, the details of what needs to be removed and what needs to be cultivated. It's up to you.[2]

That message meant a great deal to him. It was meant not just for the Regent but also for all of his students. By the way, when this talk was published in the book *Great Eastern Sun,* we decided not to mention the LSD because it seemed unnecessary. But at this time, I feel that I have to tell the whole truth. Rinpoche didn't take drugs a lot; he used them very occasionally to break through with people who were particularly stuck. That was usually when he employed something like LSD.

Maybe anyone put in the Regent's position would have gone through a period of being bloated like this. Certainly, everyone has plenty of self-deception to work through. But in the Regent's case, it was extreme, and I think Rinpoche felt that this was a kill or cure situation. It was his lineage that was at stake here, the depth of the teachings that he wanted to ensure would remain intact after his death. He was counting on the Regent to carry that forward, and I think that already by this time, Rinpoche had serious doubts that the Regent could carry this load.

After the Big No acid trip, Rinpoche and the Regent went on a vacation together to the house in Pátzcuaro where we usually stayed. They spent about ten days together, along with some other people who Rinpoche invited along, including Dapon Gimian and his wife. The Regent was very meek and gentle during that time, Rinpoche told me, but the real question was: Would it last? Would it take?

With these events, the Year of the Earth Horse came to an end in the Shambhala world. The last day of the year, February 26, 1979, there was a full solar eclipse. It was the last full eclipse of the millennium that was visible from the continental United States.

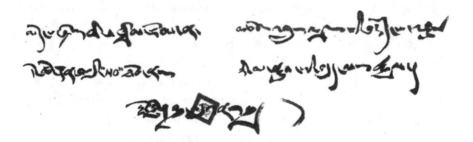

If you know "Not" and have discipline,
Then the ultimate "No" is attained,

Patience will arise along with exertion.
And you are victorious over the maras
of the setting sun.

How to Know No

There was a giant No.
That No rained.
That No created a tremendous blizzard.
That No made a dent on the coffee table.
That No was the greatest No of No's in the universe.
That No showered and hailed.
That No created sunshine, and simultaneous eclipse of the sun
     and moon.
That No was a lady's legs with nicely heeled shoes.
That No is the best No of all.
When a gentleman smiles, a good man,
That No is the beauty of the hips.
When you watch the gait of youths as they walk with alternating
     cheek rhythm,
When you watch their behinds,
That No is fantastic thighs, not fat or thin but taut in their strength,
Loveable or leaveable.
That No is shoulders that turn in or expand the chest, sad or happy,
Without giving in to a deep sigh.
That No is No of all No's.
Relaxation or restraint is in question.
Nobody knows that big No,
But we alone know that No.
This No is in the big sky, painted with sumi ink eternally.
This big No is tattooed on our genitals.
This big No is not purely freckles or birthmark,
But this big No is real big No.
Sky is blue,
Roses are red,
Violets are blue,
And therefore this big No is No.
Let us celebrate having that monumental No.
The monolithic No stands up and pierces heaven;
Therefore, monolithic No also spreads vast as the ocean.
Let us have great sunshine with this No No.

Let us have full moon with this No No.
Let us have cosmic No.
The cockroaches carry little No No's,
As well as giant elephants in African jungles—
Copulating No No and waltzing No No,
Guinea pig No No.
We find all the information and instructions when a mosquito
    buzzes.
We find some kind of No No.
Let our No No be the greatest motto:
No No for the king;
No No for the prime minister;
No No for the worms of our subjects.
Let us celebrate No No so that Presbyterian preachers can have
    speech impediments in proclaiming No No.
Let our horses neigh No No.
Let the vajra sangha fart No No—
Giant No No that made a great imprint on the coffee table.[3]

SIXTEEN

The Shambhala New Year, the first day of the Year of the Earth Sheep, was celebrated on February 27, 1979, the day after the solar eclipse. I was still recuperating in Vienna from my car accident, so, as I mentioned, I was unable to be in Boulder to attend the festivities. Rinpoche began the day by giving a sunrise talk at Dorje Dzong, the headquarters of Vajradhatu in Boulder. The entire Buddhist community, including several hundred families with infants and children in tow, packed the shrine room for his address, which he gave seated on a Tibetan-style throne at the end of the room. Following his talk, he returned to the Kalapa Court for a day of celebration, which began with an elaborate breakfast. About fifty people were invited to breakfast, and many stayed at the Court socializing throughout the day. Other community members had parties throughout Boulder to celebrate the holiday. That evening, those who had been to the Kalapa Assembly convened again in the shrine room, where Rinpoche conducted a ceremony of empowerment for his son Ösel, appointing him as the future Sakyong king of Shambhala. This event did not conclude until dawn of the next day.

As Ösel had matured from a shy young boy into a more confident teenager, we all began to see a gentle strength in him and a nascent regal quality. In particular, his connection to his father was notable. Rinpoche had had in mind for some time that Ösel would eventually take on the role of future Sakyong. He had talked to me about this in 1976, when Ösel was only thirteen years old. Rinpoche had explained to me that, in addition to the traditional Buddhist lineage that he planned to hand down, he also wanted to establish a family lineage for the Shambhala teachings. A family lineage is common in other Tibetan lineages—the Sakya and the Nyingma traditions for example—but unusual for a Kagyü teacher such as Rinpoche. However, in the context of the two important streams of teaching that he presented, it made perfect sense to have these two lineages of transmission.

Rinpoche could see things in people long before others could make them out. In any case, in 1978 he had begun talking more broadly with some of his senior students about his eldest son becoming the Sawang, which means "earth lord." That is the title that Rinpoche gave him to indicate that he was, in essence, the crown prince of the Shambhala world.

In some respects, the ceremony for Ösel was similar to earlier Shambhala ceremonies, but it was more elaborate and grand. It was referred to as the investiture of the Ashe Prince. The evening began with a *lhasang,* a traditional Tibetan ceremony that involves the burning of juniper to produce smoke. This is done to summon the *dralas,* or the Shambhala deities, the elemental forces of the Shambhala world. In this case, since the whole program took place indoors, the fire was built in a large Oriental incense pot, and Rinpoche himself fanned the fire while everyone circled around it, inhaling the smoke and chanting the Shambhala victory cry. Ösel led the procession circling the fire, accompanied by a group of Dorje Kasung members carrying Shambhala banners and flags.

During the main part of the ceremony, Ösel was questioned on his knowledge of Shambhala principles. Then, he performed the stroke of Ashe and was proclaimed the Sawang. Rinpoche had arranged for a beautiful deep-blue velvet cloak to be tailored for the Sawang and presented to him at the end of the evening. He also gave him three Shambhala awards, appointing him to the Order of Ashe, the Order of Shambhala, and the Order of the Trident. We now had these medals, which were presented at the ceremony. The Order of Ashe is the award that only the Sakyong or his heir can hold. It means that the ruler of Shambhala is connected to primordial vision and that he can join heaven and earth, or vision and practicality, by bringing down the qualities of Ashe into his own heart and into the life of the kingdom. From a Buddhist perspective, one would say that Ashe represents both the quality of *bodhichitta,* or awakened heart, and the fundamental quality of egolessness, which must pervade the Shambhala Kingdom for it to be genuine. If the person at the center of the kingdom is preoccupied with building himself up, if he is trying to use power to solidify his territory, then Shambhala would become just another oppressive model for society. Or it could just become a joke. What gives integrity and life to the kingdom is the razor knife of the Sakyong's intellect and the deep heartsblood of his compassion. This is the Order of Ashe.

The Order of Shambhala represents the accomplishment of all four qualities of warriorship: tigerlike meekness, or genuineness; lionlike perkiness, or energy; *garuda*-like outrageousness, or compassion beyond concept; and dragonlike inscrutability, which is again the quality of egolessness and not being caught in concepts. The medal is a beautiful eight-pointed star with the animals of the four dignities enameled in a circle in the center. The Order of the Trident is the highest military, or *kasung,* award. The three prongs of the trident represent piercing the heart of passion, aggression, and ignorance, the three fundamental attributes of ego.

The celebration was indeed magnificent. I sent a message to the Sawang congratulating him since I was unable to attend. It occurred to me later that it was quite interesting timing, coming just two months after the "Big No" affair with the Regent. Rinpoche now had two heirs: one Buddhist and one Shambhala. This could make for a double triumph in the future, or it could help to ensure that at least one of his lineage holders might come through for the future. Rinpoche was a realist; while he completely believed in the magic of the lineage, he also knew what could go wrong. I also found it interesting that he chose for his Shambhala heir someone from a younger generation, which seemed to me to make a great deal of sense. The Sawang was just sixteen at this time, which meant that Rinpoche could work with him during these early formative years and hopefully train him for a long period of time before the Sawang would actually have to take the reins. Among other things, Rinpoche hoped to show him that the Shambhala style of rulership was not about puffing oneself up, but that it meant accepting the heavy yoke of responsibility and working continuously for others. Rinpoche had grown up with this approach to leadership and had had the importance of duty and humbleness hammered into him from an early age.

Creating two lineages of transmission also established ongoing tension between the Regent and the Sawang. Rinpoche had in some ways encouraged a similar dynamic between me and the Regent, as I discussed earlier in describing our mutual Shambhala empowerment. Rinpoche often seemed to set up these kinds of competing energies, as a kind of system of checks and balances that prevented any one of his students from consolidating too much power.

The sixth seminary came and went in the spring of 1979 and was held that year at the Chateau Lake Louise, a grand old hotel on Lake Louise in Alberta, Canada. More than three hundred students attended. That summer, Rinpoche and the Regent taught a joint seminar entitled "The Warrior of Shambhala" at the Naropa Institute. Many of Rinpoche's talks were later included in *Shambhala: The Sacred Path of the Warrior*. The second Dorje Kasung encampment, now called the Magyal Pomra Encampment, took place in September at Rocky Mountain Dharma Center, following Rinpoche's annual summer program for the public (no longer combined with it).

In September 1979, His Holiness the Dalai Lama made his first visit to America. Members of the Dorje Kasung were very involved in the visit. They organized motorcades for His Holiness's party wherever he traveled in North America, and they worked with local law enforcement officials in major cities to help with crowd control and in general to provide security for His Holiness and his entourage. Rinpoche asked Karl Springer to greet His Holiness on Rinpoche's behalf when the Dalai Lama arrived in New York on September 3. Mr. Springer traveled to many cities with His Holiness to help assure that proper protocol was observed. In early October, when His Holiness returned to New York, Rinpoche, the Regent, and the entire board of directors of Vajradhatu flew to New York to meet with him. Rinpoche felt that it was extremely important for his senior students to meet the Dalai Lama, whom he himself had not seen for more than ten years.

His Holiness and Rinpoche had several private meetings during the visit. Rinpoche was so happy that this great spiritual figure and the leader of the Tibetan world finally was setting foot on the American continent. I was unfortunately away for much of this, but I was able to meet and spend time with His Holiness in New York just before his departure from North America. I was arriving from Europe to attend the Kalapa Assembly and spend time with Rinpoche. Although His Holiness was not able to stop in Boulder during his first visit, when he returned in the summer of 1981, he spent about a week with our community, which was a great blessing for everyone.

The second Kalapa Assembly took place in October in Big Sky, Montana, near the site of Little Bighorn—Custer's last stand. Big Sky is on the edge of the mountains in Montana, and the sky does seem very expansive there. It seemed a good place to hold the assembly. Not only was I in attendance for this, but Rinpoche made sure that I was thoroughly visible in my role as Sakyong Wangmo. My mother also made quite an impression. By this time, she had acquired her own Shambhala title. She was now the Grand Duchess of Pago, and she gave talks at the assembly on decorum. She even had a meeting to which only men were invited, so that she could talk to them about manners, grooming, and romance. I wanted to hear what she had to say, so I and another woman, Gina Jarowitz (my attendant at the time), actually crawled surreptitiously into the room under a number of tables that had long tablecloths on them. Among other topics, my mother talked about being appreciative and respectful of women and stressed the importance of good grooming. She said that women are attracted to a man when he is wearing "fresh linen, is clean shaven, looks lovely, and perhaps has a little bit of aftershave lotion." "I tell you," she commented, "it turns the girls on and it is very nice. You should be more dashing." At times, I had to control my urge to break out in laughter.

Rinpoche organized an elaborate and elegant birthday party for me at this assembly. The women came in evening gowns and the men wore tuxes. Members of the Dorje Kasung came in uniform. Rinpoche and I were seated on a raised platform. There were toasts, including spirited remarks by Rinpoche, and a cake was presented to me with a tiger, lion, *garuda,* and dragon design made from colored icing. I made the first cut in the cake with a sword that Rinpoche lent me. Then there was waltzing. Due to his paralysis, Rinpoche could not do ballroom dancing. At many of these formal Shambhala events, he would ask the Regent and me to have the first dance. We made quite a good-looking couple, I think.

However, off the dance floor, the Regent and I continued to be at odds during this time. We were really more and more distant from one another. One night during the assembly, the Regent stayed up quite late after one of Rinpoche's talks singing old fifties songs at the piano in the dining room of the hotel with a bunch of his cronies. I happened to walk through the room while he was holding forth, and I found the environment completely self-indulgent. There was a sandwich board there with information about the next day's events, and I kicked it over in disgust and yelled at him about how he had a total lack of Shambhala decorum. Then I went up to Rinpoche's bedroom in the hotel. A little while later, the Regent burst into our suite and insisted on seeing Rinpoche. He was crying and carrying on, saying, "She doesn't love me. She misunderstands me. You have to help me." Rinpoche calmed the whole thing down, somewhat, and later he made remarks to the whole assembly about this incident. Rinpoche had been talking at the Kalapa Assembly about overcoming arrogance and harmful habitual patterns. He referred to what the Regent had done as an example of "overindulging sacred outlook." Then, he asked me to explain what that meant. I talked about the difference between being caught up in personal or group neurosis versus appreciating the world as sacred, by cultivating sanity, lack of arrogance, and straightforwardness. Publicly, the issue appeared to be resolved; privately there was still quite a gulf between us.

After this incident, Rinpoche and I had a real heart-to-heart talk about my role as the Sakyong Wangmo. Rinpoche gave me very direct advice. He said, "You should never question yourself. You're the Sakyong Wangmo. Any instinct you have, just go with it. Don't second-guess yourself. Just do it." That was provocative advice because it was easy to misinterpret that to mean that anything goes. Do whatever you want. Sometimes I found it confusing to figure this out. Now, at this point in my life, I definitely think twice about things. I felt that when Rinpoche was alive, I could afford to experiment more in my decisions and my relationships with people. When Rinpoche was around I always felt that if I pushed myself too far, I would get helpful feedback from the environment that he helped to create. You could take chances, and you felt that the situation was protected. Now, I feel that I have to be more careful not to hurt others. We did a lot of crazy things in those days, which worked out okay. Even if somebody got their feelings hurt, people felt fundamentally loved and appreciated in the world that Rinpoche created. It was a more controlled learning experience. At times it was like being in kindergarten. You take chances when you're learning, and you finally figure out what works and what doesn't. Or it's like being a child learning to walk. The parent is there to catch you, kind of saying, "Yes, that's walking. Go ahead and walk."

Rinpoche said something else to me in that conversation at Big Sky, which I thought was very important. He counseled me, "You should always be impartial. When somebody comes to you and they complain about something, you've got to be able to see the other side." Then he said, "Whenever things go wrong, though, I blame myself." He continued, "The problem is always my problem when things don't work." He also advised me: "The worst thing you can do in your life is to surround yourself with yes-men. You know, you want to make sure you can trust the people you're with for genuine feedback." This was how he lived, in terms of the people around him. He insisted that the people who were close to him tell him what they really thought about things. He encouraged critical thinking in everyone.

I remember at the end of this conversation, he was sitting there looking at me sort of quizzically. He said, "How come I never get sick of you? You know, I sometimes get sick of people, but I just never get sick of you." I guess that was paying me a big compliment!

At the end of the assembly, Rinpoche talked publicly about the role of the Sakyong Wangmo in his last talk to the participants. He made extremely personal remarks about me that continue to inform and inspire me at times when I become discouraged about my life. He was so honest—not everything he said was 100 percent complimentary, but it was so true, which made him that much more lovable to me. Rinpoche said:

> Some quarters would say that keeping Diana is very expensive. I have had to tell these people: It is not keeping Diana that is expensive, but it is keeping Diana as the Sakyong Wangmo that is expensive. That expensiveness is not counted purely in pounds or

deutschmarks or Austrian schillings or American dollars or Canadian dollars. Her vision is unyielding and good. Her intention is
pure; her intention is to help elegantize the world. You know that
already, in some sense. . . . From her presence and existence in
sharing my life, the Sakyong Wangmo has provided lots of sharp
edges and lots of warm memories and lots of sad stories. . . . The
Sakyong Wangmo's vision and her fearlessness and her particular
type of impatience have brought us here [to America]. Therefore
she deserves to sit on the same platform with me as a teacher of
Shambhala vision.

I am thankful to her. Her observations are sometimes like a
bee sting—sharp and powerful. And when you try to deceive the
Sakyong Wangmo, it is like holding the stem of a rose; the thorns
prick your fingers. The Sakyong Wangmo will say, "That was a
deception. You can't even kiss me." . . . How has the Sakyong
Wangmo become such an important person? People might question how such a young English lady, an English girl, has suddenly
become a queen. How could that happen? But it is not an accident. It is the plan and the vision of the forefathers of the Mukpo
lineage. . . .

One thing is certain about the Sakyong Wangmo: she is expert
in telling the truth. And she gets very irritated when lies are told
to her, of any kind. . . . Often certain people are jealous of the
Sakyong Wangmo, and they are tempted to challenge her authority and her power. . . . But that kind of energy has never been
found in the history of all the queens in the universe. Ladies and
Gentlemen, the Sakyong Wangmo has manifested as a real disci-
plinarian and a disciplined person. She has combined the Shambhala vision, and she also takes positive pride in what happens in
our kingdom. And my profound love, love affair, and respect go to
the Sakyong Wangmo.[1]

Those remarks were both inspiring and intimidating—a lot to live
up to. I think I'm still trying to actualize what he was saying there.

There was something else that Rinpoche talked about in this lecture
that was very helpful to people, which was explaining the rationale for

the uniforms that he was wearing more and more frequently. He had designed a number of military uniforms for himself, which he had tailored in England. He wore these initially at the Magyal Pomra Encampments, but now he was also starting to wear them when he presented some of the Shambhala teachings. By this time, some of the senior members of the Dorje Kasung, particularly the Kasung Kyi Khyap and the *dapons,* also had dress uniforms that Rinpoche had designed.

People had very mixed reactions to this. Many people were concerned about this military culture at this time, and it's still the case that people are shocked when they see photographs of Rinpoche in a military uniform. That's quite understandable, actually. In his talk at the Kalapa Assembly, he said that he had been studying the history of uniforms to determine which ones were the product of aggression and which elements could be used to invoke the energy of warriorship in the positive, Shambhala sense. He talked about uniforms as bringing down the power of the *dralas,* bringing down the magic of Shambhala. On one level, he wanted to inspire people with the overpowering majesty of his dress. He also talked about transforming the perverse, aggressive energy of the conventional military into a pure manifestation of warriorship without aggression. He felt that the power of the military form was something that needed to be harnessed in the Shambhala world, because of the level of chaos and conflict that is unavoidable in modern life. Rinpoche was particularly brilliant and fearless in his ability to take on degraded cultural manifestations and transmute them into something sacred. On the individual level, he said that people would encounter terrifying visions in the *bardo* after death, and that if they could come to terms with his military manifestation during this lifetime, it would help them to work with the wrathful energy they would encounter in their journey after death.

Some people embraced his approach to the Dorje Kasung that way; others turned away. For myself, I never doubted his motivation nor was I put off at all by this approach at this point. For one thing, I was in the middle of my experience at the Spanish Riding School, where I was exposed on a daily basis to how the magnificence of military and regal traditions could be uplifting. The hall that I rode in was unbelievably brilliant and somewhat overpowering, yet that was encouragement to me in my riding and it helped to give me a better seat on the horse and more command of the energy. So this made perfect sense to me in terms of how Rinpoche was also manifesting in his dress.

When I went back to Vienna at the conclusion of the assembly, I had a truly positive sense about what Rinpoche was doing. The second assembly was a turning point for me. I felt more in tune with the Shambhala teachings and their manifestation in the Shambhala world. I began to understand how the Shambhala approach could be a skillful means of presenting Buddhism, or its essential features, in the West. Many of us in the modern Western world have lost our connection with the dignity of earth. Shambhala was bringing things down to earth, I realized, while also acknowledging the sacred or magic quality of existence. We are not a monastic society in the West, and we will never be a monastic society here. Part of Rinpoche's brilliance in how he brought dharma to the West was creating the means for people to connect with meditation outside of a monastic situation. From my perspective, if Buddhism can't become part of your life, in the way that you deal with your children, the way you do your dishes, the way you celebrate, the way you conduct your life and your business altogether, then it's not really true. It's just an idealized concept. It was very powerful the way in which Rinpoche brought the dharma into people's households and taught people how to have a dignified way of conducting their lives. This brought the members of hippie society—of which there were many in our community— back into being productive members of society at large.

When I returned to Boulder the next May, I was looking forward to spending time in the Kalapa Court. For the first time, I thought that I might be able to take my seat in that environment in a much more comfortable way. I felt that I was finally making friends with the whole thing.

For some time now, I had had attendants when I was living at the Court. Pat and Tom had been somewhat in that role in Europe, but they were so much part of the family and it was such a relaxed environment that I didn't think about it in those terms. However, Boulder was more intimidating. For one thing, there were many more people coming through the house and coming through my life as *kusung,* my personal attendants. Rinpoche stressed that I really should try to be kind and welcoming, even if I didn't feel comfortable around some people, even if occasionally I didn't like somebody. He told me that it was important to people to serve at the Court. It meant a lot to them, and I had to take this into account.

By the summer of 1980, several people had come and gone as the head of my service in Boulder. Whether it was my lack of maturity, the chemistry between me and the people in that role, or other factors, several situations had fallen apart on me already. Then in 1980, Rinpoche asked two young women to take over my service: Dierdre Stubbert (whose husband, Ron, was the director of finance for Vajradhatu) and Jane Carpenter. Something really clicked between us, and to this day, we continue to have a close relationship. They have both been immensely helpful to me, through all kinds of ups and downs. There were a number of other women who became *kusung* around this time, with whom I'm still quite connected. So perhaps it was a maturing of the Shambhala world. I wish the earlier situations could have worked out, but sadly they did not. I am still grateful to everyone who helped me and especially to those who went through the very early days, which were a learning experience for all of us.

When I came home in May of 1980, Rinpoche had developed a routine in his life in the Court, into which I tried to fit myself. As well, I developed my own routine, which included spending a good deal of time involved with the development of the Shambhala School of Dressage. While I was in Europe, as I mentioned earlier, Marie Louise Barrett had been the main instructor in my absence. Marie Louise had a background in the hunter-jumper world. She had grown up in Virginia, where she had developed her skill as a rider. She became interested in dressage and we became friends. Another woman, Beth Sproule, became the third instructor.

By 1980, we had our own rented facility. Over the years, the school was located east of Boulder in Louisville and later in Erie, which are both just outside of Boulder. We had a number of school horses on which people could learn, and some members of the community bought horses that they stabled at the school. Many *sangha* members became interested in dressage and started taking lessons. Additionally, there were a number of other riders who began training with us at the school. Many of the teenaged students from Vidya School also took lessons with us, as part of their PE requirement. For its time, the Shambhala School of Dressage was really one of the best facilities presenting classical dressage training in that part of the United States. At that time, there were very few options for people interested in this discipline.

Rinpoche took a great interest in the school. He came up with the name for the school. I had wanted to call it Windhorse Academy, but he thought that the Shambhala School of Dressage sounded more imperial, which of course he liked. At one point, he started designing the permanent facility that he thought we should build at some point in the future. The design was in some respects reminiscent of the grandeur of the Spanish Riding School. He had the innovative idea that the horses should be stabled above the indoor arena and that they would be ridden down long ramps into the arena. We never got that far, I'm afraid. After the school had been functioning quite successfully for about four years, both Marie Louise and I moved away from Boulder and the school was dissolved.

During the years that the school existed in Colorado, Marie Louise and I competed in dressage shows in the area. Once when I was riding in a show near Boulder, Rinpoche phoned me at the show grounds to say that he was coming to the show to watch me ride. I thought, "Oh no!" I still had it in mind that I wanted to keep my professional world as a rider a little bit separate from my life with Rinpoche. Up to this point, I had been fairly successful. Rinpoche arrived at the show, to my horror, in full military uniform.

In dressage competition there's a rule that spectators have to be at least ten meters from the edge of the dressage arena. Not knowing this, Rinpoche's *kusung* and *kasung* put a chair right next to the arena, so close that he could have almost put his feet up on the rail. Before the competition starts, you have sixty seconds to ride around the ring. I rode past him several times, saying, "Get back! Get back! Get back!" Finally they got the message and moved his chair back. I rode the test, feeling completely paralyzed with a combination of fear and embarrassment.

After I finished, I put the horse away, and then I went to see Rinpoche for a minute. The judge for my test, Tom Poulin, was quite prominent in the United States. He was someone I was acquainted with. While I was standing with Rinpoche, since the test was finished, the judge had a break and decided to come over. As he approached, Rinpoche said—much to my horror—in my ear, "Sweetheart, let me meet the judge!" I acted as though I hadn't heard him. I said hello to the judge, and we started to talk about my horse and how the performance could improve. Then, I heard a voice saying, "Sweetheart, introduce me to the judge." So I said, "Mr. Poulin, I'd like to introduce you to my husband, Trungpa Rinpoche." Then Rinpoche said, "You know, so many husbands are resentful of their wives riding, but I'm completely supportive. I buy my wife the best saddles, only the best." I was thinking to myself, "It's going to be all right. This is going to be okay." Then I saw Rinpoche looking into the distance at another horse, and he said, "Isn't it amazing that . . ." There was a long pause during which Mr. Poulin and I were waiting for him to finish his sentence. Finally he continued, "Dressage horses can shit and run at the same time?"

The unbelievable thing is that a few years after Rinpoche died, I saw Mr. Poulin and he said to me, "I was so sorry to read in *Time* magazine that your husband died. I was so impressed by him." So I guess you never know.

Initially, I was only going to be at home for my usual seven-week stint. (I was based in England at this time.) Rinpoche and I had been trying to have another child, and after I was home about six weeks, I found out that I was pregnant. I decided not to return to Europe. I arranged for one horse, Shambhala, to go to a facility run by Gunnar Ostergaard, a trainer on the East Coast of the United States, and I arranged for Warrior to go from England back to Herr Rehbein's facility, to be cared for until my child was born and I could take up my career again.

While I was trying to conceive a child with Rinpoche, I was still seeing Mitchell. We had slept together—with contraception—during the month that I got pregnant. (We had spent a night at the Stanley Hotel in Estes Park, which inspired the film *The Shining*.) When I found out that I was pregnant, I went into a bit of a panic, but I told myself that the baby had to be Rinpoche's. I mentioned my anxiety to Rinpoche, and he told me not to worry about it. I tried not to, but there was definitely a question mark in my mind. Mitchell and I joked that we were going to name the baby Isaac if it was his.

In the early stages of the pregnancy, Rinpoche and I decided to go to Mexico for a vacation. We invited Mitchell and Sarah to come along, and John Perks also came as the cook and butler. Beverley Webster, Rinpoche's private secretary, also accompanied us, and Ron Barnstone, who was originally from Mexico—his mother was Marty Franco—came along as driver and *kusung*. I was having a lot of morning sickness during this period, so the trip was physically difficult for me. I found it almost impossible to find appetizing food in Mexico. Sometimes I would wake up very hungry in the early morning, and there would be nothing to eat in the house. Someone would have to go to the market before we could have breakfast. John Perks did a lot of cooking. I remember being hungry one day and smelling duck from the kitchen. I went into the kitchen and lifted the pot with anticipation of getting myself some broth. There was a whole duck in the pot, with its beak, eyes, and feathers still on it. I felt very vulnerable at that time, so John's soup didn't amuse me.

While we were there, we listened to audiotapes that Louise and Roger Randolph, the owners of the Pátzcuaro house, had left at the house. They had been to see a psychic who told them that Louise was the reincarnation of Nefertiti and Roger was Akhenaten. They had made a tape of the conversation with the psychic, which we found very entertaining.

I also had an encounter with a ghost there. Rinpoche always felt strongly that I should sleep on the left side of the bed, and he would sleep on the right. It had to do with how the feminine and masculine sides of the body are viewed in tantra. When we were first married, we had a picture of Vajrayogini hanging over the left side of our bed, and a picture of Guru Rinpoche on the right. I would sleep with Vajrayogini above my head, and Rinpoche would be on the right, with Padmasambhava above him. In Pátzcuaro, we had a double bed that was not that big. It was a chilly evening, and I remember we lit the fire before we went to sleep. I woke up, and Rinpoche had crowded onto my side of the bed, so that I had only a few inches to sleep in, which was quite uncomfortable for me, especially being pregnant. I got up and I walked around to his side of the bed, where there was at least half the bed, and I thought, "Oh good, I can have some space." I fell asleep there. Suddenly, I was woken up. Rinpoche was screaming at me, "You can't sleep on my side of the bed. What are you doing here?" He was really nasty, and I was completely angry with him. I said to him, "Well then, fuck you. I'll just go and sleep by myself. Have the whole bed!" I walked out of our bedroom, and I fell asleep in the guest bedroom down the hall.

I woke up about an hour or two later. There was something in the room with me. I could almost make out the shape. It was a dark shape, and it was definitely a woman. It felt like very evil energy, and I was scared to death. I got out of bed and walked rapidly down the corridor to our bedroom. Rinpoche was sitting bolt upright in bed, with his legs crossed. The flames in the fireplace made designs on the walls of the room. Rinpoche slowly turned to me. I hadn't opened my mouth, but he said, "Don't worry, Sweetheart, she's just been here too. I've taken care of it." I returned to my allocated space in the bed and ceased all further complaints! We never saw her again.

This was, however, not the only encounter with negative energy that we had in Pátzcuaro. Over time, Rinpoche came to realize that there was a lot of black magic being practiced in that area. Once, when he went shopping in the downtown square, Rinpoche wanted to go into a little antique store. While he was there, he told his attendant, "These people practice black magic." The shopkeepers seemed very sweet and ordinary, apparently. However, at a certain point, he asked them to look for something in the back, and while they were gone, he pulled aside a curtain on one wall of the store. Behind it was an altar to the devil. He told me that it was quite creepy. The Randolphs had a lot of books in their house about Aleister Crowley, who was very involved in the dark arts. Rinpoche thought he was a malevolent person. We had some concern that the Randolphs might have gotten themselves into some of the black magic that was being practiced down there, although we didn't know for sure.

While we were there, we took a number of drives around the area. One day while driving around, we discovered some small pyramids. Rinpoche was excited about this, and he wanted to do a ceremony at the top of one of them. We went up to the top of the pyramid with an incense bowl and juniper so that we could have a little *lhasang* fire. I decided to wear a pair of expensive new shoes that I'd bought recently in New York at Saks Fifth Avenue. It was a beautiful day with a clear blue sky. There had been a drought in the area. Rinpoche did the *lhasang,* and within five minutes clouds gathered and there was a torrential downpour. I was upset at Rinpoche and I said, "Why did you do this? I just bought this nice pair of shoes and now they're ruined!"

While we were in Pátzcuaro, he also composed a new Shambhala practice called the *Werma Sadhana.* In this practice, one identifies with the primordial Shambhala lineage and connects oneself to that lineage by visualizing oneself as the Rigden, or the ruler of Shambhala. One really has to take on the power and the majesty of the Shambhala world in order to accomplish this practice.

By this time, there were a number of Shambhala texts and practices for people to do. The *Werma Sadhana* became important for everyone who completed the advanced levels of Shambhala Training. Eventually, this was a group of several thousand people. While many of the core practices that Rinpoche transmitted to his students were ancient, traditional practices from the Buddhist tradition, the *Werma Sadhana* was part of the unique cycle of Shambhala *terma,* or teachings, that he received in the West and that he gave to his Western students. He was very careful about sharing these texts and practices with other Tibetan teachers. He shared them with His Holiness Dilgo Khyentse Rinpoche and others with whom he had a strong bond, but he didn't generally want them to be propagated outside of his own teaching environment. He emphasized that students should begin with Shambhala Training and progress through the Shambhala program of education until they were ready to do advanced practices such as the *Werma* practice. I think he really felt that these transmissions were meant for the West, and he wanted his Western students to be the lineage holders of this tradition. In a sense, this was yet another reason that he put such emphasis on the Court mandala and the roles of his family and his students in that mandala, particularly myself, his son the Sawang, and his senior students who became ministers, generals, diplomats, teachers, servants, and leaders in that world.

After we came back to Boulder from our little holiday, I had a wonderful time being at the Court with Rinpoche. I was actually becoming used to daily life there. I would meet once a week with the head cook, Shari Vogler. Shari had been with us now for a very long time. She and I would design the dinner menu for the week. For a while, we had a buffet breakfast at the Court. Rinpoche was feeling healthy and energized, and we had a little more semblance of family life than usual. The buffet would be set up in the blue room for the family, and we'd often have dinner there too. We had wonderful meals there, real family gatherings. Ösel and Gesar were both living in the house, and we would all get together for meals. I remember that once Rinpoche set the table for breakfast himself. He even put English toast racks on the table.

His Holiness the Sixteenth Karmapa came for his third visit that summer. His health was in decline. He had had Bell's palsy, and a few months later he would be diagnosed with stomach cancer. It was to be his last teaching visit to America, which we did not know at the time.

While he was in Boulder, His Holiness attended another Shambhala holiday that we held each year: Midsummer's Day, which was celebrated appropriately enough on the summer solstice. For a number of years, the Shambhala community used a large acreage south of Boulder for this occasion. Ken Green, the director and minister of internal affairs, and a staff of many dedicated volunteers (and a few paid staff members from Vajradhatu) organized this spectacular festival. A raised viewing platform was set up for His Holiness, Rinpoche, myself, our family, the Regent, Lady Rich, and their children. The members of the Shambhala community lined both sides of the broad pathway that led up to the platform.

At the beginning of the day, Rinpoche and I rode in together, he on his horse Drala and I on a gray mare that a *sangha* member loaned me for the occasion. Rinpoche and I were both dressed in white, and our horses had beautiful saddle blankets and colorful pennants on their bridles. Behind us, other members of the Court and the Vajradhatu administration and staff marched in, followed by members of the Dorje Kasung and many other groups, such as the Nalanda Translation Committee, teachers at Naropa Institute, students of Alaya Preschool, Vidya School, and their teachers, and all manner of other groups in the community. Many groups carried banners with the name of their organization, and many carried decorative flags and other banners. People would cheer as each new group passed by. Almost everyone in the community was in the parade. People lining the sides of the road would leave their place in the audience to march in with one or more groups and then return to view others as they presented themselves.

After Rinpoche and I rode in, we assumed our place with His Holiness on the viewing stand. As groups arrived at the platform, they would bow and present themselves to all of us and then go off to the side. After the opening parade, there was a large *lhasang* to bless the occasion and then skydivers, hired for the occasion, landed in the field and presented themselves to His Holiness. Following that, there were many entertainments, some in front of the viewing platform and others in locations around the property. There were games for both children and adults, and everyone had a picnic. It was quite a glorious celebration of summer and wonderful to share with His Holiness.

At this time, Gesar was just a seven-year-old boy. During the Karmapa's visit, Gesar found a little bird that had fallen out of the nest. He fed it and tried to keep it alive. The Karmapa loved birds and kept an aviary at his monastery in Sikkim, so he took quite an interest in Gesar's bird and told him what to feed it. However, after the Karmapa left, the little bird died. Our family went to RMDC for the beginning of the Dorje Kasung encampment, and we decided we would bring the bird and have a funeral for it halfway up Marpa Point, which is a small peak on the land. Rinpoche and I were walking up the mountain, and Gesar was skipping ahead of us, carrying the dead bird in a box. I said to Rinpoche, "I don't think we've done a good job." And he replied, "What do you mean?" I said, "Well, Gesar's not showing any signs that he cared about his bird. He should be a little bit emotional. His bird died." Rinpoche said, "He's a Tibetan. We aren't sentimental." I thought that was quite an interesting answer, and I decided that I was going to pursue this line of questioning to find out how far he would go with his reasoning. We had a little dog at this time, a Lhasa apso named Yumtso who was absolutely devoted to Rinpoche and went everywhere with him. I said, "Well, come on. How would you feel if Yumtso died?" And he said, "That would be okay." And actually, a few years later, when Yumtso died, Rinpoche didn't have much of a reaction at all.

Then I thought of Rinpoche's horse and said, "All right then. How would you feel if Drala died?" He replied, "Well, that would be expensive." Then, very foolishly, I upped the ante, and I said, "Well, how would you feel if your wife died?" He said, "Oh well, that would be cheaper." Then he broke into a wide grin.

Although I was pregnant, I had accompanied Rinpoche to RMDC to attend part of the third Magyal Pomra Encampment. A number of my riding students from Boulder were also there, as members of the newly formed Windhorse Division of the Dorje Kasung. We worked on the equestrian version of drill, which included some rudimentary movements for a quadrille. I was not able to ride, but I worked with people in any case. It was very helpful for my training as a teacher to go through this period. I had to learn to be much more skillful in explaining what I wanted people to do and how to improve their riding.

We had purchased Drala for Rinpoche the previous year. The horse, a Lipizzaner stallion, had been sold to someone in Florida by the breeding farm in Piber, Austria, where the stallions are bred for the Spanish Riding School. This horse, originally named Maestoso Trompeta, was already quite old, about fifteen at the time. Rinpoche wanted to start riding again, and the members of the Dorje Kasung and the graduates of the Kalapa Assembly gave the horse to him as a birthday gift. We renamed the horse Maestoso Drala. Rinpoche loved him. It was amazing that, in spite of his partial paralysis, Rinpoche was quite a good rider. He started going to the stables as often as he possibly could given his teaching schedule. I asked my colleague Marie Louise to be Rinpoche's riding instructor. I didn't think it was workable for me to teach him, as his wife. The summer of 1980, we brought Drala up to RMDC for Rinpoche to ride at the encampment, now widely referred to simply as MPE (for Magyal Pomra Encampment).

I had never been able to attend an encampment, so I wanted to be there for a few days, even though it wasn't that easy for me since I was pregnant. The Dorje Kasung rented a small trailer for me to stay in. Rinpoche gave me a hard time about being such a wimp that I needed to stay in a trailer. After I left, a few days before the end of the program, I learned that he moved into the trailer!

The year 1980 was the first year that Rinpoche instituted a formal skirmish, rather than relying on random attacks by outsiders. The camp was divided into two armies, one led by the Vajra Regent Ösel Tendzin and the other by the Kasung Kyi Khyap David Rome. Before the action commenced, Rinpoche asked each of the commanders to agree to a number of rules, and they were asked to sign a document saying they would adhere to these rules. After the commanders signed off on the rules, the two opposing armies would be marched up into a series of highland meadows where the skirmish would take place. Each participant would be given a certain number of small flour bags, which they could use as "weapons." When someone was hit with a flour bag, he or she would be "dead" and would have to remain out of action. All of this was outlined in the rules. There were other rules, such as, if the opposing team gave water to someone who had been hit, that person could join the opposing army. One rule, the most important tenth rule, was only visible on the carbon copies of the document signed by the heads of the armies. Either commander could have discovered this rule; but neither did, as it was not visible on the top copy they signed.

During the battle, the two commanders were responsible for their armies' strategy, and the soldiers were expected to follow their commands. The Regent's strategy was quite aggressive; he had his army attack the other group quickly. He had many "hits" with the flour bags and killed many of the opposing team. David Rome seemed quite lost and somewhat fearful in his approach, and as a result, he marched his army into the hands of the opposing team, where they were largely slaughtered. A small band from David's army (which was led by Mitchell and included the Sawang in its ranks) did escape the first battle and spent hours trekking around Marpa's Point, trying to avoid capture or "death." In the end, they staged a final futile assault on the Regent's army and were all "slaughtered." Watching one's comrades falling down in the midst of the hazy flour smoke was quite realistic for people. They saw firsthand the devastation that war can bring. On the other hand, for many of the participants the skirmish seemed to be a lighthearted game, a fun way to spend the day.

At the end of the day, following the final battle of the skirmish, a vivid rainbow spread across the sky, filling the entire meadow where the last action took place with light. Rinpoche and his party had set up their camp that afternoon on a large outcropping of rock in the middle of this field, where he could watch the dramas unfold. When a member of either army "died," he or she was sent to Rinpoche's camp, which became known as Bardo Rock.

After the final battle, he directed all of the Dorje Kasung members to return to the main camp. There the skies opened up and the rain fell in sheets. In the midst of this downpour he discussed the results of the day's skirmish and graded the performance of the armies and their leaders. As he began to speak, people's mood changed drastically, as they began to realize that they had missed the point. Lacking a microphone, Rinpoche had to yell in order to be heard over the noise of the downpour. He was standing under a tarpaulin, but the troops had no such protection from the weather. They were being soaked by the rain. No tape was made of Rinpoche's remarks, but a "scribe" took notes, writing at a frantic speed to catch his words. Rinpoche told the assembled students that in fact they had all lost. No one had understood the main point of the exercise.

At this point, he revealed the hidden rule, the tenth rule, which was the fundamental message he was trying to convey. This rule read: "Lack of proper strategy, causing greater loss of life, is cause for loss of battle." Then he explained to everyone, "Our task at Encampment is to rewrite the Oxford English Dictionary so that the meaning of the word *war* would be 'victory over aggression.'"

Rinpoche said that before the skirmish began both armies looked quite good with their various pennants and flags flying and their energetic sense of windhorse. He gave both armies a point for that. However, the Regent had a Buddhist problem, because his approach was to kill others. He lost a point for that. David Rome had a Shambhala problem, because he allowed his own family, his own troops, to be sacrificed. He lost a point for this. Mitchell was graded down for having had the right idea and then going against his better judgment. He had the idea that he and his small band should surrender, but instead, they attacked the Regent at the end of the day, and all were killed, including Rinpoche's son. Mitchell, as the commander of this ragtag band, was also marked down for allowing the Sawang to be killed in battle. Nobody got a passing grade.

Rinpoche's remarks were an utter shock. Many of those assembled started weeping, recognizing the aggression they had put into the exercise and the problems they had overcoming it. Rinpoche told everyone that they would have to go back the next day and conduct the entire exercise again. People were exhausted, but he was not interested in how tired they were. Indeed, both armies marched back up the hill the next morning. Rinpoche switched the commanders, so that the Regent led what had been David Rome's army, and David led the Regent's original troops. They conducted a skirmish with hardly a shot being fired.

In later years, strategy progressed and there were many more skirmishes, some with no "killing," and some with a minimum loss of life. However, the first and most fundamental message—that victory or conquest could not come out of aggression—was the most profound.

Soon after the encampment ended, my doctor put me on bed rest because I was having some bleeding with my pregnancy. Rinpoche and I would hang out in bed together, and it was a very sweet, loving time for us. One evening, we had a small dinner at the Court to celebrate Mitchell's birthday. I was able to get up for this, but then I went back to bed and I watched *The Exorcist* on TV. Later I came downstairs to the kitchen to see Rinpoche. After we chatted for a while, Rinpoche went up the back stairs of the Court with his *kusung,* and I remained in the kitchen. He was in a playful mood, and he was jumping around on the stairs in a jaunty way. The *kusung* should have been behind him but was in front of him instead. Then I heard an incredible crash. I thought that somehow a chest of drawers had been pushed down the stairs. It turned out that Rinpoche had fallen and hit his head. When I found him at the bottom of the stairs, I became hysterical because he was briefly unconscious and I thought he was dead.

Mitchell was still at the Court, and he came immediately when he heard the crash. He came and examined Rinpoche, who was now awake and seemed fine—much to our relief—although upon examination, Mitchell found that he had a mild concussion. We decided to keep Rinpoche at home for the night. The next day, Rinpoche complained of a headache and said that, if he were anyone else, he "would have been licking ashtrays," referring to the intensity of the pain. Rinpoche's relationship to pain was quite different from most people's. Mitchell rushed him to the hospital at this point, where they found that he had bled into two small areas of his brain. He was allowed to come home, but he was confined to bed for a while.

We both had to stay in bed, and we started fighting. We had completely different sleeping and waking patterns, so we were constantly waking one another up. The whole atmosphere, which had been so sweet, was just awful. I now realize that Rinpoche was probably in a terrible mood because his head hurt. One night we had a horrible fight; we broke just about everything in the bedroom. I can't remember what it was about at all. I do remember both of us screaming and throwing things and breaking them. When the *kusung* came in, the whole room was in a shambles.

Rinpoche used to say that he appreciated being able to fight with me. There was nobody he could fight with like that, nobody to whom he could show such irritation, because of who he was. We didn't fight a lot, but we would have the occasional, really intense fight. Sometimes it got wild, but then it was over immediately. Neither of us ever hung onto it. The anger was never there the next morning.

In some ways, the accident on the stairs was a profound turning point in Rinpoche's life. I've always felt that he changed in a fundamental way after that. After the accident, I sometimes felt that he was no longer 100 percent in this realm. Certainly his teaching became a lot more atmospheric after that. I would say that he became less interested in transmitting the details of the teachings, but in some ways his lectures actually became more powerful because he radiated the essence of the teachings into the environment. He didn't have permanent brain damage or anything like that, but something shifted after his fall. Later, when I looked back, I felt that the accident was the beginning of a physical decline that ended with his death in 1987. I don't know exactly why I feel that.

Superficially at least, Rinpoche recovered thoroughly, and he continued with his schedule of teaching in the fall. In early January 1981, he went up to Chateau Lake Louise for the seminary again. This year it was followed by another Kalapa Assembly, where Rinpoche introduced the *Werma Sadhana* to all of the students there.

I stayed in Boulder until I was about a month away from giving birth. Then, I drove up to Lake Louise with Mitchell and moved into the suite with Rinpoche at the Chateau. I went over my due date by more than a week, and finally the doctor there decided to induce labor. I went down to the Mineral Springs Hospital in Banff to give birth.

Once again, Rinpoche proved to be a fabulous labor coach. He would tell me when to breathe and when not to breathe, and he always knew just the right time. I was in a Catholic hospital, and they had a cross on the wall of my labor room. Many of the nursing staff were nuns. I had extremely painful back labor because the baby was turned around. I was dilated at nine centimeters for several hours before the baby came out, and at the end I was screaming, "Jesus Fucking Christ, Jesus Fucking Christ," because of the pain. They wouldn't give me a decent painkiller. It was quite primitive. Later, when I came back to Boulder, my doctor there said, "I can't believe they didn't turn the baby around." At one point, one of the nuns was in the room, and she said, "Take a deep breath now." It was completely the wrong time. I screamed at Mitchell, who was also in the room with Rinpoche and me, "Get this fucking woman out of here." She disappeared and never came back.

When the baby was crowning, I asked the doctor, "What color is the hair?" and he said, "Oh, just a little darker than yours." I'm quite blond. When he said that, Mitchell ripped his surgical hat off. He was beside himself. The baby came out; he was a beautiful little boy, cherubic looking, really. He was put in a little incubator in the corner, a bassinette. Rinpoche and Mitchell both ran over and stood over the baby in the delivery room, talking about whose he was. From some point of view, it was hysterically funny. They couldn't decide who the father was, so at a certain point they decided it was theirs and not mine. It really wasn't clear to any of us. Taggie had been quite Caucasian in appearance at first, whereas Gesar looked Asian right away.

They had run out of the blue blankets they usually wrap the baby boys in, so they wrapped our son, Ashoka Alexander Mukpo, in a pink blanket. The nurses gave him back to me, and I had him in my arms, and they wheeled me out into the corridor outside the delivery room. All the members of the Vajradhatu board of directors were waiting there, along with John Perks, Mitchell's wife, Sarah, and a few others. Out I came with this very pink baby in a very pink blanket.

At that moment, I started to feel that I was bleeding. I turned to Mitchell and said, "I'm hemorrhaging." Mitchell said, "Oh, it's okay." He was somewhat distracted, to say the least. So I had to endure showing the baby to all of the directors, while all the time I knew I was bleeding. By the time they got me back to my room, I had a dinner plate–sized blood clot where the blood was congealing under me. There was blood dripping off the bed, and they had to give me a transfusion. The nurse kept saying, "Why didn't you say something? Why didn't you say something?" I just said, "Well, I tried."

When people had their babies in that hospital, the policy was that the babies would go to the nursery. I refused to have Ashoka taken there; I wanted to have him with me. I remember the nurse saying to me, "You're feeding him too often. You should have him on a feeding schedule. What are you going to do if you have to vacuum your house and the baby wants to eat?" I said, "Well, I don't vacuum my house." I was able to take him back to the hotel the next day.

SEVENTEEN

After Ashoka was born, we were at Chateau Lake Louise for several weeks. Rinpoche didn't seem concerned at all about whether or not Ashoka was his son. He loved him; he always loved him. When Ashoka was three weeks old, Rinpoche picked him up and said, "This will be the next Lord Chancellor of Shambhala!" When Ashoka was little, Rinpoche also used to say, "Something is really special about this baby."

A few weeks after Ashoka was born, we received a letter from His Holiness the Karmapa saying that Ashoka was the incarnation of Khamnyön Rinpoche, the Mad Yogi of Kham, a very important Kagyü lama who had monasteries in both Tibet and India. We decided to wait and not to make any plans about Ashoka's future at that time. There was the question of Ashoka's parentage, and we didn't know what effect that might have in the future.

When we first brought Ashoka home from the hospital, I was staying with Rinpoche in our bedroom at Chateau Lake Louise. Rinpoche thought it would be nice if the baby was in bed with us, as we had done with Gesar. We tried this arrangement, but Rinpoche's *kusung* seemed to come into the room almost every half hour. Rinpoche was having stomach problems in that era, which continued for some time. He would get nauseous frequently, which was one reason that he would ring for a *kusung* to come in.

I on the other hand was experiencing some postpartum depression, or at least my hormones were raging and I felt vulnerable and exhausted. I desperately needed to rest at night. With people coming in all night long, and the baby waking up all the time, I finally freaked out completely and started screaming at Rinpoche. We had a huge fight. Rinpoche started screaming back at me and chased me around the bedroom until I finally barricaded myself in the bathroom with the baby. He thought *I* was being unreasonable. I took a room down the corridor at the hotel so that I had a separate place to sleep with the baby. After that, we got along fine.

The Kalapa Assembly took place at Lake Louise while Ashoka was just a tiny infant. I would bring him to the talks, and there was a screen on the main stage that I used for privacy when I needed to nurse him during an evening presentation. A number of times during his presentations at the assembly, Rinpoche asked me to make remarks to the assembled students or to answer questions. He continued to want me to participate actively in the assembly.

Soon after we got back to Boulder, the Regent and Lady Rich moved out because we needed the room for the new baby. They rented their own house a few blocks away from us, which Rinpoche named the Kalapa House. I also wanted and needed to have my own bedroom at this point. Rinpoche very sweetly arranged for me to have $1,000 to decorate my sitting room, which was off of my bedroom. This was the first time that I felt I could have my own space and arrange it the way I wanted within the Court.

Right after Ashoka was born, an article was published in one of the national dressage magazines about my training in the Spanish Riding School. During this period, there was considerable interest in my riding experience, and several magazines ran features about the time I had spent at the Spanish. I saw the magazine about three or four days after giving birth, and I felt so out of shape compared to how I looked on the cover of this magazine. I thought, "Oh my goodness, it's going to take a long time to get back into this shape." Funnily enough, when I returned to Boulder when Ashoka was just a few weeks old, I got a telephone call from a television producer who wanted to do a feature on the Shambhala School of Dressage for the Arts and Entertainment network. The only time they could possibly film me was then, when Ashoka was a newborn. I had to ride for this, even though I felt inadequate. I managed to pull myself together, and it went very well, in fact. The Arts and Entertainment feature was initially aired locally, but then it was chosen at the end of the year to be shown nationally.

During the period when Ashoka was an infant, I appreciated life at the Court in many respects. I could see that it was a wonderful situation for a lot of people in the community to have contact with Rinpoche in an intimate way.

Rinpoche had a daily routine at the Court in Boulder. Of course, being Rinpoche, he constantly disrupted or changed the routine, but still there was a predictable pattern to his life. When he first woke up in the morning, his *kusung* would come in and present him with tea bowls for the main shrine downstairs as well as for the shrine in the kitchen and for the personal shrine in his sitting room. Rinpoche would add gunpowder tea to each bowl and then pour hot water into the bowls. Then the *kusung* would take the bowls and put one on each shrine, as an offering to the protectors, the forces that guard the Buddhist teachings. This daily offering is traditional in many schools of Buddhism.

Once, when Ashoka was quite little, he was in bed with Rinpoche and me. That morning the *kusung* was a man named Scott Forbes. When Scott came in with the tea offering bowls, Ashoka grabbed at one of them. I said, "No, no, don't do that. That's the Buddha's." So Ashoka sat back and let Rinpoche do the offering. A couple of hours later, we were walking through the hallway of the Court. Scott Forbes was standing in the hall. Ashoka stopped and he pointed at Scott and he said, "Look, Buddha!"

Some mornings, Rinpoche would take a shower before breakfast. He insisted that we should only have white towels in the bathroom. His philosophy was that with white towels you could see if they were dirty. Rinpoche himself didn't like to shower, but he insisted that we had to have these pristine white towels. A little later, he went through a phase where he took long baths in tepid water, uncomfortably lukewarm. He had a fear of water and disliked bathing. Somehow, however, he leaned into the bath thing and made it a regular activity for a while.

After Rinpoche had been awake for a little while, either before or after his morning ablutions, Shari would often come into the bedroom to consult with him about his breakfast. Sometimes he would get up and have breakfast downstairs or in the backyard; often he would eat in his sitting room. He liked to have what he called "bandit soup" for breakfast. This was frozen beef that Shari would shave into very thin slices and arrange artfully in a bowl. Then Rinpoche would have a small teapot containing boiling hot water, which he would pour over the strips of beef. The hot water would cook the meat a little and make a soup broth. (It was called bandit soup because when bandits were on the run, this is the kind of breakfast they could make quickly.)

Usually, Rinpoche would eat breakfast in his pajamas or his Japanese bathrobe, his *yukata*. Then he would dress for the day's work. He would indicate to his *kusung* what he wanted to wear for the day, and he or she would bring his clothing to him. He had a big walk-in closet where all his suits, uniforms, robes, and other clothing were kept. Sometimes he would go down to the office at Dorje Dzong. Other days, he would conduct business at the Court. As time went on, he spent more and more time at the Court and held many of his meetings there. He seemed in this era to be moving away from the corporate, office-based approach to business within Vajradhatu. Having seen the neurosis and limitations of that model, he began to make the Court the location for most meetings and the focus, or power spot, for decision making. The night before or first thing in the morning, Beverley Webster would bring over a typed schedule with his appointments for the day. She might also meet with him about what he was doing that day. In addition to his *kusung,* as time went on, he had an attaché, who was both like a super-*kusung* and also someone to help oversee the conduct of business. The presence of the attachés was an important part of making the Court function not just socially but as the center of the business mandala. The attachés would brief people coming to meet him; they sat in on his meetings and made lots of phone calls on his behalf, and Rinpoche often would discuss possible developments and decisions with them. He especially began to rely on this approach after David Rome moved to New York in 1982 to run his family's publishing business. Before that, David did a lot of this himself. After David's departure, Jim Gimian took over many of the functions of running the office with Beverley. There was a core group of three attachés: Mitchell, Jim, and Marty Janowitz—who was appointed the Kusung Dapon in the early 1980s after John Perks left. Rinpoche called them the "three musketeers." Altogether there was a group of about ten attachés, including several women, who rotated through the Court and also traveled with Rinpoche.

In the evening, there were often meetings, lectures, or other events that Rinpoche attended. Sometimes, this called for a change of wardrobe before going out. During this era, if nothing was scheduled in the evening, Rinpoche and I would sometimes go unannounced to somebody's house for dinner. There was one period when Rinpoche wanted to do this several times a week. We would decide whose house we were going to, and we would just show up at the door without warning. People were very hospitable, and usually they made quite a nice meal for us. Sometimes people were totally unprepared for guests and quite shocked by our arrival.

In addition to the everyday activities at the Kalapa Court, we also hosted many receptions, dinners, and celebrations of all kinds. If Rinpoche had been away for any period of time, there was a reception to welcome him home. Members of the board of directors and their spouses, staff from Vajradhatu and Naropa, and other invited guests would come to the Court the night he got home. He would greet each person, and people would join us in the blue room while he talked about the trip and about what would be happening next in Boulder. People were always anxious to see him, and these were generally very enjoyable gatherings.

Shambhala Day celebrations at the Court became more and more elaborate as the years went on. Often, Shari and other Court staff would prepare two or three elaborate meals for our guests on Shambhala Day. Sometimes a community member with culinary talent would volunteer as a guest chef for one of the meals. We could have sit-down breakfasts and dinner banquets for fifty or sixty people by turning the blue room into a dining room with long banquet tables and a head table for Rinpoche, me, and the rest of the family. During the rest of the day, people retired to different rooms to talk, have coffee and drinks, and to play board games. Rinpoche thought board games could be both engaging and edifying pastimes. He himself enjoyed the Oriental game of mingmong, which is a game of strategy, a variation of go. He detested card games and I don't think we allowed them at the Court.

One year, after breakfast I invited a group of women up to my sitting room and we pulled out the Ouija board. It was a lot of fun at first, but then we contacted the spirit of a student of Rinpoche's who had died the previous year. Then we started talking to a *lokapala,* or a worldly deity. Who knows what was real about this? Rinpoche finally came along and said that he thought it was not healthy to continue. He was not much of a fan of indulging in the supernatural, especially not in the way that Westerners use these things as a parlor game.

In later years, we had receptions at the Court for visiting Buddhist teachers, and occasionally we hosted dignitaries who came through Boulder. Once we had a reception for a representative of the Chinese government. For Rinpoche, having a Chinese official at the Court was quite a coup. He looked like the cat that swallowed the canary that evening, I thought.

On another occasion, the widow of Shunryu Suzuki Roshi was invited from San Francisco to the Kalapa Court for the opening of a Japanese tea house that Rinpoche had built in the garden. (I believe that the tea house was donated after his death to Naropa Institute and was moved onto their campus at some point.) It was a lovely occasion and wonderful to see Mrs. Suzuki again. A few years later, when some students began studying the Japanese tea ceremony, they would come to the Court almost every night of the week to take classes and practice the discipline of tea ceremony, or *chado.* That was another feature of how our house was used: it was available for classes and small gatherings, almost like a community center. Rinpoche wanted our home to be the focus for Shambhala culture, which was wonderful for the community but less satisfying for me in my desire to have a family home.

During this era, Rinpoche—among his many vocations—was quite involved with the presentation of Dharma Art, which refers to teachings on art in everyday life, as well as general aesthetics and the application of Buddhist and Shambhala principles to artistic disciplines. He spoke about nonaggression as the basis for genuine art, and in his seminars he gave demonstrations of flower arranging, calligraphy, and object arrangement, which students also worked with in small groups. At times, Rinpoche also talked about his photographs and about language and poetry in these classes. Allen Ginsberg was a participant at several of the major seminars. Jerry Granelli, the eminent American jazz percussionist and composer, helped organize early seminars in California and was quite active with the early programs at Naropa. Over the years, Rinpoche was invited to do a number of ikebana or flower-arranging exhibitions. Later, the exhibits evolved into Dharma Art "installations" in which Rinpoche placed extraordinary flower arrangements in rooms that he and his students designed and created. At the end of 1980, he and a group of students had done a major Dharma Art installation at the LAICA (Los Angeles Institute of Contemporary Art) Gallery. In September 1981, Rinpoche went to San Francisco for several weeks to give a Dharma Art seminar and to do an installation there.

As with so many other areas, his artistic endeavors drew a large group of students to him, some of them professional artists but many not. A group called the Explorers of the Phenomenal World was formed to explore the principles of Dharma Art and to work on the exhibits and installations. One of the directors of this work, Ludwig Turzanski, was a professor of art at the University of Colorado when we arrived in Boulder. Ludwig and his wife Basia were our close friends from the earliest days in Boulder.

As the interest in ikebana grew, it became common for students to come several times a week to create arrangements in various rooms of the Court. I had always loved having fresh flowers, but this took on a whole new dimension, bringing color, elegance, and wonderful fragrance into Court life.

While I appreciated the world of the Court, it had its difficulties. Although there was a sense of well-being and harmony there, at the same time, it was not entirely satisfying for me personally or for our family. For example, when Ashoka was little, his bedroom was in a corner of the Court, right next to a room we called the *kusung* station, which was where the various servers would hang out when they were not on duty. If Rinpoche rang, the *kusung* were supposed to walk around the corridor to get to Rinpoche's room. The alternative was to cut right through Ashoka's bedroom, which had two doors. I would say to them, over and over, "Please don't go through Ashoka's bedroom." But instead of taking a few extra steps, the *kusung* would usually run right through his bedroom, often when he was asleep. Most of the time, they woke him up.

During this era, I was having a difficult time in my personal life. No one was consciously admitting that Ashoka was Mitchell's child, but it was becoming more and more apparent that this was the case. On the one hand, perhaps it was irrelevant. Rinpoche accepted Ashoka, he loved Mitchell, and Rinpoche and I were getting along extremely well most of the time. On the other hand, nothing fit together for me in my life. I started to feel quite groundless. I would sometimes break down and cry uncontrollably. Finally, Rinpoche asked Ed Podvoll, a psychiatrist who was directing the psychology program at Naropa, to come and see me. I used to talk with Ed a couple of times a week, trying to resolve things. A lot of the problem, I realize now, was that, for a long time, I really couldn't admit to myself that Ashoka was Mitchell's baby. It was a struggle to continually dismiss the obvious.

As well, I wanted Rinpoche to be more involved with the family on a day-to-day basis. When he was first getting up in the morning I would go in and sit on his bed and say, "Please, I need just a little bit for me and the family. Just once a week have dinner alone with the kids and me. I know you have a duty, and you have a job. But I need something, just once a week." We'd have these conversations, and I'd always end up crying. He would promise to make time, and then usually nothing would happen. After a couple of months of doing this on almost a daily basis, I stopped. Two or three days later, he came into my bedroom and sat on my bed and said, "Why don't you come and talk to me any more in the mornings?" I replied, "It's just too painful." He said, "Oh no, you can't stop. I'm starting to rely on these conversations you have with me." And I told him, "You know, I'm not masochistic. Why am I going to come in every day? It's too painful. You don't relate to your family at all. Now I've decided to give up. I've started to move forward, and you're saying you're unhappy about that?" I couldn't believe it.

Rinpoche may have been a *mahasiddha,* but he was also a man. And like some men, he seemed to have a double standard about extramarital affairs. The fact was that I had fallen in love with Mitchell. I know that it was difficult for Rinpoche. He had a lot of relationships, but he usually didn't fall in love with these other women. After Ashoka was born, Rinpoche sometimes worried that he was losing me. In fact, I was deeply in love with Mitchell. When I was a child, my father had talked to me about how it was possible to love more than one person in your life. He had told me that love was very big; it wasn't a small thing at all, and that one's life could accommodate loving many people. I found that I loved

Mitchell more and more, and that our love for one another was genuine, strong, and growing.

There was another side to the whole thing, which was the relationship between Rinpoche and Mitchell. They were very close. One night, a few years later, the three of us were in Maitland, Nova Scotia, staying at the Great Ship Inn. I was going to bed early, and I wanted Mitchell to come to bed with me. Rinpoche was in the bathroom, and I went in there and said, "Let Mitchell off duty. I want to hang out with him." "You know, Sweetheart," he said to me, "the problem is, we're both in love with the same person." It was so very sweet. In its own way, it was workable, but there were definite difficulties. I can't deny that.

At this time, I didn't think that Mitchell and I were ever going to have a normal life together. That didn't seem possible. He was married. I was married. But we did have our time together. For me, partly it was that I enjoyed being able to share part of my life with someone who was more my own age, from my own generation. We would do simple, ordinary things like go to the movies together. We shared things that I just didn't do with Rinpoche anymore. At one point, I said something to Rinpoche about him being a father figure in my life, especially since I'd been so young when we got together. He didn't like my saying that, but there was something to it. I also did have a real craving to have a more quiet life and a more normal relationship. So there was some push and pull between Rinpoche and me, although we continued to love one another a great deal.

When Ashoka was about six months old, I took him with me over to Germany for a period of time. I had decided to go to Gronwohldhof and get back into my riding a little bit. I had sold Shambhala, one of my horses, in part because there were a number of people who had invested in buying him, and people needed to get their money out. I had Warrior with me in Germany. I was there training for several months. I felt that I had to get on with my life and that getting back into my career in riding was the healthiest thing for me to do. I did feel more of my own strength from that, and in many respects, it helped to cheer everything up in my world.

Throughout 1981, Rinpoche was preoccupied with His Holiness the Karmapa's illness. The Karmapa was very ill with stomach cancer, and Rinpoche went to visit him a number of times. He was distraught about the Karmapa's condition. Mitchell became involved in His Holiness's medical care and arranged for him to see Western doctors. In the end, His Holiness came to Mt. Zion Hospital in Chicago for medical treatment, and he died there on November 5, 1981. We all felt it as a great loss. He was truly a great leader, a dharma king. At the same time, when Rinpoche performed a funeral ceremony in Boulder for the Karmapa, he talked about His Holiness's death as a blessing to all beings and especially to the Western world. As he put it:

> Each time the departure or arrival of a Karmapa takes place anywhere in the world, it is a blessing in that particular land. . . . We do not regard His Holiness's death as an attack by unexpected obstacles. We can see it as a blessing. Never before has any realized person such as the Buddha, Jesus Christ or Mohammed set foot in the Western world. The Western world needed taming. It needed the compassion and skilful means of enlightened mind. It needed the blessings of the Karmapa to conquer the ground and bring the great fruition of the Practice Lineage.[1]

Very soon after the Karmapa died, Rinpoche went to Rumtek, His Holiness's seat in Sikkim, for several weeks. There, he spent time with all of the other Kagyü teachers, those who lived at Rumtek as well as those who descended there when His Holiness died. Because of my commitments in Europe, I was not able to accompany Rinpoche. It was the first time that Rinpoche had been back to Asia since 1968, apart from a brief visit to Hong Kong to see the Karmapa in the hospital earlier that year. He told me that when he would get up in the mornings, there would be hundreds of Tibetans waiting outside of his hotel hoping to catch a glimpse of him or to receive his blessing when he came out of the hotel.

As is traditional, His Holiness's body was preserved in salts for a period before the cremation. The body was placed within a special ceremonial closed coffin in the main shrine room at Rumtek for several weeks, and many people came to practice there and to pay their last respects. Rinpoche took a number of students with him to Rumtek, including the Regent, Mitchell, Dapon Gimian, the Dorje Loppon, as well as John Perks, Karl Springer, and several others—Ken Green, Chuck and Judy Lief, and a few assistants. They all spent time practicing in the shrine room at Rumtek with the Karmapa's body. To be able to practice in the presence of the teacher's body during this period is said to be a great blessing. After Rinpoche's death, I experienced the power of this. One can still feel the teacher's presence, and the energy of his compassion is quite available. The party could not stay for the actual funeral. (There had been a misunderstanding about the date of the cremation.) Rinpoche said that it was more important, in any case, to be there during the early period after His Holiness died.

After returning to Boulder, on the day of the cremation in Rumtek, Rinpoche conducted a funeral for His Holiness in the main shrine room at Dorje Dzong. It was during this sad and moving occasion that he made the remarks above. During the funeral, he also shared with all his students his feeling that with the death of the Karmapa his duty to the lineage became even greater. He had a sense of a heavy cloak of responsibility being placed on him. He felt more and more that the propagation of Shambhala vision was of great importance for the future of Buddhism in the West. From this time onward, he put even more effort into teaching, particularly emphasizing the advanced levels of Shambhala Training.

In May, 1982, His Holiness Dilgo Khyentse Rinpoche, who had enthroned Gesar in Berkeley, returned to the United States. At Rinpoche's request, His Holiness had agreed to perform a Shambhala enthronement ceremony for Rinpoche and me, which is generally an empowerment for a secular ruler, usually a king or queen. Khyentse Rinpoche had performed this ceremony when the current king of Bhutan was enthroned.

This empowerment is called the "Blazing Jewel of Sovereignty" and is commonly referred to in our community as the Sakyong *abhisheka*. In 1974, the Karmapa confirmed Rinpoche in the Buddhist lineage as a holder of the Vajrayana teachings, a *vajra* master. Now it was very meaningful to him that Dilgo Khyentse Rinpoche would come and confirm him as Sakyong. Rinpoche viewed this ceremony as an important landmark in the Shambhala teachings coming to the West. He told me that as part of the Sakyong *abhisheka*, His Holiness would give me the empowerment as Sakyong Wangmo. This was not a necessary part of the ceremony. Rinpoche could have asked His Holiness to do the ceremony just for himself, but he chose to make me the Sakyong Wangmo. He wanted me to feel that I was part of the ruling principle. I think this came out of his respect for women and the feminine aspect of society. He understood that Tibetan culture had become somewhat stagnant because it was such a male-dominated society. In order to create a rich society here in the Western Shambhala world, he felt that we needed to also empower the feminine principle. So while more of the focus during the ceremony was definitely on him, as it should have been, I was also empowered at the same time.

We started out wearing simple white clothing, somewhat like being on stage in our pajamas. This signified our basic human nakedness, which was adorned progressively throughout the course of the enthronement. His Holiness was on a throne to Rinpoche's right. Rinpoche started out in a normal chair. I was seated throughout the ceremony on a chair to his left. His Holiness blessed our clothing, which we then put on. For Rinpoche, there was a white naval uniform, which from then on was always called the "*abhisheka* uniform." I put on a beautiful brocade *chuba* that was custom-made for this event. Rinpoche then ascended a throne at the same height as His Holiness.

Rinpoche was given a white naval peaked cap, and His Holiness blessed a small white gold tiara inlaid with diamonds for me (a gift from Rinpoche). We also received special shoes, which in Rinpoche's case had a *vishva-vajra* (a diamond scepter with prongs in each of the four directions) drawn on the soles. Normally, you would never walk on that sacred symbol, but the king can walk on it, because for him the whole earth is regarded as a sacred golden ground covered in *vishva-vajras*. His Holiness also blessed various medals and presented them to us. These were the medals that Rinpoche had designed in 1977. We also were given beautiful velvet cloaks, which were edged with a custom-made brocade that came from Japan and included a special tiger-lion-*garuda*-dragon emblem as part of the design. (The cloaks were made by Deborah Luscomb, one of several talented seamstresses in the community who over the years made special articles of clothing or shrine cloths for members of our family. She had made the cloak for the Sawang's investiture as well.)

At a certain point, Rinpoche was given a large conch shell that he blew, signifying the proclamation of the king's command. Then a bugle played the Shambhala anthem. Many other offerings and toasts were made to Rinpoche—and to me—and he made remarks about the significance of the event. He talked about the role of the Shambhala

monarch in conquering the setting-sun or degraded aspects of civiliza-
tion. He also spoke about the need to create a Great Eastern Sun culture based on sanity, gentleness, and wakefulness. This was the role that
he saw for himself, for me, and for all the citizens of Shambhala. In our
case, the citizenry of Shambhala is spread throughout the world. While
Rinpoche established the Kalapa Court as the focus or center of the
Shambhala world, he knew that people would connect with the wisdom of Shambhala in many different places and at many different
times. While giving this wisdom a seat at the Kalapa Court, he also
wanted to extend the Shambhala principles to anyone who connected
with this path of warriorship.

All four of our boys were there: Ösel, Taggie, Gesar, and Ashoka.
When Rinpoche returned from Sikkim, he had brought Taggie back
with him. We thought that we would try having him at home once
again, since nothing much had changed while he was in Asia. We took
him to a whole new group of doctors who put him through a new
group of tests, but nothing seemed to help. At this time, Taggie was living in the Court. He had an attendant at the enthronement so that he
could witness it, although I don't think he knew what was going on.

For Ösel, this day had special meaning because he knew that he
would be receiving the same empowerment at some time in the future.
In fact, he was given the Sakyong *abhisheka* in Halifax, Nova Scotia, in
1995, conducted by another great Nyingma teacher, His Holiness Penor
Rinpoche.

Gesar was old enough to understand that this was an important
event. He held himself with restraint and dignity throughout the long
afternoon. Ashoka, meanwhile, was just a little over a year old. By the
end of the afternoon, he was climbing all over me, the stage, and Rinpoche. At one point, Rinpoche was sitting on the throne in his regal uniform with Ashoka on his lap. They seemed quite happy together.

There were about two hundred people invited to the ceremony. I
think it had a lot of meaning for everyone who was there. You know, in
telling you the slightly whacky story of my life, I worry that what gets
lost is the larger view, the larger significance of the events in Rinpoche's life. On this occasion, the whole environment was completely
luminous. It was a superpowerful event in what was a powerful environment in any case—all the time.

Rinpoche understood that the age that we live in calls for the proclamation of dharma as the imperial *yana,* the imperial vehicle. This is a
dark and confused time, a time when people have lost much of the dignity in their lives. It takes a very bright light to get people's attention because they are so lost and jaded. Rinpoche was willing to shine forth that
light, even if it was somewhat shocking, even when it was hard for people to make sense of. This was one occasion when the word "glorious"
really applied. His Holiness was also a thoroughly luminous and expansive human being. He was magnetic, powerful, and so kind. On this day,
Khyentse Rinpoche was beaming, and you could see the connection between him and Rinpoche. They were very close. It was a wonderful occasion. I didn't think so much about the implications as far as my own
path was concerned. I felt that it was an affirmation of all of us, of all of
Rinpoche's students. It also was an affirmation of hopefulness for Western society as a whole.

Shambhala Anthem

In heaven the turquoise dragon thunders,
The tiger's lightning flashes abroad.
The lion's mane spreads turquoise clouds,
Garuda spans the threefold world.

Fearless the warriors of Shambhala,
Majestic the Rigdens on *vajra* thrones.
The Sakyong king joins heaven and earth.
The Sakyong Wangmo harvests peace.

The trumpet of fearlessness resounds,
The all-victorious banner flies.
Temporal and spiritual glory expand,
Rejoice, the Great Eastern Sun arises![2]

EIGHTEEN

In the summer of 1982, not long after the Sakyong *abhisheka,* I moved up to Nova Scotia with Gesar and Ashoka. (By this time, we had concluded that nothing was going to change with Taggie. The monastery in Sikkim was willing to have him return, and Rinpoche felt this would be the kindest environment for him at the time.)

Rinpoche was talking about moving to Nova Scotia at some point in the future. He had toured the province again in 1979, and at the end of 1981, he had spent several weeks there, culminating in a seminar at the Keltic Lodge in the northernmost part of Nova Scotia, on the island of Cape Breton. He became more and more enthusiastic about the place with every visit. Beginning in 1979, a few of his students moved there from other parts of Canada and from the United States. When I arrived, there was already a small dharmadhatu in Halifax.

I thought that the sanest thing for the children and me would be to move up ahead of him and get a farm there, where I could have horses, and the children could have a more normal life. I bought a farm in Falmouth, near Windsor, Nova Scotia, which we named Willowstream Park, after the farm that my parents had owned in South Africa. I brought several horses up there, including Warrior. I had also purchased a young stallion at Gronwohldhof when I'd been in Germany the previous year. I bred him to more than twenty mares in Nova Scotia in the spring of 1982.

Rinpoche was excited that I was going to live in Nova Scotia. He saw me as pioneering the development of the Shambhala world there. For me, it was both an attempt to participate in furthering the vision that he was trying to promote and a way to have a personally sane existence. Being married to Rinpoche was sometimes like being married to a cosmic force rather than a human being. As time went on, this was more and more the case. I felt the need for a more ordinary human existence, which I thought the situation in Nova Scotia would provide.

Rinpoche had asked Jane and Tom Ryken, two senior and trusted students, to live on the farm with me. They were very committed to us and helped the family a great deal; we had quite a pleasant household for most of the year that we were there together. A student of Rinpoche's from Australia, Geoff Martin, also joined us and was a great help. We had a large vegetable and flower garden, and I used to do a lot of pickling and canning. Ashoka was happy running around on the farm, and Gesar enrolled in King's Edgehill, an excellent private school in the neighborhood. Rinpoche used to come and visit periodically, and Mitchell also came up a few times.

There was an indoor arena a half-hour from the farm where I could ride, and I started competing Warrior in a number of local shows. I received excellent scores competing at the lower international or FEI levels, and I was invited to ride in a clinic in Toronto with the Canadian Olympic coach at that time, Johann Hinnemann. At the end of the clinic, Hinneman told me that he liked the horse but felt that he would do better at Prix St. Georges, the first international level, than at the Grand Prix level, the highest level of dressage. Hinneman suggested that I sell Warrior.

After going to Toronto, I seriously got the riding bug again, and as my opportunities were so limited in Nova Scotia, I decided to move back to Europe in early 1984, to continue training and find a horse with more potential. I sold Warrior and moved over to Germany with Gesar and Ashoka, intending to stay for the whole year. After looking around a

bit for a new horse, I went back to Gronwohldhof, Herr Rehbein's facility. There was a horse there, Poseidon, that I had known about for several years, that had always appealed to me. When I rode him, he was a
beautiful mover and gave me a good feeling. I thought that I should purchase him.

Hinnemann was skeptical. He called and said, "If the horse is already
eight years old and he hasn't been successful competitively, there's something wrong and they shouldn't be selling him to you." I called Herr
Rehbein at that point, who was furious that someone was saying these
negative things. I had suddenly ended up in the middle of a political up-
heaval. I decided to trust Rehbein, so I went ahead with the purchase.

After several months training at Gronwohldhof, I began to have
doubts. Poseidon was very big, and he proved to be spooky and quite
difficult to ride. Later, I learned more about his medical history—had I
known these details earlier, I would not have purchased the horse, because the prognosis was not good. In retrospect, I don't think Herr Rehbein was malicious in selling me the horse in any way. He took an
educated gamble. He was trying to help me find a good horse that I
could afford. In the end, I lost on that gamble.

After riding the horse for more than six months, I found that he was
getting more and more difficult to ride. The difficulties with my horse
coincided with the time that I was supposed to return to North America to visit Rinpoche, who had begun a year's retreat in Mill Village, Nova
Scotia. So in the fall of 1984, I went to Mill Village, and then I spent time
in Boulder. This provided me with time to think about whether Poseidon was the right horse for me. I decided to sell Poseidon. I phoned
Rehbein at that point and asked him to sell the horse. For months, I continued to call Gronwohldhof to ask if he had been sold. Every time I
called, I was told, "No, No, he hasn't sold yet." This continued for almost
a year.

During this period, Vajradhatu experienced severe financial problems. Most of my own financial affairs were handled by the organization.
I kept asking if my bills at Gronwohldhof were being paid, and I was told
that they were. It turned out I was almost a year in arrears, without my
knowledge. The people at Gronwohldhof had basically repossessed the
horse without saying that was what they were doing. Then Poseidon

went lame. He was no longer worth anything, and Vajradhatu had let the insurance lapse. It was a fiasco.

In some quarters of Vajradhatu, there was resentment about the expenses connected with my riding, and I started to question whether it was worth going through all the negativity, especially when nothing seemed to be working out. I became depressed about my riding career. I was also quite worried about Rinpoche's health at this point, so I decided to stop riding. As it turned out, I didn't resume my career for four years, until after Rinpoche's death. Today, I find that I have more enjoyment and love for my discipline than ever before in my life. But at that particular time, that four-year hiatus was necessary.

I left Germany in the fall of 1984 and went to Nova Scotia, where Rinpoche was in retreat. He had contacted me and told me that he wanted me to come over to receive the Vajrayogini *abhisheka* from him in retreat. After all these years, I still had not had this transmission, and Rinpoche seemed to feel that this was extremely important at this time. He was planning to confer another important empowerment, the Chakrasamvara *abhisheka,* after his long retreat, and he wanted me to be able to take that as well. Chakrasamvara is the consort of Vajrayogini and a very important *yidam* in our lineage. Vajrayogini represents the wisdom aspect of the teachings, while Chakrasmavara represents the practitioner's skillful action and compassion. Since wisdom and compassion are indivisible, Vajrayogini and Chakrasamvara are joined in union in the iconography. These are some of the most profound and important teachings that Rinpoche could transmit to the West. Looking back now, I feel that he knew that his life was coming to an end, and he wanted to be sure that I received these transmissions from him.

The house he was living in was an old sea captain's house about two hours outside of Halifax. There was a large kitchen on the main floor, and people would hang out around the kitchen table at odd hours of the day and night. Near the kitchen there was a shrine room where the staff, and occasionally Rinpoche, would practice. There was a spacious dining room where Rinpoche ate at all hours of the day and night—his schedule changed a lot—and a large living room. The main cook, Joanne Carmin, who we called Machen (which means "chief cook" in Tibetan) also had a room at the very back of the house on the first floor. She spent the entire year in retreat with Rinpoche. There was always at least one attaché and one *kusung* on duty, and Rinpoche had a number of other guests who came and went. There was also a little guest bedroom on the first floor, where Gesar stayed when he visited his father for several months. Upstairs, Rinpoche's bedroom was a large room with a walk-in closet and a separate bath. Other bedrooms for the staff and visitors were also on the top floor.

The year before he went to Mill Village, Rinpoche had been on a schedule that was often totally turned upside down. He got into the habit of staying up all night and sleeping during the day. During the all-night sessions in this era, he began teaching his students elocution with an Oxonian accent, the English accent of a person educated at Oxford University. He wrote exercises that his students practiced with him at all hours of the day and night, and he also wrote a novel about life in the Shambhala Kingdom, which he liked to have read aloud in Oxonian, sometimes at three or four in the morning.

By the time he got to Mill Village, his schedule of activities was even stranger. He would often stay up for twenty-four to forty-eight hours straight, and then he might sleep that long. No one knew when he would be awake or when he might be sleeping. Sometimes, he would eat dinner three times in a day; sometimes, he would hardly eat at all. It was not very easy to be part of his staff or his household at that time.

Rinpoche's approach to retreat was quite different from the approach of a group retreat where everyone feels good and relaxes and communes with nature or with God. Rinpoche's retreats were more like the trials of Christ wandering in the desert or what ascetics in various traditions went through in their caves. Altogether, retreat in the Buddhist tradition is meant to be very tough. It is an undistracted opportunity for a student to work on unraveling ego and neurosis at a fundamental level. Rinpoche was both doing that for himself and he was also working with his students. The situation he created for himself and others in retreat was stripped bare of the conventions of everyday life. He was free to be exactly as he was, without any pretense. Even beyond the personal and interpersonal level, he was working on the karma of his whole community in North America, trying to liberate what was stuck both now and in the future.

I felt that his approach, how he worked with himself and with others in retreat, was the spiritual equivalent of the tough training that I went through in Vienna. He was creating an uncomfortable space for himself and other people, an almost ruthless space where you constantly felt groundless—you have the ground pulled out from under you so that you realize what life is about at the most fundamental level. Eventually, you might realize what buddhanature is, the heart of enlightenment, stripped of all pretenses and concepts. But while you are going through the process, you totally lose any reference point to a goal. This process is very, very uncomfortable.

Sometimes people ask me what meditation practices Rinpoche himself did, and I realize that, in some respects, it's a strange question. In a very real sense, everything he did was practice. This may be a dangerous thing to say, because if students were to take this to mean that *they* don't need to do formal meditation practice, that would be a big mistake—encouraging self-deception. However, I do feel that for Rinpoche, especially in the later years, his life was his practice. From time to time, he joined his students in the sitting practice of meditation, and he took part in the major practices he gave to people, such as the *Sadhana of Mahamudra,* the *Vajrayogini Sadhana,* and various Shambhala practices. But in general, his practice was his being, or vice versa. Very early on, in 1971, a student asked him if he ever meditated, formally. Rinpoche's response was: "That seems to depend on the situation—but formal sitting, in terms of imposing it on oneself, somehow doesn't apply anymore." The student said, "Apply to whom?" And Rinpoche responded: "To whom. That's it!"[1] I think his response here is another way of expressing the groundlessness one encountered at Mill Village. For Rinpoche, there was really no contrast between practice and everyday life, and there was nobody there to ask the question. For most of us, sharing that space was unsettling, sometimes deeply so.

Before going to Mill Village, I spent time studying the Vajrayana teachings that Rinpoche had given us to help prepare myself for the *abhisheka.* Rinpoche had phoned the Vajradhatu ambassador to Europe at that time, Steve Baker, and asked him to tutor me before I left Germany. The more I read, the less sure I felt about what I was about to do. I had a lot of questions and, one could almost say, doubt during this period of time. I didn't feel through and through that I was necessarily ready to take on this commitment. I wanted to understand what I was getting into if I took this transmission. I wasn't sure that I would be completely genuine if I took this empowerment without complete conviction. In my own way, even before I arrived at Mill Village, a spiritual crisis was growing within me, which seemed to be exactly what Rinpoche was provoking in everyone there.

When I got to Mill Village, Rinpoche said that I had to do twenty-one prostrations, twenty-one *vajrasattva* mantras, twenty-one mandalas, and twenty-one recitations of the guru yoga mantra on the day of the *abhisheka* before he would give me the transmission. I had never completed my preliminary practices. Traditionally, people do a hundred thousand of each of these practices, so he was letting me off pretty easy! However, I still resented him telling me what to do. I did the first three parts of the practice, but when I got to the guru yoga mantra, I had to visualize Rinpoche as my teacher. I was totally angry with him at that point for insisting that I take this *abhisheka*. I was conflicted about Rinpoche being both my husband and my guru. I found it difficult to reconcile these two things during this period. I thought to myself, "What the hell am I visualizing here?"

I was pushing the boundaries, wanting to discover for myself what made sense, what worked and what didn't. I had never had a chance to have a teenage rebellion, in a way, because I had married Rinpoche so young. I thought, "Why on earth am I in the shrine room doing this stuff?" So I came out and I said to him, "This is ridiculous." He got really angry with me. He screamed at me and started pounding his hand, saying, "Go back." He told me to go back and finish the practice. I was pissed off, but I went back and completed it.

I was also uncomfortable with the fact that in giving me the *abhisheka,* he seemed to be presenting Vajrayana as the highest reality. I was feeling that there were other valid positions in the world and that we were isolating ourselves as a community if we didn't acknowledge this. I was having a meltdown. The *abhisheka* was going to take place later that night. I wrote him a letter asking, "Aren't there other truths? Aren't there other realities?" In response, he wrote me this prose poem on the night that he gave me transmission:

To Lady Diana Mukpo on the Occasion of Receiving the
  Abhisheka of Vajrayogini

Why so?
Cheerful birthday once again.
You are my only eyes, heart and life as well as my breath.
Nonetheless, we haven't been together for a while.
Thinking of you is like a sudden flash of lightning in a cloudy night
    time.
Remembering your smile and your face relieves my pain.
Now and in our previous lives, we have been bound together by
    the chain of karma.
This letter was written with a combination of sadness and joy.

The reason why we are together in this lifetime is only due to the
    buddhadharma and the guru.
The little I have been able to help others is because of meeting the
    only authentic guru.
It is by the blessings of the guru that I am not insane.
However, these days, many people are insane.
Two world wars and nuclear weapons and other chaotic situations
    have occurred.
Your practising the dharma is not just for me, in the same way that
    taking of medicine is not for the doctor.
It is in order to cheer up others and blossom their lives.
The Vajrayana teaching is the highest of all.
It is the greatest magic that Buddha has ever taught.
Just as you need a mother to begin with as an infant, Vajrayogini
    practice is very necessary.
If one realizes the importance of that, one would understand all
    the Vajrayana teachings.
It is necessary to develop eyes in order to see the brilliance of
    various flowers.
Then one can develop an understanding of both spiritual and
    temporal ways.
This is not just thought up by somebody.
It is 2,500 years of wisdom.

I am presenting the *ghanta, dorje,* and *damaru* [bell, scepter, and
   hand drum] as a birthday gift.
They are like a horse and saddlery.

One might say: "Is this the one and only way? But we have become
   civilized and no longer act as cavemen."
Obviously, everyone would agree that the sky is blue.
One might ask: "Aren't there other truths, other ways?"
There might be, but mathematics must begin with zero.
One might say: "I don't want to buy any (one) else's viewpoint."
In this case, one is not buying others' viewpoint, but trees have to
   grow up from the ground.
They never take root in the air upside down.
But in any case, one is not buying somebody's view.
The Communists might say: "Lenin's view is the only way."
There are things with view and opinions.
There are also other things without view and opinion, which, as
   we know, is *shunyata* [emptiness] and is free from opinion and
   concept.
Vajrayogini herself represents nonthought.
There are ways to experience that, free from *skandhas* [ego] and
   fixed opinions and so obtain universal freedom.
That is why we have the story of the *arhats* [Buddha's disciples]
   who died of heart attacks when for the first time Buddha
   proclaimed the teachings of *shunyata.*
Once Nagarjuna said: "I have no axioms; therefore what I present is
   without dichotomy."
I would like to invite you into this enlightened world.
Once more, I would like to express that you remain as my greatest
   inspiration and companion.

With profound love and thanks,
From your best friend,
Chögyam[2]

I don't know if this will speak to others as it did to me. It was one
of those times that Rinpoche was talking directly to my heart and my

intellect at once, and he completely disarmed me. My hesitations dissolved on the spot, and I realized that my seeming irritation was actually more a reflection of my connection to him and longing for him. So I wrote this poem in reply:

Chögyie to the Rescue

Your kindness and brilliance go beyond conceptual mind.
Your generosity has transformed my life.
I was lost in the clutches of confusion
Searching for sanity and reference point
And along came Chögyie,
The first genuine person I'd ever met.
You demonstrated that the phenomenal world is merely a
    playground
To be captured with kindness and skillful means.
Your heart is unsurpassable.
You have taught me to believe in myself.
Your awakened mind is the source of my loyalty to you.
You nurture your students with loving kindness and include
    them in our Mukpo family.

I'm so glad I met you.
Please prolong your life for the benefit of others
I love you.
Your devoted wife and student.
Diana[3]

Does it seem odd that we wrote poems to one another? I suppose in a way it is, but it also was a way of reconnecting with him. In particular, I supplicated him in the poem to prolong his life because I felt that he was beginning the process of dying while at Mill Village. No one else seemed to realize this was happening at the time, which was one thing that made it so difficult for me during this period.

We proceeded with the *abhisheka*, which I felt as a breath of fresh air in what I experienced overall as a hot, crowded room. After giving the *abhisheka*, Rinpoche gave a little talk. There were several other people who received the *abhisheka,* and he gave a lecture to all of us about the principle of Vajrayogini and how to regard the practice.

During the remainder of my visit to Mill Village, I felt anything but receptive to the environment. I couldn't relax there, and I found that Rinpoche wasn't there for me in the way that I counted on him to be. It was very difficult.

During the last years of his life, Rinpoche intensified the training of a number of his close, older students—including me. I, like many others, was to be left with many unfinished lessons to work out in years to come. The story of two great figures in the lineage, Marpa and Milarepa—which I referred to much earlier in this book—involved Marpa setting impossible tasks for Milarepa, asking him first to build and then tear down building after building. This was part of purifying Mila's karma. Marpa would often be drunk and abusive when he dealt with Milarepa. These stories of surrendering are colorful when they refer to events in the past, but when they are about something that happens in your own life, it's much less easy to accept or understand. The atmosphere at Mill Village evoked those classic tales and was anything but easy.

Altogether, I was there for a week or so, and I became incredibly claustrophobic. I felt a lack of personal space; things seemed to be closing in on me. I had Ashoka with me, and that made being there more difficult. If Rinpoche slept for twenty-four hours and then was up for twenty-four hours, it was completely incompatible with being with a young child. So at one point, I said that I would like to go into Halifax and stay at the Court on Dutch Village Road for a few days. This was a house that had been recently purchased for us. Rinpoche was planning to spend an extended period of time in Halifax, probably beginning in 1986, so this house was purchased with the idea that it could be his residence at that time. In the meantime, some *sangha* members were living there and fixing it up, and Rinpoche stayed there when he was in town. He told me that it would be fine if Ashoka and I went up there. I left as quickly as I could pull my things together! When we got to the house, I spent a nice evening there. Ashoka stayed in bed with me, and we had a bath and watched movies on television together and went to sleep early.

The next morning, around seven o'clock, a *kasung* walked into my bedroom and said, "Rinpoche is on his way down." I couldn't believe it.

I finally had found a corner of privacy and space, and now he was coming there. The Sawang was staying at Mill Village at this time, also, and he arrived in the car with Rinpoche at the Court. We all gathered in the living room. By then it was close to 8 A.M. Rinpoche wanted to play a game that he loved, called the "qualities game," in which people would ask him questions about the quality of something they were trying to guess. They would ask questions such as: "If the subject of the game were a meal, what kind of meal would it be?" And he would say something like, "It would be a hot dog." Or "It would be roast beef and Yorkshire pudding." You could get a good idea about what you were guessing from the pattern of a number of answers. A British monarch might be described as roast beef, while Rinpoche was more likely to describe an American president as a hot dog.

That was the traditional way that the game was played. But starting in this era, frequently there was *no subject*. In other words, there was no correct answer and therefore no end to the game. Rinpoche would just give answers, and they weren't related to guessing anything. The game ended when he wanted it to end. Period. This was heightening my sense of being trapped and uncomfortable.

More broadly, I was increasingly upset because I sensed Rinpoche was going into another realm at this point, and I didn't know how to reverse things. He often didn't seem responsive or grounded in the way that I was used to. I felt that everything was spiraling out of my control.

I once asked His Holiness Dilgo Khyentse Rinpoche why, when you had these descriptions of how far out Vajrayana experience was, the great teachers like himself were all so kind and ordinary. He said to me, "It's that way on the outside, but if you could see into my mind, it might look completely crazy to you." So Rinpoche, in a sense, was letting people see into his mind and into their own—with nothing covering up anything.

Mill Village was the last intense opportunity he was to have to train the people around him, and he didn't let up for one moment. He didn't even say, "Now, I'm training you and this is going to be really uncomfortable." He just was the way he was, and you had to deal with it. It was outrageous in a whole new way; this time, it wasn't glorious outrageousness. It was really tough. The point seemed to be to push people in the environment until they couldn't hold it together anymore—then see what happens. He didn't relent until people lost it in some way.

At one point during this retreat, a person visiting Rinpoche asked him why he was being so tough on one particular staff member. Rinpoche had been relentlessly breaking this person down, waking him up over and over again during the night, criticizing him, and on and on. This visitor was in a car with Rinpoche and the person Rinpoche had been tormenting, so to speak. The visitor asked, "Why are you being so hard on so and so?" Rinpoche said, loud enough so he could be overheard, "I have to make him feel as bad as I possibly can." Somehow this made the person feel a little bit better. Later Rinpoche indicated that this person was really very close to him—he wasn't mad at him or anything. He just was trying to get through the facade and work with what was there.

Again, this was very familiar to me. What Rinpoche was doing at Mill Village had a similarity to the tactics at the Spanish Riding School, where they push people to such an extreme that a person discovers what he or she is made of. The difference in what Rinpoche was doing was that his approach was not based on aggression but was using aggression, turning it on its head, to break through the *fundamental* aggression. This is similar to how he worked with the Dorje Kasung discipline. It is both the heart of his brilliance and often the most misunderstood part of his teaching.

On the morning Rinpoche arrived at our home in Halifax, when the qualities game mercifully ended, I went upstairs to escape, but Rinpoche followed me. I encountered him in the upstairs hallway. He was standing with Ösel, leaning on his arm. I said to him, "This situation is terrible. It's really awful. You are getting completely crazy. You are getting completely out of control, and you're killing yourself. You're drinking yourself to death." And he said, "Well, do you know what's the matter with you? You're a punk." (He was referring to my hairstyle; I had had my hair cut short and spiky in Germany.) I came right back at him. I said, "I may be a punk, but I'm not drunk." With that, he tried to hit me, but he missed.

From my perspective as his wife, which I think is different from a student's perspective, I felt that the whole thing, my whole life, was falling apart. In earlier years, when people were having difficulty accepting Rinpoche or his latest campaign, they would come to me and ask, "Is everything okay? Is everything going to be all right?" I could always say, with complete conviction, "Everything is going to be fine." I had so much faith in Rinpoche and what he was doing. But in the later years, I would have had to say, "I don't know. I really don't know."

As Rinpoche's wife, my role seemed to be to nurture him and help to keep him on this earth, in some ways. To see him sacrificing his body and going beyond the bounds of good sense in terms of his health was excruciating. Maybe that was a lesson in itself. One of the stories about Milarepa is that the last time he was with Gampopa, his dharma heir, when they parted, Mila lifted his cotton robe so that Gampopa could see his emaciated body covered in scabs and sores. "This is the dharma. This is the truth," he said. The end of Rinpoche's life had some of that aspect to it.

When I look back at this period of time now, it still makes me incredibly sad. Yet I can see now that Rinpoche was still doing an amazing amount during this final era. Things actually weren't falling apart. During the year that he was in Mill Village, *Shambhala: The Sacred Path of the Warrior* was published, and it was a great success. Rinpoche continued to work closely with Shambhala Training, and when the administration faltered, he moved forcefully to make changes so that the project would remain strong. During this period he also directed a group of students to upgrade the facilities at RMDC, overcoming hesitations within the board of directors, so that we could hold the seminary and Kalapa Assembly on our own land starting in 1985. There were a number of projects like this, which he kept in touch with and moved forward during this period. He was also working on what I can only call a nonconceptual level in terms of planting seeds in Nova Scotia. I don't know how else to put it. He was feeling out the energy of the place, and he was putting parts of himself into the environment there. It was something like that. But as his wife, seeing that he was less and less in his body and less and less healthy, it was heart-wrenching. Sometimes, I think that he kept me away, at arms length, during this era because he knew that he was going to die relatively soon, but he just had to go forward.

Rinpoche at times was like a typhoon, or a hurricane. Viewed from afar, a hurricane appears orderly and beautiful; from inside, it is dangerous, chaotic, and difficult to endure—unless you are in the eye. The eye of the storm is absolutely still and calm. I think that for much of my life with Rinpoche, I could find the empty center, which was calm and open. I could feel the brilliance and the power, but I wasn't buffeted around by it. However in the later years, I felt that I was part of the swirling chaos. Rinpoche threw everyone into that whirlwind. I think that was deliberate on his part. After his death, I could begin to see the larger pattern again, its power, beauty, and meaning. I realize now that the immediate chaos, though painful and excruciatingly real, was a passing confusion. I find that what endures is the big picture, the vast vision that Rinpoche communicated.

Around the time that I was in Mill Village visiting Rinpoche, Mitchell and Sarah decided to separate after what had certainly been a very difficult time for them. When I left Mill Village, I went back to Boulder, where Mitchell and I were able to spend time together. The Regent and Lady Rich were living in the Court at Eleventh and Cascade. I was supposed to have stayed in Germany for the whole time that Rinpoche was in Mill Village, so we had given them the Court for the year. Rather than try to move in with them, which really didn't appeal to me, I got my own apartment, where Ashoka and I stayed. (Gesar was in Nova Scotia for the rest of the year.)

The next month I found out that I was pregnant again. Once again, it happened while I was using contraception. It was, of course, another big drama, but this time there was no question about whose child this was. David, my second son with Mitchell, was born in August 1985.

At the time of David's birth, Rinpoche was conducting the Magyal Pomra Encampment again. He asked me if I wanted him to be present at the birth, but I told him it was not necessary. My mother, however, actually came to the hospital. Somehow, she was able to accept my unconventional relationship with Mitchell, and she was delighted to have more grandchildren. Mitchell's mother was also there. The two grandmothers waited in separate rooms during my labor, as they were not overly fond of one another. After the baby was born, they both were ushered into the room. When Elaine, Mitchell's mother, saw David for the first time, she remarked, "Another Jewish doctor is born!" My mother countered, "The best part of this child is English!"

Rinpoche had the Dorje Kasung at MPE fire off the big cannon to celebrate David's birth. Rinpoche was very sweet to David when he was an infant, but Rinpoche didn't live long enough to spend much time with him. David was just eighteen months old when Rinpoche died. Rinpoche's hope was that we would name the baby Yung-lo, after the Chinese emperor who built the Forbidden City and was a great warrior-king. Rinpoche felt that this child would have a particular connection to martial energy and that this name would be very appropriate for him. Rinpoche said that this child would be the next Kasung Kyi-Khyap, the commander of the Dorje Kasung. I wanted to call my son "David." Emperor Yung-lo was also a ruthless tyrant who killed many people before converting to Buddhism, so I thought it was a strange name to saddle my son with. However, after thinking about it, I realized that all of our children had Shambhala names and that I trusted Rinpoche's inspiration. My son's birth certificate reads Yung-lo David Mukpo.

NINETEEN

In early April 1985, Rinpoche concluded his retreat at Mill Village and prepared to return to Boulder. Since he had been away for so long, there was great anticipation about his homecoming. The day before Rinpoche was scheduled to fly out of Halifax, he and the staff arranged to leave the retreat without notifying anyone in Halifax or Boulder that they were moving up the departure. They left one person behind manning the phones at Mill Village, who was instructed to maintain the illusion that Rinpoche was still there, while making him unavailable to any callers.

Rinpoche and his small band of pranksters flew out of the Halifax International Airport a day early. Their escape was not discovered until the next day, when Rinpoche did not appear for his previously scheduled flight. His whereabouts were unknown. Even I did not know where he was. The Dorje Kasung in Boston, New York, and other likely cities were asked to check the airports he might fly through, and a contingent was sent to the Denver airport. However, Rinpoche had flown into Denver before anyone was aware that he was missing, and he was staying in a hotel in Denver under an assumed name. He was not found.

The night of his expected arrival, a large welcome home gathering and blessing had been planned in the Dorje Dzong shrine room in Boulder. Although people had no idea whether he was going to appear—or whether he might be in Tahiti, for all they knew—still the community gathered and waited. There were close to a thousand people in the shrine room. The Dorje Kasung went to the airport at the hour that his original flight would have gotten in, but he did not appear there.

Finally, just at the time he was scheduled to arrive in Boulder, he and his staff pulled up to the curb of Dorje Dzong in a limousine. The Dorje Kasung were there to greet him—they were waiting there not knowing if he would come—and he entered the building, took the elevator up to the top floor to the shrine room, and he ascended the Tibetan throne from which he gave remarks and a blessing to everyone assembled. Rinpoche had always loved April Fool's jokes, and this was one of his best (although it came a few days after April 1!). People's reactions to this joke included a wide range of emotions. Some were amused; others were irritated, confused, or angry. Behind that, everyone felt a sense of empty heart and potential loss. Rinpoche's "disappearance" pointed out that we can't take anything for granted. Given that he died two years later, almost to the day, it was perhaps part of the preparation for what was to come. His death, so close to April Fool's Day—April 4, 1987—may have been the biggest joke he ever pulled.

Throughout 1985, Rinpoche continued the schedule of teaching and meetings that he had followed for many years. For the first time, both the Vajradhatu Seminary and Kalapa Assembly were held at RMDC in the summer of 1985. Hundreds of new tents had been purchased, and the facilities had been upgraded to expand the capacity of the center so that it could house hundreds of participants for months at a time. We still hold the seminary at RMDC, now called the Shambhala Mountain Center. The facilities have grown over the years since Rinpoche's death, but he laid the ground by insisting that we begin to use our own center for these large, advanced programs.

Rinpoche made his final visits to many of the city centers where he had been teaching over the last seventeen years. Of course, people did not know that it was the last time; I do not know if he knew this, although I strongly sense that he was aware that he would not live much longer. He toured Europe in December and January of 1986, where he gave the Vajrayogini *abhisheka*—the first time ever in Europe and the last time during his lifetime. He made his last visit to Karme Chöling in June of 1986, where he gave a seminar on the indivisibility of the Shambhala and the Buddhist teachings.

In April of 1986, Rinpoche conducted the Chakrasamvara *abhisheka* for about three hundred of his students in Boulder. It was very important to him to be able to transmit this teaching to people. The fact that he finally gave this transmission was a mark that he felt that the Vajrayana teachings were firmly established. The ceremony takes two days to complete. It was exhausting for him; his health at this time was quite fragile. He was, nevertheless, delighted to accomplish this. I too was delighted to be present, and I realized his kindness in having pushed me to take the Vajrayogini *abhisheka* the year before. Without that transmission, I could not have received this final empowerment from him.

Rinpoche conducted his final Kalapa Assembly early in the summer of 1986, and this was followed by the last Vajradhatu Seminary he presided over. There was also an encampment during the summer, but Rinpoche came and went from it very briefly. At the seminary, he gave fewer and shorter talks, and much to everyone's surprise, he left RMDC early and asked the Dorje Loppon Lodro Dorje to give the final talks, with the Vajra Regent conferring the Vajrayana transmission at the end.

Rinpoche had plans to go to Halifax to spend the year, beginning in the fall. Initially, this was just to be a one-year visit, after which he expected to return to Boulder. I was planning to remain in Boulder and visit Rinpoche from time to time, rather than move the whole family up for just a year. But all of that was to change, with very little warning.

One day, in August of 1986, while we were at the Kalapa Court in Boulder, Rinpoche asked for me, telling his *kusung* that it was urgent. I was somewhere else in the house at the time, but I joined him in the bedroom. He said to me, "The time has come. I want to move to Nova Scotia, permanently. We all have to go. You and the children should make plans to come with me. We should leave next week." For some reason, this seemed fine to me, even though it came out of the blue and was the opposite of what I had been intending. He was also proposing to leave several weeks ahead of schedule. It reminds me a bit of when His Holiness Dilgo Khyentse Rinpoche informed me that Gesar was a *tulku* and we should enthrone him right away. Something about how Rinpoche addressed me made me feel that I definitely should do whatever he wanted at this time. I said to him, with really almost no hesitation, "Okay, we can go."

Then, he said to me, "We're going to move into the Regent's house in Halifax. That will become the Kalapa Court." While that might sound quite straightforward, actually it was quite a bold move. In 1985, Rinpoche had asked the Regent and Lady Rich to move to Halifax to work on developing the organization and the community there, in preparation for Rinpoche to come in a year or so. Through the efforts of the Regent and other members of the community in Halifax, they had found a building on Tower Road for Vajradhatu to move into. There was one woman in our community, Martha Bonzi, who was an extremely generous patron of Rinpoche's work. She had provided funds for the Naropa Institute over the years, and she gave very generously to many other projects, such as funding the activities of the Nalanda Translation Committee. In this instance, she donated the funds to purchase the Tower Road building. There were extensive renovations throughout 1985, and in January 1986, Rinpoche had gone up for the official opening of the center, which was attended by local politicians, religious leaders, and businesspeople as well as the members of our community.

The Regent had then found a house that he thought would be suitable for himself and his family to live in. It was a three-story mansion on Young Avenue, one of the most expensive areas in Halifax. The Regent began renovating his house, and he spent exorbitant amounts of money on the project, hundreds of thousands of dollars. There were many complaints about the money he was spending and the manner in which he was preparing to live. To be fair, he and Lady Rich had a large family that included four children (they had twins born in 1981). They certainly needed a lot of space. But the approach the Regent was taking seemed over the top. It appeared that he was going to have quite a lavish lifestyle, beyond anything that Rinpoche and I had ever had. I think that he felt that he was going to assume Rinpoche's role as the head of the community, sooner than later, and this was the kind of house that he envisioned for himself when *he* was in charge. At the same time, Vajradhatu was experiencing extremely tough financial times. Everything else aside, it was questionable for us to invest so much money in his household.

Up to this point, Rinpoche had heard all the complaints, including some from people close to him whom he trusted a good deal, but he had not done anything about the situation. Then, in this one fell swoop, he dealt with the whole problem. He sent a senior student, Larry Mermelstein, to deliver the message to the Regent that Rinpoche was moving to Halifax and would need his house. Then, Rinpoche phoned the Regent to confirm this. Of course, the money had already been spent, but the Regent didn't get to live in the luxurious palace he had built for himself. As it turned out, he was building it for his teacher, a twist that was not lost on many of us. The Court on Dutch Village Road, where we otherwise would have gone, was a much more modest dwelling, both in size and the level of renovation and interior decoration. It would in fact have been extremely odd to have the Regent living in a house that was so much grander than his teacher's.

According to what I heard, the Regent suffered terribly after Rinpoche's phone call. When Larry gave the Regent the news, his first reaction was, "Whatever the guru wants." However, he then became both angry and distraught and descended into a depression that lasted for days. He didn't want to give up his house, but Rinpoche was the one person he couldn't say no to. I heard that he threw things around that night after the call, he was so angry. I believe this, because when our staff arrived at the new Court on Young Avenue in Halifax—to move in our belongings before Rinpoche and I arrived—there were holes in the bathroom walls where towel racks had been taken out of the wall, and there were large screw holes in the wall in the Regent's bedroom where a built-in shrine had been removed from the wall. They took the fixtures and the shrine with them, I guess.

The same day that Rinpoche informed me that we were all moving, he asked Mitchell and me to go for a drive with him. We got into his Mercedes, which had a custom license plate that read TLGD (for Tiger Lion Garuda Dragon). Mitchell was in the front seat. He was riding shotgun, and there was also a driver. Rinpoche and I were in the back. Rinpoche wanted to go to all the places that we had lived in Boulder and places where important things had happened. We drove up Boulder Canyon, and the first stop was the Four Mile Canyon house. He wanted to see that again. Rinpoche kept saying to me, "Tell Mitchell. Tell him about it."

After that, we went by the Red Lion Inn, which is a restaurant up

Boulder Canyon where we had many wonderful meals. We went down to the first Karma Dzong, 1111 Pearl Street, and Rinpoche kept saying, "Tell him. Tell him about it." We retraced our early life in Boulder. I began to feel concerned, because Rinpoche seemed to be saying good-bye to everything in Boulder. There was a sense of closure that made me uneasy.

This drive reminded me of a ride that I had taken with him in early 1984, shortly before I went to Germany for the last time. At that time, Rinpoche had been spending a lot of time in bed, and he seemed somewhat depressed, actually. Finally I said to him, "Come on. Let's get up and go for a drive somewhere." He wanted to take a drive up into the mountains, up Left Hand Canyon, north of Boulder. While we were out driving, I said to him, "You've got to cheer up." He was in a very black mood. I said again, "You've really got to cheer up." He didn't respond. So I said, "Come on, look out of the window. It's beautiful. It's a beautiful day. Look out. Remember, Shambhala Training, the Great Eastern Sun, and all of that." He just growled at me. So I said, "What's the matter with you?" He replied, "I'll be dead in three years." That certainly set me back. I said to him, jokingly, "You probably will, won't you, just to show me that you're right." I made light of it, but I had never forgotten that conversation. Now, this drive was feeling strangely reminiscent of that. I had the same feeling of his impending death, although he didn't mention it.

Rinpoche went ahead of me to Halifax. I went to Florida briefly before I joined him. I had taken David to a beautiful baby contest when he was seven months old, and we had won a reduced-price trip to Disney World. So Ashoka, David, and I, along with one of my *kusung,* Nancy Craig, all went on a short trip to Disney World, and after that I flew up to Halifax.

It was now September of 1986. We all moved into the Court at 545 Young Avenue. It was an impressive building, but to me it didn't have the warmth or the accommodation that the Court in Boulder had had. The Court on Eleventh and Cascade felt so open and bright. The house in Halifax always felt slightly oppressive and cold to me, even though it was magnificent. There wasn't a sense of comfort in the home. Rinpoche was very sweet to me when I arrived and seemed very happy to see me. He had invited a number of students in the Buddhist community to greet the children and me at a reception in the living room. He seemed excited at the prospect of our new life and pleased that the whole family had joined him up there.

I moved into an apartment on the top floor of the house with Mitchell and the two younger boys. Gesar had a room on the floor beneath us, close to where Rinpoche occupied the large master bedroom, which the Regent had painted gray with gray curtains. It was a sleepy room, but it had large windows that looked out on Young Avenue.

The apartment I shared with Mitchell felt like a great luxury. I had struggled for so long with needing personal space for the children and myself within the Court environment. After David was born, I had actually moved out of the Court temporarily, into a house on King Street in Boulder, to try to provide some kind of family sanity. As I described earlier, this was a struggle for many years of my marriage to Rinpoche, especially as the family grew. Having my needs accommodated within the Court in Halifax felt great. I found that I could relax and actually appreciate Rinpoche more.

In our apartment, Mitchell and I had a combined living and dining room in the apartment, and there was even a small kitchen upstairs. We usually had dinner downstairs with Rinpoche, but I could make breakfast for the kids upstairs if I wanted, and I kept snacks for them there too. There were bedrooms for us and for the children, and even a playroom. I spent a fair amount of time with Rinpoche, but I also had my own space. Mitchell and I being together was just an accepted feature of life at the Court at that point, and everyone seemed fine with it. My *kusung* would come into the apartment, but I was no longer subjected to having the people serving Rinpoche running through and forgetting that anybody else existed.

Rinpoche did not seem well physically. He looked gaunt, and his skin had taken on a dark color. He would sleep for long periods of time, and sometimes even when he was awake, he would be less than lucid. At this point, we were aware that Rinpoche had some health problems that were going to be difficult to address, especially if he continued drinking. That was one reason that he had planned to spend the year in Halifax: he was supposed to take time off from his demanding schedule to try to get a handle on his health. Rinpoche had had diabetes and high blood pressure for years, which are both diseases that many Tibetans develop in the West, perhaps due to differences in climate, altitude, and lifestyle from the environment in which they grew up. Added to that was his excessive use of alcohol over many years, which at this point in his life was overtaxing his liver.

Mitchell had come up to Halifax with us, but he was just on a visitor's visa at that time and couldn't work in Canada. He still was on the staff of St. Anne's Hospital in Denver, so after a couple of weeks, he had to fly back to Denver to work for several weeks. During that time, I stayed in the house with my three children.

One evening I went down to see Rinpoche. He was in the bedroom sitting on the side of the bed. I saw that he was bleeding from a cut on his ear. I asked him what had happened, and he said that he had fallen and cut his ear on the side table by the bed. He was trembling, and he was bleeding quite profusely. He said to me, "Look, I cut my ear. I can't stop the bleeding." He didn't want me to call anyone, but I insisted. I was very concerned about him. The *kusung* came in and we got his ear bandaged, and then they left us alone. I said to Rinpoche, "I'm worried about you. Something's not right with you. You shouldn't be lying in bed all the time. Tomorrow, let's open the curtains and let some daylight in. We can go out. What can we do for you at this point?"

He said, "It's too late. It's too late."

So I started to spend more time with him, hoping that I might cheer him up. He told me a number of things that were on his mind. He said, "The situation with the Regent is terrible. We've got to dismantle him." He was very specific about this, but I had no idea what to do. Several times he said to me, "The Regent is terrible. We should take his position away. He's dreadful." I couldn't imagine how we would go about getting rid of him. A few years earlier, I had complained to Rinpoche about the Regent, and he told me, "Fine. We'll get rid of him. But who else can you imagine? Who could do the job?" He had named some people and then broken into laughter. "Who is there?" There didn't seem to be anybody else he thought could do the job.

During this time, he also said to me, "We should reconfirm you as Sakyong Wangmo." We never did anything about that, either. Sometimes, when I tried to talk to him, it felt as though he had completely checked out. Other times, he was right there; he would come back, so to speak, and we would talk. However, the situation was tenuous. It was not easy to have an ongoing stream of communication with him during that time.

One late afternoon in late September, I had just put David to bed. The *kusung* on duty came running into my apartment, asking, "Do you have a syringe? Do you have some kind of syringe? Rinpoche's not breathing." Not knowing what they meant, I just ran downstairs with one of the bulb syringes that we had for the baby. Then I saw that Rinpoche was not just having trouble breathing; he was unconscious. I screamed at them to phone 911. Then I tried to suction out his throat, which didn't work. I remember trying to put my hand down his throat to see if there was an obstruction. It felt like ages before the ambulance came, but it was just a few minutes. I was allowed to ride in the ambulance. I remember asking, "Does he have a heartbeat?" just as they started CPR. He had definitely had a cardiac arrest. We finally arrived at the emergency room in the Halifax Infirmary, on Queen Street. They took him in the back, and it seemed like aeons while we waited, while they worked on him. We didn't know if they were going to be able to bring him back or not. Eventually the doctor came out and said that they had been able to reestablish a pulse. I was allowed in to see him, and he was completely comatose in the emergency room. Eventually, they admitted him upstairs. Later, I remembered that there had been a lunar eclipse that day.

Rinpoche was completely comatose for at least the first seventy-two hours. Yet I felt his consciousness in the room during this period. That was my perception, in any case.

Mitchell was working in Boulder when Rinpoche had his cardiac arrest. He immediately got on a flight to come to Halifax. About fifty other people got on a plane in Denver the day after Rinpoche's heart attack and flew up. The minute that Jim Gimian heard about Rinpoche, he phoned a travel agent in Boulder and booked every seat on the flights from Denver to Halifax for the next few days. (He and his wife, Carolyn, had been scheduled to come up later that month anyway. They and their infant daughter, Jenny, were going to live in the Court with us as staff for the next year.) Jim held all the available seats, and then he phoned people to offer them a seat. Everyone wanted to come. So within the next forty-eight hours, about a hundred of Rinpoche's most senior students arrived in Halifax, from Boulder and from other places, not knowing what his condition was or if he would recover. We put up about twenty people at the Kalapa Court. Every possible room was used for people to stay in.

While Rinpoche was still in a coma, two important Kagyü lamas who had been very close students of His Holiness the Karmapa, Jamgön Rinpoche and Situ Rinpoche, flew in. They went to see Rinpoche in the intensive care unit at the Halifax Infirmary. I talked with Situ Rinpoche at the Court after he had seen Rinpoche. He said, "We hope that Trungpa Rinpoche will recover, and we're doing all kinds of practices for him. But if Trungpa Rinpoche decides to change bodies, this is no problem." I thought to myself, "Well, that's easy for you to say."

Rinpoche's students—wherever they lived—gathered together to practice meditation and to do various chants and practices for his recovery and overall to express their love and devotion for their teacher.

Within a few days, Rinpoche regained consciousness, but it became apparent that he had suffered brain damage. We didn't know how much or whether it was reversible. Eventually we brought him back to the Court. We had a special hospital bed put into his room, and we hired private nurses to care for him around the clock, along with our own people. The nurses became very connected to Rinpoche and to our family, and four of them attended his funeral in Vermont the next year.

Over the next few months, his physical condition went up and down. Throughout this period, everyone in the community continued to practice intensively, alone and in group practice sessions, trying in whatever ways they could to encourage Rinpoche's return to a state of health and also to work with their own state of mind in this difficult situation. He never regained the ability to speak, really. I remember trying to get him to talk, and at one point he was actually able to imitate some of the words that I said. I felt optimistic for a short period. At a certain point, I remember clearly that he said, "I want beer." He definitely said it, although I know that Mitchell didn't believe me when I told him this.

Although there was a phase when we thought that some rehabilitation might be possible, in early March 1987, he began to degenerate again. He was readmitted to the hospital in mid-March of 1987.

I had many dreams about Rinpoche during this period. In January I dreamed that he was standing in a palatial bedroom. He was in his midthirties, at the peak of his teaching career, wearing an orange brocade robe. He was very handsome and manifested in the dream in somewhat wrathful form. In the dream, he pointed at me with two fingers, and he said, "I am going to die soon." He opened his eyes wide and said,

"The whole thing is up to you now." I interpreted this to mean that I would have to take responsibility for the Shambhala teachings he had given me, as much as I could throughout my own lifetime. In early February, I had another dream about him. He was lying in a single bed on his right side, as the Buddha lay during his *parinirvana,* or death. He said to me, "I am going to die very soon, and I am very concerned that the circumstances around my death go well."

When he was readmitted to the hospital, he had severe blood-clotting problems. At some point, they had inserted a stomach tube. Toward the end of March he began to have bleeding from the hole in his stomach. Right around this time, I was away for a couple of nights. I went down to New York to attend a trade fair because I was opening a children's clothing store in Halifax, and I had to go down to buy stock for the store. I was in close communication with people in Halifax, so that if I needed to come back right away, I could. I felt that if I continued to do ordinary things and behave as if everything were all right, maybe it would be. I was on some sort of emotional hold at that point, as was everybody. I was taking sleeping pills every night, and functioning on automatic pilot. They phoned me in New York to say that Rinpoche's condition was deteriorating, and I rushed back. The night after I returned home, I had another dream in which Rinpoche and I were in Tibet together. I was in the waiting room of a monastery there. His Holiness the Sixteenth Karmapa came to greet me. He was in the prime of his youth, wearing a brocade vest and monks' robes. Standing with him was another very great teacher, His Holiness Dudjom Rinpoche, the head of the Nyingma lineage, also in the prime of his youth, wearing a gold robe and an earring in one ear. Dudjom Rinpoche's hair was long and glossy black and styled like a yogi's hair. Trungpa Rinpoche was also there, also in the prime of his youth, and he was wearing monks' robes. He was about twenty-three or twenty-four and his head was shaved.

First, His Holiness the Karmapa entered the room. He sat on an elevated armchair. Then His Holiness Dudjom Rinpoche came in and sat on a slightly elevated couch. Finally, Trungpa Rinpoche came in and took his seat on the same couch. Then, I entered the room and sat on the floor, cross-legged in front of a coffee table, opposite Trungpa Rinpoche and facing the Karmapa. His Holiness had a very nice teacup in front of him. He was explaining something to me, something very straightforward and simple.

The next night, I had a dream in which His Holiness the Karmapa and His Holiness Dudjom Rinpoche appeared again. The Karmapa pointed to an empty seat and said that they were waiting for Trungpa Rinpoche to join them. Exactly at that moment in the dream, the beeper next to my bed went off. It was there in case of emergencies. I phoned the hospital, and they told me to come right away, that Rinpoche was having terrible bleeding. When I got there, I learned that he was hemorrhaging from the hole where the stomach tube was inserted. Basically, his entire body was breaking down. It became evident that Rinpoche was going to die soon. He had been in one of the regular wards of the hospital, but now he was readmitted to the intensive care unit.

Because of his father's dire situation, Ösel, the Sawang, returned from England where he was studying. Many, many people in Halifax came to see Rinpoche for the last time at the hospital. Many others flew in. The hospital even gave us a special sitting room for the people waiting to see him. People were allowed to file into his room in the ICU, several at a time, to say their good-byes. The hospital also allowed us to keep a number of our own staff people on duty, so we always had five or six people around Rinpoche, although there was very little to do. It was such an emotional and heartrending time for people. Many people broke down as they came into his hospital room. This went on for about a week.

On April 4, it became evident that Rinpoche's death was imminent. I, the Sawang, the Regent, and a group of close students went in and stayed with Rinpoche. We practiced all day and on into the evening. Rinpoche developed aguinal breathing, deep breathing from the brain stem. This went on for awhile, and then there were long gaps between breaths. Then, at a certain point, Rinpoche opened his eyes and stared, completely alert, completely awake, intensely into the room. I remember his eyes were as dark and as sharp as ever. At that point, I supplicated him. I said, "Please come back." He closed his eyes and took two more breaths and then he died. Although he had many of the classic health problems that develop from heavy drinking, it was in fact more likely the diabetes and high blood pressure that led to abnormal blood sugar levels and then the cardiac arrest. He died from urosepsis, a result of complications from the heart attack.

Our people, particularly Mitchell, Jim Gimian, and Marty Janowitz, had been working with the hospital to establish what would happen when Rinpoche died. Once again, the hospital was amazing in accommodating us. We had a prearranged plan. Marty had been getting information together on exactly what we should do with Rinpoche's body when he died, according to the tradition of how the body of a great teacher is treated.

Special Tibetan syllables, which are called the seed syllables of various deities, were painted on small pieces of paper and placed on his eyelids, his nostrils, his mouth, and other parts of his face and body. His body was put on a stretcher. We took him downstairs in the elevator and wheeled him out the back door. He was transported back to the Court in an ambulance. When we arrived at the Court, there had been a Tibetan throne already prepared in the living room. Everything else had been cleared out of the room. Mitchell, Jim, and Marty dressed the body in the special *chuba* that had been selected. His body was placed in meditation posture on the throne, and on his head they placed the special red teaching hat that Khyentse Rinpoche had given him and which he wore for *abhishekas.* I remember it was quite cold. It was snowing and all the windows were left open so that the body wouldn't decay as quickly. An honor guard of the *kasung* and *kusung* was placed on either side of the body, and people practiced in the room with his body around the clock. Later, we learned that for the first time in decades, ice clogged the Halifax harbor in the days before Rinpoche died.

That night, when I finally lay down for a few hours, I dreamed that I was with Rinpoche in a palace. There were four gates in the four directions: blue in the east, yellow in the south, red in the west, and green in the north. It was one large room with the four gates and many pillars. Rinpoche and I were in the center of the palace. He was dressed like a young prince. He was wearing a crown inlaid with jewels and he had a beautiful necklace and earrings. We were making love. (In the dream, he had a huge penis.) The atmosphere was luminous. He had no color and no personality. There was only intense energy. He was facing east, and we were making love lying down and standing up. Then I awoke.

Hundreds of people came to the Court to practice over the next few days. We did all of the practices that Rinpoche had given us throughout the years. Much of the time, people did the sitting meditation practice that Rinpoche had stressed as so important. We also did the *Sadhana of Mahamudra,* which he had discovered in Bhutan in 1968; the *Vajrayogini Sadhana,* which he had transmitted to so many students; and the *Werma Sadhana,* the Shambhala practice that he had written when we were in Mexico.

When a very realized lama dies, they say that the heart of the teacher remains warm for several days while the teacher remains in a state of *samadhi,* or meditative absorption. I had always been a skeptic about this. However, every day I would put my hand underneath Rinpoche's robes and feel his heart center. It remained warm. Initially, I tried to explain this to myself, thinking that the clothing was keeping Rinpoche's body warm. Then I realized: there's no obvious source of heat here, and the clothing was not going to keep a cold body warm. However, for three days, the heart center stayed warm. Also, there was never any rigor mortis with the body, which is quite unusual.

On the third day, I put my hand on Rinpoche's chest and it was cold. This was the sign that the *samadhi* was over. At this time, fluids also began to escape from his body, which is another indication that the *samadhi* has ended.

The Vajra Regent had wanted to accelerate the cremation. He thought that it should be done as soon as possible. He was in touch with His Holiness Khyentse Rinpoche to see when Khyentse Rinpoche could come over and perform the funeral ceremony. Khyentse Rinpoche said that he wanted to wait seven weeks before the cremation. The Regent did not want to postpone the funeral that long. However, he could not overrule Khyentse Rinpoche's wishes. So plans were made to hold the funeral at the end of May, and we used traditional Tibetan Buddhist methods to preserve Rinpoche's body, again according to the instructions that are prescribed for the treatment of the body of a great teacher. Rinpoche had left the outline of these instructions in his spiritual will, which he had composed during the Mill Village retreat. For the details, Marty, Mitchell, and Jim consulted with several lamas who knew what to do.

A special coffin had been built to hold Rinpoche's body after the *samadhi* was broken. At that time, his body was put in the coffin for transportation down to Karme Chöling. Karl Springer arranged to charter a special jet from Air Canada, and he got permission to transport the body across the Canadian–U.S. border. The jet was designated TLGD One. It was a large plane that would hold about 150 people. The coffin was in the front of the plane, and Rinpoche's family and many of his close students rode down on the plane. We flew directly into the airport in Burlington, Vermont, where a hearse picked up the coffin. We rode in a motorcade to Karme Chöling, which is about an hour away.

I stayed at Bhumipali Bhavan, the house where Rinpoche and I had stayed so many times, with Mitchell and my children. Taggie was still in India, and we didn't bring him over for the funeral. Everyone else was there. The Sawang had his own house near Peacham.

Two Tibetan lamas accompanied us to Karme Chöling to assist with the ongoing preparations of the body for the funeral. Lama Ugyen had been a student of Dilgo Khyentse Rinpoche. He had been working with the Nalanda Translation Committee for a number of years. Lama Ganga flew to Halifax from Los Angeles to assist us. The traditional method involves preserving the body in salts prior to the cremation. Rinpoche's body was placed in a special box in the center of the shrine room at Karme Chöling. The body was kept in an upright posture, as though seated in an armchair, and the box was covered in satins and brocades. Elaborate shrines were constructed on all four sides of the *kudung,* or "body relic," with candles and incense burning on the shrines throughout the day and night. Many of Rinpoche's uniforms and other clothing and personal objects were also displayed in the four directions surrounding the *kudung.* At the beginning and end of practice periods, students could come up and circumambulate the body and look at his belongings. There was always an honor guard in the shrine room, with several of the Dorje Kasung standing at attention on the sides of the *kudung* and others posted at the entrance to the room.

You could come in and practice at any hour of the day or night; people wandered in or signed up to practice at different times. There were also large group practices throughout this period. We did the *Sadhana of Mahamudra* and the *Werma Sadhana* at certain times, and people gathered to practice the *Vajrayogini Sadhana* together.

There were thrones and seats for the various lamas and dignitaries set up in the four corners of the shrine room as well. Throughout the month, many Tibetan teachers came to pay their respects and to practice in the shrine room. In the evenings, a visiting teacher would often give a talk. There were four main teachers from Rumtek whom the Karmapa had empowered to carry on the lineage after his death. One of them, Shamar Rinpoche, was not able to attend the funeral itself, but he was one of the first visiting teachers to arrive during the intervening weeks and he did various ceremonies in the shrine room there. He also gave a talk one evening. The other three, Jamgön Rinpoche, Situ Rinpoche, and Gyaltsap Rinpoche came for the cremation itself.

Buddhist teachers from other traditions also came to Karme Chöling, some briefly and some for an extended stay. Kanjuro Shibata Sensei, the archery master and bow maker to the emperor of Japan, who had made a very close connection with Rinpoche and our *sangha,* was at Karme Chöling for almost the entire time. He worked on painting the *purkhang,* the structure in which Rinpoche's body would be cremated. *Purkhang* literally means "corpse house" in Tibetan. It had the appearance of a small stupa. The Sawang's mother, Lady Könchok, also was there. She worked on many of the preparations for the funeral. She had first come over to visit Rinpoche and the Sawang in 1986, after a separation of many years. She was becoming a beloved part of the community, and it was wonderful to have her there.

My mother spent several weeks at Karme Chöling. She brought two of her closest English friends with her, Jack and Alex, whom Rinpoche had earlier nicknamed Thomson and Thompson, from characters in the Tintin comic books.

The Regent oversaw many of the arrangements for the funeral, and I have to say that he spared no expense. A number of major donors had given money for a trust fund that was originally intended as an endowment for Vajradhatu. There was provision, however, to use the funds for cases of extraordinary need. The Regent felt that the funds from the trust should be used for the cremation, and I think we all agreed. Vajradhatu flew many people from all parts of North America, as well as from Asia and Europe, to Vermont and paid for hotels or rental houses for many of the dignitaries. A movie crew filmed all of the preparations, as well as the cremation itself, and a corps of photographers documented the funeral and the weeks that led up to it. The Dorje Kasung set up an encampment up the hill from the main Karme Chöling building, close to the site where the cremation would take place, in a big open meadow. About 150 members of the Dorje Kasung lived there for over a month. They provided all manner of service: guarding Rinpoche's body in the shrine room, providing drivers and other help for the family and invited guests, and helping in many, many other ways.

As I mentioned, a small circular building, called the *purkhang,* was constructed for the cremation in a meadow above the main buildings at Karme Chöling. This structure was large enough so that Rinpoche's body could be elevated in the upper portion, with openings on all four sides at the height of his head. Below this was an area where the fire would be built. The *purkhang* was decorated with gold leaf and other pigments. In the four corners surrounding it, large platforms were erected. Thrones were built for His Holiness, the Kagyü teachers, and other officiating teachers. There was also space on one of the platforms for the family, the Regent, the members of the board, and other senior students.

During the last few years, after the Mill Village retreat, Rinpoche had officially appointed a group of seven women as his heart companions, or *sangyum,* which is usually a term reserved for the guru's wife. He had asked the *sangyum* both to be his personal attendants and companions during the last years of his life and to help provide leadership in the community. He had envisioned them overseeing the board of directors, and he considered them to be part of his family. So they were to be seated with us as well. All of them came to Karme Chöling and helped with the practice and other preparations.

Karme Chöling itself was filled to the rafters. Many of the regular residents generously moved out of their rooms into tents in the fields surrounding the main building, while the *sangyum,* the board, and other senior students—many of whom had brought their whole families— were given rooms in the house. There was a whole wing of Karme Chöling set aside for families with young children. The place was packed.

I have already mentioned the dreams that I had before Rinpoche died. I continued to dream about him. Sometimes one has dreams that are obviously just the product of one's discursive thoughts. Other times I have experienced lucid dreams, where I have self-awareness within the dream. In that situation, there's almost a voice in my head that says to me: "Look at this; this is it." There's some sort of reality and texture that is very different in a lucid dream. While I was staying at Bhumipali Bhavan, I had a few dreams that felt significant to me. Once, after I had gone to sleep, I woke up in my dream to find myself in the bedroom, in my dream body. Rinpoche was sitting in the room, which looked exactly the way it did when I was awake. Rinpoche was in the chair by the shrine that we always had in the bedroom. He was naked, sitting as he often did with his left leg bent at the knee, his left foot resting on the other knee. I said to him, "So here you are. What's going to happen to you? Are you going to be reborn?" And he replied. "No, not now." He said, "I think I have to rest for awhile. I'm going to go and rest in the dharmadhatu." (The dharmadhatu is a realm without form; the big, impartial space of dharma.) This dream felt very sweet and ordinary, as though he were simply explaining the situation.

Several weeks before the cremation ceremony, Khyentse Rinpoche arrived from Bhutan. I remember him coming in the door at Karme Chöling. He was such a wonderful old man: tall, massive. He was having a little trouble walking at that point. His knees weren't good, and he leaned very heavily on his attendants. I don't know how old he was exactly, perhaps around eighty. He was definitely getting on in age. You could see how exhausted he was after his long journey. He was still so gracious and kind to everybody. He gave all of us who had assembled a blessing, and he made a few remarks about how good it was to be with Trungpa Rinpoche's students, and how he was going to provide guidance to us in the days to come. Then he went upstairs to a special room that had been prepared for him. It was a large room usually reserved as a secondary shrine room, which was turned into a combined bedroom and sitting room for him. The next day, after he'd had a chance to rest, he began to check into all the arrangements that were being made. Over the next weeks, he would come down every day and practice with people in the shrine room. However, he spent a lot of time in his quarters upstairs, where he would receive people for private meetings and small gatherings.

I started to visit him every few days, which he encouraged. He told me that I should never hesitate to come to see him if I had anything to discuss. It was amazingly generous of him. He would sit cross-legged on the huge bed with his *mala,* his rosary, in his enormous beautiful hands. The whole room felt luminous to me, golden, whenever I went to see him. I found it a tremendous relief to spend time with him during this period.

I was able to discuss many issues with Khyentse Rinpoche. In particular, he wanted to know if I had had any dreams about Rinpoche. He thought these might be helpful in finding Rinpoche's reincarnation. I told him that I wasn't sure there would be an incarnation that we could find. Given Rinpoche's immersion in Western culture, I wondered at that time if there would be a *tulku* in the traditional sense. I told him that Rinpoche had told me and many of his other students that he was planning to be reborn as a Japanese scientist in Osaka. Khyentse Rinpoche said, "You shouldn't worry. Trungpa Rinpoche might have many rebirths. There might be many incarnations. It's like when you look at the moon reflected in a bowl of water. If you look in more than one bowl at a time, you may see many, many reflections. But all are reflecting the same thing." He continued, "Trungpa Rinpoche can be reborn in many different manifestations. That's possible." I didn't really understand that, and I still don't, I have to say. But this is what he said.

He also told me that the dream in which Rinpoche and I were making love was in the middle of the Chakrasamvara palace, which had never occurred to me. He said that Rinpoche was the manifestation of Chakrasamvara in that dream, and that the interpretation of the dream was that I was Rinpoche's true consort.

He also told me that any problems in my relationship with Rinpoche, which had occurred at the end of his life, were completely repaired, and that the dream was also symbolic of this. He gave me advice on how to raise my sons and promised to help educate them as they grew older. He talked about how Trungpa Rinpoche was like his son, and that they trusted one another completely, and that therefore he would definitely do whatever he could to help me and to help our community. He asked me to write and tell him about my dreams after the cremation ended, which I did. He told me that I should question Trungpa Rinpoche in the dreams about where he was going to be reborn. I tried to do this, but I didn't find anything out that was that helpful.

As the weeks went by at Karme Chöling, Khyentse Rinpoche's wisdom in allowing seven weeks between the death and the cremation became evident to me. I think it was absolutely necessary for people to have this time to process what had happened. In the days after Rinpoche died, I remember feeling how strange it was to be alive when he was dead. It seemed very strange that I could still walk on this earth when he did not. For all of us, his death was not a simple issue of burying some-body and getting on with your life. He was *the* reference point of every-body's life. Meeting him and studying with him was the most precious thing that had ever occurred in the lives of his students. Now, in the fu-ture, we would all have to sort out our entire lives without him. It's dif-ficult for me to know how to talk about this. However, I can truly say that we needed the time, those weeks, to prepare for the cremation.

The ceremony itself took place on May 26, 1987. Thousands of peo-ple came for the ceremony. Early that morning, I arrived from Bhumi-pali Bhavan dressed in a Tibetan *chuba,* and my sons were also dressed in traditional Tibetan clothing. We had rust-colored *chubas* made for the three boys. I had one that was dark green. Mitchell was dressed in his khaki uniform. He was one of the eight Dorje Kasung who carried the palanquin containing Rinpoche's body in the procession from the shrine room at Karme Chöling up a path that wound through the woods to the clearing where the cremation would take place. Among the others were the Kasung Kyi Khyap, David Rome; the Kasung Dapon, Jim Gimian; and the Kusung Dapon, Marty Janowitz. These four marched in front. In the back of the palanquin were four other senior Dorje Kasung: Hudson Shotwell, Suzanne Duquette, Jan Wilcox, and Dennis Southward. Barry Boyce held a huge umbrella on a long pole that hung above the *kudung,* providing a canopy.

The procession was led by a lone piper, who played "McPherson's Lament" and a mournful tune he had composed for the occasion. Be-hind him came a small group of Tibetan monastics as well as Western monks and nuns from Gampo Abbey, the monastery Rinpoche had started in Nova Scotia. Then there was a large contingent of the Dorje Kasung, followed by the body in the palanquin carried by the eight stu-dents. Then came the rest of the Dorje Kasung marching very slowly, ex-tremely slowly. Behind that was a procession of people who had been particularly close to Rinpoche, led by our family, including the four boys and me. The Regent, Lady Könchok, my sister and her husband, the *sangyum* (female companions), the board of directors and their wives, and others all marched in the procession. Khyentse Rinpoche and the other high lamas who were going to lead the ceremony were already up the hill on their thrones when we approached. The entire procession passed under a large wooden gate, which had been erected for the occasion, and slowly approached the *purkhang*. The four pallbearers then placed the body in the *purkhang*.

When we completed the climb up the hill, we took our seats. I was seated with the Regent and the Sawang on a wooden platform close to the *purkhang*. The other members of the family, the *sangyum,* members of the board, and other close students were also nearby. Khyentse Rinpoche was seated on a throne on the main platform to the left of me. He was leading the practice and his seat directly faced the *purkhang* containing Rinpoche's body. Before the practice itself began, everyone assembled there was invited to circumambulate the *purkhang* in a clockwise direction and to offer a white scarf, a *khata,* as they walked past the front of the stupa. The Sawang, the Regent, and I led the offering procession. We were told to try to throw our *khatas* through the ornate window opening in the front of the *purkhang,* through the little hole where you could barely see Rinpoche's face screened from view but sort of peeking out. I remember that my *khata* went right into that opening. There were thousands of people attending the funeral, so it took quite a long time for this *khata* offering. From time to time, the honor guard around the stupa would have to remove the hundreds and hundreds of white scarves that were accumulating on ropes strung in front of the *purkhang*.

It was tremendously colorful up there in the meadow. I noticed how beautiful the *purkhang* was, ornamented with its gold designs and with the Mukpo colors: brilliant white, bright red and orange, and deep blue. These colors were used in the Mukpo family emblems that adorned the corners of the monument. While everyone was walking around the *purkhang* to pay their respects, I had the opportunity to look out and see the thousands of people who were assembled there. It had been cool and misty in the early morning, but the sun burned off the mist, and it was a brilliant sunny day with hardly a cloud in the sky. People were standing or sitting on chairs and blankets they had brought with them, and the crowd spread out across a great expanse. There were also tents for special guests and invited dignitaries. James George was there, the Canadian High Commissioner to India and Nepal, whom Rinpoche had met in the 1960s. Ato Rinpoche was there from England. Several Zen teachers with whom Rinpoche was close also attended the funeral. There were many dignitaries who had come to his cremation.

After everyone completed their circumambulation, we began the ceremony itself. The main text that the Western students used was a fire offering connected with the *Vajrayogini Sadhana* that Rinpoche transmitted to so many of us. All of us practiced this together. His Holiness and the other Tibetan teachers practiced a number of other fire offerings in Tibetan. After the practice had gone on for some time, the fire for the cremation was lit. According to tradition, no one who had known Rinpoche could light the fire. So they had to search for someone with no physical connection to him. One of the monks from India, I believe, performed this service. At a certain point, which was a different point for different people in the audience, I think almost every one of us broke down. It was impossible not to weep, not to be overcome with the tremendous sadness of this moment. As the flames were lit, a cannon was fired off, and for many of us, that was the moment when the tears started. Not surprisingly, many of us wore our dark glasses that day. While the flames were burning, Shibata Sensei and three of his senior students performed a traditional ceremony, which is done when an emperor dies. At the four corners of the *purkhang,* they plucked empty bows and then offered straw sandals to the fire.

When the fire offerings were finished, there was one announcement, the only announcement during the entire day. "Ladies and gentlemen, the Shambhala Anthem." We sang as we wept.

At the end of the afternoon, as the fire subsided, after the body had been consumed in the flames, we looked in the sky and there was a succession of rainbows. The most dramatic was a circular rainbow that circled around the sun in the sky above the *purkhang*. It was absolutely circular and quite vivid. This was written about in the press as an amazing phenomenon. A white cloud in the shape of an Ashe appeared, and three hawks circled and circled. Other small clouds in the sky looked to many onlookers like tigers, lions, *garudas,* and dragons. They too were tinged with rainbow light at one point. Two of the senior teachers accompanying His Holiness Khyentse Rinpoche later interpreted some of the auspicious signs: fog in the morning, which was neither too high nor too low, and which hung like a protective parasol over the area; then the rainbows, then the clouds shaped like *khatas,* ritual scarves; and finally the three hawks, *dakinis* or celestial maidens, who had taken the form of birds and were welcoming Rinpoche.

After the formal part of the cremation had ended, I remained up in the meadow to have the opportunity to talk with people. It was very moving to see and speak with so many of the people who came to the cremation ceremony. I realized even further what a profound impact Rinpoche had had on people's lives. Speaking with people who were so filled with love and sadness, it was impossible not to be affected.

Several days after the cremation, I had to go back up to the meadow. This time there were very few of us. Traditionally, several days after the cremation of a great teacher, there is a ceremony where the *purkhang* is opened and the bones and ash are removed. As Rinpoche's consort and his wife, I was expected to accompany the lamas up to the *purkhang*. Someone opened the section where Rinpoche's remains were, and they told me that I should be the first one to reach in and pull out a bone. Dzongsar Khyentse Rinpoche, a young teacher who was being trained by His Holiness, was in charge of this ceremony. As I looked into the *purkhang*, I saw a pile of charred bones. I hadn't expected to be so shocked, but it was very traumatic. I kept thinking, "I never thought I'd see you in this condition. I never thought I'd see you like this." While I was peering into the stupa, somewhat stupefied, Dzongsar Rinpoche said, "Go on, go on." He handed me a *khata,* and I had to lean in and draw out a bone, which I finally did. Then the rest of Rinpoche's bones were taken out. Some, including a section of his pelvis and part of his skull, were preserved to be placed in the Great Stupa of Dharmakaya that we were planning to build at RMDC. Many others were pounded down to make *tsa-tsas,* which are small sculptures in the shape of stupas that are made from various substances including the bone relics and ashes of the teacher. Later, these would be given to various of Rinpoche's disciples and to the many meditation centers he founded, as objects of veneration to be kept on the shrines in each center. Some of his major disciples were also given one of his teeth to keep as a relic. One of these was later placed in the Great Stupa of Dharmakaya.

During the seven weeks between Rinpoche's death and the cremation, we could ride on the energy of the situation most of the time. We were carried along by all the work that needed to be done to prepare properly for the cremation. Khyentse Rinpoche's presence also buoyed people's spirits. During the weeks that led up to the cremation, it was almost as if the power of Rinpoche's energy kept him alive for us. With the conclusion of the cremation, there was a huge deflation. His presence had definitely moved on.

Everyone was left with the realization that now they had to live their lives without the support and presence of Rinpoche. There was a quality of emptiness and loss. Something unfathomably precious had been lost from this world. Something amazing had passed through this world and now was gone.

At the end of the spiritual will that Rinpoche wrote in 1984, he said,

Altogether we are happy to die. We take our joy along with us. It is unusually romantic to die:

> Born a monk,
> Died a king—
> Such thunderstorm does not stop.
> We will be haunting you, along with the *dralas*.
> Jolly good luck![1]

I know that for me, I will continue to long for him, as long as I have breath. I am left, however, not only with a broken heart but with a tremendous appreciation of my life. I remember one evening sitting with him in a restaurant by the water, and he said to me, "You know, you should appreciate this. This is our life. This is our marriage. It won't be like this forever." I laughed him off a little bit. Now, in retrospect, I realize that he was saying something profound about impermanence and the importance of appreciating one's life. I learned from him to appreciate the world as sacred.

As his wife of seventeen years—in a marriage that not only had tremendous highs but also had its low points, which were not easy—I can attest to the fact that Rinpoche was not an ordinary human being. His actions cannot be imitated, neither should they be interpreted by conventional reference points. Rinpoche had no other motivation in his life than to enrich the lives of others and to make the world a better place. He gauged all his successes in those terms. His sole motivation was to enrich the lives of others and create a world in which others could flourish.

He taught me that in order to save the world, one must begin with oneself. One of the main thrusts of his teachings was to trust oneself and to rely on one's own basic sanity. I have tried to take that teaching to heart. He devoted his life to showing others that path. His every moment was devoted to helping other people. To be able to live one's life with a fraction of the wisdom and compassion that permeated his would make one an exceptional person.

As the model of sanity and compassion in my life, he continues to guide me. Throughout my life, I continue to question myself as to how he would want me to handle one situation or another. He is no longer outside of me, so when I turn to him, I turn to my own wakefulness. He will always be my gold standard.

There is a song that Rinpoche loved by Robert Burns. It is called "The Winter It Is Past." He owned a treasured recording of the Scottish vocalist Jean Redpath singing this melancholy ballad. Later, one of Rinpoche's students, Jane Condon, used to sing it to him in a beautiful soprano voice. Sometimes when I think of him, especially when I long for him, I hear this song in the background:

Oh the winter it is past and the summer's come at last
And the small birds sing on every tree
Their little hearts are glad but mine is very sad
For my lover is parted from me

Oh the rose among the briar by the water running clear
Has charms for the linnet and the bee
Their little hearts are blessed but mine can know no rest
For my lover is parted from me

For my love is like the sun, in the firmament does run
Forever constant and true
But his is like the moon that wanders up and down
And every month it is new

All you who are in love and cannot it remove
I pity the pains you endure
For experience makes me know that your hearts are full of woe
A woe that no mortal can cure.[2]

EPILOGUE

To my astonishment, it will have been almost twenty years since Rinpoche's death when this book is published. Contemplating this, two things come to mind. One is how quickly life passes. In some respects, the years since Rinpoche's death seem like the blink of an eye. Also, when I think of what Rinpoche accomplished in just seventeen years in North America, I am in awe.

Even in sickness and death he continued to have enormous influence. Following Rinpoche's cardiac arrest, during the period leading up to his death, and for several years after he died, a stream of students moved to Nova Scotia from the United States, other parts of Canada, and Europe. Several hundred of his most senior and closest students settled in Halifax and other areas of the province. While he was alive, I think that people felt that they had all the time in the world to fulfill Rinpoche's wish that we would join him in Nova Scotia. Now it became clear that we had no time left at all. This inspired people to pick up and move themselves, their families, and businesses to this new homeland.

Whether they joined in this odyssey or not, wherever they were, all of Rinpoche's students now had to take responsibility for the teachings they had received from him. Rinpoche appreciated and magnetized people with talent and intelligence. During his lifetime, he supported everybody, and, at the same time, he expected a lot of people. He asked them to live up to their own highest expectations. The people who were close to Rinpoche have developed into remarkable human beings. Uniquely, individually, his students have led incredibly productive lives, which I feel have had a profound and beneficial effect on other people.

When the teacher dies, it is like breaking a vase; the air that was held in the container mixes with the whole of space. It is partially in this sense that the teacher's death is a blessing. Similarly, Rinpoche's students, who were held together in the circle of his life, were released and let go to find their own way. Many have remained in Nova Scotia, Boulder, and other major centers he founded, but many others are spread around the world.

In its own way, his death was the beginning of a tremendous period of growth for a lot of people, including myself. However, it was not a particularly easy time for any of us. During his lifetime there had been a dependence upon Rinpoche for sanity and for a confirmation of our personal worth. After his death, when that external reference point was gone, people hit rock bottom in states of depression, anger, and psychological poverty. Then slowly, as people began to internalize his teachings and turn those teachings into their life path, realization began to occur on many different levels. It is like the story of Ananda, a monk who attended the Buddha for many years. It's said that Ananda didn't fully understand the Buddha's teachings when the Buddha died, and that was when his personal journey really began to move forward.

Following Rinpoche's death, the Vajra Regent moved immediately to consolidate power, and he began to slowly weaken the community's financial and psychological support for my family. Within days after Rinpoche's death, I learned that his life insurance policy had already been cashed in before his death to help pay Vajradhatu's bills. I began to panic a bit about how I would provide for my family. I went to see the Regent and reminded him that Rinpoche had intended to put the house at Mill Village, which Vajradhatu now owned, into my name. I told him that I wanted to sell the property and put the proceeds in a trust for my children's education. The Regent agreed, and the house was put on the market. At the time of the sale, however, I was only given something like ten thousand dollars. The rest went to Vajradhatu. Initially, the Regent offered me a monthly stipend, which I think was $1,400 a month to cover my living expenses. (The mortgage on the Court was covered by the organization.) Less than a year after Rinpoche's death, however, the Regent told the comptroller of Vajradhatu, Bill Karelis, to stop sending me a monthly check. To his credit, Bill refused to cut us off, a kindness that I have never forgotten.

I felt that I should continue to support the *sangha* in whatever ways I could, and this included teaching within Shambhala Training, something that Rinpoche had always encouraged me to do. The year after Rinpoche died, when I was asked to teach an advanced level of Shambhala Training in Texas, the Regent wrote to me, telling me that I was only qualified and authorized to present the most elementary levels of the teachings. This was typical of how he attempted to belittle the family. He began to refer to the Sawang as "the little prince," a term he employed in the most derogatory fashion.

Rinpoche had left instructions that a committee consisting of myself, the Regent, the Sawang, the Kasung Kyi Khyap, and the two *dapons* was to be convened to help with the transition after his death. I was to chair this committee. The Regent never once brought this group together. Rather than seeing it as his role to support the family and to advise the Sawang as he grew into his maturity, the Regent obviously felt threatened by us.

In late 1988, the community learned that the Regent was HIV positive and had developed AIDS. A young man in the community who had had a brief sexual encounter with the Regent was diagnosed with HIV and could only trace his illness to the Vajra Regent. I did not know about the Regent's condition until this all came out. I learned later that Rinpoche had arranged for the Regent to be tested for HIV, without his knowledge, in the mid-1980s. Rinpoche had then met with the Regent to inform him of his illness and to warn him to be careful not to infect others. The Regent didn't heed Rinpoche's warning, it seems.

There was an uproar in the Buddhist community—and in the press. The Regent, without actually being stripped of power, was forced by actions of the board and other community members into retreat in California. Finally, with the intercession of His Holiness Dilgo Khyentse Rinpoche, the Regent gave up his attempt to exercise authority over Vajradhatu and he was in a sense exiled into retreat for the remainder of his life. Early on in this crisis, I traveled from Halifax to Boulder where I gave a talk to the community in which I said that I thought that the Regent should step down, for the good of everyone. Although I was criticized in some quarters for taking this public stand, I feel that it was necessary, and I have no regrets. The Regent's family and a small group of students who remained loyal to Ösel Tendzin established a community in Ojai, California, where a few of them remain today. The Regent died there, from complications of AIDs, in 1990. We are as of this writing still working to have a genuine reconciliation of the two communities, based on dignity and truth on both sides. This troubling chapter in the history of our community continues to haunt us, as perhaps it should. It serves as a powerful, ongoing reminder of the dangers of self-deception, especially on the spiritual path. It was not just the failure of one individual. In a sense, we all failed. Sometimes I think that it will be the sum total of the achievements of all of Rinpoche's students that will ensure that his wisdom remains. In that sense, we are all burdened with the responsibility for transmitting his teachings and seeing that his legacy endures.

In the years following Rinpoche's death, I found that some people were looking to me for leadership, but many also wanted to tell me how to behave and what to do. There was no malicious intent, but people started to become domineering and brittle with one another. In Rinpoche's absence, not surprisingly perhaps, numerous power struggles developed. Vajradhatu was having tremendous financial problems, and some of the negativity about this became focused on me.

Rumors also abounded during this period. At times, they were quite petty. To give an example, at one point, Ashoka had a pet turtle that ate small quantities of ground beef. One evening, I went down to the kitchen and found out that we had run out of this food. A volunteer was preparing shrimp for dinner, and I cut a small sliver of one of the raw shrimps to feed the turtle. A few days later, I heard that a story was going around the community that Lady Diana had a pigeon that only ate lamb chops!

Under financial pressure, the board of directors decided to sell the Kalapa Court and only informed me after the decision had been made. I was to be given the money from the sale, with the expectation that I would buy a house somewhere else in Halifax. I felt like a pawn in a male power play. The negativity was permeating my family life as well as my public life. Criticism sometimes came in the form of poisonous letters, some anonymous and some not. Eventually, I reached a point in my life where I experienced no personal joy at all. Strangely, it reminded me of how I had felt growing up in England. People seemed to have tremendous expectations about how I should behave, which had no relationship to my own experience or instincts. The situation weighed on me very heavily.

Eventually, in 1989, Mitchell and I decided to move the family away from Nova Scotia to Hawaii—just about as far away as we could get. We expected this to be a temporary move. We had been through such a stressful time that we needed to go to a place that was isolated and relaxing. Mitchell wanted to get back into his medical career, and he was able to get a good position in a hospital in Honolulu. Our family needed the time to heal. We stayed in Hawaii for three-and-a-half years. Mitchell and I married in 1990, in a small family ceremony in a Buddhist temple there. In Hawaii, we were able to discover some family unity and provide a normal environment for the children, which was very important.

Soon after Rinpoche's death, the Sawang traveled to India to study with His Holiness Dilgo Khyentse Rinpoche. He remained there until 1990 when, with the death of the Vajra Regent, he was called upon to assume the leadership of the Vajradhatu community. In 1995, he received the Sakyong *abhisheka* from His Holiness Penor Rinpoche. Penor Rinpoche also recognized Ösel as the incarnation of Mipham, a great Tibetan teacher who died at the beginning of the twentieth century. Ösel Mukpo is now widely known as Sakyong Mipham Rinpoche. In the mid-1990s he changed the name of the organization from Vajradhatu to Shambhala. He continues to propagate the dharma teachings of his father. In 2005, he married Semo Tseyang Ripa in a private ceremony in Boulder, Colorado, and they plan a large public celebration in Halifax in 2006. I have been asked to conduct the public ceremony for them, and I am delighted to be able to welcome Lady Semo Tseyang into our Mukpo family in this way.

Taggie returned from Sikkim soon after Rinpoche's death. For many years now, he has been living at Bhumipali Bhavan at Karme Chöling. Although things have not changed a great deal with him, I have recently been extremely pleased to see that he is more cognizant and has an improved ability to converse with people about simple subjects. His seizures have finally been controlled. I think he is content, and I am so grateful to all those who have supported his care.

Gesar had a turbulent adolescence, and we went through a period when communication between us was difficult. We are now extremely close. I have been delighted to see him mature and to take on many of his father's qualities. He is tremendously intelligent and has exceptional artistic talent, which I believe he will develop more over time. After Rinpoche's death, Gesar studied with Dzongsar Khytenste Rinpoche and spent time in India, where he received teachings from His Holiness Dilgo Khyentse Rinpoche. Later, he traveled to his predecessor's monastery, Sechen, in Tibet, when it was very difficult to do so, and he also joined the family when we visited Tibet in 2002.

Gesar was already on his own when we moved to Hawaii, but he did join us there for several months. He spent a number of years in California, where he attended community college, played football, and worked on several Hollywood films. Gesar moved back to Nova Scotia in 2003, where he married Anna De Nicola, the daughter of longtime *sangha* members. In 2004, their daughter Chokyi Sofia Mukpo was born. I am a proud grandmother. Chokyi is a very special little girl.

Ashoka graduated from Georgetown University with a B.A. in political science in 2004. In 2005 he attended the seminary at the Shambhala Mountain Center. Earlier, in 2002, he was enthroned in Tibet as Khamnyön Rinpoche during our family's trip to visit the Surmang monasteries that Rinpoche came from. Hundreds of Tibetans mobbed our hotel in Jyekundo, the last town before Surmang, to see Ashoka and receive his blessing when we arrived there.

From time to time, we get phone calls in the middle of the night from Ashoka's monasteries in Nepal or Tibet. I pick up the phone at 3 A.M. and someone says loudly into the line on the other end, "Khamnyön Rinpoche?" I respond, "Sleeping." They continue repeating Ashoka's name until I get him to the phone.

Within the next few years, Mitchell and I plan to travel with Ashoka to his monastery in Tibet. It is located in the Tibetan Autonomous Region. Ashoka made a deeper connection to the Tibetan world when we traveled there in 2002. He was initially extremely skeptical about assuming any position as a teacher. Through the course of our trip, he began to realize the suffering of people there and how he could help them in his role as a teacher. He particularly was taken, not just with the poverty of the people, but also by the treatment of dogs and other domestic animals in Tibet. He made strong pronouncements to people there that they needed to stop mistreating their animals. Later, we said that this was his first dharma talk.

He has just become engaged to be married to Bianca Velez, whom he met at Georgetown. They both plan to attend graduate school within the next few years, and Ashoka hopes to have a career in the field of human rights. Rinpoche talked about Ashoka having the potential to be a great statesman. It has been interesting to see his interest in political science, and I feel that great things lie ahead for him.

David graduated from high school in 2003. He also attended the seminary in 2005. Currently, he is traveling for a year with his brother, Sakyong Mipham Rinpoche, in the role of an attaché and *kusung*. This will be excellent training for him, whatever direction his life takes. He plans to attend university in 2006. David has shown a great connection to the Dorje Kasung since he was a small boy. He is constantly cheerful, empathetic with others, and a delight to me.

Altogether I am very proud of my boys, especially as I see more and more that they feel a connection to Rinpoche and to his teachings. They feel a responsibility to help care for Rinpoche's legacy and to continue the work that he began. This makes me especially pleased.

Rinpoche and I had always wanted a daughter, and we wanted to name her Chandali, but we were never blessed by one. He even wrote a poem to Chandali Mukpo. In 1988, Mitchell and I heard about an eight-year-old Tibetan girl who was in quite dreadful circumstances. She had been adopted by a woman in North America who mistreated her and had placed her for awhile in foster care. We decided to adopt her. So Chandali Mukpo joined our family at that time. Chandali is currently in nursing school in Providence, Rhode Island. She is a beautiful, gentle young woman. Altogether I am pleased that we are a closely knit family.

My mother, Elizabeth Pybus, died in Chatterwood Nursing Home in Hampshire, England, on September 8, 1998. She was eighty-eight. Recently, our family suffered a tragedy when my sister, Tessa, passed away. She was diagnosed in 2001 with hepatitis C. Tessa worked very hard to help raise funds for a Shambhala center in Providence in the years prior to her death. In the spring of 2006 she received a liver transplant but she did not recover, and she died on the evening of March 28, surrounded by members of our family. I was reading to her from the *Tibetan Book of the Dead* when she died. She had a peaceful and luminous death. I miss her profoundly.

While in Hawaii, I started riding again, and found that my passion for it returned with a vengeance! While we were living there, I was able to arrange for Rinpoche's horse, Drala, to be flown over. I found a place where he could spend his last days on the island of Hawaii. The woman who took him used to feed him strawberries in the field. When he finally died, around the age of twenty-five, they discovered that the mare with whom he'd been pastured was pregnant. I attempted to buy the foal, but it was not for sale.

After a few years in Hawaii, both Mitchell and I felt ready to move back to the mainland. I moved the family to Seattle ahead of Mitchell while he was investigating work possibilities. There, I connected with a wonderful group of people interested in dressage. Within a very short period of time, I developed quite a good teaching and training business, and I continue to travel regularly to Seattle to teach. However, Mitchell did not find a good position there, and after about a year, we moved to Providence, Rhode Island, where we have remained. Mitchell became a professor in the division of pulmonary and critical care medicine at Brown University.

Although my life may have been unconventional, I have had two marriages in which there's been a tremendous amount of love. I feel that I've had very good fortune in my life in terms of the men I've been married to. For me, my marriage to Mitchell is in fact a continuation of my relationship with Rinpoche, in that Mitchell and I both have a commitment to bringing the Shambhala vision into our lives. We have supported each other in developing ourselves and our lives as Rinpoche encouraged us to do.

During Rinpoche's lifetime, Mitchell and Rinpoche worked together on creating an organization called Amara to explore how to treat sickness from the Buddhist perspective. After Rinpoche died, Mitchell threw himself into his career 100 percent. He is now one of the foremost physicians in critical care in the United States, and in 2009 he becomes the president of the Society of Critical Care Medicine. He has been instrumental in bringing into the mainstream of Western medicine the compassionate care of the dying and providing support for their families.

For my part, I have been very actively involved in my dressage career for the last ten years or more. Currently, I spend about six months a year in Florida, teaching and training horses. I have had many horses over the course of my career. Currently, I have excellent horses to ride. There are many vicissitudes of life and of horses, but I find that I take more and more delight in the day-to-day discipline of dressage.

When Rinpoche and I first came to America, I tried to keep the dressage world and the dharmic kingdom separate. Over the last ten years, I've noticed a change, so that many of my friends who are interested in dressage are now also interested in spirituality. I have great respect for the people I meet who have taken their discipline to its pinnacle. To do so, one must go through a process of working with one's own state of mind. I know many people who are extraordinarily open-minded Shambhalian people in their own right. For me, the situation becomes more and more comfortable, so that I no longer have to keep the two worlds apart.

Khyentse Rinpoche was helpful to our community in every way. After Rinpoche's death, he gave advanced Vajrayana teachings at Karme Chöling and then traveled to Halifax and to Boulder to give the same empowerments. These were teachings that Rinpoche had always hoped could be transmitted to his students. As he had promised, His Holiness took a role in the education of my two sons who were old enough to study with him. His advice and loving kindness were invaluable to everyone during the difficulties surrounding the Vajra Regent's illness and death. Following the Regent's death, His Holiness counseled everyone to remember the preciousness of Rinpoche's teachings and to work together. He left letters to that effect that still continue to guide us. His Holiness died in Bhutan in September 1991, and the Sawang led a large delegation to His Holiness's funeral.

In 2001, the Great Stupa of Dharmakaya That Liberates upon Seeing, dedicated to Rinpoche's life and Buddha activity, was consecrated at RMDC, now renamed the Shambhala Mountain Center. Khyentse Rinpoche gave that name to this monument. It is the largest stupa in North America. More than a thousand of his students attended the consecration ceremonies. The stupa is an exquisite and very powerful expression of the devotion of his students, and represents an outpouring of generosity from many people. A small stupa was consecrated that same year at the monastery that Rinpoche started in Nova Scotia, Gampo Abbey, in Pleasant Bay on Cape Breton Island.

At the time of the consecration of the stupa, I had begun to feel that it was very important for me to travel to Tibet and visit Surmang, Rinpoche's monastery there. I wanted to take the children with me, except for Taggie, of course, and Sakyong Mipham Rinpoche—who had already gone the year before, leading an official delegation from Shambhala. In the summer of 2002, Mitchell and I journeyed there with Gesar, Ashoka, David, and Chandali. It was extraordinary to see the place that Rinpoche came from and to meet so many people there who were still so dedicated to him. We spent quite a lot of time with the Twelfth Trungpa, who is now a teenager. We also met a number of members of Rinpoche's family, including his nephew Karma Senge Rinpoche, who had traveled all over Tibet collecting the teachings that Rinpoche had written and transmitted to people before leaving there in 1959. Karma Senge has now made two trips to North America. Rinpoche's brother, Damchöd Rinpoche, was also at Surmang when we were there, and he and Karma Senge will be coming this summer to Halifax for Sakyong Mipham Rinpoche's wedding.

When we first arrived at Surmang, it was two or three o'clock in the morning. The monks greeted us wearing wrathful *mahakala* masks and playing Tibetan horns, drums, and cymbals, which make an unearthly music. I was profoundly affected by the primordial feeling. In the morning, we were able to see the state of Surmang, and it was heartbreaking and somewhat shocking to realize that the monastery had not been rebuilt, and that people were living in extreme poverty.

I was very moved throughout our visit, not only by the physical hardship people had endured, but also by the knowledge that they had also suffered from losing Rinpoche so early in his life. We got so much from him; they gave up so much. Since that visit, I have been spearheading the work on a number of projects to rebuild Surmang Dutsi Tel. We have started the Könchok Foundation as the umbrella organization for this work. Currently, the monastic school, or *shedra,* is being rebuilt, and we have also been raising funds for the education of the Twelfth

Trungpa. I am particularly interested in providing education for the laypeople as well as for monastics, and I would like to work on sustainable economic ventures for Surmang. For one thing, I want to donate 100 dris, female yaks, to help establish the dairy business there.

Before Rinpoche died, he had received letters from Surmang asking him to return. He had written back, saying that he was not well enough to travel there by jeep or horse, but that he might try to helicopter in. That never happened. In the years after Rinpoche's death, when much of Tibet opened up to Westerners, for various reasons, our community neglected the rebuilding of Surmang. However, now we are striving to make up for lost time. I am very pleased the project is moving forward. In the end, I hope that Surmang will become a place where our students can go to practice, and also that we can send people there to share the teachings that Rinpoche gave us. While I was there, for example, I gave the transmission of the *Werma Sadhana* to several hundred people.

During Rinpoche's lifetime, he wrote more than a dozen books. Since his death, more than two dozen additional books of his teachings have been published based on his lectures, which are preserved by the Shambhala Archives in Halifax. In 2004, an eight-volume, three-thousand-page collection of *The Collected Works of Chögyam Trungpa* was published. There are plans to publish many more volumes of his teachings. We are particularly looking forward to the publication of several volumes based on the teachings that Rinpoche gave at the seminaries, a project that is being headed up by Judith Lief. There is certainly no dearth of material overall. When we added up all of the talks he had given in North America, we discovered that there were more than two thousand of them! Between now and the twentieth anniversary of his death, the Archives is digitizing all of the audiotapes on which his lectures were recorded, and centers around the world will have digital libraries of this material.

We are now in the initial stages of planning a Chögyam Trungpa Foundation and Institute that will help to ensure that the publication of his work will continue and that generations of students can continue to study what he taught.

Every year on April 4, the anniversary of Rinpoche's death, students around the world gather to practice together and to share with one another stories of his life and teachings that he gave. Rinpoche planted the seeds for the teachings to flourish in the West. Because of the depth of his intention and his actions, and because what he gave us was absolutely unadulterated, I know that Buddhism will firmly take root in the Western world, as another link in the chain that began with the Buddha. When Padmasambhava brought the teachings of Buddhism to Tibet, he was able to present their essence, transmuting them into the Tibetan culture. Similarly, Buddhism is taking root here in a uniquely Western way, based on Western sanity and wisdom, independent of the crutch of other cultures. This is due, in part, to the purity and the intensity of Rinpoche's efforts. I have no doubt that he will be with us for a long time, and that my grandchildren, as well as their children, will come to know him.

PUBLISHER'S AFTERWORD

I first met Chögyam Trungpa Rinpoche and Diana Mukpo in 1970, soon after they arrived in the United States. I had recently published the American edition of Rinpoche's book *Meditation in Action* and had invited him to the San Francisco Bay area to teach and promote his book. I was very much looking forward to meeting him in person. At thirty-one, Rinpoche was already a revered Tibetan Buddhist master, but he was not yet well known in this country.

In those days, I had little idea of the impact this meeting would have on my life, both personally and professionally. My relationship with Rinpoche was one that gradually evolved from the traditional rituals of publisher to author into the spontaneity of a profound friendship. Then at some point I realized that he was no ordinary person but someone who fully embodied the teachings of the Buddha. At that point our relationship changed and I formally became his student. If one put aside or suspended habitual conceptions, it was clear that Rinpoche was the most extraordinary person, specifically his unwavering dedication to benefit others at his own expense. He always considered other people and beings (including animals) before his own comfort. In all the seventeen years I knew him I never saw him do anything that was just for himself.

Rinpoche was a person you could never pin down—he was a man who possessed an infinite variety of faces, totally in and of the moment.

In the future there will likely be many more memoirs and biographies published by various people who were associated with Trungpa Rinpoche, as well as those who will feel inspired to study him from a distance. This book sets the proper tone and context for any books that might follow by telling the story in an uplifted manner, and without holding back seemingly unpleasant details. Diana Mukpo's fearlessness and candor, the very qualities that Rinpoche so appreciated in her, are abundantly present throughout. She has done a great service to her husband and to the vast array of his students—not only for those who met him, but for those that will meet and be inspired by him through his teachings, and now, through this book.

In my view, the history of Chögyam Trungpa in the West is analogous to that of the eighth-century Indian Buddhist master Padmasambhava, who was principally responsible for bringing the complete teachings of Buddhism to Tibet. Likewise, Chögyam Trungpa is arguably the most important figure in the transmission of Buddhism to the West—through his activity, speech, and writing, the power and compassion of the Buddhist path of enlightenment have been clearly presented.

I once heard Chögyam Trungpa Rinpoche describe his "family business" as "caring for others." During his lifetime, Chögyam Trungpa presented himself in many different forms: as a monk, a married man and father, a crazy wisdom yogi, a university founder, an artist, a monarch, and so on. In Sanskrit, a man like Trungpa Rinpoche is described as a *mahasiddha*—one who not only has achieved great accomplishments through practice, study, and realization, but who has also transcended the bounds of ordinary social expectation or behavior. In the Buddhist tantric tradition, a *mahasiddha* is an individual that manifests in order to reveal the ultimate truth for the benefit of anyone he or she encounters, through their activity, through their speech, and through the profundity of their mindstream. It is said that it doesn't matter if the person meeting the *mahasiddha* is attracted or repelled. In the Indian tradition of Tantric Buddhism, there are many accounts of these iconoclastic masters called *mahasiddhas*. The most well-known have been collected in *The Lives of the Eighty-Four Mahasiddhas*, an assemblage of life stories both revered and studied by Tibetan scholars and practitioners. Many of the great teachers of Tibet are considered to be emanation rebirths of these *mahasiddhas*. In fact, Trungpa Rinpoche is traditionally considered to be an emanation of the *mahasiddha* Dombi-Heruka. The biographies of these *mahasiddhas* present extraordinary examples of enlightened behavior that not only transcend duality, but also avoid the ordinary norms of materialism with activities that might seem, to the uninitiated, both outrageous and miraculous.

Even though Padmasambhava and the *mahasiddhas* lived at another time, in another place, if one understands the timeless realities and truths of their essential natures, one can also realize that it's entirely possible for such beings to exist in different cultural contexts. It is my belief that Trungpa Rinpoche is one of the great *mahasiddhas* of our time. Like the *mahasiddhas* of the past, he transcended the ordinary bounds of social convention, sometimes employing outrageously innovative means to encourage others to realize fearlessness, compassion, and ultimately complete enlightenment.

The Buddhist teachings emphasize that we should not look outside of ourselves to discover the truth. I often heard Chögyam Trungpa repeat this point to his students, urging us not to look to him or any spiritual teacher as a savior. The seventeen years that Trungpa Rinpoche taught in North America were like a golden age. What he was able to accomplish and inspire others to accomplish was completely magical. His love of life and honesty about the human condition provided fertile ground to plant the seeds of Buddhadharma.

This book can inspire one to be a decent human being in whatever one does and not become bound by cultural and social conformity. Rinpoche was true to himself and to his tradition. Because he was an honest person who didn't hide anything, the details of his life were not off-limits to his students. There was no wizard behind a curtain. If you want to know something about the man, this is the book to read—his day-to-day life was the core of his teachings, the display of his enlightened activity. Rinpoche's transcendent qualities of compassion and wisdom will, over time, be appreciated as his major contributions to our society. Those qualities are illustrated in this book.

Thank you, Diana Mukpo.

Samuel Bercholz
Wesak Day, 2006

COAUTHOR'S AFTERWORD
AND ACKNOWLEDGMENTS

It is said that sometimes truth is stranger than fiction. This is certainly one of those times. Looking at Chögyam Trungpa's life is like looking into a cloudless night sky. It is impossible to count the stars; impossible to name them all; impossible to describe all the possible constellations. So this book does not try to tell *the* life, but one life of many. In this case, perhaps, the advantage is that the storyteller is the Moon, who reflects the light of the Sun rather well. It seems that way, at least, to me.

Diana Mukpo and I began work on this project in late 1998. It took us almost eight years to complete. The manuscript is based on more than a hundred hours of taped conversations, which took place in Providence, Rhode Island, and in Wellington, Ocala, and West Palm Beach, Florida. Additionally, Diana Mukpo recorded a number of reminiscences on microcassettes. To verify dates, places, and occurrences described here, we drew heavily on both published and unpublished teachings by Chögyam Trungpa. Unpublished material in the Shambhala Archives was an important source of information, as were issues of the *Varjadhatu Sun*. We also relied on eyewitness and second-party accounts offered to us. We thank all those who have offered information and helped us to solve various puzzles. Where there have been disagreements or discrepancies, we have relied on the author, Diana Mukpo, as the principal witness. For errors of fact or omission, we apologize.

We have not "composited" any characters knowingly. However, in a few cases we have knowingly changed or omitted names. We regret that we could not include or name hundreds of people who played important roles in Chögyam Trungpa's life.

Many people contributed to this book. Again, it is impossible to name them all. Thanks to all of the members of the Mukpo, Levy, Pybus, and Gimian families who appear in this book and were supportive in so many, many ways.

We would like to thank our agent, Joe Spieler. Melvin McLeod, editor of *The Shambhala Sun,* convinced us to show him an early draft of the manuscript and published two articles based on the material. We might never have finished the book if he hadn't had this inspiration. Thanks also to Trish Rohrer for editorial help with the second article. My husband, James Gimian, helped me through many rough times and spots with this book, and I cannot thank him enough. I would also like to thank my father, Edward Rose, who taught me much about reading, writing, and listening that was helpful in preparing this manuscript. Tessa Pybus provided information about her mother Elizabeth Pybus and other events in the book. Larry Mermelstein and Walter Fordham read the book carefully and made many helpful comments. For their general support and love, in addition to those already mentioned, we thank Lisa, Winnie, Jenny, Amy, and Rosie.

Eden Steinberg, our editor at Shambhala Publications, has been remarkable to work with. Thanks also to Sam Bercholz, Peter Turner, Jonathan Green, Hazel Bercholz, Kendra Crossen Burroughs, Steve Dyer, Julie Saidenberg, Ben Gleason, and Art McCabe for their support and contributions.

We would like to thank all those who read and commented on the manuscript in draft and penultimate form. In addition to those already named, thanks to Rudy Wurlitzer; he has been supportive in so many ways. Thanks also to Michael Herr, Pema Chödrön, Steve Silberman, Andrea McQuillin, Liza Matthews, Gail Flynn, Dierdre Stubbert, Jane Carpenter, Fabrice Midal, Larry Shainberg, Art McCabe, Bill Turpin, Lindsay Brown, and Barry Boyce. At the time that this is being written, a number of other people are reading the manuscript, and we thank them in advance for their input. We are also grateful to the photographers whose work appears here, including Andrea Roth, Blair Hanson, George Holmes, Tharpa Chotron, and others as yet unidentified. We also thank the Spanish Riding School for permission to reproduce a photograph of Diana Mukpo riding at the school, and we offer our thanks to the Shambhala Archives both for access to their photo collection and for their efforts to preserve these images.

For the privilege of having known Chögyam Trungpa Rinpoche and having served him, we offer profound thanks. For the opportunity to share in writing this book, we offer a deep Shambhala bow to him and to one another.

By the confidence of the golden sun of the Great East
May the lotus garden of the Rigden's wisdom bloom.
May the dark ignorance of sentient beings be dispelled.
May all beings enjoy profound brilliant glory.

NOTES

Chapter One

1. Chögyam Trungpa, *The Collected Works of Chögyam Trungpa,* vol. 1 (Boston: Shambhala Publications, 2004), p. 265.
2. Chögyam Trungpa, *The Collected Works of Chögyam Trungpa,* vol. 7 (Boston: Shambhala Publications, 2004), pp. 299–300.

Chapter Two

1. Chögyam Trungpa, from a letter to Bob Copley, October 31, 1969, unpublished.
2. Ibid.
3. Ibid.

Chapter Four

1. Chögyam Trungpa, *Great Eastern Sun: The Wisdom of Shambhala* (Boston: Shambhala Publications, 1999), pp. 73–74.

Chapter Five

1. From an address to the Naropa Institute Conference on Christian and Buddhist Meditation, August 9, 1983, as quoted in *Speaking in Silence: Christians and Buddhist on the Contemplative Way,* ed. Susan Walker (Halifax: Vajradhatu Publications, 2005).
2. Chögyam Trungpa, letter, unpublished.
3. Chögyam Trungpa, *True Command: The Teachings of the Dorje Kasung,* vol. 1 (Halifax: Trident Publications, 2003), pp. 138–139.
4. Chögyam Trungpa, *The Collected Works of Chögyam Trungpa,* vol. 1 (Boston: Shambhala Publications, 2004), pp. 282–283.

5. Chögyam Trungpa, *The Collected Works of Chögyam Trungpa,* vol. 1 (Boston: Shambhala Publications, 2004), p. 283.
6. Chögyam Trungpa, *The Collected Works of Chögyam Trungpa,* vol. 1 (Boston: Shambhala Publications, 2004), p. 266.
7. Chögyam Trungpa, *The Collected Works of Chögyam Trungpa,* vol. 1 (Boston: Shambhala Publications, 2004), p. 279.

CHAPTER SIX

1. Chögyam Trungpa, in "Ten Years in America," *Vajradhatu Sun* special issue, 1980.
2. Chögyam Trungpa, "Tenth Anniversary Dharma Celebration," *Vajradhatu Sun* 3, no. 3 (February–March 1981).
3. The approach to the sitting practice of meditation that Chögyam Trungpa taught was always based on the highest teachings of the Tibetan Buddhist tradition. Because he emphasized the simplicity and formless aspects of the practice, sometimes people thought that his approach was elementary. In fact, he taught his students the technique of mixing mind and space by placing an emphasis on the outbreath. He taught his students to go out with the outbreath, as he often described it, and then to allow a gap. The inbreath, he said, would happen naturally, without any emphasis. This approach was expansive and encouraged one to develop a broad sense of the environment. He further emphasized the openness to space by having his students sit with their eyes open, facing the central shrine rather than facing the wall or otherwise closing themselves in. While in the beginning he allowed a loose approach to the physical or bodily aspects of the practice, he slowly introduced more discipline, with particular emphasis on good posture, which he termed good "head and shoulders." Rinpoche always stressed the importance of receiving personal meditation instruction from someone trained in the discipline.
4. Chögyam Trungpa, "Opening Talk: Alaya Preschool," March 1978. Boulder, Colo., unpublished.

CHAPTER SEVEN

1. Thomas Rich, in "Ten Years in America," *Vajradhatu Sun* special issue, 1980.
2. Chögyam Trungpa, "Vajracarya's Birthday Address," *Vajradhatu Sun* 1, no. 4 (April–May 1979).
3. Chögyam Trungpa, poem, unpublished.

CHAPTER EIGHT

1. The Five Buddha Families—buddha, vajra, karma, padma and ratna—refer to five distinct styles of both enlightened and confused behavior. Each family has both a sane and a neurotic manifestation. The buddha family relates to spaciousness or openness on the one hand and ignorance on the other. It is associated with the color white, and its symbol is the wheel. It is connected with the element of space, which is considered to be the fifth element in the Tibetan Buddhist view. *Vajra* energy is connected with intellectual penetration or precision, on one side, and with the cutting quality of anger and aggression on the other. Its element is water, its color is blue, and the symbol for *vajra* is the tantric scepter, which itself is called a *vajra,* or *dorje* in Tibetan. Karma, which simply means action, is connected with appropriate action and spontaneously fulfilling one's endeavors on the enlightened side and with jealousy, or competitiveness, on the other. It is associated with the color green, with the element of wind, and the symbol of karma is a sword. *Padma,* which literally

means lotus, is connected with communication, discrimination, and compassion in its sane embodiment and with neurotic grasping and unbridled passion in its neurotic form. The symbol for *padma* is the lotus itself, it is connected with the color red, and its element is fire. Finally, there is the *ratna* family. *Ratna* means jewel, and the jewel is the symbol of this family. It represents enriching and equanimity, appreciating all situations, or on the other hand its neurotic side is a sense of poverty and envy, coveting what others have. It is connected with the element of earth and the color yellow.

2. Rinpoche wrote an article about his view of a proper relationship to alcohol and drinking. "Alcohol as Medicine or Poison" can be found in *The Collected Works of Chögyam Trungpa,* volume 3, pages 456–460. Here are a few excerpts that give some sense of his view of the problematic as well as the positive possibilities connected with drinking. He had much more to say about this, and for those interested, I would recommend reading the whole article.

> There seems to be something wrong with an approach to alcohol that is based entirely on morality or social propriety. The scruples implied have solely to do with the external effect of one's drinking. The real effect of alcohol is not considered, but only its impact on the social format. . . . It seems that alcohol is a weak poison which is capable of being transmuted into medicine. . . . Nevertheless, alcohol can as easily be a death potion as a medicine. The sense of joviality and heartiness can seduce us to relinquish our awareness. But fortunately there is also a subtle depression that goes with drinking. . . . Psychologically, intoxication with alcohol is a process of coming down, rather than, as with the other substances [such as LSD, marijuana, and opium], of going up into space. Whether alcohol is to be a poison or a medicine depends on one's awareness while drinking. Conscious drinking— remaining aware of one's state of mind—transmutes the effect of alcohol.

3. Chögyam Trungpa, diary entry, unpublished, translated from the Tibetan by John Rockwell.

CHAPTER NINE

1. The Nalanda Foundation, which oversaw the operations of Naropa for a number of years, was incorporated in January 1974. The original Board of Directors of Nalanda consisted of Chögyam Trungpa, John Baker, Marvin Casper, Kenneth Green, Fran Lewis, Thomas Rich, John Roper, and Steve Roth. The Naropa Institute Executive Committee, which had more hands-on responsibility for the running of Naropa, was originally John Baker, Martin Fritter, Jeremy Hayward, Marty Janowitz, and Rinpoche.

2. Chögyam Trungpa, *Great Eastern Sun: The Wisdom of Shambhala* (Boston: Shambhala Publications, 1999), p. 38.

3. Chögyam Trungpa, excerpt from "Wait and Think," in *The Collected Works of Chögyam Trungpa,* vol. 7 (Boston: Shambhala Publications, 2004), pp. 395–396.

CHAPTER TEN

1. A horse's height is measured in hands, which each represent four inches. A sixteen three hand horse would measure 16 × 4 inches plus three inches for a total of 67 inches. The measurement is from the ground to the highest point of the withers— the bone that arches at the base of the horse's neck.

2. The title "His Holiness" is usually reserved for the head of one of the major lineages of Tibetan Buddhism. Although Dilgo Khyentse Rinpoche was not the formal head

of a lineage, Rinpoche felt that he was a man of such realization and presence that he should be called by this title. For this reason, I have kept this title and used it frequently in the manuscript to refer to Khyentse Rinpoche, although I know that some of his students would not agree that it is accurate. Nevertheless, it reflects my own feeling about his extraordinary qualities, as well as what Rinpoche instructed us.

CHAPTER ELEVEN
1. Chögyam Trungpa, *Great Eastern Sun: The Wisdom of Shambhala* (Boston: Shambhala Publications, 1999), p. 100.
2. Chögyam Trungpa, poem, unpublished.

CHAPTER TWELVE
1. Chögyam Trungpa, poem, unpublished.
2. Chögyam Trungpa, poem, unpublished.
3. Chögyam Trungpa, poem, unpublished.

CHAPTER THIRTEEN
1. Elizabeth Pybus, letter to Chögyam Trungpa, 1977, unpublished.
2. Chögyam Trungpa, letter to Diana Mukpo, 1977, unpublished.
3. Chögyam Trungpa, *Great Eastern Sun: The Wisdom of Shambhala* (Boston: Shambhala Publications, 1999), p. 110.

CHAPTER FIFTEEN
1. Chögyam Trungpa, *Court Vision,* unpublished manuscript.
2. Chögyam Trungpa, *Great Eastern Sun: The Wisdom of Shambhala* (Boston: Shambhala Publications, 1999), pp. 140–141. (The version presented here is an earlier version of the book, before the reference to LSD was removed.)
3. Chögyam Trungpa, *The Collected Works of Chögyam Trungpa,* vol. 7 (Boston: Shambhala Publications, 2004), pp. 515–518.

CHAPTER SIXTEEN
1. Chögyam Trungpa, *Kalapa Assembly Transcripts* (Boulder: Vajradhatu Publications, 1979), pp. 77–79.

CHAPTER SEVENTEEN
1. Chögyam Trungpa, "He Raised the Dharma Victory Banner in All Directions," *Vajradhatu Sun* 4, no. 2 (December 1981–January 1982): 1.
2. Chögyam Trungpa, "Shambhala Anthem," in *Great Eastern Sun: The Wisdom of Shambhala* (Boston: Shambhala Publications, 1999), p. 207.

CHAPTER EIGHTEEN
1. Chögyam Trungpa, *The Collected Works of Chögyam Trungpa,* vol. 7, p. 258.
2. Chögyam Trungpa, poem, unpublished.
3. Diana Mukpo, poem, unpublished.

CHAPTER NINETEEN
1. Chögyam Trungpa, excerpt, spiritual will, 1984, unpublished.
2. Robert Burns, "The Winter It Is Past," 1788.